This is a profoundly meaningful a
beautiful writers and have keen eye
perfect for anyone who has visited ;
eyes more to things they saw. For someone trying to decide whether to go to the
Holy Land, this wonderful book will make you realize how important it is to go,
and how deeply meaningful the experience will be. And for those planning to
go, this book should be your constant companion. The research for this book is
staggering, and the authors share amazing insights, smarts, positive energy, and
humor.

—Joe Armstrong. Publisher and Editor-in-Chief of New York Magazine;
Publisher and COO of Rolling Stone; Top advisor to the President of ABC
NEWS and anchor Peter Jennings.

Here is a delightful and engaging account of the authors' travels to the Middle
East as they and their family sought out all the key locations referred to in the
Bible. With geographical and biblical precision, along with colourful descriptions
of the family's experiences, this book opens our eyes to the beauty and wonder
of the ancient Near East. There is nothing dry, dusty or arid in this account. For
those who have an interest in Biblical history, and in the culture of this region,
this is a "must read" that will both inform and entertain.

—Rev Dr. Stafford Carson, Principal Emeritus,
Union Theological College, Belfast.

Roy and Evelyn Turkington have masterfully married biblical archaeology to the
Judeo Christian Scriptures in an entertaining, personal, humorous and incredibly
informative book. It contains a wealth of information and is a must read for
anyone interested in the very real connection between Middle East archaeology
and Christianity. Their powerful narrative details the dangers they encountered
while gathering research for the book, which is not only riveting but speaks to
the incredible commitment these intrepid authors possessed to complete their
mission. If only this resource existed in the 1970s when I visited Israel as a
21-year-old!

—Christopher P. Chanway, Professor, University of British Columbia,
Vancouver, BC, Canada

'No stone left unturned' is a beautiful, one-of-a-kind travel adventure through the Bible lands. It is humble, funny, inspiring, and a reminder that the journey is the adventure. The book is compelling, truthful, and inspiring. It is a journey in faith and reflection in which theology and scripture are brought to life. Roy and Evelyn with their children travelled throughout the lands of the Bible and visited virtually every known biblical location - this is no small feat. Each adventure gently showcases the values of the authors and family. The larger narrative and links to the Scriptures throughout the text provide a sound anchor to all stories and an amiable flow to the book. This book is a must read for those that love travel, the Middle East, the Lord Jesus Christ, and have an open and inquiring heart.

—Christopher Lortie, Professor, York University, Toronto

The reality of the bible comes to life through the words of the Turkington's. It is easy to place yourself in the footsteps of the people on the ground. Whether you are planning a trip or wanting to experience a biblical journey through the written word to strengthen your faith, this is a phenomenal book to dive into. One of the core values of Awana is "Equipping"; this book will do just that, equip your understanding, love for the bible and faith in its truth.

—Eric Provost, Executive Director, Awana International Canada

Don't miss out on this modern day family adventure through ancient Bible lands. The Turkington's found themselves rocked and robbed multiple times, yet they finished their mission!

—Jack D Eggar, President, Global Children's Network

ROY AND EVELYN TURKINGTON

ST NO ONE
LEFT UNTURNED

A Fourteen Year Travel Adventure
through the Bible Lands

ISBN: 978-1-4866-2182-8
eBook ISBN: 978-1-4866-2183-5

Word Alive Press
119 De Baets Street Winnipeg, MB R2J 3R9
www.wordalivepress.ca

WORD ALIVE
—P R E S S—

Cataloguing in Publication information can be obtained from Library and Archives Canada.

*We lovingly dedicate this book to the seven little jewels in our lives
— Maisie, Ellie, Talya, Samuel, Ozzy, David, and Deborah.*

CONTENTS

PREFACE

It was November 1991. We had already decided to spend our sabbatical year in Israel and to live in Jerusalem. One of the research technicians at the Hebrew University in Jerusalem, Nechama Rivlin,[1] had been making arrangements for us. I received a message from Nechama, "I have an apartment arranged for you; you have an address in Jerusalem." I remember sitting back in my office chair and pondering: *"We have an address in Jerusalem; this is the Holy City, the City of the Great King."* From the following August until June 1993, my family and I lived in Jerusalem. I was on sabbatical from the University of British Columbia and used this time to foster new research links with colleagues at the Hebrew University of Jerusalem and the Ben Gurion University of the Negev. Our apartment was in Bet Hakerem, about three kilometers from the Old City of Jerusalem and about seven kilometers from Bethlehem.

This became a very special year for us. We spent most weekends exploring and visiting various parts of the country and beyond — to Egypt and Jordan. Both of our children, Alistair and Andrea, accompanied us to almost every site in Israel, Egypt, and Jordan, and both were with us for the duration of our sabbatical year in Jerusalem from 1992–93. At that time Alistair was fourteen years old and Andrea was twelve. Andrea was with us during our sabbatical in Turkey, in 1999–2000, and joined us for our travels in Turkey and Greece.

While we lived in Jerusalem, Alistair was proceeding through the Junior Varsity program of the AWANA[2] ministry. One of the requirements was to do a project, and we decided to search for Bible references for the various sites we had visited in Israel. This turned out to be a wonderful little project, with about two hundred Scripture references. Our interest was piqued because we had actually visited many of the sites that most people could only dream about and many sites that many had probably never heard of. Besides, many of the locations were

---

[1] In July 2014, Ruvi Rivlin was sworn in as President of Israel. Ruvi is the husband of Nechama who was a good friend while we lived in Israel and in 2014 Nechama became Israel's First Lady. We kept in touch since we first met in 1992 until her death in 2019.

[2] The name AWANA (http://www.awana.org) is an acronym for Approved Workmen Are Not Ashamed and is based on 2 Timothy 2:15 which says, "Be diligent to present yourself approved to God, a worker who does not need to be ashamed, rightly dividing the word of truth."

extremely difficult to find. It became our objective to follow God's commission to Abram, to walk through the length and width of the land (Genesis 13:17).

We tried to visit the site of every recorded Bible event in Israel, provided there was some evidence that the site and location could still be identified with some degree of certainty — a number are rather tenuous — and a number are based on human invention rather than scriptural or archaeological authority. Together, as a family, we beat our way through bushes, drove through farmers' fields, along tracks rather than roads, through fruit groves, through shallow rivers, around military bases, and into some quite dangerous areas, all to experience this land. Such is the pace of development in Israel, that maps become outdated notoriously quickly. Consequently, we often got lost, needed directions, were stoned, and we were robbed, but we just about met our objective.

As we traveled around, we took about ten thousand photographs, made notes, sketched maps, and after encouragement from many sources, we compiled all this information as a book, published under the title *"Arise, Walk Through the Land"* by Palphot in Israel. After publication, we lived in Turkey from July 1999 to February 2000, and subsequently, we visited Italy, Greece, Syria, Lebanon, and Iraq — and in June 2004, during a visit to Iran, we turned our backs on the tomb of Cyrus the Great, walked away, and realized that we had just about completed our fourteen-year journey through the Bible lands. An updated and revised edition of *"Arise, walk Through the Land"* was published in 2017.

But these books were lacking one major dimension — our experiences. The books were purely factual guides to Bible sites in Israel and Jordan. As we gave public presentations, we realized that we had a story to accompany almost every slide or PowerPoint image. Often these were funny, exciting, frustrating, sometimes daring, and on occasion a little dangerous. Many of these experiences were documented but many were simply stored in our heads. After some gentle encouragement from well-meaning friends, we embarked upon this compilation of our travels. We trust that as you read this book you will share the experiences of our adventures.

INTRODUCTION

It was early September 1992, and we decided to make a trip to Galilee. Evelyn was driving, and I was reading maps. I recall saying to Evelyn: "Do you realize that we are going to drive past Armageddon in about twenty minutes?" "We really must stop to see it." We did stop, and while there, we discovered that there was another biblical site, Jezreel, less than a ten-minute drive away. This was the site of Naboth's vineyard, where Queen Jezebel was killed. This location is almost unparalleled in terms of the number of biblical events and locations that are nearby, and we decided to visit them. We drove the short distance to the spring where Gideon chose his three-hundred men to do battle with the Midianites. This spring is at the base of Mount Gilboa where Saul and Jonathan were killed. Then, on to Mount Moreh, Shunem (Elisha and the Shunammite woman), Nazareth, Nain (where Christ raised the widow's daughter), Gath Hepher (the birth place of the prophet Jonah), Cana of Galilee, Mount Tabor (the traditional site of the transfiguration), and the day ended with a visit to En Dor where Saul's last tragic days brought him to the witch of Endor. All of this was done in one day, and we didn't drive more than about sixty kilometers. But of all these twelve sites, only three were marked with directions — Megiddo, Nazareth, and Cana of Galilee; the rest required some map reading, guesswork, and asking. The exhilaration of finding so many unmarked sites in such a small area stimulated our early interest and desire to find and visit as many Bible sites as possible. We had no way of knowing that this day was the beginning of a fourteen-year journey.

This book is designed to introduce the reader to many of the major narratives of the Bible beginning with Abraham in Ur, other patriarchs, Israel's Judges and Prophets, Jesus Christ, Paul, and John's Seven Churches in Revelation. This covers considerable geography from Iran (biblical Persia) and Iraq in the east, through Jordan, Egypt, Syria, Israel, and Lebanon, to Turkey, Greece, and Italy in the west. It is not a theological text, but mostly our travel logs from 1991–2004 when we had the opportunity to visit almost all known Bible sites.

Occasionally we describe in detail some obscure or difficult-to-access sites, but the emphasis is on our experiences. These vary from being funny, exciting, frustrating, sometimes daring, and on occasion a little dangerous. Together, often with our two children, sometimes with other friends, we beat our way through bushes, drove through farmers' fields, along tracks rather than roads, through fruit groves, through shallow rivers, around military bases, and into some quite dangerous areas. And on our journey, we had stones thrown at us at least five times, robbed three times, stopped by the police or army five times, had many exciting border crossings (including once where we were within seconds of being shot by Israeli border guards), and we even had a car accident — all to experience these biblical lands. This book is our attempt to recreate these stories and experiences, which were accumulated during our adventures traveling throughout the lands of the Bible. Because these adventures took place over a fourteen-year period, often involving numerous repeat visits to some sites, we have tried to package them into groups of sites that loosely hang together to tell a biblical narrative.

Our approach to traveling and visiting was quite unique because most travelers to the Bible Lands, especially Israel, are restricted to a predetermined tour schedule and visit sites marked by impressive churches or ancient ruins. In contrast, few travelers consider the more obscure biblical sites as places of interest. Yet, many places throughout the region offer the visitor food for thought, meditation, and inspiration. Many of these towns and villages are off the beaten tourist track, nevertheless, they witnessed some of the most inspiring stories of the Old and New Testaments. There is a tremendous sense of history all around. Every hill and valley, town and village, seems to have some claim to fame. Bible stories take on a whole new dimension as they become real historical events that involved real people. It is exhilarating to follow the footsteps of Abraham, Moses, Joshua, David, and Jesus Christ, and to retrace the journeys of Paul. We climbed to Cave 1 at Qumran, climbed Mount Sinai (two of them!), traveled across deserts, stood atop the ruins of the Tower of Babel, and visited the tombs of many Old Testament heroes, including Abraham, Sarah, Jacob, Queen Esther, and the Persian kings. We stood on the spot where Jezebel was killed and the city gates where Haman was hanged. We used buses, taxis, flights, boats, rental cars, camels, and foot, to visit every biblical site possible — but we never did make it to the island of Patmos.

If our travels and our visits were merely aimed at ticking names off a list, this would have been of limited value. Of course, it was much more. It was a time of great learning and of great growth in our Christian lives. Before visiting any site, we did a thorough preparation by reading all the pertinent biblical passages and then following up with Bible dictionaries and archaeological texts. We knew most of these sites intimately before we arrived — and then we visited and put real, live flesh on our mental images. Often we took the time to simply sit down at a site, open the Scriptures, read some passages, and watch the scriptural narratives unfold before us.

For example, Shushan is today's city of Shush in western Iran. This was a royal city of Persia under Darius I and his successors. The famous Code of Hammurabi was uncovered here in 1901. Like so many archaeological sites, you need to have a vivid imagination to conjure up their past grandeur. The major attraction is the ruins of the palace of King Darius. Little remains of the palace itself, except for the great hall of columns known as the throne-room of Artaxerxes, the setting for the narrative in the first chapter of the book of Esther. But tucked away at an unannounced location behind all the ruins is a rather insignificant, but magnificent site — the city gate and inner courtyard. The city of Shushan was the location of the entire book of Esther, and the city gate and courtyard feature prominently in that narrative. It was here that Mordecai discovered a plot to assassinate King Xerxes (Ahasuerus).

> *When virgins were gathered together a second time, Mordecai sat within the king's gate. Now Esther had not revealed her family and her people, just as Mordecai had charged her, for Esther obeyed the command of Mordecai as when she was brought up by him. In those days, while Mordecai sat within the king's gate, two of the king's eunuchs, Bigthan and Teresh, doorkeepers, became furious and sought to lay hands on King Ahasuerus.* (Esther 2:19-21)

It was also here that Mordecai refused to acknowledge Haman:

> *And all the king's servants who were within the king's gate bowed and paid homage to Haman, for so the king had commanded concerning him. But Mordecai would not bow or pay homage. Then the king's servants who were within the king's gate said to Mordecai, "Why do you transgress the king's command?"* (Esther 3:2-3)

And, although not explicitly stated in Scripture, it is likely that Haman and his ten sons were hanged in this courtyard (Esther 9:13-14). What a goosebump privilege to stand in the city gate and in the square. Today, although only a shadow of their former glory, they provide a memorable mental picture of the narratives of Esther.

A few days later, in June 2004, we visited the archaeological ruins at Pasargadae. Pasargadae was begun under Cyrus the Great in about 546 BC, but it was soon surpassed by the magnificent city of Persepolis about sixty-five kilometers to the south. Many travelers don't visit Pasargadae because there is little to see, and what there is to see is not well preserved. Even the setting is not particularly inspiring, sitting in a hot, deserted plain. However, near the entrance is the imposing tomb of Cyrus the Great. It was Cyrus that allowed the Jewish captives to return to their homeland in Jerusalem (Ezra 1:1-4), and to rebuild the Temple (Ezra 6:1-12). The book of Ezra contains many reports on the progress of the work related to the decree of Cyrus. And God has something to say about Cyrus, calling him "God's shepherd" and "the Lord's anointed."

> *Who says of Cyrus, 'He is My shepherd, And he shall perform all My pleasure, Saying to Jerusalem, "You shall be built," And to the temple, "Your foundation shall be laid."'* (Isaiah 44:28)

> *"Thus says the Lord to His anointed, To Cyrus, whose right hand I have held—To subdue nations before him And loose the armor of kings, To open before him the double doors, So that the gates will not be shut..."* (Isaiah 45:1)

We stopped and looked at the imposing eight-meter-high structure. We walked around it, examined it from every angle, and reminded ourselves that God had named Cyrus in these two verses, 150 years before Cyrus was even born! As we turned and walked away from the tomb of Cyrus the Great towards our vehicle, we realized that we had experienced it all — we had just completed our fourteen-year journey through the Bible lands — except for Patmos.

I.
THE PATRIARCHS IN THE BIBLE LANDS

By late 2000, we had visited almost all accessible Bible sites, except for those in Iran and Iraq. We knew that we could visit Iran sometime in the future, but Iraq was a different story. Iraq was the cradle of civilization, part of the Fertile Crescent, and the likely location of the Garden of Eden. This was the land of Sumer, Babylonia and Assyria. This was Mesopotamia, meaning "between two rivers," the Tigris and the Euphrates. This was the homeland of Abram's family. It was here that human beings first began to cultivate their land and where writing was invented. Unfortunately, this is all history, and Iraq today is a very different country.

With the UN embargo imposed after the Gulf War of 1991, Iraq had no international flights. Both the northern and southern portions of the country were designated "no-fly" zones, and poverty was rampant. Based on all of this, we had simply drawn a circle around the biblical sites of Babylon, Ur, and Nineveh, realizing that these were sites we would never visit. But one night in late 2,000 we were watching the late-night news and that all changed. The news showed an aircraft landing in Baghdad airport. So it was possible to get into Iraq? I sent a letter to the Iraqi embassy in Ottawa explaining that I was writing a book on the biblical sites of the Middle East and that this included some sites in Iraq. I got a polite response indicating that the Iraqi embassy had not issued a tourist visa in the eleven years since the Gulf War; they had only issued visas to some journalists, aid workers, and UN personnel. But we wanted to go to Iraq and the travel bug had hit. We thought and prayed, and then had an idea — we were not tourists, we were authors.

Rather than writing again to the Iraqi embassy, I decided to phone. After many conversations, we convinced them that we were legitimate, and they agreed to forward our request to Baghdad. It took more than two months, but the Iraqi embassy in Ottawa finally cleared us through Baghdad, and we were issued visas as guests of the Ministry of Tourism.

Even though we had visas in hand, the process of getting to Iraq was another issue. A visa simply meant that we had permission to enter the country; it didn't guarantee a way of doing so. Information was hard to come by. Lonely Planet and other guide books were publishing nothing on Iraq. Likewise, there was little forthcoming from the Canadian government. The situation was extremely volatile, UN sanctions were strangling the Iraqi economy, unemployment was high, crime was increasing, and US and British forces were occasionally bombing military installations. Iraq was a military dictatorship under Saddam Hussein, and Uncle Saddam wasn't exactly making his country welcoming to tourists. The US and Canadian governments, along with most other western governments, had issued travel advisories warning their citizens against traveling to Iraq.

> Canadians are advised not to travel to Iraq. Canadians there should leave. Canadians who choose to be in Iraq, despite this warning, should maintain close contact with the Canadian Embassy in Amman, Jordan, or the Department of Foreign Affairs and International Trade in Ottawa, Canada. Conditions throughout Iraq remain dangerous and could further deteriorate without notice. Regional conflicts continue in the north. Periodic military action continues between Iraq and coalition aircraft enforcing "no fly zones" in the north and south of the country. Iraq is under long-term UN sanctions.[3]

The only people we told about our plans were our son Alistair and daughter Andrea because we knew that many would try to dissuade us from going. After many phone calls, we concluded that flights were non-existent, but we could get a taxi from Damascus to Baghdad. Two months later we were in the final few days before leaving Canada to go to the Middle East. The news wasn't good. The Iraqis had just shot down an unmanned US drone-spy aircraft, and the Americans had threatened retaliation. If they retaliated now, then we would most likely not be allowed across the border.

In spite of these obstacles, a few weeks later we were in Damascus and had a taxi. It cost us $160 USD for the 7½ hr, eight-hundred kilometer journey to Baghdad ($90 USD on the return journey!). We left Damascus at about 8:00 a.m.; it was a hot 40°C; when we arrived in Baghdad, it was 49°C. It was desert the entire journey, and the road was mostly four-lane in Syria and then six-lane in Iraq. Our driver was clearly on a mission to return to Bagdad as he drove the Baba Ganoush out of our comfortable air-conditioned Chevy Caprice for most of the way between 130–160 kph. The trip was relatively uneventful except for the two-hour crossing of the Iraqi border. We pulled up to Syrian customs. This was a fairly rapid procedure, probably about twenty minutes, but nothing out of the ordinary. Then just a few minutes to the Iraqi customs. The taxi pulled up to a building, and our driver jumped out.

---

[3] https://travel.gc.ca/destinations/iraq, accessed March, 2001.

"Passports over there," he pointed to us, as he opened the trunk of the taxi. We went to the trunk to get our bags, but he indicated we didn't need them. We felt a little uneasy with our bags exposed in this part of the world and not being there to watch them. We headed off in the direction he indicated, and then a man appeared and indicated that we should follow him. We followed him into a large but sparse room with benches, which, at one time, were clearly used for searching baggage when this was a busy border crossing. We stood there alone. No one else was crossing this border, yet we saw about twenty others who were apparently working here. Heaven only knows what they were employed to do.

After about five minutes, four officers appeared and stood looking at us as though we were a circus peep show. It was amusing yet a little frustrating. Nobody was doing anything. We were standing at a bench being watched by four officers, yet our bags were still in the trunk of the taxi. I had my camera bag and Evelyn her carry bag — we would never leave these unattended. Our driver then brought in our one small case, and I went to open it, but one of the staff indicated that I didn't need to. Then, finally, after having been there for at least twenty minutes, someone appeared and beckoned us into an office. He spoke just a little English, pulled out a form, and tried to document that we had two cameras and a pair of binoculars. Within a few minutes, there were seven or eight men trying to fill out this form. Evelyn and I tried very hard to cover the evident smiles appearing on our faces as we watched this total incompetence.

"Why are you laughing?" one of the officers asked. I think they were slightly embarrassed. They weren't angry or offended at our laughing; I think they wanted to know why we were laughing because it isn't common to see much fun or laughter in many of these countries. "It is like Canada," I replied, "one man working and three or four others watching!" We were given a copy of the form and told to declare it as evidence on leaving the country (evidence that we didn't leave the cameras or binoculars in Iraq). We went back out into the large room — and stood again. It was at this point we met another person crossing the border. He was a Canadian from Calgary and was working on computer systems in Baghdad. He had already been in Baghdad, had left to go to Canada for a hernia operation, was now returning, and was clearly not too happy at having to do so. We chatted very briefly and then he abruptly asked, "Who in Hell are you anyway? Why are you coming into this country?" "Oh, we are just coming into Iraq so as to visit Babylon, Ur, and Nineveh," I replied. We deliberately remained quite vague with him because he was clearly quite surprised, and puzzled, that we had a visa and even more surprised that we wanted to go to Iraq.

"You will regret the moment you ever set foot in this country," he said, and he went on to describe how much he disliked the place.

"Let me give you two pieces of advice. Never take photographs of anything without lots of permission because you will find your camera at your feet. In addition, guard every word you speak because, although they all claim not to speak English, there are a lot of ears and they understand a lot. These guys standing here are probably not too happy that we are talking right now."

This Canadian man then disappeared into another office for about five or ten minutes. Meanwhile, we stood there just looking at each other, with some small talk to break the deafening silence. When the Canadian man came out, we were beckoned in with our cameras and binoculars. This turned out to be only five minutes, and it was an official wee man who filled out another form and then said:

"There is a charge for this service."

"How much?" I responded.

"As you wish," was his response.

"Ah, you want a baksheesh?" Evelyn asked.

When he realized that we genuinely didn't have any US dollars (at least any that we were going to tell him about), he backed down a little, and we gave him about $2 USD worth of Syrian money. He didn't seem to be too displeased. And then we were out into the big room again. We never did open our bag, and our driver brought the bag back to the taxi. We held on to our camera and shoulder bags. We'd been at customs for nearly an hour when we were directed to another office. This time three or four of the officers who had been standing watching us for most of this last hour wanted a tip. We tried to play ignorant of their requests, pretending we didn't know what their hand signals meant. Then it got too much and we simply and firmly said "no." We now had a young official who spoke very good English, and he apologized for the conduct of his colleagues especially after we explained that "In our country, we only give tips for services rendered." What a load of piffle. For the next hour, we sat in a very comfortable, well-furnished waiting lounge, with a huge portrait of Saddam Hussein watching over us. There was no one else but ourselves and another official, who was in some way connected with the Ministry of Tourism. There was writing at the bottom of our visas, which this man told us said: "guests of the Minister of Tourism." He spoke relatively good English, and for a long time we chatted with him and milked him for all sorts of good information about traveling in Iraq. Why we sat for so long, who knows, and what they were doing with our passports for so long, who knows? But suddenly, after two hours, it was all over and we were on our way towards Baghdad.

Our taxi driver delivered us and checked us into the Al-Hayat Tower Hotel. We don't know who made this choice, but we certainly had no input. The young lad at reception was called Davir, and he spoke good English. When we checked in, Davir took our Canadian passports and said, "You are from the US?" We instantly corrected him because being a westerner in Iraq was already risky, but to be an American would be absolute folly.

The Al-Hayat Tower was a four-star hotel. Well, it was probably a four-star hotel eleven years earlier, and with years of trouble and low revenue, there was little to spend on maintenance. The swimming pool had no water, the restaurant had no food, cracks in large windows were sealed with duct tape, carpets were thread bare, and almost everything was sparse. We didn't know exactly where this hotel was, except that we'd crossed to the eastern side of the Tigris River. We had no idea if we were to the north or south, near the city center, or near the edge of the city. There were no tourist facilities, so we were totally on our own. No maps, no travel books or brochures, no organized bus tours… nothing. This also meant that we were totally reliant on taxis even though the Canadian government travel advisory said that "Visitors should not travel alone in taxis," because of the excessively high crime rates. The only positive we had so far was that Davir spoke good English, and he became very useful to us.

We didn't find a restaurant until the end of our third day, so we found little food, and what we could find was terrible. Consequently, we ate mainly Mars bars for four days. Breakfast was interesting and always consisted of a bread roll that we couldn't swallow and a spread that was probably some type of molasses — we never did figure it out. Coffee took half an hour to prepare, and there was no milk or sugar. We will digress to say that we decided to leave Baghdad a day earlier than planned.

This was a strange decision because I really wanted to see the Iraqi Museum in Baghdad, which had a wonderful archaeological collection, and Evelyn wanted to see New Baghdad, which had been reconstructed since the Gulf War. As it was, we felt prompted to leave early. The ever-dependent Davir had an early taxi ready for us. As we were leaving, Davir passed some remark about us being Americans. Again, we quickly corrected him but he responded with a spine-chilling remark that "You are all the same to us." We moved quicker than usual into the taxi and sped our way across the desert for eight-hundred kilometers back to Damascus, most likely following a route similar to that of the Jews returning from exile in Babylon with Ezra and Nehemiah.

We arrived at our hotel, put our bags down at reception, and CNN was just reporting that the US had bombed targets in southern Iraq. It might not have been as easy to have left Iraq the following day — the Lord directed us in a meaningful way. Little did we know that twenty-one months after our visit, US tanks would be in the streets of Baghdad toppling the regime of Saddam Hussein.

We are getting ahead of our story, so let's return to the Al-Hayat Tower Hotel and to Davir. We had informed Davir the previous evening that we wanted to travel to Ur the next day. Sure enough, Davir arranged for a taxi to be at our hotel quite early. However, we needed cash. We had $500 USD, and there was a currency exchange (a corner store) across the street from our hotel. Now the difficult part. At that time, Iraq had no coins in circulation and only one banknote — a 250 Iraqi Dinar bill. There were 3,125 dinars to the US dollar, so a single 250-dinar bill was worth seven–eight US cents. We decided to exchange $300 USD, which gave us 937,000 dinars, which were 3,750 dinar bills — we had a stack of bills about sixteen inches high. We put the stash in a black plastic shopping bag, followed by the usual breakfast of a piece of dry bread, and soon we were on our way to Ur.

There wasn't much to remember about the journey except the utter desolation of most of the country, the pervasive military presence, and the ever-present paintings and photographs of Saddam Hussein. The taxi cost us $40 USD for the entire day for the 750 kilometers round trip to Ur. When our driver pulled in to fill up with gas, even we were shocked to see a cost of 1 cent per liter; less expensive than water! Ur is only a few kilometers south of Nasiriyeh. We stopped briefly in Nasiriyeh to pick up a few more liters of water. As we left Nasiriyeh, we could almost immediately see the great ziggurat of Ur in the distance. Our first impression was one of being overwhelmed by the desolation of the place.

The founder of Ur was the biblical King Nimrod. Its location as the birthplace of Abram is generally accepted, and few dispute this. Muslim tradition identifies ancient Ur as the city of Urfa in southeastern Turkey near the border with Syria. It's possible that Urfa is the site of biblical Ur of the Chaldeans, but it is more commonly accepted as being in southern Iraq. Besides, we were now in southern Iraq, and this is where we wanted Ur to be! This is the native land of Harran, Terah, Abram, Lot and Sarah. This is one of Iraq's most imposing ancient sites. Ur was the capital of the ancient civilization of Sumeria. As we drove towards the site, we couldn't help but remember the words of Joshua when he challenged the people of Israel:

… choose for yourselves this day whom you will serve, whether the gods which your fathers served that were on the other side of the River, or the gods of the Amorites, in whose land you dwell. But as for me and my house, we will serve the Lord. (Joshua 24:15)

Joshua was referring to Ur, the birthplace of Abram, and Ur was "on the other side of the River," referring to the River Euphrates, and it was here on this ziggurat that their fathers worshiped pagan gods. The huge ziggurat was the Temple of Sin, god of the Moon, the chief god worshiped by the people of Ur, built around 2000 BC — that makes it four thousand years old! As we drove closer, the massive structure assumed its real size. Unfortunately, it looks better today than it has done throughout most of its history because of a delusional notion by Saddam Hussein to 'fix it' with questionable attempts at repairing the structure.

When we were within a kilometer, we came to a military checkpoint, probably about the tenth we had negotiated on our journey from Baghdad. We heard the usual chatter between the driver and the military, understanding none of it, except for a periodic injection of "Canadienne". However, this checkpoint didn't seem to be as effortless as the previous ones. Typically, we would be asked to show our passports and shortly be on our way. Not this time, and for a moment we thought we weren't being allowed to proceed. It turned out to be simple — we were not merely passing through a checkpoint — we were entering a military zone! After much more chatter and many more "Canadiennes," we were allowed entry. We're not sure what happened, but we assume that the driver convinced the soldier to allow us entrance, even though it was a military zone. After all, we were guests of the Minister of Tourism! And to keep the whole process kosher, the soldier got into our taxi and accompanied us. We drove for a few moments to the base of the ziggurat and climbed out of the taxi. Blast Furnace! It was a steaming 52^0C in Ur — and the wind was blowing. It felt as though someone was holding a hair drier about thirty centimeters from our faces.

After wandering around the huge structure, we skipped up the eighty or so steps to the top — and then almost fainted in the heat. We were quickly followed to the top by the soldier who was very careful to tell us that we weren't permitted to point our cameras to the south because this is a militarily sensitive area. Quite honestly, the desolation in all directions didn't entice us to point our cameras in any direction. We wandered around the summit and marvelled at the construction, even though only one layer remains of the three or four that probably formed the original structure. The ziggurat was constructed with bricks that were cemented together with pitch. We shouldn't have been surprised at this because this is exactly as prescribed for the most famous of all ziggurats, the Tower of Babel: *"Then they said to one another, 'Come, let us make bricks and bake them thoroughly.' They had brick for stone, and they had asphalt for mortar"* (Genesis 11:3).

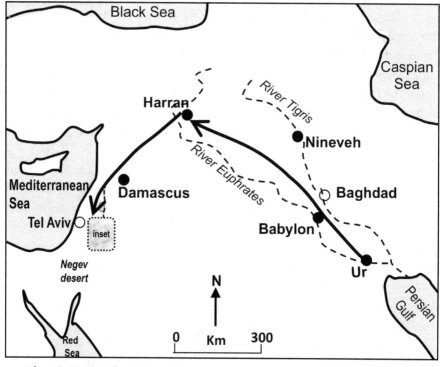

Abram's Journey from Ur to Canaan. The inset map is expanded on page 15.

And then, about two hundred meters away, we could see a man approaching at something between a fast walk and a slow run. He was wearing a white shirt and red-checkered keffiyeh, and he appeared to be on a mission. I turned to Evelyn and said, "Wouldn't it be funny if he is coming to sell us an entrance ticket?" He was, and he did! This guy probably hadn't seen a tourist in ten years, and no doubt he was waiting just for today. But give him credit, he was extremely knowledgeable, and gave us a wonderful guided tour, pointing out other temples and palaces, some royal tombs, and all sorts of things that we would definitely have missed without him.

But then trouble struck. I've already said that it was hot — blast furnace hot. After about thirty minutes Evelyn said to me, "I'm going to faint." Being the sensitive man that I am, I interpreted this to mean "it's hot." A few moments later Evelyn repeated her statement, and this time I interpreted it to mean "it's very hot." It was only when Evelyn began to wobble that I realized what she really meant to say was that she was going to faint!

The taxi driver and I grabbed Evelyn and supported her down into a shady spot where she sat in the doorway of a four-thousand-year-old royal tomb for the next twenty minutes. This was quite an anxious time because not only were we in the middle of nowhere, but we didn't want to end up in an Iraqi hospital. While Evelyn is a nurse and knew exactly what to do, at least while she was lucid, I'm not a nurse and didn't have a clue what to do. If Evelyn would have passed out, we'd have been royally scundered. As she rested, got some fluids, and cooled a little, we convinced the driver to bring his taxi, as best he could, across the bumpy ruins to meet us, and again we supported Evelyn back from her temporary shelter and into the taxi. We drove a short distance to a residential area, and our guide tried to show us the home where Abram lived! This was the end of our visit, and as we pulled up to the checkpoint, we slipped the soldier a few dollars for accompanying us. Given the annual income of most Iraqis we probably tipped him close to a week's wages.

As we pulled away from the checkpoint we were reminded that this was the beginning of a long journey for the patriarch Abram as he left Ur and headed towards the land of Canaan via Harran and Shechem:

And Terah took his son Abram and his grandson Lot, the son of Haran, and his daughter-in-law Sarai, his son Abram's wife, and they went out with them from Ur of the Chaldeans to go to the land of Canaan; and they came to Haran and dwelt there. (Genesis 11:31)

As Abram traveled north he probably followed the Euphrates River towards Babylon and on to Harran. At 2,900 kilometers, the Euphrates is the longest river of Western Asia. Along with the Tigris, these are the two major rivers in Mesopotamia, which means "between the two rivers." The source of the Euphrates is in the mountains of eastern Turkey. From there, it flows through Syria and Iraq, and finally joins the Tigris River before entering the Persian Gulf. As it flows south, it passes within forty kilometers of Harran, Abram's first destination, and so the Euphrates forms a natural traveling route joining Ur and Harran, providing food and water along the way.

The first major stop on Abram's journey was probably Babylon even though this is not recorded in Scripture. The ruins of ancient Babylon are situated on the River Euphrates near the modern city of Al-Hillah about ninety kilometers south of Baghdad. Babylon was an ancient city-state and the Hebrew text says:

Therefore its name is called Babel, because there the Lord confused the language of all the earth... (Genesis 11:9)

Hammurabi, king of Babylon, about 2000 BC, was a contemporary of Abram. The city rose to prominence about 1,830 BC but didn't reach the height of its glory until the reign of Nebuchadnezzar II, beginning in 605 BC. Nebuchadnezzar's city included vast fortifications, famous streets, canals, temples, and palaces, and of course the famous Hanging Gardens. This was one of the most magnificent cities ever to be built and was one of the wonders of the ancient world. The prophet Jeremiah (Jeremiah 51:7) describes it as "a gold cup in the Lord's hand." The book of Daniel records that King Nebuchadnezzar was walking on the roof of the royal palace of Babylon and said:

... *"Is not this great Babylon, that I have built for a royal dwelling by my mighty power and for the honor of my majesty?"* (Daniel 4:30)

The population of greater Babylon in Nebuchadnezzar's day has been estimated at about a half million. Daniel was taken captive from Jerusalem in 605 BC by Nebuchadnezzar and the armies of Babylon. Daniel lived and ministered in the city of Babylon, and the book with his name was written about 605 BC. Ezekiel was about twenty-five years old when he was taken captive to Babylon in 597 BC, and the book he authored was written from Babylon about 570 BC. While in captivity, the Jewish people longed to be home:

By the rivers of Babylon, There we sat down, yea, we wept
  When we remembered Zion.
  We hung our harps
  Upon the willows in the midst of it.
  For there those who carried us away captive asked of us a song,
  And those who plundered us requested mirth,
  Saying, "Sing us one of the songs of Zion!" (Psalm 137:1-3)

Babylon elicited mixed reactions. Our first reaction was a great thrill just to be at Babylon, even though it was 50C. However, the little soda pop salesman knew that we would give in before he would as he followed us around from a distance. When we finally gave in to the temptation of having a pop, we were more than willing to pay what no doubt were excessively inflated prices, and then to have a second one! Our second reaction was awe at the impressive structures on-site, including the watchful eyes from one of Saddam's palaces that overlooked the site from a height to the northwest. Our third reaction was disappointment that these structures were mostly reconstructed during the mid-1980s. All that remains of ancient Babylon are parts of the original main street that ran through the city — the Processional Way,[4] and The Lion of Babylon, which is over 2,600 years old. The statue was built by king Nebuchadnezzar II (605-562 BC). Virtually everything else is piles of rubble. Almost all of what we see today is a rather questionable attempt at reconstructing Nebuchadnezzar's Palace. No doubt Babylon was more impressive in ruins than after Saddam tried to 'fix it.' It is believed that Nebuchadnezzar had his royal seal stamped onto bricks in the original palace. And while we didn't see any evidence, it is seemingly well authenticated that Saddam Hussein has immortalized himself by stamping his seal on the new bricks:

> In the reign of the victorious Saddam Hussein, the president of the Republic, may God keep him the guardian of the great Iraq and the renovator of its renaissance and the builder of its great civilization, the rebuilding of the great city of Babylon was done in 1987.

And we weren't fooled by the remodeled Ishtar Gate at the site entrance. This is also a recent construction. The primary sites to be seen are the ruins of Nebuchadnezzar's southern palace; this includes the famous banquet hall of Daniel 5 that hosted Belshazzar's feast and the ominous writing on the wall:

> *And this is the inscription that was written: MENE, MENE, TEKEL, UPHARSIN. This is the interpretation of each word. Mene: God has numbered your kingdom, and finished it; Tekel: You have been weighed in the balances, and found wanting; Peres: Your kingdom has been divided, and given to the Medes and Persians.* (Daniel 5:25-28)

But make no mistake, this was remarkable to visit, and little did we know that within eighteen months of our visit, a US army base would be located on site.

We wanted to go to another site about one kilometer to the south. For a fleeting moment, we considered walking through a few palm trees, a citrus orchard, and a grassy field — it might have been a pleasant walk had it not been 50C. So we returned to our taxi, but for some reason, the driver wasn't too happy even though this had been agreed upon before we left our hotel. Finally, we convinced him to follow a rough track to an enormous pile of rubble about one kilometer south of Nebuchadnezzar's reconstructed palace. But this was no ordinary pile of rubble. Probably this was the remains of the original Tower of Babel (a term not used in Scripture), the original ziggurat, which subsequently became the blueprint for hundreds of similar structures

---

[4] Much of the original glazed clay bricks that adorned the walls of the Processional Way are on display at the Pergamon Museum, Berlin. The museum also houses the Ishtar Gate and other artifacts from Babylon.

throughout Mesopotamia. We struggled up the rubble pile in the intense heat and realized that it was just past midday in early August and probably one of the hottest times of the year. It took about five minutes to get up there, but what a strange feeling when we reached the top. This was the place referred to where they said:

> … *"Come, let us build ourselves a city, and a tower whose top is in the heavens; let us make a name for ourselves, lest we be scattered abroad over the face of the whole earth."* (Genesis 11:4)

And where the Lord:

> …*scattered them abroad from there over the face of all the earth, and they ceased building the city. Therefore its name is called Babel, because there the Lord confused the language of all the earth; and from there the Lord scattered them abroad over the face of all the earth.* (Genesis 11:8-9)

And the view to the north over Nebuchadnezzar's Palace, Saddam Hussein's Palace, and the Euphrates River was awesome. As we raised our cameras for the obvious photograph, we were quickly interrupted and reminded, as we had been about two hours earlier, that there were to be absolutely no photographs of Saddam's palace. Our taxi driver spoke no English other than "police, police" as he held his two wrists together to indicate the consequences of being caught photographing Saddam's Palace. We thought about the consequences of ending up in an Iraqi prison, for about a nanosecond, and instantly decided against taking any photographs. There was a large flat area between us and the city. This was a large public area at the time of Nebuchadnezzar and quite likely the site of the giant ninety-foot-high golden image described in Daniel, regarding Daniel and his friends and the fiery furnace (Daniel 3), and Daniel in the lion's den (Daniel 6). We picked up a few small stones from the site as a memento and returned to the taxi. As we drove away, we were reminded of how Babylon was described prophetically:

> *And Babylon, the glory of kingdoms, The beauty of the Chaldeans' pride, Will be as when God overthrew Sodom and Gomorrah. It will never be inhabited…* (Isaiah 13:19-20)

From Babylon, Abram and his migratory family would have continued to follow the River Euphrates north to the region of Harran through the region that would come to be known as Assyria. Assyria was a kingdom between the Tigris and Euphrates Rivers, dominating the ancient world from the ninth to the seventh century BC. Its principal city and its third, and last, capital was Nineveh (but we will not write about this city until we meet Jonah in a later chapter).

Abram's next major destination was Harran. We drove towards Harran from the west and en route crossed the Euphrates River; although still about 1500 kilometers from the sea, it is already an enormous river, and there was a great sense of awe as we crossed into Mesopotamia. Harran is close to the Syrian border.

> *And Terah took his son Abram and his grandson Lot, the son of Haran, and his daughter-in-law Sarai, his son Abram's wife, and they went out with them from Ur of the Chaldeans to go to the land of Canaan; and they came to Haran and dwelt there. So the days of Terah were two hundred and five years, and Terah died in Haran.* (Genesis 11:31-32)

As we approached the settlement, we could see the obvious ruins of ancient Harran, surrounded by crumbling walls, on the hill in front of us. Harran is one of the oldest continuously inhabited places in the world. This is the hometown, or area, of Rachel, Rebecca, and all the children of Israel, including Dinah and Joseph, but not Benjamin. Harran was the birthplace of the Jewish people; I guess it never quite struck us before that in today's geography, the Children of Israel were all Turks! This was a fascinating place with its unique bee-hive shaped mud-brick buildings designed to be warm in the cold of winter and to be cool in the relentless heat of the summer.

Sooner than anticipated, we had an escort of about ten grubby little children with beautiful care-free smiles, and almost before our feet had hit the ground we found ourselves resting in the relative cool of a mud-brick bee-hive home. Our host offered us a glass of çay then we doddled a short distance up to the ruins. The major site is the ruins of the Great Mosque dating from the seventh or eighth century; it has a square minaret which is unusual in Turkey. The large arch in the center of the ruins is what remains of a large, ancient Islamic university. On the hill behind the major ruins is a pair of door-posts marking a home where tradition indicates that Abram met Sarah — isn't tradition wonderful — there would be far fewer sites to visit if we could only eliminate the traditional sites.

Today's village of Harran spreads a short distance beyond the crumbling walls, and just beyond the edge of the village is a long, low, flat concrete structure that covers an ancient well. The locals told us that this is the only well for miles and that this is Jacob's well, Bi'r Yakub. Sadly, it's quite a cesspool today and evidently used by many as a rubbish dump. This is quite likely the well where Jacob met Rachel, and where Eliezer met Rebekah:

> *And he [Eliezer[5]] made his camels kneel down outside the city by a well of water at evening time, the time when women go out to draw water. Then he said, "O Lord*

---

[5] Most interpretations identify the unnamed "servant" as Eliezer (Genesis 15:2, 24:2).

God of my master Abraham, please give me success this day, and show kindness to my master Abraham. Behold, here I stand by the well of water, and the daughters of the men of the city are coming out to draw water. Now let it be that the young woman to whom I say, 'Please let down your pitcher that I may drink,' and she says, 'Drink, and I will also give your camels a drink' -- let her be the one You have appointed for Your servant Isaac. And by this I will know that You have shown kindness to my master." And it happened, before he had finished speaking, that behold, Rebekah, who was born to Bethuel, son of Milcah, the wife of Nahor, Abraham's brother, came out with her pitcher on her shoulder. (Genesis 24:11-15)

It was time to leave Harran, and as we drove out of the village we were quite possibly following the same tracks trodden by a famous adventurer almost four thousand years earlier. It was at Harran that God gave His great commission to Abram:

Now the Lord had said to Abram:
　"Get out of your country,
　From your family
　And from your father's house,
　To a land that I will show you.
　I will make you a great nation;
　I will bless you
　And make your name great;
　And you shall be a blessing.
　I will bless those who bless you,
　And I will curse him who curses you;
　And in you all the families of the earth shall be blessed."
So Abram departed as the Lord had spoken to him, and Lot went with him. And Abram was seventy-five years old when he departed from Haran. Then Abram took Sarai his wife and Lot his brother's son, and all their possessions that they had gathered, and the people whom they had acquired in Haran, and they departed to go to the land of Canaan. So they came to the land of Canaan. (Genesis 12:1-5)

Harran marked about as far east as tourists may travel in Turkey with absolute safety. At this point we were getting into the Kurdish region and, unfortunately, in the recent past, a few tourists had been kidnapped. However, there was currently relative quiet. We visited Harran on September 13th, our twenty-fourth wedding anniversary. We thought back over the years and couldn't remember anything we had done on any of our previous anniversaries other than go out for a meal. But this one we wouldn't forget! Only after we returned from this trip did we discover that all the locations we had visited on September 13th were in a zone where the US and UK governments had issued a travel advisory to stay away! C'est la vie!

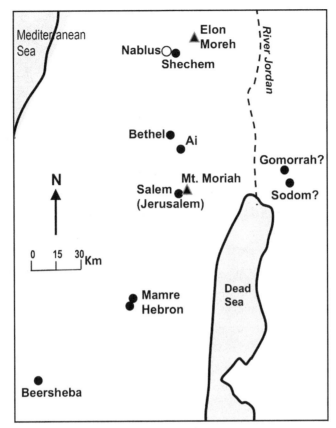

The patriarchs in Canaan.

Genesis 12:6 says:

Abram passed through the land to the place of Shechem, as far as the terebinth tree [more often translated as oak tree] of Moreh. And the Canaanites were then in the land. (Genesis 12:6)

The phrase "passed through the land" is a euphemism referring to a journey of seven hundred kilometers, probably passing through Alleppo, Ebla, Hamath, Damascus, Galilee, Hazor, and finally to Shechem. After a journeying perhaps eighty kilometers from Harran, Abram would have passed through Carchemish — a region which some thirteen hundred years later would be the site of one of the most significant and decisive battles in ancient history. Carchemish was an ancient capital of the Hittites, and it was at Carchemish in 605 BC that the advancing Egyptian armies of Pharaoh Necho were defeated by Nebuchadnezzar II of Babylon.

...Concerning the army of Pharaoh Necho, king of Egypt, which was by the River Euphrates in Carchemish, and which Nebuchadnezzar king of Babylon defeated in the fourth year of Jehoiakim the son of Josiah, king of Judah: (Jeremiah 46:2)

The Egyptians suffered a crushing defeat, permitting the Babylonians to gain control of the Syrian-Palestinian region. Before the battle of Carchemish, King Josiah of Judah tried to block the advance of Pharaoh Necho in his march northward. Josiah was fatally wounded in the Valley of Megiddo (2 Chronicles 35:20-24).

The ruins of Carchemish sit more-or-less astride the Turkish-Syrian border. On the Turkish side is the village of Karkamiş, and on the Syrian side is the town of Jerabalus. On the southern edge of Karkamiş is an army checkpoint. Apparently, on rare occasions, the army will escort you to the ruins, but they wouldn't escort us. Two years later, we tried to gain access from the Syrian side. Although the border guards invited us into their office and supplied us with çay for about thirty minutes, we had the same problem as before — the officers were convinced we wanted to cross the border into Turkey. Not even Abram would have had this amount of bureaucratic trouble traveling in this area. The Scriptures say that: "Abram passed through the land to the place of Shechem, as far as the terebinth tree of Moreh ..." (Genesis 12:6).

Moreh is located on Mount Kabir which is only a few kilometers northeast of Shechem. The summit is marked by a large oak tree, which some traditions claim was perhaps the great tree of Moreh at Shechem, or the oak of Moreh. If this were true, then this is one of the most special locations in Israel; this is the place where God promised the land to Abram when he first entered Canaan:

Then the Lord appeared to Abram and said, "To your descendants I will give this land." And there he built an altar to the Lord, who had appeared to him. (Genesis 12:7)

The huge, spreading, and very old (perhaps five hundred years) oak tree is just beyond the Jewish community of Elon Moreh on Mount Kabir. But there was a problem — the site is close to Shechem. The name Shechem might not sound dangerous, but its modern equivalent name, Nablus, is a hotbed of Palestinian activism and a center of violent anti-Israeli hostilities. A second problem was that we absolutely needed our own transport. We could easily catch a shared taxi from Jerusalem to Nablus, but then how would we ever travel the remaining five kilometers beyond Nablus to the Jewish community of Elon Moreh? You can easily walk five kilometers but not in that part of the world — the Arabs think you are Jewish and the Jews think you are an Arab; either option was unacceptable in that volatile region.

Elon Moreh is a Jewish community, and its very presence raises enormous anger among most Palestinians. For this reason, the community is like an armed camp, yet we had to enter it and pass through to the other side to reach Mount Kabir. The solution to all of this was to rent a car, but, you guessed it, this was also a problem! Why? Well, because of Palestinian hostilities, international car rental companies such as Avis, Hertz, Budget, and the local Eldan company, do not allow their cars to be taken into the West Bank.[6] That's not quite true; you can take the car to the West Bank if you wish, but it's not covered by insurance. And besides, the yellow license plates are a real give away because yellow plates indicate a Jerusalem car and therefore a Jewish car. Oh, dear.

We badly wanted to go, but the possibilities of trouble were high, so we made a quick decision to proceed in a car, with yellow plates and without insurance coverage. We reasoned that Nablus and the territories had been relatively 'quiet' in the preceding weeks, and if there was any serious chance of trouble, then the Palestinian Authority police would stop us and send us back. It takes just under an hour to drive to Nablus from Jerusalem. We were rather nervous when the Palestinian Authority police stopped us on the outskirts of Nablus and were quite amused that we were "traveling around." From there, we easily made our way to Elon Moreh, and, surprisingly, it was all too easy to get past the guard at the gate, through the community, and on to the top of Mt Kabir. And then there it was, the huge spreading oak tree, and the view was magnificent. It was spectacular. To the south we could see Shechem (Nablus), to the west was the site of Joshua's altar on Mount Ebal, to the north we could see Tirzah (an ancient capital of the northern kingdom of Israel) and Thebez (where Abimelech was killed), and to the east was a deep, beautiful valley heading toward the River Jordan valley. This truly is a site where one can stand and ponder!

Despite the importance of Shechem to the biblical narrative, the Scriptures are relatively silent on Abram's visit. However, we will return to Shechem in later chapters with Jacob, Joseph, Joshua, and Jesus. Our first visit to Shechem

---

[6] The "West Bank" refers to the territory that sits on the west bank of the Jordan River and the Dead Sea. The name was used after it was captured by Jordan in the 1948 Arab–Israeli War. Jordan annexed the territory in 1950 and held it until 1967 when it was recaptured by Israel during the 1967 Six-Day War. This region is variously referred to as Palestine, The Occupied Territories, and The Administered Lands and its borders corresponds very closely with biblical Judea and Samaria. Because we are describing experiences while searching for Bible sites we will generally use the names Judea (south of Jerusalem) and Samaria (north of Jerusalem). When writing about more recent political events we will use the term West Bank.

was in 1993 with Pastor Musa, the pastor of the First Baptist Bible Church in Ramallah. It was quite unsafe to travel in the West Bank, so we rented a taxi for the day. Although we were in an Arab taxi with an Arab driver, we could sense a certain amount of tension as we traveled north through Ramallah to Shechem. The ruins lie at the eastern end of Nablus and are being encroached by a car graveyard.[7] Although there isn't much to see, what is available is significant. The northern portion of the perimeter wall is impressive, but there is also a single rather inauspicious-looking standing stone about 1.5 meters tall. This stone probably once guarded the entrance to what was an imposing temple-fortress at Shechem. This temple was the site of numerous biblical incidents, including Abimelech's infamous slaughter of one thousand Shechemites.

> *Now when all the men of the tower of Shechem had heard that, they entered the stronghold of the temple of the god Berith. And it was told Abimelech that all the men of the tower of Shechem were gathered together. Then Abimelech went up to Mount Zalmon, he and all the people who were with him. And Abimelech took an ax in his hand and cut down a bough from the trees, and took it and laid it on his shoulder; then he said to the people who were with him, "What you have seen me do, make haste and do as I have done." So each of the people likewise cut down his own bough and followed Abimelech, put them against the stronghold, and set the stronghold on fire above them, so that all the people of the tower of Shechem died, about a thousand men and women. (Judges 9:46-49)*

While we stood at the ruins pondering the biblical texts that came alive at this location, suddenly our four-thousand-year-old dreams were shattered by twentieth-century technology. As two Israeli air force jets screamed just overhead, producing an enormous sonic boom, I felt the legs of my pants vibrate and quiver. "They do this to remind the natives they are being watched," explained Pastor Musa.

Genesis 37 relates the story of Joseph having two dreams in which he learned that one day his father, mother, and brothers would bow down to him and that he would lord it over them. It may not have been Joseph's most prudent moment when he told his parents and his brothers about his dreams! Joseph was already his daddy's favorite, and is it any wonder that his brothers despised him? Later in the chapter, Joseph's father sent him to Shechem to visit his brothers who were tending sheep. Joseph arrived in Shechem and asked a man if he knew about his brothers :

---

[7] When we returned to Shechem (Tel Balata) in 2017, we were pleasantly surprised to find that it had been developed, preserved, and renovated as an Antiquities site under the control of the Palestinian Authority.

And the man said, "They have departed from here, for I heard them say, 'Let us go to Dothan.'" So Joseph went after his brothers and found them in Dothan (Genesis 37:17)

Dothan is about thirty kilometers north of Shechem.

Now when they saw him afar off, even before he came near them, they conspired against him to kill him. Then they said to one another, "Look, this dreamer is coming! Come therefore, let us now kill him and cast him into some pit; and we shall say, 'Some wild beast has devoured him.' We shall see what will become of his dreams!" (Genesis 37:18-20)

The oldest brother, Reuben, exercised some maturity and convinced the other brothers not to kill Joseph.

So it came to pass, when Joseph had come to his brothers, that they stripped Joseph of his tunic, the tunic of many colors that was on him. Then they took him and cast him into a pit. And the pit was empty; there was no water in it. And they sat down to eat a meal. Then they lifted their eyes and looked, and there was a company of Ishmaelites, coming from Gilead with their camels, bearing spices, balm, and myrrh, on their way to carry them down to Egypt. So Judah said to his brothers, "What profit is there if we kill our brother and conceal his blood? Come and let us sell him to the Ishmaelites, and let not our hand be upon him, for he is our brother and our flesh." And his brothers listened. Then Midianite traders passed by; so the brothers pulled Joseph up and lifted him out of the pit, and sold him to the Ishmaelites for twenty shekels of silver. And they took Joseph to Egypt. (Genesis 37:23-28)

As we approached Dothan, we asked the taxi driver to stop so that we could take some photographs and video. While taking the video, an Israeli military police vehicle drove past. They screeched their brakes and reversed to us at high speed. We barely had time to think or react. They said we weren't allowed to take video in the area and started to ask the usual questions — where do you live, what are you doing in Israel, what are you doing here, and what are you photographing? It didn't help that we had a Palestinian taxi driver, were in an Arab taxi, with a Palestinian man who was a Baptist pastor. The police demanded that we rewind the video so that they could replay and see what video we had taken. They seemed to accept our story and bid us on our way. And in case you are interested, no, the pit that Joseph was placed in has not been found; that story happened 3,800 years earlier.

Joseph's dreams were fulfilled; he became the Prime Minister of Egypt and ruled over his family. Joseph died and was buried in Egypt, but when God delivered the Hebrew slaves from bondage four hundred years later, the Children of Israel brought the bones of Joseph with them:

The bones of Joseph, which the children of Israel had brought up out of Egypt, they buried at Shechem, in the plot of ground which Jacob had bought from the sons of Hamor the father of Shechem for one hundred pieces of silver, and which had become an inheritance of the children of Joseph. (Joshua 24:32)

The traditional tomb of Joseph was a beautiful and tranquil little building only a few hundred meters from the ruins of ancient Shechem and a short distance from the well that his father Jacob had dug — we will visit this well later when Jesus meets the woman at Jacob's well in John 4. Unfortunately, the building housing Joseph's tomb was destroyed by Palestinian rioters in 1999. Josephus explains that Joseph's bones were moved from Shechem to the Tombs of the Patriarchs at the Cave of Machpelah in Hebron.

Abram then moved south to Bethel and Ai and mostly lived and traveled in southern Samaria and in Judea. His sons and other descendants also moved around in the same general region. The sites that Abram frequented are nearly all situated on the one main road that runs north-south through the length of the West Bank from Nablus to Ramallah, Jerusalem and Hebron, and then on to Beersheba. Both Bethel and Ai feature prominently in many biblical narratives, and we will return to both in later chapters. Abram moved through this region and Scripture tells us:

And he moved from there to the mountain east of Bethel, and he pitched his tent with Bethel on the west and Ai on the east; there he built an altar to the Lord and called on the name of the Lord. (Genesis 12:8)

The two towns are only three kilometers apart, and today they are separated by the Ramallah By-Pass Road. Just off the eastern side of the bypass road and about one kilometer west of Ai is a small hill with a Byzantine monastery. Why should an otherwise unremarkable hill have a monastery? Could it be that in Byzantine times this site was commemorated as a revered site? This hilltop might be the place where Abram pitched his tent and built an altar. Geographically it fits the scriptural description. It is relatively easy to visit this site if you aren't easily intimidated — intimidated by the Israeli tank sitting at the end of the dirt road used to gain access to the hill, or by the restless natives that live in the nearby villages of Deir Dibwan and Beitin; we will tell you later about our rather tense first visit to the site of Ai — and the size of rocks the children were holding!

A significant event in the life of Jacob, Abraham's grandson, happened at Bethel.

Now Jacob went out from Beersheba and went toward Haran. So he came to a certain place and stayed there all night, because the sun had set. And he took one of the stones of that place and put it at his head, and he lay down in that place to sleep. Then he dreamed, and behold, a ladder was set up on the earth, and its top reached to heaven; and there the angels of God were ascending and descending on it. (Genesis 28:10-12)

At this juncture, God renewed and confirmed his covenant with Jacob that he had earlier made with Abram.

Then Jacob awoke from his sleep and said, "Surely the Lord is in this place, and I did not know it." And he was afraid and said, "How awesome is this place! This is none other than the house of God, and this is the gate of heaven!" Then Jacob rose early in the morning, and took the stone that he had put at his head, set it up as a pillar, and poured oil on top of it. And he called the name of that place Bethel;... (Genesis 28:16-19)

Bethel is only about four kilometers northeast of Ramallah, so it should have been easy to find especially with the help of Pastor Musa from Ramallah Baptist Church. But Pastor Musa didn't know where it was and even the local Arab taxi driver that we hired didn't know. We got to the general area but couldn't pinpoint the location despite us asking directions innumerable times. This reinforced a lesson we had repeatedly learned in the previous eight months — most religious Jews and Muslims pay little attention to biblical 'holy sites'; this seems to be a singularly Christian thing to do.

We gave up that day, but not to be deterred, we chatted to some of our colleagues at the Hebrew University in Jerusalem. One of them was in Israeli intelligence during the Six-Day War of 1967, and he had military maps. These maps, although twenty-five years old, were extremely detailed and showed every trail and track in the country. He obviously wouldn't let us have the maps, but we quickly found Bethel. Again, we rented our trusty Avis car and went Bible-site hunting in the West Bank. As always, this was a nervous and anxious pursuit, especially as we passed by the Qalandiya[8] refugee camp south of Ramallah, and as we passed through Ramallah. We came to the general region, and with a few quick enquiries along the way we soon arrived at Bethel. Most of ancient Bethel is buried under the present village of Beitin. Nevertheless, this was a special spot, and not only for Abram and Jacob. Some nine hundred years later, Jeroboam the first king of the northern kingdom would build a shrine with the idolatrous golden calf, and a few years after this we learn an important lesson about showing respect for the follicly-challenged:

---

[8] In the early 2000s this became the location of the Israeli Security Barrier and the official border when traveling between Jerusalem and Ramallah.

Then he [Elisha] went up from there to Bethel; and as he was going up the road, some youths came from the city and mocked him, and said to him, "Go up, you baldhead! Go up, you baldhead!" So he turned around and looked at them, and pronounced a curse on them in the name of the Lord. And two female bears came out of the woods and mauled forty-two of the youths. (2 Kings 2:23-24)

DETOUR ONE:
THE NAME OF GOD ENGRAVED IN THE HILLS

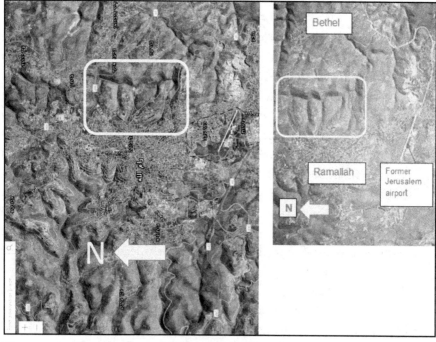

This is an interesting musing and nothing more. This aerial image shows the region between Bethel (House of God) and Ramallah (Hill of God). We were shown this by an airplane pilot while taking us on a sightseeing flight over Samaria. The pilot believed the image, produced by valleys and shadows, to be the name Yahweh or Jehovah, the God of the Israelites, whose name was revealed to Moses as four Hebrew consonants (YHWH) and translated "The Lord" in the Old Testament.

When I returned to Vancouver, I visited a lunchtime meeting of a society for young Jewish adults at the University of British Columbia. I walked through the room and showed the unlabeled photograph to six individuals chosen at random; I didn't know anyone in the room. I deliberately handed the photograph to each person "on its side" i.e. north pointing towards me. I simply asked, "can you identify any writing on this photograph?" Four of the six identified "YHWH" almost immediately, but all qualified that it was a little rough, yet nevertheless discernable. Although not very scientific, it is interesting to have the name of God engraved on the hills between the House and Hill of God! Try recreating this using Google maps; it works quite well.

While Bethel has mostly been associated with the village of Beitin, a more recent proposal places the site of Jacob's dream and King Jeroboam's Altar at the northern end of the Jewish community of Beit El. As we drove through the community, we followed signposts to "Jacob's dream" and "Jacob's ladder." Although there is a parking lot (beside a school) about 250 meters before the site, we ignored it and continued along the rough track to the site. Only a few meters from where we parked, was a large, flat rock platform that has been labeled the site of Jacob's dream; a rock in the center of the platform is identified as Jacob's pillow. About twenty meters beyond the flat area is another area identified as the location of King Jeroboam's altar. While wandering around and staring at the site, we were startled out of our wits when a group of ten Israeli soldiers seemed to appear from the bushes out of nowhere. They were very friendly, and within minutes we were all together taking photographs.

Okay, let's move south and leave tents, dreams, ladders, youths, and bears behind us.

Then Abram moved his tent, and went and dwelt by the terebinth trees of Mamre, which are in Hebron, and built an altar there to the Lord. (Genesis 13:18)

Some of the most significant events in the life of Abram took place at Mamre. It was here that God changed Abram's name to Abraham, and, debatably,[9] where God made an unconditional covenant with Abram, promising him that his descendants had been given the land from the river of Egypt to the River Euphrates. This is more commonly known as the Covenant of the Pieces because of the nature of the sacrifices and ceremonies that took place.

It was probably easier for Abram to get to Mamre than it was for us. During the year that we lived in Israel, the first Intifada was quite tense, and traveling in the

---

[9] Many authorities are of the opinion that the Covenant of the Pieces took place on the western slopes of Mt. Hermon in the northeast of Israel.

West Bank was either ill-advised, cautious, or downright foolish. It was only after much arm-twisting and vigorous negotiations with Pastor Musa, from Ramallah, and Pastor Naim, from Bethlehem Baptist Church, that we persuaded them to take us to Hebron, and we will tell you all about that in a few pages. On the journey, we were only within one kilometer of Mamre, but we didn't get to visit on that occasion — primarily because we didn't know where it was. We finally made it to Mamre two years later but all under rather intimidating circumstances.

We rented a car from Avis in Jerusalem and began to drive south, for about thirty-five kilometers. In hindsight, this was silly because rental cars aren't covered by insurance in the West Bank, and the natives were still restless during the Intifada. However, we reasoned that if we stayed on the main road until the northern outskirts of Hebron, we would be okay. But even that was a challenge because we had to pass through the restless town of Beit Jala and a Palestinian refugee camp just south of Gush Ezion. Although it took only forty-five minutes, it felt like an eternity because of the tension, and we finally reached the northern outskirts of Hebron.

According to our map, we would come to a major intersection, and we should turn left for about one kilometer. We reached the intersection but it was blocked by a very tight Israeli army security barrier – concrete blocks and bollards forced us to drive slowly in a zig-zag route to reach the soldiers and checkpoint, all the time being watched by at least a dozen soldiers with their M-16s[10] at the ready, accompanied by about six jeeps. And we had heard it all before, "ID please, who are you, where are you going, and why? Does Avis know you have a car in Hebron? You really shouldn't be here with yellow license plates. Okay, proceed, it is about one kilometer," as the soldier pointed and confirmed the road we should take. Oh, to be young and adventurous!

It only took a few moments to arrive. The site is surrounded by a large Herodian wall built of enormous ashlars. We parked in an alley beside a furniture store and then chuckled. There, just at an opening in the perimeter wall, sitting in a ticket booth, was a little bespectacled man with a huge, totally toothless smile. A ticket booth! Surely he was sipping a cup of coffee because he couldn't be selling tickets. But he was, and specifically, he was selling us tickets. "When did you last have visitors to this site?" we asked. He understood, but just chuckled and mumbled as he handed us our tickets. Inside the Herodian enclosure is an old well called Abram's well and the ruins of a church. In the center of the compound is a platform. This platform is bedrock, raised above the atrium. This is speculated

---

[10] In 2009, the Israeli Defense Forces gradually began the process of replacing their M-16 rifles with the Tavor X95 as the standard-issued weapon of the Israeli infantry.

to be the exact spot where God appeared as a firepot, moved between the rows of sacrificial offerings, and delivered His unconditional promise to Abram.

So He said to him, "Bring Me a three-year-old heifer, a three-year-old female goat, a three-year-old ram, a turtledove, and a young pigeon." Then he brought all these to Him and cut them in two, down the middle, and placed each piece opposite the other; but he did not cut the birds in two. And when the vultures came down on the carcasses, Abram drove them away. Now when the sun was going down, a deep sleep fell upon Abram; and behold, horror and great darkness fell upon him. Then He said to Abram: "Know certainly that your descendants will be strangers in a land that is not theirs, and will serve them, and they will afflict them four hundred years. And also the nation whom they serve I will judge; afterward they shall come out with great possessions. Now as for you, you shall go to your fathers in peace; you shall be buried at a good old age. But in the fourth generation they shall return here, for the iniquity of the Amorites is not yet complete." And it came to pass, when the sun went down and it was dark, that behold, there appeared a smoking oven and a burning torch that passed between those pieces. On the same day the Lord made a covenant with Abram, saying: "To your descendants I have given this land, from the river of Egypt to the great river, the River Euphrates..." (Genesis 15:9-18)

Abram was living in Mamre when he received the news that his nephew, Lot, had been captured by King Chedorlaomer. Abram gathered a group of trained men and pursued Chedorlaomer as far as Dan, which is on the northern border of Israel. Dan is a remarkable combination of Nature Reserve and Antiquity Site and one of the most fascinating and beautiful sites in Israel. The main trail in the Reserve meanders through a thousand bubbling springs all contributing to the headwaters of the River Jordan. The Antiquity Site, when we first visited in 1993, had little for tourists to see.

Then, I was viewing an exhibit in the Israeli Museum in Jerusalem and realized that there are some very important discoveries to see, but they were evidently not yet on display for visitors. So I headed back towards Dan, a large site, and wandered around the trails for about two hours without finding either of the two discoveries I wanted to visit. Then bingo, I saw a younger man disappearing into the bushes with a pick and shovel and a bucket. He wasn't carrying his lunch, so I followed through the bushes at a distance behind him, scrambled under some "keep out" tape, and after about five minutes I arrived in a clearing. There before me was a sacrificial altar, probably the one built by King Jeroboam.

Therefore, the king [Jeroboam] asked advice, made two calves of gold, and said to the people, "It is too much for you to go up to Jerusalem. Here are your gods, O Israel, which brought you up from the land of Egypt!" And he set up one in Bethel, and the other he put in Dan. (1 Kings 12:28-29)

I was in a dilemma. I wanted to get closer and see the altar, but I didn't want to push my luck seeing I was in a restricted zone. My dilemma was short-lived when a few of the staff spotted me and beckoned me over. Not only did I have a personal tour of the altar, they provided me with detailed directions on how to find the second site I was looking for.

The second site is the only eighteenth-century BC mud gateway in the Middle East dating to Canaanite times. The workmen were working away excavating around the area, and the whole structure was covered by what looked like a large glasshouse, designed to keep the rain and elements from deteriorating the newly exposed mud brick. Sadly, about ten years after my initial visit, it seems that birds were finding the clay brick to be a convenient place to dig holes and build nests, so damage was occurring. But think about it — Abram probably wandered through this gate 3,800 years ago as he pursued King Chedorlaomer and the kings of the north to rescue his nephew Lot:

Now when Abram heard that his brother was taken captive, he armed his three hundred and eighteen trained servants who were born in his own house, and went in pursuit as far as Dan. (Genesis 14:14)

Mamre is also the place where Abraham met the three visitors who promised Abraham and Sarah a son in their old age. In a corner of the compound, an unusual patterning of the limestone slabs leaves a space, and this has convinced some archaeologists that this was the location of the terebinth trees:

Then the Lord appeared to him [Abraham] by the terebinth trees of Mamre, as he was sitting in the tent door in the heat of the day. So he lifted his eyes and looked, and behold, three men were standing by him; and when he saw them, he ran from the tent door to meet them, and bowed himself to the ground, and said, "My Lord, if I have now found favor in Your sight, do not pass on by Your servant... Then they said to him, "Where is Sarah your wife?" So he said, "Here, in the tent." And He said, "I will certainly return to you according to the time of life, and behold, Sarah your wife shall have a son."... (Genesis 18:1-3, 9-10)

But before we leave Mamre, we must pay a visit to the Russian Church at the western edge of Hebron. The Russian Church believes this to be the real location of Abraham's oak, and they still have a tree to prove it. As we left Mamre, we began to retrace our tracks. We spotted two young Arab lads sitting chatting in a car, seemingly with lots of time. "Do you speak English?" we shouted. We must have asked that question a thousand times during our travels, and the answer was almost invariably "a little," but the reality was usually "not a word." But it was a point of contact.

After showing the young lads our maps along with a few photos, we were soon speeding our way through Hebron following a beaten-up Peugeot 405. In ten minutes we arrived at these huge imposing gates to the Russian compound, at least three meters high, and they were locked and spiked at the top. The young lads, in typical Arab fashion, indicated that we should climb over. We could see the tree about one hundred meters along a driveway inside the gates, and we desperately wanted to get closer. We couldn't climb the high wall because it was topped with barbed wire and glass pieces, so it had to be the gate!

I gingerly climbed the gate getting my feet into secure footholds, but I was getting desperately dirty and oily. I reached the top and gingerly worked my way over the top; I certainly didn't want to get my noolies impaled on a Russian Orthodox gate, in Hebron, with a Jewish car! Cautiously, I made my way down the other side. Evelyn passed the camera through the gate to me, and I walked up to the tree hoping that no one would spot me or challenge me. The tree was braced and strapped with enormous metal supports, but it is apparently only about six hundred years old —personally, I think it's dead. Okay, this was probably not the tree, and this was probably not even the location of Mamre, but it was a wonderful moment just to stand, ponder, and to think about getting back over that gate!

Abraham then moved to Gerar, and Isaac also lived here for a short time. It was in is this region of the northern Negev that Abraham spent much of his life. The exact location of Gerar is uncertain, but archaeologists have proposed two major possibilities. The first proposed site of Gerar is about twenty kilometers west of Beersheba on the road to Gaza. Gerar isn't well marked and is a little awkward to find. When we finally turned off the road, we could see the mound of Gerar about one kilometer distant across the fields, but we had no idea how to get there. Perhaps rather arrogantly, we turned down a driveway alongside a home, passed the garage, drove through someone's backyard, and passed a vegetable patch before starting to drive through grain fields and cash crops to reach the mound — only to join up with the main track into the mound! It was here at Gerar that Abraham lied to Abimelech about Sarah being his sister, and Isaac likewise lied about Rebekah being his sister.

And Abraham journeyed from there to the South, and dwelt between Kadesh and Shur, and stayed in Gerar. Now Abraham said of Sarah his wife, "She is my sister." And Abimelech king of Gerar sent and took Sarah. (Genesis 20:1-2)

And the men of the place asked about his wife. And he said, "She is my sister"; for he was afraid to say, "She is my wife," because he thought, "lest the men of the place kill me for Rebekah, because she is beautiful to behold." Now it came to pass, when he had been there a long time, that Abimelech king of the Philistines looked through a window, and saw, and there was Isaac, showing endearment to Rebekah his wife. Then Abimelech called Isaac and said, "Quite obviously she is your wife; so how could you say, 'She is my sister'?" Isaac said to him, "Because I said, 'Lest I die on account of her.'" (Genesis 26:7-9)

The story of Abraham continues with his sojourn in Beersheba, which became the center of patriarchal life. Throughout Israel's settled history, it was recognized as the southern boundary of the country, with at least ten biblical references defining Israel as stretching from Dan to Beersheba. Genesis 22:19 tells us that Abraham dwelt at Beersheba. Archaeologists have uncovered the original city gates and city walls. We plundered around the ruins for about an hour looking at old storehouses, the city center, city gates, and homes in the city wall. Notably, there are two particularly significant finds — a great horned altar and an ancient well.

There were many quarrels over water and wells, and ultimately Abraham and Abimelech made an agreement at Beersheba. This well is probably about twenty-five meters deep and dates to the twelfth century BC. While the well is too young to have been used by the patriarchs, it was probably very close to the site of the well where Abraham and Abimelech made their oath (Beersheba means "the well of the oath" or "the well of seven") because it is immediately outside the city gate.

An event of major historical significance took place either at Beersheba or in the regions nearby including Mamre and Gerar. The account is recorded in Genesis 15 when God promised Abraham that he would have a son; however, by chapter 16, Abraham's wife Sarah, had still not borne him any children. Sarah suggested to Abraham that he should take Sarah's Egyptian slave, Hagar, and build a family through her. So Abraham slept with Hagar and she became pregnant. Understandably, Sarah became jealous and chased Hagar into the desert. An angel appeared on the scene and sent Hagar and her child back to Abraham and Sarah's home, but with a historic promise:

Then the Angel of the Lord said to her [Hagar], "I will multiply your descendants exceedingly, so that they shall not be counted for multitude." (Genesis 16:10-11)

Then, in chapter 17, Hagar is back home, and the son Ishmael is born at Mamre when Abraham was eighty-six years old. God once again confirms His covenant with Abraham to provide him and Sarah with their own son. Finally, in chapter 21, the promised son is born:

And the Lord visited Sarah as He had said, and the Lord did for Sarah as He had spoken. For Sarah conceived and bore Abraham a son in his old age, at the set time of which God had spoken to him. And Abraham called the name of his son who was born to him—whom Sarah bore to him—Isaac. (Genesis 21:1-3)

DETOUR TWO:
HOW TO BOARD AN EGGED BUS IN ISRAEL

We can't leave Beersheba without relating a few of our adventures while traveling by bus. Often, the real experience occurs before getting on the bus. On my first visit to Israel in 1991, I traveled by bus from Tel Aviv to Beersheba; that part was civilized. In Beersheba, I had to change buses and catch a bus into the Negev desert to Sede Boqer. Initially, things were civilized — everyone waiting for the bus was lined up in an orderly fashion, and I was fairly far up the line along with my two medium-sized carry-on bags. Then, the bus pulled into the loading bay, and everything fell apart! Mayhem unleashed. There was mad pushing and shoving as at least seventy people tried to get on to a forty-five-seater bus. At one stage, both of my feet were literally off the ground as I clung to my bags. When I was finally deposited, I was closer to the bus door, but fifty other people had arrived before me, the doors slammed shut, and I was left standing. I caught the next bus forty-five minutes later. I found it slightly unnerving to be one of the few passengers on the bus that wasn't a soldier. Almost everyone on the bus had weapons, and the chap sitting beside me calmly laid his M-16 across my lap!

On another occasion at Beersheba, I was left behind by the bus because I didn't have any bags! Again, the pre-boarding decorum was civilized, then the bus arrived, and the post-arrival mayhem ensued. I noticed something that I hadn't seen before: passengers, quite far back in the line-up, would simply walk around the outside of the mayhem, put their bags in the luggage storage under the bus and calmly enter the front of the lineup. So, the act of having baggage seemed to promote a person to the head of the lineup. Perhaps seven or eight people did this.

This time, I was just about to step onto the bus when the driver closed the door. The bus was full, very full, and I was the last person but at least I would be first for the next bus. Then the unthinkable happened. Someone reached over my shoulder, banged the door of the bus, the driver opened the door, the guy clambered over me, climbed into the bus, and the door closed! How did that happen? Then another arm over the shoulder ... and two more people did the same thing. Okay, I can play this game, so I banged the door. I must not have banged the door in Hebrew because the bus reversed out of the loading bay! When I realized that people with bags had jumped the line, and others had climbed over me, I muttered, *"this will never happen again!"* and it didn't. I got good, really good, at getting on board buses.

One day, Alistair and I went to the Central Bus Station in Jerusalem to catch a bus to Beersheba. Usual arrangement — a fairly orderly pre-boarding lineup. The bus pulled into the loading bay. I had already done my count and realized that it was unlikely that we would get on the bus. I nudged Alistair and said, "Follow me." We walked around the group, put our tiny little bags in the storage compartment, walked to the top of the line, climbed on, and realized that we had just become Israelis!

Isaac was born at Gerar when Abraham was one hundred years old and Sarah was ninety. But all wasn't well in the Abrahamic household — one wife, one slave, and Abraham had fathered a son to each of them!

> *And Sarah saw the son of Hagar the Egyptian, whom she had borne to Abraham, scoffing. Therefore she said to Abraham, "Cast out this bondwoman and her son; for the son of this bondwoman shall not be heir with my son, namely with Isaac." And the matter was very displeasing in Abraham's sight because of his son. But God said to Abraham, "Do not let it be displeasing in your sight because of the lad or because of your bondwoman. Whatever Sarah has said to you, listen to her voice; for in Isaac your seed shall be called. Yet I will also make a nation of the son of the bondwoman, because he is your seed." So Abraham rose early in the morning, and took bread and a skin of water; and putting it on her shoulder, he gave it and the boy to Hagar, and sent her away. Then she departed and wandered in the Wilderness of Beersheba. And the water in the skin was used up, and she placed the boy under one of the shrubs. Then she went and sat down across from him at a distance of about a bowshot; for she said to herself, "Let me not see the death of the boy." So she sat opposite him, and lifted her voice and wept. And God heard the voice of the lad. Then the angel of God called to Hagar out of heaven, and said to her, "What ails you, Hagar? Fear not, for God has heard the voice of the lad where he is. Arise, lift up the lad and hold him with your hand, for I will make him a great nation." Then God opened her eyes, and she saw a well of water. And she went and filled the skin with water, and gave the lad a drink. (Genesis 21:9-19)*

Ishmael was circumcised at thirteen years old, the age at which Arabs and Muslims still circumcise. Isaac and Ishmael's mothers were quarreling almost 3,800 years ago, and their descendants continue that fight today — a bus bomb exploded in Beersheba only three weeks before we wrote this part of our story.

And Hebron remains one of the most dangerous cities in Israel with frequent clashes between the descendants of Isaac and Ishmael. The story ends by saying:

So Abraham returned to his young men, and they rose and went together to Beersheba; and Abraham dwelt at Beersheba. (Genesis 22:19)

One of the best-known stories in all of Scripture begins with:

Then He said, "Take now your son, your only son Isaac, whom you love, and go to the land of Moriah, and offer him there as a burnt offering on one of the mountains of which I shall tell you." (Genesis 22:2)

The narrative goes on to tell how Abraham took Isaac and went to the land of Moriah as God had commanded them:

Then on the third day Abraham lifted his eyes and saw the place afar off. And Abraham said to his young men, "Stay here with the donkey; the lad and I will go yonder and worship, and we will come back to you." So Abraham took the wood of the burnt offering and laid it on Isaac his son; and he took the fire in his hand, and a knife, and the two of them went together. But Isaac spoke to Abraham his father and said, "My father!" And he said, "Here I am, my son." Then he said, "Look, the fire and the wood, but where is the lamb for a burnt offering?" And Abraham said, "My son, God will provide for Himself the lamb for a burnt offering." So the two of them went together. Then they came to the place of which God had told him. And Abraham built an altar there and placed the wood in order; and he bound Isaac his son and laid him on the altar, upon the wood. And Abraham stretched out his hand and took the knife to slay his son. (Genesis 22:4-10)

The early part of this story may seem depressing and suggest a tragic ending. But then the sky clears, the sun comes out, and a beautiful scene unfolds, that begins with *but...:*

But the Angel of the Lord called to him from heaven and said, "Abraham, Abraham!" So he said, "Here I am." And He said," Do not lay your hand on the lad, or do anything to him; for now I know that you fear God, since you have not withheld your son, your only son, from Me." Then Abraham lifted his eyes and looked, and there behind him was a ram caught in a thicket by its horns. So Abraham went and took the ram, and offered it up for a burnt offering instead of his son. And Abraham called the name of the place, The-Lord-Will-Provide; as it is said to this day, "In the Mount of the Lord it shall be provided." (Genesis 22:11-14)

And so is presented one of the most beautiful pictures in all of Scripture. Josephus posits that Isaac was twenty-five years old, and some rabbis say that he was thirty-six. My guess is that he was probably about thirty-three, the age at which the great fulfillment, Jesus Christ, was offered up. Isaac was a relatively young man in the prime of life yet he submitted to his father who must have been frail and at least 125 years old. This story beautifully typifies the sacrifice of Jesus Christ, almost two thousand years later, probably on this same Mount Moriah. In both cases, the father himself offers up his only-begotten son, and the father himself binds the son to either the wood or the cross. In neither case is the son forced to yield. The angel said to Abraham that God would provide a lamb. He provided a lamb instantly, the one caught in the thicket, but it cannot go unnoticed that Abraham called the place "the Lord will provide" on the Mount of the Lord.

The great temples built by Solomon, Zerubbabel, and Herod, the places of sacrifice, were later built upon this same Mount Moriah. And the place of Calvary where Christ was crucified was most likely about seven hundred meters to the northwest on the same mountain ridge. Today, Mount Moriah is occupied by the Muslim Golden-Domed ornamental shrine known as the Dome of the Rock.[11] This was the site of Araunah's threshing floor (2 Samuel 24:18-25; 2 Chronicles 3:1), and it is called the Lord's holy mountain. It is also a place where I was "verbally abused." We had entered the shrine as visitors,[12] and I was looking over the top rail of the wooden barrier that surrounds the rock in the middle of the shrine. Our daughter Andrea was only twelve years old and too short to see over the rail. As any dad would do, I picked her up to let her peek over the top. Not a good thing to do in a Muslim holy place! No touching, no holding hands, no nothing. At least I knew exactly what they wanted me to do — there was no ambiguity.

<hr />

DETOUR THREE:
CELEBRATING THE FESTIVAL OF EID AL-ADHA AT ACHMED'S TENT

Before we leave the story of Abraham and Isaac we will divert briefly to Abraham and Ishmael. During our time working in the Negev desert, we became friendly

---

[11] For the Jewish people, the Temple Mount is the holiest place on earth. This is where their two temples once stood. The First Temple was built by King Solomon and destroyed by the Babylonians in 586 BC; the Second Temple, built by Zerubbabel in the sixth century BC and massively renovated and extended by Herod the Great was destroyed by the Romans in 70 AD. Many believe that the Holy of Holies inside the Temple was located on the rock where the Dome of the Rock now stands. For Muslims, the Temple Mount is known as *Haram al-Sharif* and is the third holiest site in Islam. Muslims teach that The Dome of the Rock is built over the Foundation Stone which marks the spot where Muhammad ascended into heaven in the seventh century.

[12] Visitors were allowed into the Dome of the Rock in the early 1990s. At some stage in the mid-1990s, Muslim authorities imposed restrictions so that non-Muslims could no longer visit.

with a Bedouin man called Achmed. He didn't speak a word of English, nor we a word of Arabic, yet in a strange sense we communicated and became good friends. Achmed often said that sometime he would like to have us visit his tent. The Bedouins are (were) nomadic people, and the Israeli government was making a lot of effort to settle them in more permanent homes. In 1996, Evelyn and I received a formal invitation to visit Achmed's tent on the festival of Eid al-Adha.

This festival commemorates the occasion when (according to Muslim tradition) Abraham was willing to sacrifice everything, including his own son Ishmael. Since Muslims believe that Allah spared Ishmael by substituting a sheep in a thicket, Muslims honor the day by slaughtering an animal and distributing the meat among friends, family, and the needy. We were accompanied by two other colleagues who could translate.

Achmed's tent is in a sizeable Bedouin settlement in the Negev desert on the southern outskirts of Beersheba and pitched in the shadow of a large Israeli prison. The directions we were given were quite good. Although we drove almost entirely around the prison, carefully avoiding a few camels, donkeys, and children, we eventually found his tent. Interestingly, we drove past a tent covered by a very large, bright, yellow tarpaulin — exactly like the one we had ordered to cover large sand piles at our experimental sites in Sede Boqer about forty miles to the south, exactly like the one we had stolen about one week earlier! (And talking about sandpiles, we often joked about making one of the world's largest sandboxes — thirty trenches, each two meters by five meters by 1.20 meters deep, filled with six hundred tons of sand specifically transported in for the work).

We were invited into Achmed's tent, sat down on floor mats, and had numerous cups of very sweet black tea. The only things inside were a mat, a small table, and a cooking pit in the floor in the middle. We were introduced to Achmed's family, including both of his wives, both decked-out and dripping with gold jewelry for this special holiday. For the first few years we knew Achmed, he only had one wife. This was the first time we had had a chance to chat with him since he married again. I spoke to my colleague-translator and asked her to ask Achmed why he had married a second wife. He paused, then chuckled with a broad almost toothless grin and replied, "It seemed like a good idea at the time." They were both beautiful women, very friendly and hospitable towards us, and apparently very friendly towards each other.

We chatted for some time, intrigued by the cooking methods and the tent's air conditioning. It was very hot outside, and although the tent provided shade, it was still relentlessly hot. The air conditioning was simple. There was a nice breeze blowing through the tent. Achmed had simply set up a hose to sprinkle the ground outside the tent on the up-wind side. The cooling effect was remarkable, and I was immediately thrown back to my high school physics classes where we were taught about the latent heat of evaporation. Basically, as hot air moves over the wet ground, heat is used to evaporate the water with a consequent cooling of the air that continues to flow into the tent.

Achmed had five children, who were keen to show us the family's animals and the rest of their home. We were surprised by the high quality of the furniture and furnishings, and this especially so because these were all in tents, on an uneven and sloping earthen floor. The family zoo was small and included several sheep and goats, a few donkeys, and two camels.

When we returned to the tent, one of Achmed's wives was cooking sheep on a wood fire built in the small hollow in the middle of the tent. Apparently, the sheep had just been slaughtered at the back door of the tent, so this was fresh. Frequently, pieces of meat would fall off the metal grill or even fall through the grill, but that didn't phase the cook. Like lightning, she would grab into the fire, pick up the meat, and after a quick blow and a gentle shaking of the meat, it was back on the grill.

There was plenty to eat, but we didn't eat a lot. Although we have traveled a lot, experienced a lot, and eaten in many trying situations, the combined mixture of it being a very hot day, the cooking conditions, and the flies, was beyond the threshold of our appetite; however, what we did eat was very good and none of us got sick. After a lot more chatting, it was time to go home. As we said our farewells and exited the tent, there, lying on the ground, was the head, wool, entrails, and other bits of the sheep we had just eaten — just as well we didn't see that before dinner!

Our journey with Abraham closes in the city of Hebron. Hebron is the city of the patriarchs, and there, in the middle of the city, is an enormous Herodian structure containing the burial sites of Abraham, Sarah, Isaac, Rebecca, Jacob, Leah, and Joseph. In Hebron, David was crowned king of Judah, where he ruled for seven years. David had six sons born in Hebron including Absalom, Amnon, and Adonijah. Sounds nice; and it even has a tranquil ring to it, but this doesn't reflect the present-day reality of Hebron.

Hebron is a troubled city. It is the largest city in the West Bank having over 200,000 Palestinians and 750 Israeli Jews living in proximity. The Jewish population lives in a neighborhood using the old biblical name for Hebron, Kiriath Arba (Genesis 23:2):

And the name of Hebron formerly was Kiriath-Arba (Arba was the greatest man among the Anakim)... (Joshua 14:15)

Few tourists visit Hebron for safety reasons. We had lived in Jerusalem for nine months and still hadn't been able to visit Hebron. However, in chapter 10, we will describe in detail how we ultimately convinced Pastor Musa from Ramallah Bible Baptist Church and Pastor Naim from Bethlehem Baptist Church to take us to Hebron, specifically to the tombs of the patriarchs — exciting, interesting, and frightening. A few years later, Evelyn and I decided to make another trip to the tombs of the Patriarchs in Hebron. A year or so earlier, in 1994, a Jewish settler from Kiriath Arba, Baruch Goldstein, had entered the building and shot and killed twenty-nine Palestinian Muslim worshippers and wounded more than 125 others, in what has become known as the Cave of the Patriarchs massacre. Consequently, to prevent a repeat of this horror, security was stepped up an enormous degree. In addition, the building was now divided in half so that Jews have access to the tombs of Joseph, Judah, Leah, Sarah, and Abraham, and Muslims have access to Isaac, Rebecca, and Abraham.

Now it was 1996, a partial peace plan was in effect, and the social and political environments were a little more settled. We were on a day trip, and Evelyn had brought a few sandwiches, a whole tomato, and a small knife to cut the tomato. If you have any imagination, you can probably guess what happened next. As we approached the security police (Israeli soldiers), we remembered we had the knife. What to do? We walked up to the security police in front of the scanner, and we informed them that we had a knife. This caused no end of amusement. They took the knife from us for safekeeping until we left the building. We then walked through the scanner, were frisked and searched and proceeded up the steps to the entrance. There we were met by another group of security guards who asked:

"Are you the people with the knife?"

"Yes," we replied, "but the guards downstairs took the knife from us."

We never determined if they were suspicious or whether this was protocol, but we went through another security scanner, more frisking, and more examination of our bags, finally gaining entry to the Jewish side of this wonderful building. After our visit, we returned the way we had come and reclaimed our knife at the security check. From here it is about a two-minute walk around to the backside of the building where we would enter the Muslim side. Rather than go through a repeat security performance, we walked over to our rental car and popped the knife into the glove compartment. Upon arrival at the security check to the Muslim mosque we were greeted with:

"Are you the people with the knife?"

"Yes, but we put it in the car," we replied.

And, yes, it all happened for a third time: the scanner, the frisk, and the bag check. This was now becoming amusing (if not a little frustrating) although we could understand why security was so tight. The Israelis didn't want a repeat performance of the massacre. In fact, Israeli soldiers guarded both the synagogue and the mosque. However, it wasn't all over yet, because there ahead of us, at least ten meters beyond our third checkpoint, was yet a fourth checkpoint.

"Are you the people with the knife...?" (and you know the rest)! Otherwise, we had a wonderful visit to the Tombs of the Patriarchs at the Cave of Machpelah in Hebron.

Then, in 1997, I took a couple of friends to the tombs. This time we arrived from the north, and I wasn't as familiar with that end of the city. Hebron is quite disorganized and chaotic and not easy to get around — this is a euphemism for saying that it is easy to get lost. We did! We asked for directions, and a young Arab lad jumped into the back seat of our rental car and said he would take us to the tombs. He seemed to drive us endlessly around streets and alleys but then I recognized the familiar Tombs of the Patriarchs. Just at that moment, I spotted about twenty meters ahead of me an armed Israeli soldier sauntering out onto the road and beckoning me to stop. The little Arab guide in the back seat was a little nervous and adamantly said, "Don't stop because there will be trouble with me being in your car." Thankfully, some things happen so quickly in life that we don't have time to think. If I had the time to sit back, strike a committee, and made a logical and informed decision, there is no doubt that I would have stopped for the soldier. After all, an armed Israeli soldier is nothing to be messed with. But instead, I just kept driving staring straight ahead pretending I didn't see the soldier, trying to look as if I were lost! I can still see the rather startled soldier in my rear-view mirror. We went around the corner, dropped off the young lad, gave him a tip, parked, returned to the soldier, apologised, and then walked over and entered the building. It seems that it is not possible to visit this building without a little excitement.

Next, on what turned out to be the last tour we led to Israel, we managed to get our group to Hebron and into the Tombs of the Patriarchs. We were on the Jewish side, and it seemed to be particularly busy this day. It was obvious there had been a meeting of some kind and then everyone scattered pushing the chairs in every direction, making a chaotic mess. Despite the untidiness, there was a lot of celebration and singing. As a group, we were walking around rather aimlessly when a little, elderly, Jewish grandmother spotted us and beckoned us over to where she was standing. It was a circumcision! We thought we were being intrusive, but on the contrary, we were invited right inside the room to watch the procedure. About twenty young Jewish men dressed in religious apparel danced in a circle around the rabbi and child, singing loudly and happily. Evelyn has been an operating room nurse for more than forty years and had seen many of these procedures before, but there was one difference. Apparently, there is typically a lot of bloody gauze all over the place, but here there was barely a drop of blood and a cut as clean as a whistle. The original welcoming grandmother now had the child and was dancing and showing it to everyone. What a wonderful celebration and experience.

The Scriptures tell us that:

Sarah lived one hundred and twenty-seven years; these were the years of the life of Sarah. So Sarah died in Kirjath Arba (that is, Hebron) in the land of Canaan, and Abraham came to mourn for Sarah and to weep for her. (Genesis 23:1-2)

So the field of Ephron which was in Machpelah, which was before Mamre, the field and the cave which was in it, and all the trees that were in the field, which were within all the surrounding borders, were deeded to Abraham as a possession in the presence of the sons of Heth, before all who went in at the gate of his city. And after this, Abraham buried Sarah his wife in the cave of the field of Machpelah, before Mamre (that is, Hebron) in the land of Canaan. (Genesis 23:17-19)

Then Abraham breathed his last and died in a good old age, an old man and full of years, and was gathered to his people. And his sons Isaac and Ishmael buried him in the cave of Machpelah, which is before Mamre, in the field of Ephron the son of Zohar the Hittite, the field which Abraham purchased from the sons of Heth. There Abraham was buried, and Sarah his wife. (Genesis 25:8-10)

And so we leave Abraham and Sarah to rest. However, not far south of Hebron, we had some excitement. This has absolutely nothing to do with the life of the patriarchs, but we had to squeeze this story in somewhere. This trip had no obvious danger, but it was tense, and in the words of Pastor Musa, "The Lord delivered you." By 1995, we'd traveled everywhere imaginable in Israel. We'd been in many nervous situations, talked our way out of many problems, and perhaps were getting a little complacent. I had badly wanted to visit the cities of Carmel and Maon in the hill country of Judah. Maon was the hometown of an infamous character called Nabal, and his beautiful wife Abigail.

Now there was a man in Maon whose business was in Carmel, and the man was very rich. He had three thousand sheep and a thousand goats. And he was shearing his sheep in Carmel. The name of the man was Nabal, and the name of his wife Abigail. And she was a woman of good understanding and beautiful appearance; but the man was harsh and evil in his doings... (1 Samuel 25:2-3)

David was on the run from King Saul and had sent ten young men to Nabal to request supplies. The hard-hearted Nabal refused, but Abigail...

...made haste and took two hundred loaves of bread, two skins of wine, five sheep already dressed, five seahs of roasted grain, one hundred clusters of raisins, and two hundred cakes of figs, and loaded them on donkeys. And she said to her servants, "Go on before me; see, I am coming after you." But she did not tell her husband Nabal. (1 Samuel 25:18-19)

Abigail personally brought the supplies to David and paid him homage and asked for forgiveness for her scoundrel husband.

Then David said to Abigail: "Blessed is the Lord God of Israel, who sent you this day to meet me! And blessed is your advice and blessed are you, because you have kept me this day from coming to bloodshed and from avenging myself with my own hand. For indeed, as the Lord God of Israel lives, who has kept me back from hurting you, unless you had hurried and come to meet me, surely by morning light no males would have been left to Nabal!" So David received from her hand what she had brought him, and said to her, "Go up in peace to your house. See, I have heeded your voice and respected your person." Now Abigail went to Nabal, and there he was, holding a feast in his house, like the feast of a king. And Nabal's heart was merry within him, for he was very drunk; therefore she told him nothing, little or much, until morning light. So it was, in the morning, when the wine had gone from Nabal, and his wife had told him these things, that his heart died within him, and he became like a stone. Then it happened, after about ten days, that the Lord struck Nabal, and he died. (1 Samuel 25:32-38)

The story could have ended here with a sad and tragic ending, but David was a mover and shaker:

So when David heard that Nabal was dead, he said, "Blessed be the Lord, who has pleaded the cause of my reproach from the hand of Nabal, and has kept His servant from evil! For the Lord has returned the wickedness of Nabal on his own head." And David sent and proposed to Abigail, to take her as his wife. When the servants of David had come to Abigail at Carmel, they spoke to her saying, "David sent us to you, to ask you to become his wife." Then she arose, bowed her face to the earth, and said, "Here is your maidservant, a servant to wash the feet of the servants of my lord." So Abigail rose in haste and rode on a donkey, attended by five of her maidens; and she followed the messengers of David, and became his wife. (1 Samuel 25:39-42)

The ruins of these towns are about fifteen kilometers southeast of Hebron. I was traveling alone, with not-so-good maps, in an Israeli yellow-license-plate car. I drove through Hebron with no problem and continued south on the road towards Beersheba. I spotted the signpost I had been looking for: Yatta. Yatta was about seven or eight kilometers to the east of the main road, and I knew that if I could get there, I'd already be over halfway to my destination. I turned left and was barely two hundred meters along the road when a UN vehicle hurriedly came alongside me.

"Where are you going?" I was asked.

I explained that I was trying to find the biblical ruins of Carmel and Maon.

"You can't go into this area because it is much too dangerous," I was told.

I asked, "Are you telling me I shouldn't go, or that I am not allowed to go?"

"We can't stop you," the UN officer said, "but this is a dangerous area especially since you have a car with yellow plates."

For the first time in my visits to Israel, a little voice told me to forget this one, and return to Jerusalem. "Okay," I agreed, "I will just go a few meters down the road, and I will turn around."

We bid each other some pleasantries, and I drove about two hundred meters along the road to a spot where the road widened. I was in the process of doing a U-turn when a stretched Merc drew up along side with six Arab lads. Again, all the usual questions, "Who are you?" "Where do you live?" "Where are you going?" "Do you speak Hebrew?" and of course, "Do you speak Arabic?" and most of this was in very broken English. In the best way I was able, I told them that I was turning around and going to Jerusalem. However, somehow in the midst of this, they seemed to know what I was looking for. They had clearly spoken to the UN folks. I knew I had made the correct decision to return to Jerusalem when one of the lads punched a clenched fist into his open palm five or six times and said, "Throw stones, throw stones."

"That's okay, I'm going back," as I indicated with my finger the direction I intended to go. Before I knew what was happening, one of the lads jumped into the car beside me and seemed to indicate that he would go with me. Now what do I do? What does this mean? I tried to indicate to this fellow that I was going to Jerusalem, but he seemed to insist that I was going to Yatta.

So I drove off along the road towards Yatta. Within a few minutes, we arrived in a little village which I initially thought was Yatta — it wasn't. I was feeling rather uneasy and tried to communicate with my new passenger, but this was to little avail. In the middle of the village, my passenger quite calmly said, "Here, stop," and with that, he climbed out of the car. Was I to stay here? Was my passenger coming back? This was soon answered when my passenger returned with two bottles of Coca-Cola. Again, I drove off while the two of us drank our Coke. Then we arrived at Yatta, which was a chaotic jumble of streets. Little did I know that it was going to take almost an hour to ask directions about forty times (slight exaggeration!) before finding the direction we needed to leave Yatta and head the few kilometers to Carmel and Maon; by now I was relieved to have my young companion with me. Part of the problem was language, part was that I didn't have a very good map, but part of the problem could have been nasty. You see, I didn't realize that there were two Carmels and two Maons. Not only were there scant remains of the ancient biblical cities, but there were also two new Jewish communities with these names! Oh, dear, yellow plates in Yatta and asking for directions to Jewish communities!

We finally found our way out of Yatta and traveled the short distance to Carmel. The roads were paved but in terrible disrepair, and they seemed to twist and turn in every direction. The road was only a single lane but had a rather noticeable ridge along its center. To place the wheels on either side of the ridge meant scraping the underbelly of the car, but to drive with one wheel on the ridge meant that the other wheel was on the grass verge — what a mess. Once arriving in the village, it only took a short time to locate the ruins, but by this time I had picked up yet another passenger, one who spoke relatively good English. We arrived at an abandoned piece of land, littered with garbage, parked, and walked a short distance to the ruins. They were scant, but I was overjoyed to see them. Then the fellow asked: "Would you like to go to Maon?"

Still nervous, but eager, I was in a real dilemma. I knew there wasn't a chance in the world that I would ever be able to visit this area again. My heart and my head were having an intense, rapid-fire debate. My head was saying get out of here, you are in danger, but my heart was telling me that I wanted to visit Maon. Even though I was suspicious if this fellow even knew where Maon was, my heart won. I believed him when he pointed to a large hill about two kilometers to the south of where we were standing and said "That's it, right there." From what I knew of the geography of the area, I knew he was correct. He jumped into the car, and now I had three passengers, heading even farther away from anywhere I was familiar with. We drove along a very bumpy track (thank goodness for Avis rental cars) for about a kilometer until we came to an opening in a stone fence. They pointed to the opening. I pulled in to park, believing that we were going to walk the remainder of the way.

In a single chorus they all indicated that I should drive through the opening and follow the series of ruts that ran along the edge of this field. No way should a car be in a place like this. It just kept getting worse as we climbed higher past a few homes, through more openings and finally we were within fifty meters of the summit of the hill of Maon. It was on a rather steep incline, so I pulled the hand brake very tightly. We couldn't drive to the top because a few Bedouins had built an encampment. Then my blood pressure went up, my heart beat noticeably faster and I didn't know how to react to one of the lads who said: "You take him up to the summit, and we will watch the car."

What an irony! Two young Palestinian men wanting to watch my yellow-license-plate car to protect it from the Bedouins. I did the only thing I could do and walked to the summit, but I never, for the slightest moment, let that car out of my sight. I hurriedly looked around (there was virtually nothing to see), snapped a few quick photographs, and headed straight back to the car. I was able to convince them that I really had to be on my way to Jerusalem. The four of us bumped our way down the hill, back to Carmel, dropped off two passengers, through Yatta, and back to the main Hebron-Beersheba road where I dropped off my final passenger. At this stage, I was getting ready for a request for money. After all, this fellow had spent three hours with me, traveled about thirty kilometers, bought me Coke, and he was the main factor in getting me to two very difficult sites — and to my utter embarrassment he never asked for a penny.

As I drove north to Hebron and on to Jerusalem, I had plenty of time to reflect on what had just happened — it was exciting, it was fascinating, but it sure wasn't funny and perhaps not too bright! Shortly after this, I was speaking with Pastor Musa by telephone and told him what had happened. His only response: "Did you not know that this is where Hamas have their headquarters? Roy, the Lord delivered you." And to cap this story, two years later, the Intifada had eased a little, and I returned to the sites of Carmel and Maon with Evelyn.

II.
AROUND THE DEAD SEA

On the journey from Jerusalem towards the Dead Sea you pass a signpost that says, "Sea Level." This is unexpected particularly since we're driving through the middle of the Judean desert. What is perhaps even more unexpected is that for the next twenty minutes we continue driving downhill, even farther below sea level, and we see mountain peaks below us. Upon arrival at the Dead Sea, we are 396 meters below sea level[13] — the lowest point on the earth's surface — and the sea itself is between 300–400 meters deep. The Dead Sea is just over eighty kilometers long and averages about fifteen kilometers wide.

The Dead Sea valley is the northern extension of the great East African rift valley that extends north from Tanzania through the Red Sea and continues along the Arabah, the Dead Sea, the River Jordan Valley and into the Sea of Galilee. This is the largest fracture on the earth's surface. In Scripture the Dead Sea is also known as the Vale of Siddim, the Salt Sea, the Arabah Sea, and the East Sea. Because road access is easy, and expensive resort hotels dot the western shore, it is easy to overlook the fact that this region is a barren desert with an inhospitable climate. The Dead Sea area is extremely dry and temperatures are high all year round; an average year has only five centimeters of rainfall. The water of the Dead Sea is about four to five times more saline than that of ocean water and feels smooth and oily, disgustingly bitter to the taste, and absolute torture on the eyes. The very dense water gives everyone the opportunity to take the obligatory float, lying on their back, reading a newspaper or magazine. It is impossible to sink in this water. I have a slight build, and can barely stay afloat long enough to swim the length of an average swimming pool; but in the Dead Sea, I can effortlessly bob vertically like a fishing float, with the water circling about twenty centimeters below my chin. It was like 'standing' in the water. But a word of cautious reflection: when we first got into the Dead Sea, we were made painfully, very painfully, aware of all sorts of cuts and scratches that we never knew we had.

---

[13] In 2018, the waters of the Dead Sea had receded to 430 meters below sea level — this is an average annual rate of about 110 centimeters. This recent receding water level has been caused by enormous reductions in the amount of water entering, primarily due to rivers being damned and diverted upstream and water used for drinking, domestic use and agriculture by Israel, Jordan, Syria, Lebanon and the Palestinian Authority, The receding water level has exposed large areas that were once underwater and created sinkholes that threatens soil stability.

The geography of the Dead Sea is changing. Between them, the Jordanians and the Israelis are extracting so much water from the Dead Sea that the whole lower basin from Masada to the south is totally dried up. The upper basin is also drying, the water level receding, and as a result the lowest point on the earth's surface is steadily getting lower. A great example of this is to be seen at the northern end of the Dead Sea. There, a mere shadow of its former glory, stands a lone hotel that was built by the Jordanians before the war of 1967. The hotel was built so that patrons in the hotel bar could sip their booze while dabbling their feet in the waters of the sea. The hotel has long been closed, but today it stands some four hundred meters from the new shoreline, and patrons, if there were any, would be squelching mud between their toes.

If a road existed to completely encircle the Dead Sea, the journey would be less than two hundred kilometers. But because of political history and today's political reality, such a journey isn't possible. Both the Israelis and Jordanians have a road along the full length of their respective shores, and, although one of the most heavily-armed border crossings in the world[14] joins the two roads at the north, there is no such southern connection. So in our journey around the Dead Sea, we will pretend that such an encircling road exists and we will take you on a counter-clockwise tour beginning at Qumran at the northwestern end of the sea.

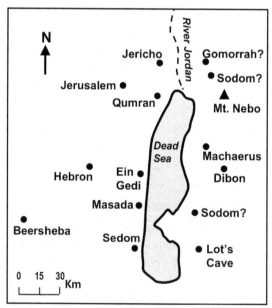

Bible sites around the Dead Sea.

---

[14] The Allenby Bridge border crossing is between Jordan and Israel and crosses the Jordan River about ten kilometers north of the Dead Sea.

Qumran is on a small hill overlooking the northwestern shore of the Dead Sea, thirteen kilometers south of Jericho, with beautiful, high cliffs as a backdrop. On an alluvial plateau below the cliffs, is the site of an ancient building complex which has a main building including a dining room, kitchens, dormitory, workshops, cisterns, and pools, and a room where manuscripts were prepared. This community numbered between 200–400 people, from about 140 BC until AD 67. The Jewish historian Josephus identified this community as the Essenes, a sect of Judaism.

This area lay in ruins for almost 1,900 years until, in 1947, Bedouin shepherds found the first of the Dead Sea Scrolls in caves close to the ancient settlement; further finds occurred until 1956.[15] It is fascinating that the first fragments of the scrolls were purchased in Bethlehem by the Hebrew university on exactly the same day of the UN resolution to establish the state of Israel. The caves uncovered what is the greatest archaeological find of the twentieth century, perhaps of all time.

Ancient manuscripts and fragments were found of almost all books of the Old Testament along with other non-Scriptural writings. Cave 4 produced the greatest finds with about fifteen thousand different fragments including the "*Acts of Torah*" and the very important "*Son of God*" text, which includes the phrases "*Son of Man*" and "*Son of the Most High.*" Another cave produced the Psalms Scroll that contains thirty eight psalms from the Bible. In addition, the cave contained seven Apocryphal Psalms, three of which weren't previously known. One of them reads as follows:

> Smaller was I than my brothers and the youngest of the sons of my father,
> so he made me shepherd of his flock and ruler over his kids.
> My hands have made an instrument and my fingers a lyre; and so have I
> rendered glory to the Lord, thought I, within my soul.
> The mountains do not witness to him nor do the hills proclaim; the trees
> have cherished my words and the flocks my works.
> For who can proclaim and who can bespeak and who can count the deeds
> of the Lord? Everything has God seen, everything has he heard
> and he has heeded.
> He sent his prophet to anoint me, Samuel to make me great;
> My brothers went out to meet him,
> handsome of figure and appearance.
> Though they were tall of stature and handsome by their hair,
> the Lord chose them not.

---

[15] More recent finds from 2000 onwards have all been shown to be forgeries.

> But he sent and took me from behind the flock and anointed me with holy
> oil; and he made me leader of his people and
> ruler over the sons of his covenant.[16]

The Psalms Scroll also provided the 'missing' verse 14 from Psalm 145. Psalm 145 is an acrostic Psalm, with each verse beginning with the next letter of the Hebrew alphabet, so scholars have always known that verse 14 was missing. It has now been inserted into the New International Version as an extended verse 13 (compare vs. 13 in the New King James and NIV).

Your kingdom is an everlasting kingdom,
And Your dominion endures
throughout all generations.
(Psalm 145:13, NKJV)

Your kingdom is an everlasting kingdom,
and your dominion endures
through all generations.
The Lord is faithful to all his promises
and loving toward all he has made.
(Psalm 145:13, NIV)

Many of the caves where the scrolls were found are accessible with a little effort. So, being dragged off by two young teenagers, our children Alistair and Andrea, we took off climbing the hills. One of the closer caves to the Qumran ruins is Cave 6. A guide at the main Qumran site advised us that there was absolutely nothing to see in this cave except for bird ****. This turned out to be true, but the climb was wonderful. It was nice to go inside one of the caves, and the view from the cave overlooking the ruins and the Dead Sea was quite awesome. On a later visit, we climbed to see Caves 3 and 11, and unfortunately spent a lot of time, at least three visits, going to the Cave of the Column mistakenly thinking that it was Cave 1. The Cave of the Column was so-named by an eccentric Texan, Vendyl Jones.

Vendyl Jones spent at least thirty years of his life searching for the lost Ark of the Covenant. If we remove the first letter 'V' and the last letter 'l' from Vendyl we are left with Endy; yes Endy, or Indiana Jones. Although George Lucas and Steven Spielberg apparently deny this, it is commonly believed that Vendyl was

---

[16] This version of the Psalm was taken from Emmanuel Dehan's "Our Visit to Israel" (1989 edition). Other translations include:

- Brownlee, William Hugh. "The 11 Q Counterpart to Psalm 151, 1-5." Revue de Qumrân 4, no. 3 (15) (1963): 379–87. http://www.jstor.org/stable/24600883.

- Psalm 151 and the Dead Sea Scrolls

by Peter W. Flint. https://www.bibleodyssey.org/passages/related-articles/psalm-151-and-the-dead-sea-scrolls - Psalm 151 and TextCritical Issues http://ccat.sas.upenn.edu/rak/courses/735/textcrit/Ps151.html

the inspiration for *"Indiana Jones and the Raiders of the Lost Ark."* There are too many parallels for this proposal to be ignored completely.

Jones was born in 1930, did a Masters in Theology from the Bible Baptist Seminary, and for a short time was a Baptist pastor. He finally gave up on most of Christianity and considers the New Testament to be a fraud. In 1964, the Copper Scroll was found in Cave 3 at Qumran. Jones was fascinated that this Scroll listed [or so he claimed] the hiding places of sixty-four sacred articles, which included the Tabernacle and the Ark of the Covenant. This catalyzed a personal quest that was to change his life. Vendyl conducted several major excavations primarily around Qumran although he was in continuous confrontation with the Israeli Antiquity Authorities; few archaeologists grant him much credibility. He claims to have identified the Cave of the Column, and inside he claims to have found the Holy Anointing Oil[17] from the Holy Temple, and over four hundred kilograms of spices he believes is the Holy Incense. Vendyl's exploits became a screenplay entitled *"The Search of the Ashes of the Red Heifer."*

In the spring of 1998, a few of us went to see some of the caves at Qumran. Driving along a rough but quite good track to a parking spot, we were surprised to see a fairly beaten-up VW Camper van. As we were leaving our vehicle, an older lady emerged from the VW and chatted to us, mostly about her daughter Donna.[18] She seemed disorientated but lucid, but who was she with, how did she get there, and what was she doing there in the middle of nowhere, in 38C heat, with apparently no one else in sight? We decided to leave her, visit the cave, and check in with her on the way back, probably in about thirty minutes.

We clambered the short distance up to the cave and while we were wandering around the entrance three people appeared and an older gentleman said to us,

"Hello, I'm Vendyl Jones; who are you?"

Initially, I was rather surprised, "Vendyl Jones?" I questioned. "This must be candid camera; this can't be happening; I thought you were dead!"

"There might not be much of me," he replied, "but this is it."

We stood there in the blazing heat for about half an hour and had a great chat although we found it difficult to separate fact from fantasy. He was a gracious, old gentleman, and he related to us the boring yet intricate details of how he discovered Gilgal, the first place the Children of Israel encamped after crossing

---

[17] The holy anointing oil was an integral part of the ordination of priests and the High Priest, and in the consecration of articles used in the tabernacle (Exodus 30:26) and subsequently the temples in Jerusalem. The primary purpose of the holy anointing oil was to scanctify, or to set apart, a person or object as holy (Exodus 30:29). The oil was made from liquid myrh, sweet-smelling cinnamon, sweet-smelling cane, cassia, and olive oil (Exodus 30:23–24).

[18] As best we can recall this is the correct name.

the River Jordan. Despite its importance, the true site of Gilgal was, for a long time, lost, until Vendyl came along — at least that is what he claimed. He told us about his excavations in the hills around Qumran, and for a few moments, Jones almost had us convinced that he had built the Ark of the Covenant — and had probably written the Dead Sea Scrolls!

Time was moving on, but before we parted company we asked about the VW camper and the elderly lady. "Oh, that's my mom," responded the young woman. "Ah-ha, so you must be Donna." We established that the old lady had Alzheimer's but was otherwise healthy. "Tell her we will be down in a few minutes," said Donna. We bid our farewells and scrambled down the slope to our car. As we approached the VW, the lady greeted us again along with her little Pomeranian dog which she had nicely snuggled into her chest.

Then doggie made a jump for freedom and took off across the rocky landscape. In a moment of horror, Mrs. Jones raised her two hands to the top of her head and was clearly upset. Momentarily, I glanced to my two colleagues. Being only half my age, I expected one of them to retrieve doggie. But, as doggie got farther away, and neither of my colleagues looked too motivated to run in 38C, I decided to run. The dog wasn't fast, and I caught up quickly, but she was maneuverable and agile. Thankfully, the dog was wearing a leash that became lodged between a few rocks, and I was finally able to pick her up. I looked back, and I was about eighty meters from the VW along with its three spectators. As I walked back, I held on to doggie quite tightly because this little escape artist wasn't going to be permitted a repeat performance. My mind was obviously doing an instant replay of what had happened, and I began to smile. Then, about ten meters from my spectators, I began to laugh at the moment. Who would ever believe this story? Here was I, standing in the middle of nowhere, in the blazing heat, holding the dog belonging to Indiana Jones's wife. I laughed so hard that I wet my pants — and I almost lost the dog again!

After all of this, we still hadn't visited the first cave found by the Bedouin shepherds. We drove back along the track for only a few hundred meters and parked. Cave 1 is not difficult to get to if know where it is, but it can be difficult to find because it isn't visible from the road. A few weeks earlier I had spoken with Professor Martin Abegg[19] at Trinity Western University, and he had given me directions. We savored this moment as we reflected upon the impact of the Bedouin's find — and then we turned around and enjoyed a magnificent view of the Dead Sea.

---

[19] Martin Abegg is Emeritus Professor of Religious Studies and former Director of The Dead Sea Scrolls Institute at Trinity Western University on the outskirts of Vancouver, Canada. (https://www.twu.ca/research/institutes-and-centers/university-institutes/dead-sea-scrolls-institute)

Next, we drove south past the very scant remains of six towns mentioned in Joshua 15:20, 61-62. The last of these is Ein Gedi. Today, Ein Gedi is a beautiful nature reserve, and from the parking lot, it's an easy thirty-minute amble through luxuriant vegetation along a little river to the waterfall at Nahal David. Ein Gedi is a botanist's dream. The combination of the reserve's location, topography, year-round warm temperatures, and abundant water allow a variety of plant species to survive here, representing different regions. Ein Gedi has plant species from the Mediterranean flora and also has the densest concentration of tropical plants growing in Israel, some being exceedingly rare. In some cases, Ein Gedi is the northernmost point at which some of these tropical species can be found. In addition to the Mediterranean and tropical flora, there is a diversity of wetlands vegetation and desert flora.

Ein Gedi was the location of that wonderful story of Saul and David. Scripture tells us that David went "and dwelt in strongholds at Ein Gedi." King Saul had been chasing the Philistines, and upon his return, he was informed that David was in the Wilderness of Ein Gedi. Saul gathered three thousand men to hunt David and his men and …

So he came to the sheepfolds by the road, where there was a cave; and Saul went in to attend to his needs. (David and his men were staying in the recesses of the cave.) Then the men of David said to him, "This is the day of which the Lord said to you, 'Behold, I will deliver your enemy into your hand, that you may do to him as it seems good to you.'" And David arose and secretly cut off a corner of Saul's robe. (1 Samuel 24:3-4)

Saul then left the cave, oblivious to what had happened. When he was a short distance from the cave David made his move:

[David] …called out to Saul, saying, "My lord the king!" And when Saul looked behind him, David stooped with his face to the earth, and bowed down. And David said to Saul: "Why do you listen to the words of men who say, 'Indeed David seeks your harm'? Look, this day your eyes have seen that the Lord delivered you today into my hand in the cave, and someone urged me to kill you. But my eye spared you, and I said, 'I will not stretch out my hand against my lord, for he is the Lord's anointed.' Moreover, my father, see! Yes, see the corner of your robe in my hand! For in that I cut off the corner of your robe, and did not kill you, know and see that there is neither evil nor rebellion in my hand, and I have not sinned against you. Yet you hunt my life to take it." (1 Samuel 24:8-11)

This story continues:

So it was, when David had finished speaking these words to Saul, that Saul said, "Is this your voice, my son David?" And Saul lifted up his voice and wept. Then he said to David: "You are more righteous than I; for you have rewarded me with good, whereas I have rewarded you with evil. And you have shown this day how you have dealt well with me; for when the Lord delivered me into your hand, you did not kill me...And now I know indeed that you shall surely be king, and that the kingdom of Israel shall be established in your hand. (1 Samuel 24:16-20)

We have no idea about the identity of this cave, and given the friable nature of the rocky substrate, a cave from three thousand years ago has likely been long eroded.

A few kilometers south of Ein Gedi we approach Masada, which looks bleak and ominous in the distance. Masada may have been David's stronghold (1 Samuel 22:4; 1 Samuel 24:22). It was one of Herod's fortresses, and it is the great symbol of the Jewish nation. The flat-topped summit is over thirteen hundred feet above the Dead Sea (which means that the summit is about one hundred feet below sea level!), and this immense rock has an area equivalent to about twenty football fields. Here was the scene of one of the most remarkable and tragic last stands for independence made by the Jews against the Romans. This story is well-known although it can sometimes differ in the details.

After the fall and destruction of Jerusalem in AD 70, a group of 960 Jewish patriots, including men, women, and children, barricaded themselves on the summit of Masada. They were pursued by Roman legionaries under the command of Flavius Silva. The Jews held the fortress for three years, but when their defeat seemed imminent and the Romans were ready to claim victory, the historian Josephus Flavius tells us that the commander of the zealots, Eleazar Ben-Yair, spoke to his people. He urged each man to die by his own hands rather than fall into the hands of the enemy. Ten men were chosen by lot to kill all the rest, including women and children. When these ten men had killed all the others, they again cast lots, and one man killed the other nine before killing himself. When the Romans eventually scaled the summit, they found ample food demonstrating that it wasn't a lack of provisions that caused the Jewish surrender. What the Romans found were a pile of corpses and deathly silence. Masada's defeat, in AD 73, marked the end of Jewish independence until 1948.

There are three routes to the top of Masada — two easy routes and one a little more difficult. The easiest route to the top is by cable car, and the other easy route is to take the short ten-minute climb along the ramp the Romans used almost two thousand years ago. But why take an easy route when a difficult one is available?

On our first visit we climbed using the Snake Path, which rises steeply on the eastern side of the plateau. The temperatures were relatively low, 18–20C, but the climb was tough and took about forty-five minutes. We returned to Masada on many occasions, and on one of these visits our son Alistair raced up in twenty minutes, but his face was such a deep red we thought his head was going to explode! In 2018. I was accompanied by our son-in-law Fergus — a 2.04 meter tall bag-of-muscles fire fighter. Fergus climbed via the Snake Path while I photographed him from the cable car; it was only 41C. His ascent was impressive, but he badly needed his firefighter colleagues to put him out when he reached the top.

Regardless of how often we visited Masada, it never failed to grab our emotional strings as we reflected upon the events that happened there. To the tourist, the most important finds at Masada are probably King Herod's palace, the storehouses, steam rooms, synagogue, and the Byzantine church. To the historian, the most important finds are the various biblical and non-biblical scrolls that were uncovered, including a description of Eleazar Ben-Yair's historic address to his doomed comrades. To the archaeologist, the whole place is important. But to us, the most significant discovery was made on the northwestern edge of the plateau. In a section of the casemate wall, overlooking the Roman camp of Flavius Silva below, archaeologists discovered a house of worship, and a synagogue, a special communal hall for prayer, which would have been a most fitting act of deeply Orthodox religious Jews, which the zealots were. As excavators dug the floor, they discovered various scrolls. One of these scrolls turned out to be a passage from the book of Ezekiel, and apparently it was open at that magnificent portion in chapter 37 which, rather appropriately, prophesies the rebirth of Israel as a nation. In part, it reads:

The hand of the Lord came upon me and brought me out in the Spirit of the Lord, and set me down in the midst of the valley; and it was full of bones. Then He caused me to pass by them all around, and behold, there were very many in the open valley; and indeed they were very dry. And He said to me, "Son of man, can these bones live?" So I answered, "O Lord God, You know." Again He said to me, "Prophesy to these bones, and say to them, 'O dry bones, hear the word of the Lord! Thus says the Lord God to these bones: "Surely I will cause breath to enter into you, and you shall live. I will put sinews on you and bring flesh upon you, cover you with skin and put breath in you; and you shall live. Then you shall know that I am the Lord."'"

So I prophesied as I was commanded; and as I prophesied, there was a noise, and suddenly a rattling; and the bones came together, bone to bone. Indeed, as I looked, the sinews and the flesh came upon them, and the skin covered them over; but there was no breath in them.

Also He said to me, "Prophesy to the breath, prophesy, son of man, and say to the breath, 'Thus says the Lord God: "Come from the four winds, O breath, and breathe on these slain, that they may live."'" So I prophesied as He commanded me, and breath came into them, and they lived, and stood upon their feet, an exceedingly great army.

Then He said to me, "Son of man, these bones are the whole house of Israel. They indeed say, 'Our bones are dry, our hope is lost, and we ourselves are cut off!' Therefore prophesy and say to them, 'Thus says the Lord God: "Behold, O My people, I will open your graves and cause you to come up from your graves, and bring you into the land of Israel. Then you shall know that I am the Lord, when I have opened your graves, O My people, and brought you up from your graves. I will put My Spirit in you, and you shall live, and I will place you in your own land. Then you shall know that I, the Lord, have spoken it and performed it," says the Lord.'" (Ezekiel 37:1-14)

Of particular interest to us is that archaeologists discovered hundreds of inscribed pottery shards. Among them was a group consisting of ten names, including the name 'Ben Yair.' Archaeologist Yigael Yadin linked these shards with Josephus's story of the drawing of lots on that final night of the revolt.

Then, another botanist's dream. In 2008,[20] a paper reported the germination of a 1,900-year-old date seed collected from Masada, and a later paper[21] in 2020 confirms the long-term survival of date palm seeds. The date seeds were found buried under rubble close to the remains of an area identified as a food storage site. These are the oldest authentic seeds ever to have germinated.

We don't want to indulge in too much speculation, but some is permissible at this time. Some of the scrolls found here at Masada are similar to some of the Dead Sea Scrolls found at Qumran. Most of these scrolls date back to the same general time. It should be recalled that Masada is less than fifty kilometers to the south of Qumran. Again, it is fascinating to us that the first fragments of the Dead Sea scrolls found their way into Israel on exactly the same day of the UN resolution to establish the state of Israel — when all those dead bones came to life! Isn't verse 14 exciting? It says:

"...and I will place you in your own land. Then you shall know that I, the Lord, have spoken it and performed it," says the Lord.'" (Ezekiel 37:14)

Somehow the Scriptures of antiquity have an enduring and ever-present relevance to today.

The road from Masada continues south along the shores of the Dead Sea in the general direction of a rather obscure location. Scripture describes this as the cities of the plain (Genesis 19:29), and the five cities are identified alongside the kings' names as follows:

And the king of Sodom, the king of Gomorrah, the king of Admah, the king of Zeboiim, and the king of Bela (that is, Zoar) went out and joined together in battle in the Valley of Siddim (Genesis 14:8)

[20] Sallon, S. et al. (2008). Germination, genetics and growth of an ancient date seed. *Science* 320, 1464.

[21] Sallon, S. et al. (2020). Origins and insights into the historic Judean date palm based on genetic analysis of germinated ancient seeds and morphometric studies. *Science Advances* 05 Feb 2020: Vol. 6, no. 6, eaax0384 DOI: 10.1126/sciadv.aax0384

The names of these cities are by-words in our modern society. When ministers are said to be preaching fire and brimstone, the allusion is to Sodom and Gomorrah. The names, especially Sodom, are inextricably associated with sin and wickedness, particularly sexual immorality. We have the legal term sodomy to describe unnatural sex acts. Four of the cities were destroyed because of their wickedness.

Also I have seen a horrible thing in the prophets of Jerusalem: They commit adultery and walk in lies; They also strengthen the hands of evildoers, So that no one turns back from his wickedness. All of them are like Sodom to Me, And her inhabitants like Gomorrah. (Jeremiah 23:14)

...as Sodom and Gomorrah, and the cities around them in a similar manner to these, having given themselves over to sexual immorality and gone after strange flesh, are set forth as an example, suffering the vengeance of eternal fire. (Jude 7)

The exact location of these cities is uncertain. Indeed, some scholars argue that they never existed. A short distance south of Masada is a dilapidated signpost indicating Sedom, but this is not the location of biblical Sodom. Today, the only evidence of life is that of a huge, ugly chemical production plant. A prevalent argument is that the cities were located beneath the shallow waters of the southern basin of the Dead Sea. However, after extensive excavation in the 1970s, a compelling argument can be made for the ruins at sites in a region to the east and southeast of the Dead Sea in Jordan. These sites are Bab ad-Dhra (Sodom?), Numeira (Gomorrah?), Safi (Zoar?), Feifeh, and Hanzir. All of them are situated beside oases, and, except for Safi, were fortified by walls.

Our adventures to Sodom and Gomorrah began when we rented an Avis car in Aqaba in southern Jordan. We made our way north, spent a day at Petra, which was the setting for the movie *Indiana Jones and The Last Crusade*. The next day we arrived at the area of Sodom but not before a quick visit to a rather special cave named the Monastery of St. Lot. There are remains of a small monastery and church at this site. During the Byzantine period, early Christians built a church and monastery around this natural cave that was first occupied over five thousand years ago.[22] Although we only had a short visit, it was long enough for us to stand and ponder and reflect upon the biblical account of the events that

---

[22] About one hundred kilometers to the north of St. Lot's Monastery is the Jordanian city of Madeba. In the city is a sixth century Greek Orthodox church of St. George. The church has an enormous mosaic tile map (estimated to have two million tiles) embedded in its floor. This is the oldest surviving map of the Bible lands and shows the entire Middle East region from the River Nile through to Turkey. The map is centered and focused on the city of Jerusalem but many other sites of biblical interest are also indicated including St. Lot's monastery.

happened at this spot. Lot was here. His two daughters were conceived here. The Moabites and the Ammonites originated here.

And it came to pass, when God destroyed the cities of the plain, that God remembered Abraham, and sent Lot out of the midst of the overthrow, when He overthrew the cities in which Lot had dwelt. Then Lot went up out of Zoar and dwelt in the mountains, and his two daughters were with him; for he was afraid to dwell in Zoar. And he and his two daughters dwelt in a cave. Now the firstborn said to the younger, "Our father is old, and there is no man on the earth to come in to us as is the custom of all the earth. Come, let us make our father drink wine, and we will lie with him, that we may preserve the lineage of our father." So they made their father drink wine that night. And the firstborn went in and lay with her father, and he did not know when she lay down or when she arose. It happened on the next day that the firstborn said to the younger, "Indeed I lay with my father last night; let us make him drink wine tonight also, and you go in and lie with him, that we may preserve the lineage of our father." Then they made their father drink wine that night also. And the younger arose and lay with him, and he did not know when she lay down or when she arose. Thus both the daughters of Lot were with child by their father. The firstborn bore a son and called his name Moab; he is the father of the Moabites to this day. And the younger, she also bore a son and called his name Ben-Ammi; he is the father of the people of Ammon to this day. (Genesis 19:29-38)

It is only a short distance from St. Lot's monastery to one of the proposed locations for Sodom. Sodom is a huge mound about two kilometers from the eastern shore of the Dead Sea and a mere twenty kilometers due east of Masada. Initially, we were disappointed because the site was totally enclosed by a rusty, dilapidated, but still quite impenetrable fence. Besides, it was a blistering 40C, we had quite a tight schedule, and we were temped to take a token photograph and keep driving off to Gomorrah. But this was Sodom; this is one of the few biblical cities that everyone — believer and pagan, Jew and Gentile — has heard of. Our heads over-ruled our hearts, and we went looking for a hole in the fence. Luckily, we came to a gate that had a space just large enough to allow us to wriggle through on our bellies. In! Sodom! We didn't know if this really was Sodom; nevertheless, we stood awestruck at the historical memory of events that happened here perhaps four thousand years ago.

So why is there difficulty in identifying the location of Sodom? Scripture seems to imply that Abraham could see Sodom and Gomorrah and the valley from the oaks of Mamre, which is at Hebron. Further, Genesis 14:3 says that Sodom is in the Vale of Siddim, which is the Salt Sea (Dead Sea).

Then the Lord appeared to him [Abraham] by the terebinth trees of Mamre, as he was sitting in the tent door in the heat of the day. (Genesis 18:1)

Then the men rose from there [oaks of Mamre] and looked toward Sodom, and Abraham went with them to send them on the way. (Genesis 18:16)

Then the men turned away from there and went toward Sodom, but Abraham still stood before the Lord. (Genesis 18:22)

And Abraham went early in the morning to the place where he had stood before the Lord. Then he looked toward Sodom and Gomorrah, and toward all the land of the plain; and he saw, and behold, the smoke of the land which went up like the smoke of a furnace. (Genesis 19:27-28)

However, Genesis also seems to indicate a different general location about fifteen kilometers northeast of the Dead Sea:

So Abram said to Lot, "Please let there be no strife between you and me, and between my herdsmen and your herdsmen; for we are brethren. Is not the whole land before you? Please separate from me. If you take the left, then I will go to the right; or, if you go to the right, then I will go to the left." And Lot lifted his eyes and saw all the plain of Jordan, that it was well watered everywhere (before the Lord destroyed Sodom and Gomorrah) like the garden of the Lord, like the land of Egypt as you go toward Zoar. Then Lot chose for himself all the plain of Jordan, and Lot journeyed east. And they separated from each other. Abram dwelt in the land of Canaan, and Lot dwelt in the cities of the plain and pitched his tent even as far as Sodom. But the men of Sodom were exceedingly wicked and sinful against the Lord. (Genesis 13:8-13)

Tel Hammam (Sodom) and Tel Kafrayn (Gomorrah) are also proposed locations and are eighteen kilometers due east from Jericho, in Jordan. Coincidentally, Tel Hammam is located on the eastern edge of the Plains of Moab where the Children of Israel were encamped east of the Jordan, This one is easy to find once you know where it is, and it has more interesting ruins than the other sites. As we wandered over this mound and reminisced on what God did to this place and to its people, we had a certain amount of uneasiness. The fate of Sodom and Gomorrah is used as a warning to those who reject the gospel:

Assuredly, I say to you, it will be more tolerable for the land of Sodom and Gomorrah in the day of judgment than for that city! (Matthew 10:15)

And you, Capernaum, who are exalted to heaven, will be brought down to Hades; for if the mighty works which were done in you had been done in Sodom, it would have remained until this day. But I say to you that it shall be more tolerable for the land of Sodom in the day of judgment than for you." (Matthew 11:23-24)

But I want to remind you, though you once knew this, that the Lord, having saved the people out of the land of Egypt, afterward destroyed those who did not believe. And the angels who did not keep their proper domain, but left their own abode, He

has reserved in everlasting chains under darkness for the judgment of the great day;
as Sodom and Gomorrah, and the cities around them in a similar manner to these,
having given themselves over to sexual immorality and gone after strange flesh, are
set forth as an example, suffering the vengeance of eternal fire. (Jude 5-7)

DETOUR FOUR:
DO YOU WANT TO TAKE A PICTURE OR A PHOTOGRAPH?

We stopped briefly at Dibon, but there was really very little to see beyond a few remnants of walls that a previous generation of archaeologists had left untidied. Nevertheless, I wanted to photograph the mound and the surrounding areas to provide a context for the few photos I had taken on site. We drove to various vantage points but none were very satisfactory until we were driving past a row of homes in the local village. From here, we could get the contextual photograph I wanted, but it would mean entering and walking through someone's property.

As we approached the house, a middle-aged man, apparently a mechanic, looking rather disheveled, covered in oil and grime, emerged from under an old car that he was repairing. He was accompanied by four quite bedraggled children. I apologized for interrupting him and then said, in my slowest, clearest voice possible, "Do you speak English?" "Yes, I speak very good English," the man replied. I was rather taken aback by his English proficiency and proceeded to ask him, "Would you mind if we went to the back of your property to take a picture of the mound of Dibon?" His response took me a little off guard. "Do you want to take a picture or a photograph?" He went on to explain the difference that one draws or paints a picture but takes a photograph. He said, "There's a reason we have wedding photographers because they take photographs!" He was very kind and took us to a location where we were able to take a picture — I mean photograph. Not only did we learn a little nuance of the English language but had a lesson in humility because we had assumed that someone covered in oil and repairing a car in a remote part of Jordan couldn't possibly speak much English — he was a high school English teacher, chatted with us for a long time, and told us all we ever wanted to know about Mesha the King of Moab and the Moabite Stone. A wonderful man.

There was only one other site we needed to visit on our journey around the Dead Sea. In early 1993, we arrived in Aqaba and rented a Lada. This vehicle had a top speed of about seventy kilometers per hour, and at that speed we couldn't speak to each other over the noise. Besides, none of the windows closed very tightly, and there seemed to be breezes and wind coming from every direction, including through the floor. We could count the white lines on the King's Highway through the floor of the Lada! And then there was a gearshift which in most cases required double-clutching and a lot of brute force. We traveled north on the King's highway, the ancient biblical road, which today joins Aqaba in the south and Amman in the north.

We visited Petra and arrived at Dibon. It was here in 1868 that a German missionary found a stone slab over a meter tall. This stone was inscribed with the accomplishments of Mesha, the King of Moab around 850 BC. The King brags of having driven the Israelites out of his land. This Moabite Stone, sometimes called the Mesha Stele, is one of the earliest finds that mentions biblical people, and it is currently housed in the Louvre in Paris with a copy in the British Museum in London.

Then, a little farther north, we turned left towards the fortress of Machaerus, following a narrow road to the village of Deir el-Makwar. The site was being developed and didn't have a visitor center. In fact, there was nothing to tell us where we were. Only after speaking to a few children were we brought to the site. Machaerus is a fortress, similar to Herodium in the Judean desert. This was one of the fortresses of Herod the Great, and, according to the Jewish historian Josephus Flavius, this is where John the Baptist was imprisoned and beheaded in about AD 26.

> For Herod had laid hold of John and bound him, and put him in prison for the sake of Herodias, his brother Philip's wife… But when Herod's birthday was celebrated, the daughter of Herodias danced before them and pleased Herod. Therefore he promised with an oath to give her whatever she might ask. So she, having been prompted by her mother, said, "Give me John the Baptist's head here on a platter." And the king was sorry; nevertheless, because of the oaths and because of those who sat with him, he commanded it to be given to her. So he sent and had John beheaded in prison. And his head was brought on a platter and given to the girl, and she brought it to her mother. (Matthew 14:3, 6-11)

There wasn't much to see here. The Jordanian authorities were constructing a wide path to the summit, and unfortunately, they were planting cypress trees all around the slopes. The climb was a bit of a grind, but not exhausting. If we had come here to see great archaeological remains, this would have been an extremely disappointing site. However, paramount in our visits to any site was the impact of the events that happened there. We've had two subsequent visits, and there is now a well-constructed path to the top of the mound, which has had extensive excavation. In recent years (2012), the actual dance floor on which Salome danced before King Herod has been uncovered.

> *But when Herod's birthday was celebrated, the daughter of Herodias danced before them and pleased Herod. Therefore he promised with an oath to give her whatever she might ask. So she, having been prompted by her mother, said, "Give me John the Baptist's head here on a platter." And the king was sorry; nevertheless, because of the oaths and because of those who sat with him, he commanded it to be given to her. So he sent and had John beheaded in prison. And his head was brought on a platter and given to the girl, and she brought it to her mother.* (Matthew 14:6-11)

As we stood at the top of the mound, we reminisced about this story and wondered where John might have been imprisoned. Then we remembered that it was John the Baptist who spoke those immortal words:

> *…Behold! The Lamb of God who takes away the sin of the world!* (John 1:29)

DETOUR FIVE:
THE PASSPORT SHUFFLE

While in Cairo, we had to make a few 'arrangements' in preparation for a future trip to Jordan. In central Cairo, across Tahrir square from the Egyptian Museum, is a massive, dull, grey government building called the Mogamma; this was the passport-visa office, and apparently about five thousand people work in this building. With only a little difficulty we found our floor and waiting area. We waited a long time, but when it was our turn, I walked forward to the window, wicket 93, and requested:

"I would like to transfer our Egyptian visas from our British passports into our Canadian passports."

"That can't be done," the lady replied quite coldly.

"I believe it can and have spoken with people who have done it," I replied.

"No, I can't do it, but you should go to wicket 98 and ask there."

So, I explained to Evelyn and the children what was happening and went to 98.

"I would like to transfer our Egyptian visas from our British passports into our Canadian passports."

"That can't be done," I heard again.

"Yes, it can," I said to the lady who didn't really want to talk to me.

"Go to wicket 93."

"But I have already been there, and she sent me to you," I protested.

"Please go to 93 and tell her that you have been to see me."

I had no idea what this would achieve but I dutifully did as requested, and as expected, it achieved nothing except,

"If this can be done it can be done at 98."

So back to 98, and one more round between 93 and back to 98 until I'm convinced both women were sick of the sight of me — I clearly wasn't going away. Finally, the woman at 98 instructed me to go to a particular room one floor up. The four of us climbed upstairs and found that we had been sent to see the Chief of Police. We sat down until I was beckoned in. I entered the office and said,

"I have a problem."

"Problem? My friend, there are no problems in Egypt," replied the chief.

"Fantastic," I replied, because "I would like to transfer our Egyptian visas from our British passports into our Canadian passports."

"You can't do that," he replied.

"But you just told me there were no problems in Egypt," I protested.

"Why do you want to do this?" he enquired.

His question indicated that my request might be possible.

I explained that I wanted to take my family to visit Jordan. To do so we would have to cross into Jordan from Egypt, and to do that would require an Egyptian visa in our passport. However, our Egyptian visa was in our British passports, and this also had Israeli stamps, and this would bar our entry to Jordan. Therefore, I was requesting that our visas be transferred from our British passports into our 'clean' Canadian passports.

"Where is your family?" he inquired. This time I played my ace card — our daughter Andrea. Andrea was a cute little twelve-year-old with blue eyes and fair hair. Egyptians love children, especially ones like this. I pointed out his door to where Evelyn and the children were seated. He wanted to see Andrea, and I knew we had struck oil! I brought Andrea into his office, he chatted for a short time and then agreed to our request, but we still had a problem.

"This process will take about seven days," he informed us, "and you must have a letter from the Canadian embassy."

"That's fine," I replied, "because we plan to be in Egypt for about 8–10 days." He then asked me to turn over our passports and call back in a week.

"But we can't do this" I argued, "because according to Egyptian law we cannot travel around your country without our passports, and we plan to travel to Luxor, Aswan, Abu Simbel and other places."

He smiled at my response, and this seemed to clinch it ... and 2½ hours later we had our Egyptian visas in our Canadian passports. Somewhere in this process, we visited the Canadian embassy and obtained the required letter. Now we were traveling in Egypt with a British passport without a visa; the old visa had a huge CANCELED stamped across it. It would only become apparent to us three months later that the new visas in our Canadian passports listed us as temporary residents of Egypt!

We left the building, quite pleased with ourselves, but in the back of our minds we knew that we had to leave Egypt (to return to Israel) with passports showing a canceled Egyptian visa — would the fastidious customs officers understand all of this?

About ten days later we went back to Israel, and we approached the Rafia crossing to return to Israel. As we came to passport control, I nonchalantly passed our passports through the window. It didn't take long until I heard the obvious question:

"Why is your visa canceled?"

I spent some time explaining the whole saga to the officer. Reluctantly, I produced our Canadian passports to convince him that we were legal visitors to Egypt. He explained to us that he would have to cancel our Egyptian visas.

"No, please don't do that," I pleaded. "We will be returning to Egypt in a few months to go to Jordan, and if you cancel our visas, then I will not be able to take my family to Jordan." He seemed sympathetic but equally compelled to put an Exit Stamp across the newly-acquired visas in our Canadian passports.

"I have to stamp something," he said quite strangely, and then a brainwave struck me,

"Why don't you stamp the already canceled visas in our British passports?" I asked.

"But they are already stamped and canceled," he responded.

"That's okay, stamp them again." I suggested.

With that, he took our British passports, stamped our already canceled visas (the visas were now canceled twice) with an Exit Stamp, and told us to proceed. We had done it. We were now heading back into Israel with clean Canadian passports that had valid Egyptian visas. A few months later we would return to Egypt en route for Jordan.

———————

III.
EGYPT

Except for our travels in the Sinai, we only had one other short trip to Egypt. Unfortunately, we didn't get to visit many of the more notable biblical sites in Egypt, especially those associated with the time that Israel was in bondage, such as Pithom, Rameses, Goshen, Marah, Elim, Succoth, and Rephidim.

We had been in Israel for almost three months. Our Israeli visas were good for only three months, so it was time to renew. We could either go to the rather dingy offices and nasty people at the visa office in Jerusalem, or we could leave the country, re-enter, and receive a new three-month visa. This was a great opportunity for the four of us to visit Egypt, the only neighboring country that wasn't officially at war with Israel. It was October 1992 when we took the bus from Jerusalem to Cairo. This took a mere fifteen hours. Our bus left Jerusalem early in the morning. We went to Tel Aviv to pick up more passengers and then took a rather circuitous route south towards the Rafia border crossing at the Gaza strip. Our bus pulled into a large, open, and rather sparse parking lot, surrounded by a high fence. A few other buses were mere spots in this rough, large compound. We were still in Israel but a rather surly official checked our passport and our papers for Egypt. We were traveling on our British passports, but we also had our Canadian passports.

After transferring into a smaller bus, within minutes we were driving on a road along the border between Israel and Egypt. This was no ordinary road, being lined on both sides by a huge amount of barbed wire and other fencing, perhaps to a height of 3–4 meters. I started to take video out of the front of the bus. The rather nervous guide asked that I put my camera away, and we quickly arrived at the official border. We weren't sure if this first set of offices were Israeli or Egyptian, and they turned out to be Israeli. This part was relatively straightforward although it was interesting to have our luggage searched while leaving a country.

Into the bus again and a few short moments brought us to another set of halls and offices. First, there was the passport check and the all-important Egyptian entry stamp that said Rafia. Unfortunately, this Rafia stamp indicates that the passport holder has come from Israel which makes it impossible to use this passport to go to any other Middle Eastern country, but the concealed Canadian passports had no Israeli stamps and so were considered 'clean.' The remainder of the experience through Egyptian customs was more amusing than anything else.

After passport control, we had our luggage thoroughly checked, very thoroughly, and another stamp in the passport. Because we had a video camera, we got special treatment and had to have it registered. A little man registered the video camera directly into the passport. He used up an entire passport page noting the serial number, registration number, make and model, and a general description, and then another stamp. This procedure is done to ensure that the camera is taken out of the country after the visit. Then, we had to report to the border police. They stamped a little triangular-shaped stamp in the passport which indicated that we were to report to the security police in Cairo if we planned to stay in Egypt for more than fifteen days. Finally, another little man stamped the passport; we think as a check that all the previous wee men had checked and stamped where appropriate … and, having secured five stamps in our passports, we were through. These proceedings finally over, our bus came to take us, in convoy, with an armed guard on the bus, across the Sinai desert, across the Suez Canal, to Cairo.

It was marvelous to see northern Sinai, to cross the Suez, and to see all the scrap tanks and equipment — a testimony to the three relatively recent wars fought in this area. Egypt can't be photographed, put on video, or described — it has to be experienced — noise, smells, horns, incredible squalor, donkeys, carts, street vendors, etc., yet there is a lot of contrast between this and hi-tech video and computer stores and quite up-market residential areas.

Our children, who were only twelve and fourteen years old, attracted a lot of attention because most tourists were either students or older couples, or bus tours, and we didn't see another family. Also, being fair and having blue eyes, Andrea attracted attention; even a traffic policeman on duty at a very busy intersection gave her a big wave, in through the taxi window! And then there were all the girls coming out of school trying to touch Alistair through the taxi window! While walking down a main street in Cairo, an Arab fellow approached Alistair and asked him if Andrea was his wife! When Alistair rather emphatically said 'no' the young lad then turned to Evelyn and offered her three thousand camels and a kilo of bananas for Andrea. Evelyn explained that Andrea was too young to be married, and besides, how could we get three thousand camels home to Vancouver, and where would we keep them?

Although we visited a lot of sites, various episodes stand out as being memorable. We won't document all the detail because most of our visits had little or nothing to do with biblical sites. After a visit to the fascinating Tutankhamun exhibition in the Egyptian Museum, we went to see a bunch of mosques, and then we asked our taxi driver to take us to the Great Pyramids at Giza. Par for the course, we were first brought to a papyrus store at which the driver would get a percentage of whatever we spent. Then, instead of taking us to the pyramids, he brought us to his friend who had camel rides to the pyramids. I'm not sure why we agreed, but we did. We struck a deal with the camel owners and off we went on a twenty-five-minute ride to the pyramids.

However, a problem arose because I wasn't very good at sitting on the hump! I was trying to take video and necessitated that I 'hold steady' but you can't do that on a lumbering camel. After less than a minute, I was sure I was going to coup off, but, when I was shown how to sway with the camel, it wasn't so bad. We had spent some time inside the pyramids, argued with an attendant who wanted baksheesh, went inside the king and queen's burial chambers, more arguments about baksheesh, visited the Sphinx, more baksheesh, and finally, we returned to the camels.

Typically, the camels are sitting down on the ground, the rider climbs on, and then in an awkward set of movements, the camel gets up on its back legs tending to throw the rider forward, and then it gets up on its front legs, and presto. My old camel was sitting where it should have been when I approached. I had one leg barely over the camel's hump when it decided to stand up leaving me dangling off one side and holding on for dear life. My only grip was the halter on the saddle and one leg half-over the hump. It is amazing how far you get lifted off the ground when these beasts stand up. Meanwhile, the owner was beating this poor old thing to make it sit, but it didn't. However, I managed to hang on and then pull myself up. Now I was a pro; everyone thought this was funny — and I did a little later!

Our taxi driver then took us south to Zoser's pyramid at Saqqarah, which was the first-ever stone pyramid built some 4,700 years ago. And nearby was Memphis. Memphis was known to the Hebrews as Noph, and Ezekiel prophesied that it would be destroyed:

Thus says the Lord God: "I will also destroy the idols, And cause the images to cease from Noph; There shall no longer be princes from the land of Egypt; I will put fear in the land of Egypt...And set a fire in Egypt; Sin shall have great pain, No shall be split open, And Noph shall be in distress daily." (Ezekiel 30:13,16)

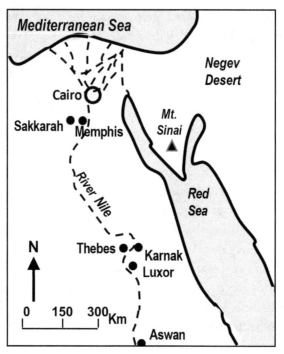

Some of the Biblical sites in the Lower Nile region, Egypt.

Memphis was an important ancient Egyptian capital situated on the River Nile about twenty-five kilometers south of Cairo. King Zoser embellished the city and constructed the monumental step pyramid. Practically nothing remains now of ancient Memphis. In fact, our ill-planned journey delivered us to Memphis, and it was closed. All we could do was peer through a rather dilapidated iron gate and dysfunctional fence at a few unlabeled bricks and stones on the other side.

We returned to Cairo to board the night train for the fifteen-hour journey to Aswan. We arrived early at Rameses[23] Station, but the lineups were already long. We were told, however, that it is customary in Egypt that women do not stand in lineups. It is acceptable, perhaps expected, that ladies automatically go to the front of the line. Our "Western" mindset said "no," but our desire to be on this train said, "let's try it." Evelyn promptly navigated her way through the hordes of men, while I stayed behind with the two children. About five minutes later she returned triumphantly with tickets in hand. Even though this was a night train, we got very little sleep on the fifteen-hour journey to Aswan. At Aswan we visited the great Aswan high dam and the Philae temple and took a trip to the temple of

---

[23] Rameses, also commonly spelled Ramesses or Ramses is the name conventionally given to many Egyptian pharaohs of the later New Kingdom period, between the thirteenth and the eleventh century BC.

Abu Simbel. Of the various Bible versions, only the New International Version refers to Aswan:

Therefore I am against you and against your streams, and I will make the land of Egypt a ruin and a desolate waste from Migdol to Aswan, as far as the border of Cush. (Ezekiel 29:10, NIV)

This is what the Lord says: "The allies of Egypt will fall and her proud strength will fail. From Migdol to Aswan they will fall by the sword within her, declares the Sovereign Lord…" (Ezekiel 30:6, NIV)

We had an interesting episode at Aswan. Because we were only in Egypt for a week, traveling on a limited budget, we couldn't afford to get sick. So, we traveled mostly by train and ate well, but as lightly as possible. This meant getting a good breakfast, then having a very good meal in mid-afternoon that doubled as lunch and dinner. While in Aswan, we went to a restaurant in a five-star hotel overlooking the Nile and Elephantine Island. Our daughter Andrea ordered spaghetti. The very smartly-dressed waiter appeared with our meals and there, perched exactly center and on top of Andrea's spaghetti, was a small piece of garnish, probably parsley — no —on closer inspection, it was a fly. We were at first a little embarrassed because we thought it was a garnish, but even more embarrassed to find it was a fly. Without touching anything, we called the waiter. He looked and waved his hand over it to try shooing the fly away. It wasn't going anywhere — it was dead. But no problem, after profuse apologies, they threw the meal out and provided a new meal.

Our visit to Egypt then took us to Rameses II's greatest masterpiece, the great Temples at Abu Simbel. We were up early because our minibus was leaving at 4:00 a.m. for the four-hour trip from Aswan through the Nubian Desert to Abu Simbel. The driver ate sunflower seeds the entire journey and spit the husks at his feet. There wasn't a blade of grass to be seen; this was desert at its most barren. After about two hours, the driver stopped the van, went to the side of the road, pulled up his robe, and had a pee. No bushes in this part of the world. And then we arrived at the Great Temple to be greeted by bureaucracy at its best (or worst).

There was a little shack that doubled as a ticket office and snack store. A few other buses had pulled into the parking lot alongside us, and we hurried along to avoid the rush. We were about tenth in line. But there was a problem with the ticket price. Rather than having a flat rate for entrance, say twenty or twenty-five Egyptian pounds, they had a "combined ticket." The combined ticket included the price of admission to the grounds (six pounds), the large temple (six pounds), the smaller temple (five pounds), guides for both temples (two pounds each), for a total of twenty-one pounds. Like most of us, the lady at the front of the line had twenty pounds, and twenty-five, but not twenty-one, and the ticket office had no change. She offered twenty-five and said she would do without her change. They wouldn't accept that either. None of us had change, the lineup was growing, time was short, tempers were getting short, and finally, a few of us walked forward, placed twenty-five pounds on the ticket desk, and just kept walking —nobody ever asked to see our tickets, and we never did see a guide!

Next, we retraced our tracks, literally, and went by train to Luxor. In the NIV, NASB and ASV, Luxor is called Thebes, and in the KJV, NKJV and RSV Luxor is called No.

> *The Lord of hosts, the God of Israel, says: "Behold, I will bring punishment on Amon of No [Thebes; Luxor], and Pharaoh and Egypt, with their gods and their kings -- Pharaoh and those who trust in him.* (Jeremiah 46:25)

> *I will make Pathros desolate, Set fire to Zoan, And execute judgments in No [Thebes; Luxor]. I will pour My fury on Sin, the strength of Egypt; I will cut off the multitude of No.* (Ezekiel 30:14-15)

Thebes is an ancient and large city that spreads on both banks of the Nile, and it boasts some of the world's greatest tourist attractions. On the east bank are the temples of Karnak and Luxor, and on the West Bank is a monumental series of mortuary temples: Qurna, Beir-el-Bahri, the Rameseum, the Colossi of Memmon (Amenhotep III), the temple of Deir-el-Medineh, and Medinet-Habu. We visited three of these, but the most enticing was surely the mortuary temple of Queen Hatshepsut at Beir el-Bahri. Immanuel Velikovsky argues the case that Queen Hatshepsut was the Queen of Sheba that visited King Solomon, but I'm not aware that any reputable scholars agree with this identification. To cut a long and complicated story short, Hatshepsut was the daughter of Thutmose I, and she appointed herself Pharaoh. In the temple, her birth and coronation are described in paintings and other works of art, along with a description of an expedition to the Land of Punt, located near the Red Sea, possibly in present-day Somalia.

Close by we visited the Rameseum to view the "vast and trunkless legs" of which the English poet Percy Bysshe Shelley wrote. Shelley's poem was titled "Ozymandias" which was the Greek name for the Egyptian pharaoh Rameses II, who many believe was the pharaoh of the Israelite bondage. Rameses II was a megalomaniac and built colossal monuments of himself, many of which can still be seen at Luxor and Karnak Temples and at Abu Simbel. The poem reads:

> I met a traveler from an antique land
> Who said: 'Two vast and trunkless legs of stone
> Stand in the desert. Near them, on the sand,
> Half sunk, a shattered visage lies, whose frown,
> And wrinkled lip, and sneer of cold command,
> Tell that its sculptor well those passions read
> Which yet survive, stamped on these lifeless things,
> The hand that mocked them and the heart that fed.
> And on the pedestal these words appear --
> "My name is Ozymandias, king of kings:
> Look on my works, ye Mighty, and despair!"
> Nothing beside remains. Round the decay
> Of that colossal wreck, boundless and bare
> The lone and level sands stretch far away.'[24]

Those "vast and trunkless legs" still stand, surrounded by various bits of ancient rubble, and beside it, a broken face half-buried in the sand. Brilliant!

In the same vicinity of these temples are the Valley of the Kings, the Valley of the Queens, and the Valley of the Nobles. This was our first time to be introduced to the Egyptian practice of "baksheesh," otherwise known as a tip or a bribe. We had purchased our entrance tickets to the various sites and photograph tokens. Each person was permitted five photograph tokens for each site. Before taking a photograph, a token was to be given to the attendant at the site. This system is apparently set up to reduce the amount of flash photography and so protect the ancient artifacts, but as you might imagine, it doesn't quite work that way in Egypt. We quickly found that in virtually every temple, or tomb, one US dollar was worth more than all the tokens in the ticket office.

At one particularly interesting tomb of a Noble, the attendant had a large mirror at the entrance, and this was used to reflect the bright Egyptian sun through the door into the tomb. Then, for a small baksheesh, he had another reflector that looked something like a tea tray covered with aluminum foil, and this was used to reflect the light onto whatever part of the artwork we wanted to photograph. Ingenious, creative, innovative, but also illegal and immoral; and no, we didn't pay him or use his reflectors, we simply gave him our tokens. However, we were also taking video, and this caused an interesting situation in another nearby tomb. No one said anything to us at the ticket office about tokens for video, only for photography, presumably flash photography. In addition, I had run out of regular tokens. When I produced my camera, the wee attendant wanted baksheesh. I handed him $1 USD, and as he was reaching out to receive

---

[24] Cited from a tourist brochure provided with our entrance tickets.

it, I produced my video camera. Suddenly, he wanted $15 USD for the video. But I wasn't born yesterday, and I had been warned about this type of situation. I allowed him to get his fingers on the $1 USD bill while I held on tightly. Once they get the feel of the greenback in their fingers there is no limit to what they will do. I gently tugged the bill as if to say, "It is yours if I can video, but I will take it back if you insist on anything more." No contest: it took about two seconds, no it was more like a millisecond, for him to say, "Okay, okay."

Next on our itinerary was the intriguing Valley of the Kings where most of the New Kingdom Pharaohs are buried. Specifically, we wanted to see the tombs of Rameses II who is popularly thought to be the pharaoh under which the children of Israel spent many years in bondage and Merneptah who is popularly thought to be the Pharaoh that died while pursuing the children of Israel.[25] Unfortunately, the tombs of King Tut and Rameses II were both closed for restoration, but we visited six tombs including that of Pharaoh Merneptah. It almost leaves you speechless to realize you are looking at the sarcophagus and burial place of the Pharaoh whose heart God hardened. The mummies of both Rameses II and Merneptah are in the Egyptian Museum, but at that time these displays weren't open to the public since Muslims requested President Sadat to close the gallery in 1981.

We ventured back across to the east side of the Nile and to the great temples of Karnak and Luxor that almost defy description. Karnak is an especially great marvel, its architecture a wonder of construction skill. Its great hypostyle hall contains 132 columns, the tallest over twenty meters high and almost four meters in diameter. The pillars and the hall are awesome, an unforgettable forest of colossal, towering, sandstone pillars. There is no vantage point to get an overview of the whole place, and all we could do was stand and stare at the dizzying spectacle. The hall itself is almost one hundred meters long and every stone and column a library in itself. Karnak also has impressive obelisks, the tallest over thirty meters high. And the temple of Luxor is wow! The enormous compound is almost 275 meters long, built primarily by Amenhotep III, with additions by Rameses II.

After our visits in Luxor, we found ourselves a few hours ahead of schedule, so we decided to go to the railway station and get the 4:00 p.m. train north to Cairo rather than waiting until the next morning. Evelyn and the children waited outside the station while I went inside to change the tickets. Nothing is easy here! After being bounced around between about ten offices, I was finally directed to

---

[25] There is a lot of debate about the identity of the Pharaohs that were contemporaries of the Children of Israel, so these identifications aren't definitive.

the proper office and to the director of ticketing; but not a chance. Yes, there were empty seats on the train we wanted; yes, it was on schedule; but no, you can't change reserved tickets.

After a prolonged and totally useless dialog, it was clear that I couldn't win —unless I used my trump card — our blonde, blue-eyed as cute-as-a-button twelve-year-old daughter Andrea. I'd pulled this trump card out of the hat before with success in the Mogamma building in Cairo.[26] I looked at this officer and gave a huge, fake sigh of total desperation, forcing every last cubic centimeter of air to drain from my lungs, and then looked forlornly at the floor. "My daughter is going to be so disappointed," I said, "because she so dearly wants to go to Cairo tonight." "How many people are you?" he asked. "Bring me your daughter." Under my breath, I said *thank you Lord* and went outside to get Andrea. Five minutes later we had new tickets, and an hour later were on the train to Cairo. Don't ask me what mental processes went on in that poor man's head; perhaps there weren't any, but they produced our desired outcome.

So, another overnight train journey, a day in Cairo, and that was Egypt – it wasn't very long or extensive, but we loved it!

---

[26] We wrote about this at length earlier, in Detour 5. Briefly, we had to get our Egyptian visas transferred from our British passports into our Canadian passports. There was absolutely no way this could be done — until we produced our trump card. Presto! There are no problems in Egypt!

IV.
THE EXODUS FROM MOUNT SINAI TO THE PROMISED LAND

Sadly, this journey is quite incomplete for us because, in all our travels, we never managed to trace the route of the early part of the Exodus from Egypt to Mount Sinai. It's also worth remembering that there are more than ten different contenders for the real Mount Sinai and, therefore, the various routes leading to and from the mountain in southern Sinai may be speculative. Also, we were limited to the available roads and couldn't necessarily wander along valleys as Moses and the Children of Israel did. Part of the 'traditionally accepted' route wanders back and forth across today's Egyptian-Israeli border, which of course isn't possible today; because of this, we didn't get to visit Kadesh Barnea,[27] which is in Egypt but not too far across the border from the Israeli town of Nizzana.

Now, having given you the excuses and reservations, let's begin our journey — it's still a good one. There are essentially three parts to this trip: from Mount Sinai to Ezion Geber (today's seaside resort of Eilat); the circular tour through the Negev Desert and back to Ezion Geber; and the journey from Ezion Geber through Jordan to Mount Nebo and to the Promised Land.

Mount Sinai, also called Horeb in Scripture, is one of the most venerated and important sites of the world's three great monotheistic religions: Judaism, Christianity, and Islam. This is the Mountain of God, the mountain of revelation, where God gave Moses the Ten Commandments and many other laws that still form the backbone of western ethics and morality. The exact location isn't certain, but the peak in Egypt's southern Sinai desert called Gebel Musa (Moses Mountain) is the most widely acceptable location. Another potential is Har Karkoum in the western Negev — but more about that fascinating site later.

It was in February 1993 that Evelyn and I and the two children began making plans to go to Mt Sinai. From Jerusalem it is two hundred miles to Eilat, over the Egyptian border, and then another one hundred miles into the Sinai desert to St. Catherine's monastery at the base of the mountain. This journey required a rental car, a border crossing, a visa for entering the Sinai Peninsula, another car

---

[27] Tell el-Qudeirat, about eight kilometers east of the Egyptian village of Quseima is widely considered to be the location of the biblical Kadesh Barnea. This places it about ten kilometers west of the current Israel-Egypt border in the region near Har Karkoum, but the precise location is unknown,

rental, and overnight accommodation. We hoped that this wouldn't be a wasted journey. It rarely rains in the Sinai. The Sinai is incredibly bleak with barely any sign of plant life. No wonder Scriptures describes it as:

... that great and terrible wilderness which you saw on the way... (Deuteronomy 1:19)

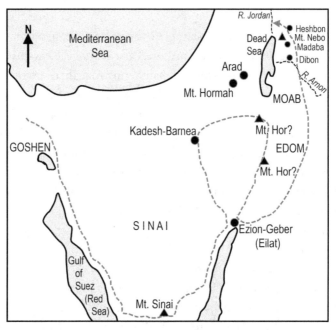

A proposed route of the exodus from Egypt to the Promised Land.

We left Jerusalem early on Friday morning and drove for about four hours to Eilat. The border crossing into Egypt is only a few miles south of Eilat, but we had a rental car to deal with. This proved to be troublesome. Because of high security in the region, we couldn't find a parking garage that would keep our car overnight. This led to a calculated risk. We simply drove our rental car into the parking lot of a hotel close to the border. We parked, removed our travel bags from the trunk, locked up, and walked off towards the border praying that our car would still be there when we returned the following evening — it was!

Our journey through Israeli customs was uneventful, and it was a short walk to the Taba Hilton where we hoped to rent a vehicle for our travels in Sinai. This hotel became the target of a horrific bomb attack a few years later. It took more than an hour for the agent to finally admit to us that they had no vehicles, and they weren't expecting any returns within the next 4–5 hours. It was only about a mile between Israeli and Egyptian customs, but because we had to walk and drag our bags, it seemed like a lot more. Immediately upon entering Egypt, we were ambushed by what seemed to be a thousand taxi drivers all wanting to take us to Mt. Sinai. We quickly made a deal, and were on our way to the Mountain of God.

Just as darkness was falling, we arrived at St. Catherine's monastery, and we stayed in a dormitory there overnight (there was nowhere else to stay except at the monastery). The small dorm room had ten narrow, single beds squeezed into it, and it had an opening in the wall that was called a window — but it was actually a hole in the wall! In addition to the four of us, there were two, young Scandinavian women. I don't know if they were lesbians or just smart, but when they entered the room, they immediately jumped into the same bed. It's difficult to comprehend how at least one of them didn't fall out.

The night was cold, very cold, below zero. We jumped into bed with all our clothes on and huddled tightly with lots of blankets. We were still very cold. Sometime in the middle of the night, Evelyn and I also got into the same bed so that we could warm up a little. The wall on one side of the bed, and the cupboard on the other side, prevented us from falling out.

The next morning after breakfast we toured the monastery, which is the oldest in the world, built between AD 542–551 by Emperor Justinian, and has been continuously inhabited ever since. It was an interesting tour even though it was led by a few crotchety and very grumpy old monks who appeared to have been there since the sixth century. We were shown the skulls of many monks who had died there over the centuries and had described to us in detail a number of the quite hideous icons and relics. The library is not open to the public, but it used to house the Codex Sinaiticus, which is a Greek manuscript of the Bible from the fourth century AD. This is a Greek Orthodox monastery and claims to be built on the site where Moses encountered the burning bush — which is still growing for all to see! The burning bush is one of the most amazing stories in Scripture, and whether it happened here or somewhere else does not detract from the enormity of the miracle that happened or from the subsequent events that resonated from Moses's encounter with God:

> *And the Angel of the Lord appeared to him in a flame of fire from the midst of a bush. So he looked, and behold, the bush was burning with fire, but the bush was not consumed. Then Moses said, "I will now turn aside and see this great sight, why the bush does not burn." (Exodus 3:2-3)*

As we left the monastery, I was struck by the fact that Mohammad had been here. Mohammad had been forced to flee from Mecca and Medina, and when he came to the monastery, the monks provided him with protective sanctuary. History records that when the Muslim armies later came through this region, the monastery was spared because it had previously given Mohammad sanctuary. Even though to a Christian Mohammad is only another historical figure, nevertheless, this left an impression — Mohammad was here at this very spot. "But dad," said our son Alistair, "Moses was here as well, and so was God." I almost felt chastised. It bought home in a forcible way that we can become so familiar with Bible stories and biblical characters that there's a danger of treating them almost as fantasy, placing them in the same category as Santa Claus, Cinderella, and the Jolly Green Giant. Strange as it may sound, it then hit me — yes, God was here!

Outside the monastery were many Bedouins with their camels. Evelyn and Andrea hopped on board their respective camels and were brought about two-thirds towards the summit. Alistair and I walked along with the camels. The two Bedouin camel drivers were jolly, but they had virtually no English, so conversation was minimal. In contrast to other places we have been to, the Bedouins treat their animals very well, their camels in particular.

As we walked along, it didn't take long to notice that the two camels had their own unique characteristics. One seemed to fart cabbage about every ten strides, and the other was constipated. The camel driver had an interesting remedy for constipation — every time the camel tried to unload, the driver shoved his finger into the camel's rear end and poked the excrement out. Will someone please remind me not to shake hands with this guy when we finish our journey? From the point where the camels drop off their passengers, it is only about a ten-minute walk until our path joins with another route.

From this junction to the summit, it is stepped all the way. The entire climb from the monastery to the summit took just over two hours — it was quite a climb near the end. No wonder poor old Moses was angry when he came down, saw the people of Israel misbehaving, and then had to go back up again! The summit is at 2,281 meters (7,483 feet), it is about a 760 meter (2,500 foot) climb from the monastery, and the air is thin. Near the summit, there was some snow lying around, but we weren't cold. Even though it was mid-February there were quite a few people on the mountain. The sky was cloudless, the views stunning, and it seemed we could see forever. It was only now that the impact started to dawn. This mountain (if it is the correct one) was the site of probably the single most momentous series of events in history. I'll let Scripture take over from here:

Then the Lord said to Moses, "Come up to Me on the mountain and be there; and I will give you tablets of stone, and the law and commandments which I have written..." (Exodus 24:12)

And when He had made an end of speaking with him on Mount Sinai, He gave Moses two tablets of the Testimony, tablets of stone, written with the finger of God. (Exodus 31:18)

And Moses turned and went down from the mountain, and the two tablets of the Testimony were in his hand. The tablets were written on both sides; on the one side and on the other they were written. Now the tablets were the work of God, and the writing was the writing of God engraved on the tablets. (Exodus 32:15-16)

And the Lord said to Moses, "Cut two tablets of stone like the first ones, and I will write on these tablets the words that were on the first tablets which you broke. So be ready in the morning, and come up in the morning to Mount Sinai, and present yourself to Me there on the top of the mountain." (Exodus 34:1-2)

On the summit are a little chapel and four Bedouin shacks selling tea, coffee, pop, and cookies. The Bedouin at the summit stay for five days before being replaced. One of the Bedouin shacks is in the traditional site where God hid Moses in the cleft of the rock while His glory passed by:

Then He said, "I will make all My goodness pass before you, and I will proclaim the name of the Lord before you. I will be gracious to whom I will be gracious, and I will have compassion on whom I will have compassion." But He said, "You cannot see My face; for no man shall see Me, and live." And the Lord said, "Here is a place by Me, and you shall stand on the rock. So it shall be, while My glory passes by, that I will put you in the cleft of the rock, and will cover you with My hand while I pass by. Then I will take away My hand, and you shall see My back; but My face shall not be seen." (Exodus 33:19-23)

We went inside the cleft and had a Coca-Cola and a chat with a local tribesman. We stayed at the summit for perhaps an hour, mostly soaking up and savoring the incredible vistas but also taking time to contemplate what happened here.

The whole trip was a wonderful experience. Now when Moses came down from Mount Sinai he had to go back up again; when we came down, we grabbed a taxi, drove like crazy through the Sinai, over the Israeli border, into Eilat, picked up our illegally parked car, and went to the Pizza Hut!

Professor Anati from the University of Florence, Italy, proposes a not-too-widely accepted theory, that Har Karkoum is the real Mount Sinai. Har Karkoum is located in the western Negev desert about forty kilometers southwest of Mitzpe

Ramon. It wasn't until 1999 that I had the opportunity to visit Har Karkoum. This site boasts 35,000 petroglyphs, the largest concentration of rock art in the Negev. The mountain is about twenty-five kilometers west of the main road going south through the Negev and is only accessible using four-wheel drive. I wish I could relive the details of how we got to this site. The easiest method is to drive along the road that runs along the Israeli-Egyptian border, and then turn inland at the appropriate time.

However, this is a military road and there are some conditions attached to diving on it. Typically, there must be a minimum of two vehicles in convoy, at least one person in the party with a gun and with a telephone, and knowledge of how to use both. Even in 1999, there were still some fears, largely unfounded I think, that some nasty Egyptian terrorists may slip across the border.

Arthur duMosch, owner-operator of *"Out of the Wilderness Travel"* was our driver and guide. About fifteen years later I was able to return to the site with Evelyn, again with *"Out of the Wilderness Travel."* Arthur wasn't deterred by the potential of meeting terrorists, but he had a healthy respect for the regulations and Israeli soldiers. However, we were one vehicle, and we had no guns. There is a direct road from Mitzpe Ramon going west to this border road with an Israeli checkpoint at the intersection. When we were about seven or eight kilometers from intersecting with the border road, Arthur took off cross country, following ravines and riverbeds, until we emerged onto the military road about four or five miles beyond the army checkpoint. The Negev is fantastic — everything is legal if you don't get caught. Even if you are caught, nobody seems to be too bothered. We drove to the base of the mountain and were introduced to something quite amazing: twelve standing stones, in two rows of six, with the rows being about a meter apart. These weren't large, perhaps no more than 30–50 centimeters tall, but they reminded me of:

> *And Moses wrote all the words of the Lord. And he rose early in the morning, and built an altar at the foot of the mountain, and twelve pillars according to the twelve tribes of Israel.* (Exodus 24:4)

We then scrambled for about ten minutes up to the top of the mesa. Rock art was everywhere, innumerable reminders that, for centuries, this was a center of religious worship. The top of this flat-topped mountain must have stretched for five or six kilometers, and we walked endlessly. It was an unbearably hot day and we consumed enormous quantities of water. I have no idea if this is the real Mount Sinai or not, but I'm glad that Professor Anati gave us the excuse to go and visit.

The Negev desert is a dry scrubland and desert from Beersheba to the south of Israel. It is the eastern extension of the Sinai and is described by Isaiah the prophet as:

...a land of trouble and anguish, from which came the lioness and lion, the viper and fiery flying serpent... (Isaiah 30:6)

It is a land of sparse springs and little rainfall. The word Negev comes from a root meaning "to be dry," implying the "dry" or "parched regions." It supports lots of grazing animals, mostly sheep and goats in the winter and spring, but there is a long, very hot summer drought. It is a land much better suited to nomadic life than settled inhabitants. The Negev was the setting for much of Abram's wanderings; it was here that Hagar met with the angel, and Isaac and Jacob both lived there. Moses sent the twelve spies from this region, and many of the exploits of David occurred here. Prophetically, when describing the future glory of Zion, Isaiah says:

The wilderness and the wasteland shall be glad for them, and the desert shall rejoice and blossom as the rose; (Isaiah 35:1)

Today, many believe that this prophecy is being fulfilled as the Israelis have built an impressive irrigation system that channels water from the Galilee to this dry, parched region of the Negev.

The four major locations of biblical interest are: the Wilderness of Paran, Taberah, Kadesh Barnea, and the Wilderness of Zin. The exact locations of three of these are questionable, and Kadesh Barnea is extremely difficult to access. Paran may have been the general wilderness region of the central and southern Negev, with the wilderness of Zin being to the north and extending as far west as the area of Kadesh Barnea. Today, the name applies to a spectacularly beautiful valley that crosses the Negev about forty kilometers south of Beersheva, at Sede Boqer.

In 1991 I visited Israel for the first time. I had gone on a field trip with colleagues from The Ben Gurion University of the Negev. We were doing vegetation monitoring at a site called Bir Ada in the Wadi Faran, and even though it was only about six kilometers to the west of the main road, this was four-wheel drive country. The word 'bir' is Arabic for well, and if Professor Anati is correct about his identification of Har Karkoum with Mount Sinai, then his subsequent arguments identify Bir Ada with Taberah, the site of a rather notorious event in the saga of the Children of Israel:

Now when the people complained, it displeased the Lord; for the Lord heard it, and His anger was aroused. So the fire of the Lord burned among them, and consumed some in the outskirts of the camp. Then the people cried out to Moses, and when Moses prayed to the Lord, the fire was quenched. So he called the name of the place Taberah, because the fire of the Lord had burned among them. (Numbers 11:1-3)

This is a seriously harsh environment, and it didn't take long to stake out our plots and to monitor the vegetation. The itinerary for our trip involved spending one night under the stars. We had made camp for the evening, and I went around a corner along a little gully to have a pee. I was climbing up the face of quite friable rock, and I can still see the following flash across my mind — I was near the top, perhaps with my feet only three meters above the bottom. I wrapped both of my arms around a particularly large stone and was just about to pull myself to the top of the ledge. But the stone came loose. And so did I. I momentarily passed out, but when I came around, I was lying in the middle of an acacia thicket. This was the only acacia in sight, and while it may have cushioned my fall, I spent the next four weeks pulling tiny spines out of my backside.

I was also a bloody mess. There were a lot of flint-like stones in the substrate, and one of these produced a deep gash in my left forearm that went to the bone; the rest of me looked awful. Although these were mostly superficial scratches, there were lots of them, and they produced a lot of blood. I rejoined my group, and they were horrified. We didn't have a first-aid kit, so I was washed down, and my left arm bandaged with kitchen roll and masking tape. I had a restless and uneasy night. The next day, after finishing our fieldwork, we made our way back to the main road and drove north to the town of Mitzpe Ramon. Here there was a local office of Magen David Adom, the Israeli equivalent of the Red Cross. I was initially concerned because the nurse had only one needle, which she used to give me a little anesthetic, then an antibiotic. The nurse was very kind, then she gave me a scolding for delaying for almost sixteen hours before coming to see her; she was concerned that at this late stage the stitches might not take. She stitched my arm anyway, sent me on my way, and the stitches were just fine.

Kadesh Barnea is in northeastern Sinai, an eleven-day journey from Mount Sinai (Deuteronomy 1:2). Here the children of Israel camped for about thirty-eight years during the Exodus. Kadesh was their headquarters during these years, and it was from here that the people began their final march to the Promised Land.

Then the children of Israel, the whole congregation, came into the Wilderness of Zin in the first month, and the people stayed in Kadesh; and Miriam died there and was buried there. (Numbers 20:1)

We couldn't get to Kadesh Barnea from Israel. However, because it is only about eight kilometers across the border in Egypt, we decided we would get as close as we could but stay on the Israeli side. We drove to the small town of Nizzana, which sits right against the Egyptian border. We were surprised to discover that there were no barriers to prevent us from driving along the road that traces the line of the border — and a few meters away, on the other side of the fence, there is a parallel road in Egypt. We'd been advised several times that traveling on this road required a convoy of a minimum of two cars, a gun, and a cell phone. We failed on all three counts, but we were on the road anyway. After about five minutes, both Evelyn and I had that strange feeling we were being watched, or to put it another way, a strange feeling that we shouldn't be there. We tried to set our baseless feelings to one side and kept driving, but they wouldn't go away. Finally, after about eight kilometers, we decided to turn around and return to Nizzana.

It was then that we spotted an Israeli army jeep barreling down upon us. They screeched to a halt beside us and immediately wanted to see our IDs. Now we were in a pickle because we didn't have our passports, but I did have my Canadian Citizenship card. I presented this to the officer and he immediately replied, "Are you a diplomat?" It was tempting! I said, "No, this is my Canadian citizenship card. It is not as authoritative as a passport, but it is genuine." They seemed satisfied. They asked us the usual thousand questions and they especially wanted to know how we had accessed the road and made it past the checkpoints. We were genuinely puzzled because we hadn't seen any checkpoints, nor had we seen any signs. However, they were very nice and let us go with a "I will let you go this time."

As we returned to the main road, it became apparent where we had gone astray —the warning sign "Border ahead, entry prohibited" had been knocked down and was lying flat on the ground. Apparently this was a sensitive military zone. I'm not sure why because ten years later we had occasion to drive this road again, this time legally without convoy, gun, or cell phone, and there were no checkpoints or warning signs. On several occasions along this road, blowing sand had actually covered the entire border fence, making it possible to walk across the border road without hindrance — we were tempted, but we didn't (honestly!).

The Wilderness of Zin marked the southern boundary of ancient Israel (Numbers 34:3). It was somewhere around here that Moses's sister Miriam died and was buried and where Moses disobeyed God. Because of Moses's unbelief in this place, he was barred from ever entering the Promised Land.

Then Moses lifted his hand and struck the rock twice with his rod; and water came out abundantly, and the congregation and their animals drank. Then the Lord spoke to Moses and Aaron, "Because you did not believe Me, to hallow Me in the eyes of the children of Israel, therefore you shall not bring this assembly into the land which I have given them." (Numbers 20:11-12)

The Wilderness of Zin is best viewed from the David and Paula Ben Gurion burial grounds beside the Sede Boqer campus of the Ben Gurion University of the Negev. This is one of the most awe-inspiring landscapes in all of Israel. During the year we lived in Israel, we visited here regularly. It was a popular walk with our children, and on one occasion Alistair rode parts of it on a borrowed mountain bike. Often in the late afternoon, a few ibex would appear, and it was fun to watch them scurry around on the steep slopes. And the sunsets were for the romantic. The sun rapidly drops in the western sky at these latitudes, and the light reflecting from the red-yellow sand and stones changes color and hue by the minute — sometimes verging on spectacular, but always too short.

Scripture then tells us that:

They moved from Ezion Geber and camped in the Wilderness of Zin, which is Kadesh. They moved from Kadesh and camped at Mount Hor, on the boundary of the land of Edom. (Numbers 33:36-37)

But let's continue with Moses and travel to Mount Hor. There are two widely touted sites, and although one is in Israel and one in Jordan, geographically they are only about forty kilometers apart. The most widely proposed location for Mount Hor is near Petra in Jordan. However, for our purposes we will travel to Har Zin or Har Haran (Mount Aaron) at the eastern end of the Zin and near the Arabah. Getting to this site is tricky because Har Zin can only be accessed along a private road, which is owned by the Negev Oron Phosphate Plant.

Although roads come to Har Zin from both the west through Yeroham and Oron, and from the east from Hazeva, access is only possible from Hazeva. We know because, when we approached from Yeroham, we arrived at a control barrier near the Phosphate Plant; the security guard wouldn't allow us through. This was understandable because the Phosphate Plant is an enormous industrial operation with monster trucks on the roads. Later we stopped beside one of these behemoths, and its wheels were about 4.5 meters in diameter (yes 4.5 meters), and the truck was probably higher than a two-story building; these brutes can carry up to 250 tons of ore. The last thing management needs is a sniveling little one-liter Fiat Uno to be squashed like a fly beneath a behemoth ore truck.

Now what should we do? We desperately wanted to visit Mount Hor, and we weren't getting access by this route. We then embarked on a long, circuitous tour so that we could approach the Phosphate plant from the other side, from Hazeva. From Hazeva we drove for about fifteen kilometers along normal roads, then we turned a corner and instantly were confronted by enormous signs warning of all sorts of nasty things to those who entered without permission. It was also crystal clear that this was the private property of the Negev Oron Phosphate Plant.

But there was a mild dilemma that we took advantage of. Alongside the NO ENTRY signs there were the ubiquitous orange signs of the Israeli Nature Reserves Authority, pointing to Har Zin. We decided that we weren't going to the Phosphate Plant but we were going to the Nature Reserve. No one could quite explain to us why the Nature Reserve signposts would direct us along a private road. The road was very wide, perhaps as much as thirty meters, to accommodate the ore trucks, and very bumpy. We scraped the underbelly of our little Fait Uno more than once, and too often I feared for its survival as we repeatedly banged the muffler and exhaust pipe. Nevertheless, we slowly bumped along, following the orange Nature Reserve signs for about six kilometers, and then the mountain became obvious. It is a high, double-peaked flat-topped mountain to the south.

We drove as far as we could, to within a kilometer of the base of the mountain, and it was immediately apparent that we wouldn't get any closer either by car or on foot. This was a mining area that had been ravaged by surface mining. Much of the substrate was very soft underfoot with a consistency of flour. We spotted a wide, paved area that would take us about two hundred meters closer to the peak, and we ventured in that direction. This wasn't a good idea, and I started to have that 'sinking' feeling — literally! I knew that our little Fiat Uno was sinking into the crushed rocks. Perhaps these large ore trucks having enormously wide wheels wouldn't sink, but our little Uno did. Rather than make the problem worse, we stopped, we all got out of the car, and assessed the situation. We came to the simple conclusion that if we were able to drive this far with four people, then with a driver only we should be able to reverse along the tracks that we came in — it was a little nerve-wracking, but it worked. This was one of those places to stand and ponder even though there were frequent interruptions as the huge trucks thundered by. This was possibly the place where Aaron, the brother of Moses, died and was buried:

> *Then Aaron the priest went up to Mount Hor at the command of the Lord, and died there in the fortieth year after the children of Israel had come out of the land of Egypt, on the first day of the fifth month.* (Numbers 33:38)

Now we had to leave, and we had two options. We could drive on a properly paved road for a few kilometers back to the security barrier at which we were blocked earlier in the day —and pray that the wee man at the gate would allow us to leave. Alternatively, we could retrace our tracks and follow the unpaved, very bumpy road, but this would take an extra two hours.

We decided to go for the easier option. As we left our viewpoint, the road immediately climbed steeply, and after about three minutes, we were afforded a spectacular view of Har Zin. We stopped and climbed out of the car to get another photograph; it was a captivating view, and we just stood and looked. We paid little attention to the car that zoomed past at about 120 kph until it screeched to a halt and rapidly reversed to where we were standing. We were about to meet a security guard, and a particularly obnoxious one at that. We had the usual hundred questions about who we were, what we were doing, did we have ID? He made it abhorrently clear that we had to leave the area immediately, with no tolerance for our argument that we were following the orange Nature Reserve signs. We tried to pull the old 'stupid and lost tourist' routine and calmly showed him our map and where we wanted to go. This was unfortunate because our map marked this road as "strictly private," and he repeatedly banged his finger into our map as he made this point. We still don't know why there were signposts for the Nature Reserve. He also made it clear that we had to leave the area by the route we had entered, and we couldn't travel to the security barrier. We faked a lot of apologetic sorrow, hung our heads, apologized, and told him we would leave after we took one more photograph. By the time we had taken our photograph he was back in his car and drove off downhill as if he were being chased by an ore truck. He was soon out of sight, we jumped into our car, and, contrary to his directions, we drove to the security barrier where the very friendly gateman asked us no questions and allowed us to exit.

Moses and his cadre trekked from Har Zin to Eilat, about 150 kilometers, most likely following the valley of the Arabah. The road runs south and parallel to the Jordanian border. This region rarely gets rainfall, the flora is sparse and characterized by the umbrella-shaped acacias, tamarisks, and broom. Israel narrows to a point here at Eilat, and it is only ten kilometers from the Egyptian border on the southern outskirts of Eilat to the Jordanian border to the east.

Eilat is unlike anywhere else in Israel, except perhaps Tel Aviv. It is a major port and gateway to Africa and the Far East. Modern Eilat has no ancient history at all and didn't exist before Israel became a state in 1948. Today it is an up-market resort and tourist center with little evidence of the Jewishness so apparent everywhere else.

There are no camels, sheep or goats, and few keffiyehs. ATMs had an English option, and driving was relatively civilized. It has luxury hotels, desert tours, and excursions in glass-bottomed boats, a wonderful marine center and aquarium, McDonald's, Pizza Hut and Kentucky Fried Chicken. It doesn't seem Middle Eastern at all, especially when we pop into the Red Sea Gulf of Aqaba for a swim, or for a snorkel among some of the finest coral in the world. With this as a backdrop, it is difficult to imagine the children of Israel camping nearby at Ezion Geber:

> *They departed from Abronah and camped at Ezion Geber. They moved from Ezion Geber and camped in the Wilderness of Zin, which is Kadesh.* (Numbers 33:35-36)

Biblically, Eilat was known as Elath and it was an important harbor during the time of the Kingdom of Judah:

> *King Solomon also built a fleet of ships at Ezion Geber, which is near Elath on the shore of the Red Sea, in the land of Edom.* (1 Kings 9:26)

> *Jehoshaphat made merchant ships to go to Ophir for gold; but they never sailed, for the ships were wrecked at Ezion Geber.* (1 Kings 22:48)

———————

DETOUR SIX:
GETTING FROM JERUSALEM TO AMMAN
WHEN ISRAEL AND JORDAN WERE AT WAR

It is only three or four kilometers from Eilat to the Jordanian city of Aqaba, but visiting Jordan created a problem. In early 1993 Jordan and Israel were officially at war, and Jordan didn't recognize the existence of Israel. We had Israeli stamps in our passports, which prevented us from visiting Arab countries (except Egypt). So how did we get into Jordan? Good question, *long* answer; it is called the passport shuffle. We traveled light, real light, on this trip. From Eilat we arranged for a taxi to take us to the Egyptian border at Taba; it is only a few miles. We entered Egypt on our British passports and kept our clean Canadian passports out of sight, not that the Egyptians would have cared one way or the other. Because we were only going to the Sinai and not going farther into Egypt, it was possible to get a Sinai permit rather than a full visa for this entry, and these permits were issued at the border. And again, we had to go through the whole process of having the video camera described in detail and hand-written into a page in my passport — this would become a real problem later. The border crossing was relatively straightforward. The only problem was that it is a distance of at least 1½ kilometers between the Israeli and Egyptian checkpoints … and there is no option but to walk. Once we were processed, we hopped on board a rickety old bus for the journey to Neweiba, which took about 1–2 hours. Neweiba was the ferry terminal for passenger service across the Gulf of Aqaba to the city of Aqaba in southern Jordan. We stayed overnight in Neweiba, and to our surprise, we were given discounted prices at the hotel because we were "temporary residents of Egypt" according to our visas.

The events of the next day were memorable. We had no idea what to expect, so we were up early and went to the ferry terminal. We were traveling on a tight budget and we had hoped to get second-class tickets, but we weren't given that option. We were automatically sold first-class tickets. We were then ushered into this huge outdoor paddock. It had a roof of sorts, but it was more of a shelter. To our chagrin, we weren't first in line for the ferry. There seemed to be thousands of people waiting for the ferry, and as far as we could tell, they were all men — not a woman in sight, except for Evelyn and Andrea. Talk about being conspicuous and wondering if we were just being a little bit crazy. It was a seething mass of Arab men, all being kept very much in order by officials in uniform, walking around and waving these rather nasty-looking sticks. Without more than a few words, we were pointed to a seat. Would we get on to the ferry? Would we get lost in this huge crowd? Should we ask someone, or tell someone, that we needed to be on this ferry?

We didn't wait too long when, out of nowhere, a man came and beckoned us to follow. I don't know if it was eerie, scary, or amusing, to be led through the middle of all these piercing eyes; it was probably a mixture of all of these emotions. We were then led through a door, and into a cavernous warehouse, and here was yet another seething mass of Arab men. We were feeling very uncomfortable at this stage, yet strangely excited by the whole experience. We were brought to a couple of flat tables and had our bags searched and passports checked. At this point, we became Canadians and no longer British. Everything was in order except "The video camera?" the customs officer questioned. I knew exactly what he was asking because the entire description, serial and registration numbers, etc., were all recorded in the British passports, which were now out of sight. My vain attempts to act as though I were ignorant were short-lived. This officer was letting us go nowhere until we could explain how we got the video camera into Egypt without having it registered in our passports.

At this point I thought our game was finished. I produced the British passports and explained what we were trying to do, that we had left Israel and entered Egypt on British passports because we had to keep our Canadian passports clean. We now wanted to use our Canadian passports to enter Jordan. I felt sick because the only reason we had been caught was because of this silly video camera. If we had left the camera in Jerusalem, there wouldn't have been a problem. Anyway, the officer seemed rather unperturbed but basically told us that we probably couldn't do what we were trying to do. Then he beckoned that we follow him, and we walked the full length of this warehouse, past thousands of pairs of eyes, and they all seemed to be on us, past enormously long lineups, and to the head of the line. Something was muttered, and we had our passports checked, and then we went into a small side room for another piece of paper to fill in (who knows what for), and then an officer had a chat with us:

> It doesn't matter to us Egyptians what you are doing, but if the Jordanians catch you, you will be sent back on the next boat here to Neweiba. You are now cleared to go onboard the boat, but before you board, ask for the captain of the boat. Tell him what you are attempting. If he is an Egyptian captain, he will take you to Aqaba. If it is a Jordanian captain he will probably not let you on board.

So off we trundled to the ferry. As we were about to board, we showed our tickets, and asked for the captain. This seemed to be a strange request, but there was no fuss, and the captain appeared. We explained our game — and he was Egyptian! However, he also explained that if we got caught at Aqaba, we would be sent back on the next ferry and would have to pay for the journey. We nodded, acknowledging that we understood, then went on board. We were among the first passengers to get onboard. We had hoped to look around the ferry, but there was no chance. We were hurriedly directed and led into the first-class lounge; no question about being allowed to go anywhere else.

The ferry ride was an experience to fully appreciate and remember. We estimate there were 2,000–2,500 people on the ferry literally packed wall-to-wall, mostly standing room only, much like cattle or sheep in a wagon on the way to the slaughterhouse. Alistair and Andrea called it the refugee boat. We counted about ten non-Arabs, six women, and only two other children. Although we apparently traveled first class, the only thing separating us from the life jackets under our seats was a row of springs. The backs of the seats each had the insignia of Pan Am, meaning that our first-class cabin seats were actually rejected Pan Am airline seats. At one point during the three-hour journey, I decided I would like to go up on deck. I brought one of the children with me, and we only got halfway up the steps. This ferry was jammed-packed full —standing room only, passengers sitting on the edge of the ferry with their feet dangling through the rails and over the side. Then we arrived at Aqaba in Jordan. As tourists, we were whisked off the ferry before anyone else and walked a few hundred meters along the jetty towards immigration.

We each took a quick glance over our shoulders at the boat that had just ferried us from Egypt. Oh, for a photograph, but we wouldn't dare. It was crawling with people, mostly migrant workers going from Egypt to Saudi, and one wonders how it remained afloat. We couldn't help but wonder if we would get through customs. This was our last hurdle. By this stage, we knew that we had nothing on our possession that would give away the fact that we had been to Israel (except our hidden British passports) — no Israeli coins, and no products with Hebrew writing such as toothpaste! As we entered the customs hall, we first had to purchase our Jordanian entry visas (a whopping $50 USD each), then customs. There were quite a few tense moments as the officer did a very thorough search of our luggage — but the one place he didn't check was the outside pocket of Evelyn's handbag, yep, where we had the passports. We were through; we were in Jordan; all totally legal yet the Jordanians wouldn't have been happy had they found out what we had done. Our journey from Aqaba to Amman is described later.

While driving through Eilat, a woman decided to take a shortcut through the passenger door of our rental car. Evelyn was driving, and I ended up with a lap-full of shattered glass, but no one was hurt. Our rental car, which had eight thousand kilometers on the clock, was badly hurt! The woman had tried to do a U-turn on a busy street, and when we were alongside her she made her move — bang! She accepted full responsibility for the accident. Luckily, Avis car rental was almost opposite the site of the accident, and they quickly got us a new car and sent us on our way.

We traveled from Eilat through Neweiba, across the Gulf of Aqaba to Aqaba in Jordan. After clearing customs, we went straight into the city of Aqaba and rented a vehicle. From Aqaba, there are only two roads north, one that follows the Rift Valley and the Dead Sea, and the other the King's Highway. We know that Moses didn't use either of these roads because they were specifically refused passage through Edom and the King's Highway:

> *Now Moses sent messengers from Kadesh to the king of Edom... Please let us pass through your country. We will not pass through fields or vineyards, nor will we*

*drink water from wells; we will go along the King's Highway; we will not turn aside
to the right hand or to the left until we have passed through your territory.'" Then
Edom said to him, "You shall not pass through my land, lest I come out against you
with the sword." So the children of Israel said to him, "We will go by the Highway,
and if I or my livestock drink any of your water, then I will pay for it; let me only
pass through on foot, nothing more." Then he said, "You shall not pass through."...*
(Numbers 20:14, 17-20)

The King's Highway was the main highway in biblical times running through
Edom, Moab, and the land of the Amorites. It passes close to Petra and goes
through the cities of Karak and Madeba. The route of the Exodus was to the east
of this highway and thus bypassed Petra and Karak. However, Scripture tells us
that the Israelites were at Aroer on the rim of the Arnon gorge, so it was probably
in this general area that they joined the main King's Highway and continued
north to Madeba. We rented vehicles twice in Aqaba and drove north along the
King's Highway to Amman and beyond. Both trips evoke memories for us.

This first journey was in early 1993. We rented a Russian Lada and started
driving north towards Petra. This was a journey to remember, and frankly, I don't
ever recall having a worse driving experience. We left Aqaba just as it was getting
dark. The road had no lane markings, no markings on the side of the road, lots of
guard rails, no signs or warnings, many potholes, and was initially very steep as
we climbed from sea level up out of the rift valley. It seems that the road climbed
for at least forty-five minutes, but the fact that we were driving in a low-geared,
rickety old Lada didn't help. The road was very busy with enormously over-laden
trucks. This was white-knuckle and eye strain at its very best.

After perhaps two hours we were concerned that we had not seen any signs
to Petra. This concern was intensified when we lost the side of the road — we just
couldn't see it. Later, we would discover that on occasion the Jordanians simply
widen their roads for about a mile so that they can land aircraft during times of
emergency. Now get this picture: It is dark, the Lada has poor lights, there are
no road markings, and suddenly a 'normal' four-lane, fifteen-meter wide road
becomes perhaps forty meters wide. We saw a light just off to the right, so we
drove towards it. Luckily, it was a police officer checking vehicles although I
suspect most of them drove right past him. Anyway, he was able to tell us that
we had missed our turnoff to Petra many miles back, but that there was another
just a short distance ahead. Obviously, we made it and pulled into a cold little
hotel that evening in Petra — we will never forget having to move the kerosene
heater out of our very cold bedroom into the hallway because the fumes from the
heater were choking us.

Four years later we were back in Aqaba, and this time rented a Renault. It had quite a powerful engine, but otherwise, it wasn't very good. Things got off to a bad start when the rental agent gave us money to have the car cleaned; it was very dirty both inside and out. It had no horn, the brakes squealed, there were no rear-view mirrors, the handle on the gear stick was held in place with Kleenex tissues and fell off every time I changed gears. The indicators only worked to the right, and there was no high beam. Oh, and did I mention that there were no handles on either of the back windows?

About fifty kilometers out of Eilat we were driving through a small village and noticed this guy hitching a ride. We thought it prudent, that as tourists in a rental car in a foreign country, we shouldn't stop to pick up a total stranger. As we drove past, we screeched to a halt when we realized we were driving past a police officer. He had almost no English, but it was clear that he wanted a ride. He hopped in the back seat and we drove him to his post some twenty-five kilometers farther along the road. When he tried to get out of the car we discovered that the back doors could only be opened from the outside. I felt rather chauffeur-ish as I jumped out of the car and opened the back door while the officer got out.

We had the car for five days, and along with the extortionate drop-of charge at Amman, this rental was approximately $100 USD per day (in 1996). When we got our MasterCard statement we had been charged in Jordanian dinars instead of US dollars meaning we had been charged double at almost $200 USD per day for a heap of junk! When I wrote a letter of complaint to Avis, and described the car, they canceled the entire transaction! Thumbs up to Avis.

Back to Petra — which is stunning, awesome, astounding, awe-inspiring and breath-taking. This is one of the great wonders of the world, and if you are only going to see one thing in the Middle East, this is it. This magnificent site is a combination of extraordinary geology and outstanding workmanship. This was the capital city of the Nabateans and is referred to as The Rose-Red City because of the layered red and multi-colored sandstone infused with white, grey and yellow stripes, and mottled pinks. The city has a one-kilometer long entrance through a canyon, the siq, about four meters wide and up to 125 meters deep. Petra has few free-standing buildings, and most are chiselled out of the rock. It is a rock-hewn necropolis with over eight hundred tombs, buildings, and monuments, all delicately chiselled, including an eight-thousand-seat theater. All visitors travel through the siq, and when the siq emerges for the first time to the open, visitors are greeted by one of the most magnificent views in the entire city

— this is the famous Treasury Building, the Khazneh, a full forty-meter high grandiose façade carved into the sandstone; this was the site of an epic battle by Harrison Ford in *Indiana Jones and the Last Crusade*. From here visitors may scatter all over the site and can easily spend 2–3 days doing so.

It is a particularly rewarding climb for just over an hour to the Monastery (al-Deir), a massive square building cut out of yellow sandstone, and at forty-eight meters tall it is the largest structure in Petra. From here, in the distance, and another few hour's walk, is a little mosque sitting on top of a high hill, and the more traditional site of the tomb of Aaron — Har Harun, Mt. Aaron. Oh, how I dearly wish we would have had a little more willpower, and pushed through the heat and tiredness, and pressed to the tomb of Aaron — perhaps next time.

The highway north is truly historic because from Karak and to the north it follows the route followed by the children of Israel on their trek to the Promised Land — the River Arnon, Dibon, Madeba, Mount Nebo, and Heshbon. The road follows the undulating contours through the land of Moab and the land of Ammon. The tribes of Reuben and Gad would later return to settle in this region. The area is intensely cultivated and provides a livelihood for the many villages scattered around the countryside.

It was perhaps 150 kilometers north of Petra that we came to the gorge of the River Arnon, known locally as the Wadi el Mujib, and deservedly has the name Grand Canyon of the Middle East.

From there they moved and camped on the other side of the Arnon, which is in the wilderness that extends from the border of the Amorites; for the Arnon is the border of Moab, between Moab and the Amorites. (Numbers 21:13)

"But we have shot at them; Heshbon has perished as far as Dibon. Then we laid waste as far as Nophah, Which reaches to Medeba." (Numbers 21:30)

As we traveled northbound and reached the rim of the canyon, the view was truly breathtaking. It is about five kilometers from one side of the canyon to the other, and the space between is empty, jagged, and barren, with only the occasional patch of vegetation. This valley marked the boundary between the kingdoms of Ammon to the north and Moab to the south. The road drops steeply and circuitously to the canyon bottom but has a gentler ascent on the northern side. Within five minutes of emerging from the northern rim, we arrived at the small village of Dibon. It was here that the famous Moabite Stone was discovered in 1868, the details of which we described earlier. After a brief visit to the site and the token photographs taken with all the local children, we headed north for about twenty kilometers to Medeba.

We went to Medeba to see the famous mosaic tile floor in the Greek Orthodox Church of St George. This floor is one of the most remarkable in all the Middle East. It was uncovered in 1896 when the present Church was being rebuilt on the foundations of an ancient Byzantine Basilica. The mosaic is a map of the Middle East from the sixth century AD stretching from the Nile Delta and Cairo to southern Turkey. It is incomplete and damaged, probably suffering from many earthquakes over its 1,400-year existence. The complete map would have been almost thirteen meters wide, 4.5 meters deep, with almost two-million tiles. The map shows amazing detail of Jerusalem, and the locations of over 120 other cities. There are remarkable details such as fish in the River Jordan, palm trees in Jericho, the Damascus Gate, the Church of the Holy Sepulchre, and a row of forty-five columns lining the Cardo in the old city of Jerusalem. The map also shows an assortment of animals such as bears, foxes, lions, and sheep.

Moses then led the Children of Israel those last few miles north, set up camp in the Plains of Moab, and prepared for two major events: the changeover of leadership from Moses to Joshua, and the entry and conquest of the Promised Land:

> So Moses did as the Lord commanded him. He took Joshua and set him before Eleazar the priest and before all the congregation. And he laid his hands on him and inaugurated him, just as the Lord commanded by the hand of Moses. (Numbers 27:22-23)

> See, I have set the land before you; go in and possess the land which the Lord swore to your fathers—to Abraham, Isaac, and Jacob—to give to them and their descendants after them. (Deuteronomy 1:8)

When the Israelites were encamped on the plains of Moab, we find one of the most amusing and perplexing narratives of the Old Testament. Balaam, a magician or soothsayer, was summoned by the Moabite king Balak to curse the Israelites before they entered Canaan. But by the intervention of God, he was utterly unable to fulfill Balak's wish, however much he tried. And he didn't give up. Three times Balaam tried to speak against Israel, but he was always overruled by God so that instead of cursing them he blessed them and pronounced magnificent prophecies. On one of his attempts, we have the narrative usually referred to as Balaam's donkey:

> Then the Angel of the Lord went further, and stood in a narrow place where there was no way to turn either to the right hand or to the left. And when the donkey saw the Angel of the Lord, she lay down under Balaam; so Balaam's anger was aroused, and he struck the donkey with his staff. Then the Lord opened the mouth of the

donkey, and she said to Balaam, "What have I done to you, that you have struck me
these three times?" And Balaam said to the donkey, "Because you have abused me. I
wish there were a sword in my hand, for now I would kill you!" So the donkey said
to Balaam, "Am I not your donkey on which you have ridden, ever since I became
yours, to this day? Was I ever disposed to do this to you?" And he said, "No." Then
the Lord opened Balaam's eyes, and he saw the Angel of the Lord standing in the
way with His drawn sword in His hand; and he bowed his head and fell flat on his
face. (Numbers 22:26-31)

Not only is this story amusing because of a talking donkey, Balaam spoke back to the donkey! Numbers chapter 33 reflects upon, and describes in some detail, the itinerary of the children of Israel from Egypt to the plains of Moab by the Jordan, across from Jericho. It was here that Moses delivered perhaps the longest sermon in the Scriptures — the book of Deuteronomy. The entire book highlights God's power and control of nations and nature, God's faithfulness and total dependability, God's love, and God's requirement of undivided allegiance from His people. The purpose of Moses's sermon was to confirm Israel as the people of God before he handed leadership over to Joshua and the people went out to conquer Canaan. Also, a purpose of Deuteronomy was to call for new commitment to the covenants by the new generations entering Israel and move Israel to faith and obedience. The book also gives a retrospective on some of the history of the Jews. It describes the good life lived in fellowship with God and enjoying his blessings, and contrasts this with the awful results of neglecting the covenant. The book is centered on a focal verse:

I call heaven and earth as witnesses today against you, that I have set before you
life and death, blessing and cursing; therefore choose life, that both you and your
descendants may live; (Deuteronomy 30:19)

Moses obviously knew that his life was coming to an end. God had told him back in the Wilderness of Zin that, because of his disobedience, he would not be allowed to enter the Promised Land. Now they were at their final encampment before the conquest. Today the Jewish people commemorate their forty years in the wilderness with the Sukkot holiday, which follows about one week after Yom Kippur.

Yom Kippur, the Day of Atonement, is the holiest day in the Jewish calendar, and the whole country of Israel stops; only emergency vehicles are allowed on the roads. It gives children with bicycles and skateboards a great opportunity to ride the main boulevards. It was delightful to see Hertzl Boulevard and the Jaffa Road without a car in sight, aside from a few delinquent Arab taxi cabs, but abuzz with children engaged is street-play. And about a week later, Sukkot, or the Feast of Tabernacles, is one of Israel's most beloved holidays. It is sometimes referred to simply as *"The Holiday"* or *"The Feast."* The Feast of Tabernacles is the last in a series of God-ordained festivals given to Israel (Leviticus 23:33-43). Sukkot was the third and final occasion on which all Jewish adult males were required to make a pilgrimage to Jerusalem to appear before the Lord. Sukkot is a joyful holiday filled with celebration. It is known in Scripture as the Feast of Ingathering because it was held at the end of the harvest season when God's provision was so clearly in view. The Feast of Tabernacles had a commemorative purpose as well. It looked back to the time when the children of Israel dwelled in temporary shelters or booths as God led them through the wideness and provided for all their needs.

Of all the requirements surrounding Sukkot, the most conspicuous is building the temporary shelter or booth called a sukkah. Booths are built at homes and often at synagogues. In Israel, it is common to find booths located on apartment rooftops, balconies, and courtyards. According to rabbinical teaching, the walls of a hut can be built with anything, but the roof must be made of vegetation and should be covered with enough leaves and straw to provide shade without blocking the view of the stars at night. To help accomplish this, the Jerusalem city council dumps enormous piles of palm branches (actually they are leaves) all over the city for people to use. Jews will sleep in these sukkah for the week of Succoth, and the most Orthodox ones will not leave the sukkah during the week.

In both biblical and rabbinical teachings, Sukkot typifies the days of the Messiah, an age when the glory of God, representing the presence of God, will dwell, or tabernacle, or sukkah, among men. Sukkot is often used in the New Testament to affirm the messianic credentials of Jesus. To Christians, Jesus not only celebrated the holiday of Sukkot, but He was also its fulfillment. For example:

> *And the Word [Jesus] became flesh and dwelt [tabernacled] among us, and we beheld His glory, the glory as of the only begotten of the Father, full of grace and truth.* (John 1:14)

On one occasion, while celebrating Sukkot in Jerusalem, Jesus made a remarkable declaration.

> *On the last day, that great day of the feast [Hoshana Raba], Jesus stood and cried out, saying, "If anyone thirsts, let him come to Me and drink. He who believes in Me, as the Scripture has said, out of his heart will flow rivers of living water."* (John 7:37-38)

To those listening, pouring the water on the altar at Sukkot symbolized the pouring out of the Holy Spirit in the days of the Messiah. Applying that symbolism to Himself, Jesus was declaring that He was the Messiah and that God was now dwelling with man just as He had done in the wilderness.

The final hours of Moses's life are simply described in Scripture:

> *Then Moses went up from the plains of Moab to Mount Nebo, to the top of Pisgah, which is across from Jericho. And the Lord showed him all the land of Gilead as far as Dan, all Naphtali and the land of Ephraim and Manasseh, all the land of Judah as far as the Western Sea, the South, and the plain of the Valley of Jericho, the city of palm trees, as far as Zoar. Then the Lord said to him, "This is the land of which I swore to give Abraham, Isaac, and Jacob, saying, 'I will give it to your descendants.' I have caused you to see it with your eyes, but you shall not cross over there." So Moses the servant of the Lord died there in the land of Moab, according to the word of the Lord. And He buried him in a valley in the land of Moab, opposite Beth Peor; but no one knows his grave to this day.* (Deuteronomy 34:1-6)

We have visited Mount Nebo six or seven times, but only once did we see the view that Moses saw (the other times were hazy). And on that one occasion, what a stunning view. Then, as now, the view extends to the imaginary four corners of the earth, down to the Dead Sea that lies one thousand meters below to the west. We could see long distances north along the Jordan River valley and south along the Dead Sea. To the west, we could see the Russian Church of the Ascension atop the Mount of Olives some seventy kilometers away.

Today at the site is the Moses Memorial Church, which is one of the most venerated sanctuaries in Jordan. Inside, the church has large, exquisite, mosaic floors. Outside, there is a contemporary sculpture of Moses with the brazen serpent commemorating;

> *Then the Lord said to Moses, "Make a fiery serpent, and set it on a pole; and it shall be that everyone who is bitten, when he looks at it, shall live."* (Numbers 21:8)

We have a few favorite spots in the Bible lands, each of which evoke a great sense of awe, wonder, serenity, and a sense that we are reliving a great moment in history. As we looked out towards the Mount of Olives and Jerusalem, looked below to the Dead Sea and Jericho, and gazed at the bronze serpent, it was amazing to stand and ponder: it was at this spot that God spoke to Moses and showed him the land that was to become the inheritance of the Children of Israel. It was here that Moses died, Joshua took on the leadership mantle and led the people down from Mount Nebo to the Jordan River and camped on the large flat plain below us known as the Plains of Moab. Joshua now plans to cross the Jordan into the Promised Land.

Clearly, this is an important location, but it is also important for other reasons. In this same general location, Jesus Christ was baptized by John, Elijah went to Heaven in a chariot of fire, and today we have the Allenby Bridge border crossing, officially called the *King Hussein Bridge* by Jordanians and the Al-Karameh Bridge by Palestinian Arabs. But we aren't going to cross for a few more pages. We can't leave Jordan without a brief visit to Amman, the capital city, which is about a fifty-minute drive from the River Jordan.

During our first visit to Amman, Israel and Jordan were still officially at war, and Jordan had very few tourists. At times we felt as if we were the tourist attraction. We walked around downtown Amman and attracted much attention — it was quite embarrassing, especially being accompanied by a beautiful young daughter with fair blonde hair and blue eyes. However, it was while we were in Amman that we saw something quite unusual in the city center. A kid, probably about ten years old, ran out in front of a taxi and was knocked down. The taxi driver was out of the car in a flash, gave the kid a tongue lashing, cuffed him on the ear a few times, jumped in his car, and drove off! Lawyers wouldn't survive long in Jordan. Coincidentally, this incident occurred at the base of a hill, the citadel, in central Amman. The citadel is the place where David sent Uriah the Hittite to his death:

> *It happened in the spring of the year, at the time when kings go out to battle, that David sent Joab and his servants with him, and all Israel; and they destroyed the people of Ammon and besieged Rabbah [today's city of Amman, Jordan]... And he [David] wrote in the letter, saying, "Set Uriah in the forefront of the hottest battle, and retreat from him, that he may be struck down and die." So it was, while Joab besieged the city, that he assigned Uriah to a place where he knew there were valiant men. Then the men of the city came out and fought with Joab. And some of the people of the servants of David fell; and Uriah the Hittite died also.* (2 Sam 11:1, 15-17)

On another one of our visits to Amman, we decided to attempt a day trip into Damascus, Syria. We left all our luggage in storage at our hotel and told the staff that we would probably return that day, but that it might be two days. I had cold feet about this journey, and I had this sneaky feeling we were going to get caught — but Evelyn encouraged me to keep going. After all, although we had Syrian visas in our passports, and Jordan was now at peace with Israel, Syria was still at war with Israel. Any evidence of having been in Israel was an automatic refusal of entry to Syria, even with the visas.

We went into downtown Amman to the servis taxis (shared taxis) to Damascus. Servis taxis simply wait until they are full, then take off. We waited for perhaps ten minutes and were on our way. There were six passengers in the taxi, one of whom was an Arab woman totally covered in black, along with her chaperon. The journey to Damascus would normally take about 3–4 hours and cost only a few dollars. This time we knew we would have to play a very careful game of passport shuffle. Evelyn was wearing a jacket that had two inside pockets; the one on the left had our British passports and the one on the right had our Canadian passports. We would have to leave Jordan on our British passports (because we had left Israel and entered Jordan on the British) but enter Syria on our Canadian passports. We came to the first checkpoint, which was probably military police. These police were at the passenger side of the car (Evelyn and I were in the front seat of the taxi along with the driver), so we simply passed our passports through the window. They checked our passports — no problem.

We then pulled into a rather official-looking place with flags, many buses, and many other taxis, so we knew this was Jordanian emigration proper. On entering the building, to our horror, there were different lines for locals and for foreigners. We didn't like the look of the "foreign" lineup one little bit. It was long, looked more like a scrum, was chaotic, and most of e those in the melee looked to be bus operators — each one of whom seemed to be holding a fist full of passports, probably the entire passenger list of their respective buses. This was going to take hours, but we couldn't wait for hours —there were other people in our taxi who would doubtless want to be on their way. Evelyn and I discussed what we would do. We decided to go to the woman in black who was standing over by the door. We don't know if she spoke much English or not, but Evelyn, using a mixture of words, pointing, and other hand signals, explained that we were going to be a very long time. The women said nothing, but she took our passports, pushed her way to the front of the line, banged on the glass, said something, the passports were handed over the top of the glass, and within about three or four minutes we had our passports back and were on our way. We drove for a few minutes from this spot until we came to another road check. This time, we assumed we were entering Syria, so Evelyn dipped her left hand into her right inside pocket to produce the Canadian passports.

"Are these Syrian soldiers?" I asked the driver.

"No. Still in Jordan," came the response.

With lightning-quick sleight of hand, Evelyn put the Canadian passports back into the appropriate pocket and produced the British passports. We don't know the reason for all of these checkpoints. It seems the first check is to ensure you have proper documentation before reaching the border, and the third is to ensure you have performed all the necessary procedures at the main office. Anyway, again Evelyn passed the British passports out the taxi window, no problem, and we were on our way. From here it was easy except we went through three or four more checkpoints, plus the formal Syrian immigration, and we were now using our Canadian passports out of the correct pocket!

We arrived in Damascus at about 11:00 a.m. We experienced an enjoyable day in Damascus and visited the House of Ananias and Straight St., both made famous by the Apostle Paul, and the well-known Damascus Grand Bazaar. We bought Andrea a gold bracelet in the bazaar, and we bought Alistair an ornamental knife that would later cause us problems at the Israeli border. However, all day we were just slightly uneasy, and since we had seen all that we had come to see, we decided not to stay overnight and to return to Amman that night. We took a local taxi out to the servis center, and wouldn't you know it, we got the same driver that had brought us from Amman in the morning. We were soon on our way, and within about an hour we were at the border. This time the border police were at the driver's side window. As we approached the first checkpoint, Evelyn produced the Canadian passports for the driver. Immediately something clicked in his mind.

"You are not Canadian," he stated, "you are British," as he obviously recalled our conversation earlier in the day.

"No no no. We are British, living in Canada, and our British passports were issued in Ottawa."

I'm sure he was utterly confused, as we had hoped he would be, and he was probably as keen to get back to Amman as quickly as we were. We got through the Syrian side without issue, but when we reached the Jordanian side, our taxi (along with all the other taxis) was taken off to one side and into a shelter where we drove over the top of a mechanics pit. Every car was thoroughly searched inside and out, and even underneath. We were later told that this was done as security for Jordan. Jordan had signed a peace treaty with Israel, but Syria had not. Jordan was afraid that their rather tenuous peace deal could be derailed if Syrian terrorists assaulted Israel from Jordanian territory, hence the tight security entering Jordan. We were caught unawares by this detailed search, and now they wanted to see our bags. The only luggage we had was a shoulder bag that Evelyn was carrying. When the officer opened the bag the first thing that greeted him was a roll of toilet paper, which is an absolute necessity when traveling in the Middle East.

"Oh, this is personal," he said as he smiled, and with that he closed the bag. We then went through the passport formalities. As we left the parking lot, there were several buses blocking our exit route. As it turned out, we had just met up with tens of thousands of Muslim pilgrims returning from the Hajj at Mecca. There were buses everywhere, and true to typical Middle-Eastern chaos, they were everywhere, and it wasn't possible for us to get through. But there are no insoluble problems in the Middle East. Our taxi driver took to the hard shoulder, into the fields, along field-side tracks, and who knows where for at least a few miles, and then finally wriggled between a few buses, and we were liberated. We estimated that there were at least a thousand buses lined up at the border. A few hours later we were back in Amman.

When our visit to Jordan was complete, it was now time to return to Israel. From Amman, it is only about ninety kilometers to Jerusalem even though it took us four days to get to Amman from Jerusalem. Thankfully, we didn't have to retrace our steps through Aqaba, Newiba, Taba, and Eilat but could enter Israel directly from Jordan; crossing in the opposite direction from Israel to Jordan wasn't possible. We went to the appropriate offices in Amman and applied for a "West Bank Permit"; you do not apply for a visa to Israel because you aren't visiting Israel, rather you are visiting the West Bank. Let me explain. The problem occurs when you consider two points of view. To the Israelis, when you cross the River Jordan to the West Bank you are crossing from Jordan into Israel's Judea and Samaria. To the Jordanians, you are simply crossing from one part of Jordan into another part of Jordan because, at that time, the Jordanians didn't recognize that Israel captured the West Bank in the 1967 Six-Day War. So it is obvious what to do. You apply for a West Bank permit which is good for one month. Once you enter the West Bank, just keep going to Jerusalem.

We have crossed the Allenby border on many occasions. Typically, it ranges from slow to excessively slow (six hours on one occasion). The Allenby Bridge crosses the Jordan River, which is the most heavily fortified border crossing in the world. It is only a few miles from Jericho. Crossing the Allenby Bridge isn't always easy, as Evelyn and I were to discover. A shuttle bus took us the one-kilometer journey from Jordanian passport control to the bridge and to Israeli security. Fortunately, our bags were first to be taken out of the bus, so we took them and were the first to enter the customs hall. We set our single, rather large suitcase on the conveyer belt, went through passport control, and waited for our bag to come out the other end. It didn't come. After waiting for at least twenty minutes and watching everyone else's bags come through, we knew something had gone wrong. Perhaps our bag had fallen off the conveyer belt? We asked various people in uniform but nobody seemed to know anything. We finally got our answer when we were beckoned into a small room off to the side, and there was our case up on a table. The knife. I bet it's the little ornamental knife that we had bought for Alistair in Damascus. We were directed to a few chairs and told to sit down.

"Is this your luggage?" the officer asked rather curtly.

"Yes, and...?" I was sharply interrupted with,

"Do you know everything that is in this bag?"

"Yes, and ..." and again she interrupted. It was clear that this lady wasn't playing any games and was in no mood to listen.

"And everything in this bag is yours?" she asked.

I stood up to open the zip to show her the knife when I was met with a very sharp command to stay seated. Okay, what do we do in a situation like this? We knew what she wanted, we could tell her what she wanted to know, but she was in the driving seat, and she wasn't going to listen. So we just sat there and watched and let her go through her intimidation routine. She then opened the case and started to take everything out piece by piece, and not in a very organized or tidy way. She moved her hands all through our stuff obviously looking for something. We knew it was the knife, and we even knew that it was in that outside pocket, but why tell this dragon-lady? She had a routine to follow, and this included intimidation and not listening. After all this, she still hadn't found the knife but clearly she knew there was one. No doubt the scanners on the conveyer belt had detected it. With everything lying on a pile on the table, we ventured again:

"You are probably looking for the knife we have with us. We left it in the bag by mistake. We had planned to transfer it into our hand luggage, but we forgot."

"Where is it?" she snapped. With this invitation, I got up from my seat, and we showed her the knife. It was small, perhaps fifteen centimeters long, with an ornamental handle and blade, the blade was curved and blunt and perhaps 7–8 centimeters long. It was a harmless thing. After we received the mandatory scolding, she walked of and left all our stuff lying in a pile. We repacked our bags and carried on our journey to Jericho and finally to Jerusalem.

This first part of the big story is complete. The Israelites had left Egypt, and under the leadership of Moses, they wandered in the wilderness. And now with a new leader, Joshua, they were ready for part two — the entry and conquest of the Promised Land. God now speaks to Joshua:

"Moses My servant is dead. Now therefore, arise, go over this Jordan, you and all this people, to the land which I am giving to them—the children of Israel... "Pass through the camp and command the people, saying, 'Prepare provisions for yourselves, for within three days you will cross over this Jordan, to go in to possess the land which the Lord your God is giving you to possess."' (Joshua 1:2, 11)

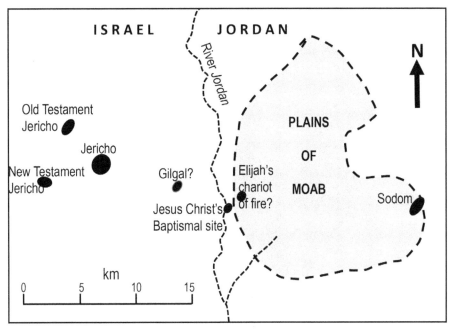

Geography of the Plains of Moab where Israel encamped before crossing the Jordan into the Promised Land. We thought it interesting that the Plains of Moab (where Israel camped before crossing the Jordan River) may have had Sodom on its eastern border. Jesus Christ would later be baptized on the encampment's western border.

V.
JOSHUA'S ENTRY TO THE PROMISED LAND

This is a fascinating journey through many parts of Judea and Samaria, the West Bank. We have listed the various sites in more-or-less the same order in which Joshua conquered them, but this part of the story begins with the crossing of the Jordan River.

So it was, when the people set out from their camp to cross over the Jordan, with the priests bearing the ark of the covenant before the people, and as those who bore the ark came to the Jordan, and the feet of the priests who bore the ark dipped in the edge of the water (for the Jordan overflows all its banks during the whole time of harvest), that the waters which came down from upstream stood still, and rose in a heap very far away at Adam, the city that is beside Zaretan. So the waters that went down into the Sea of the Arabah, the Salt Sea, failed, and were cut off; and the people crossed over opposite Jericho. Then the priests who bore the ark of the covenant of the Lord stood firm on dry ground in the midst of the Jordan; and all Israel crossed over on dry ground, until all the people had crossed completely over the Jordan. (Joshua 3:14-17).

Adam is on the eastern bank of the River Jordan and almost on the border between Jordan and Israel, and, therefore, in a military zone. We could see how to get there from our maps, but maps don't get you past military road checks. We drove north along the Jordan Valley Road (on the Jordanian side) and were just slowing down for an army road check about fifty meters ahead when we spotted our road to the left. We made a rather impulsive left turn and took off down this road. It was only then we realized that this must have raised tremendous suspicion at the army checkpoint because the road we had just entered doesn't go anywhere. Well, actually it does. It goes for about five kilometers to another army road check; this is the end of the road because beyond is the military zone, the Jordan River, and then Israel on the other side. The checkpoint had two young soldiers who spoke very broken English. We muttered and spluttered and pointed, and drew a very raw map, and they finally realized that all we wanted to do was to drive 200m to that mound sitting beyond their gate. We aren't sure what happened at that point, but the gate was opened and we were beckoned in.

We drove to the mound and clambered up to the top. This was a place to stand and ponder. As we looked north and south along the Jordan Valley the contrast was stark. Because of the geography of the area and the prevailing wind directions, the land to the west (that is Israel) is dry and barren, yet the Jordan Valley and the land to the east (that is Jordan) is lush and productive. Just below the mound an army of workers were harvesting beans. Although this site is nothing more than a thirty-meter-high mound, nevertheless it is packed with meaning. The Scriptures tell us that when Joshua and the people crossed the River Jordan into the Promised Land, the waters of the Jordan backed up to this point. As we stood we began to contemplate the enormity of the miracle that took place right here. We allowed the words of a well-known song to run through our minds, the beginning of which is: "He is able, more than able to accomplish what concerns me today..." This song is based on the New Testament verse that says:

> *Now to him who is able to do exceedingly abundantly above all that we ask or think, according to the power that works in us,* (Ephesians 3:20)

We were very tempted at this point to walk down towards the River Jordan. However, we had already pushed our luck getting this far, and, realizing that we were already in a military zone, and probably being watched, that we had better return to the car. We scrambled down the mound, made our way through the bean field, and drove back towards the main Jordan Valley road. As we headed north, we approached another military checkpoint. We slowed down, stopped, and greeted the soldiers. This time they wanted me out of the car to check the trunk. This was unusual because we had already been through three or four checkpoints where we had been checked, documents had been checked, and presumably, this far along everything should be okay.

But while I was at the trunk of the car with one soldier, the other soldier was making advances to Evelyn. He wanted to see inside her day bag. This was a medium-sized fabric bag that was sitting on her lap. As Evelyn opened the bag the soldier reached in ostensibly to put his hands in the handbag but meanwhile was groping at Evelyn through the fabric. Evelyn sternly said to him, "Men don't do that in our country," and gave him a penetrating look. Although this happened in an Arab nation, it is a sad commentary on our own culture that we have sent a message of complete and flagrant licentiousness to the rest of the world. While the soldier can't be excused for his behavior, he nevertheless treated Evelyn just as he thought men would treat her 'normally' in North America. After this little episode with the randy soldier, we were on our way.

We arrived at a little village. It was hot, and we decided to stop for a soft drink. We entered an inauspicious little store and pointed at the cans of Sprite in the fridge and indicated with our fingers that we would like two of them. The cheerful old lady gave us the cans and wrote-down on a piece of paper, one dinar. This was equivalent to about $1 USD per can, which we knew to be exorbitant. In Jordan, the price of canned pop is laser-sprayed on the bottom of the cans, so rather nonchalantly, I turned the can upside down, pointed to the bottom, and raised my eyebrows in a puzzled look. The price was listed as 200 fils - 20¢, and without even the slightest hint of embarrassment the lady charged us 40¢ for the two cans, and we were on our way.

A quick look at any map of the Bible Lands shows a remarkable correspondence between the lands that Joshua successfully conquered, Judea and Samaria, and the lands today that are referred to as "The West Bank." During our first eight months in Israel, we delayed visiting most of this area in the vain hope that the political instability and attendant dangers might improve. Instead, the situation grew progressively worse and mirrored the conditions in the same region some 2,500–3,000 years earlier:

> *In those days it was not safe to travel about, for all the inhabitants of the land were in great turmoil* (2 Chronicles 15:5, NIV)

After living in Israel for about eight months, we had developed an almost consuming desire to visit as many biblical sites as possible and to experience this land in its entirety, including Judea and Samaria. Often this meant taking risks, although in most cases the risks were only marginal. However, on some occasions, we underestimated how fine that margin of risk might be.

An additional problem is that most Old Testament Bible locations aren't marked on most maps. However, many Israelis seem to know almost every detail about the geography and history of their country. A few of these Israelis were my colleagues in the departments of Botany and Zoology at the Hebrew University. One of them had military maps, and he used these to transpose locations of the sites we wanted to visit onto our regular tourist maps —biblical places such as Gibeon, Gibeah, Geba, Michmash, Bethel, Mizpeh, Baal Hazor, Ophrah, Shiloh, Lebonah, Tirzah, Thebez, Dothan, Samaria, Shechem, and others — these are only the sites that are north of Jerusalem, biblical Samaria.

The early part of our story follows the journey of the Ark of the Covenant from the River Jordan to Gilgal, and (described in a later chapter) we will pick up our story from there. Jericho is at once both exciting and boring. It is exciting because it is at the center of some of the great stories of the Bible. It is boring because today it is just a dusty little unhurried town that time seems to have left behind. It is about 250 meters below sea level, making it the world's lowest town.

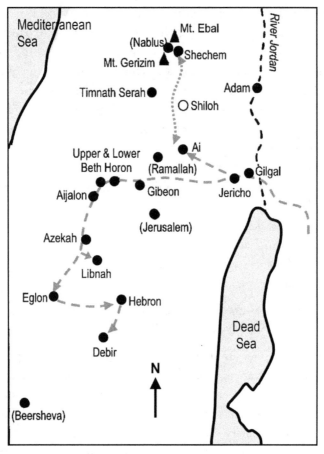

Joshua's entry and conquest of the Promised Land.

There are three different Jerichos, each about two kilometers from the other two: New Testament Jericho, Old Testament Jericho, and today's modern Jericho. The ancient city lies on the northern outskirts of today's Arab town. Jericho is called the 'City of Palm Trees' (Deuteronomy 34:3). It was the first city captured by the Israelites under Joshua when "Joshua fought the battle of Jericho and the walls came tumbling down." This was the home of Rahab the harlot (Joshua 2:1-21), where Elisha purified the water, where Jesus healed two blind men including Bartimaeus, and where Zacchaeus climbed the sycamore tree to see Jesus. Not bad for a city of a few thousand people!

Our first visit to Jericho happened because it was a wet and cold Saturday in Jerusalem. Our whole family took a sherut and were delivered to city center Jericho. In contrast to Jerusalem, Jericho was pleasantly warm with a beautiful, clear-blue sky. We walked a short distance to the bicycle rentals. Now, this was a surprise to the senses! We came across this ramshackle old garage with bits and parts of old cars and bicycles strewn untidily around the place. We gingerly ventured to ask, "Is this where we rent bicycles?" When the young man replied in the affirmative we expected he would go and get some real bicycles. But no, the dilapidated pieces of junk parked against the walls of the garage were what we were going to rent.

We looked at each other, smiled, then laughed out loud at the prospects of riding these things around Jericho — we were going to have a blast. While bartering for a rental rate, another lad arrived on his bicycle, and he had a flat rear tire. The attendant got a little enthusiastic with the inflation, and the resulting explosion sounded like a bomb in the streets of Belfast. We left a $5 USD deposit for the four bicycles and agreed on a rate of $1 USD per hour. Evelyn and I took the two bicycles that had no brakes. Well, that's not quite correct: there were brake handles, but they weren't connected to anything. We took off on our adventures in Jericho, laughing all the way. Thankfully, most of our journey was on flat ground because we had no gears, and the chains groaned and creaked as they moved around the cog — a little oil would have helped enormously, but then it wouldn't have been such a good story.

Within five minutes, we were riding past one of the homes of Yasser Arafat. It was nothing extraordinary in a Western context, but it was rather ostentatious given the standard of living of everyone else in the region. After bumping into a few things, we got used to riding without brakes. When we wanted to stop we simply jumped off the bicycle. Another ten minutes brought us to Hisham's Palace. We parked our bicycles at the entrance, not worried in the slightest about anyone stealing them because no one would want these babies. Hisham's Palace is really a hunting lodge and was first thought to have been built by the Umayyad Caliph Hisham bin Abdul Malek (AD 724-743), who ruled an empire stretching from India to the Pyrenees. Many from the Umayyad dynasty had such hunting lodges. It was probably built by Hisham's nephew and successor, Al-Walid bin Yazid. He was assassinated a year after coming to power, so the palace was never completed. However, a small room in the northwest corner of the complex has one of the most beautiful and elaborately decorated mosaic floors in the world —the 'Tree of Life' mosaic. The mosaic is about four to five meters square, completely intact, and the colorful design has a fruit tree, a lion, and gazelles.

The Tree of Life is a universal motif, found in almost every ancient culture. With its branches reaching into the sky, and roots deep in the earth, it is a symbol of the uniting of heaven and earth, spiritual nourishment, and even enlightenment.

Click on Google Images and you will see an amazing assortment of motifs ranging from Cultic, New Age, religious, astrological — and in evolutionary biology as the Tree of Life project. The Tree of Life Web Project[28] (ToL) is a collaborative effort of biologists from around the world. On more than four thousand World Wide Web pages, the project provides information about the diversity of organisms on Earth, their evolutionary history, and their characteristics. Each page contains information about a particular group of organisms and attempts to illustrate the genetic connections between all living things.

The expression "tree of life" occurs in three places in Scripture: (1) in the story of the Garden of Eden, (2) in the Book of Proverbs, and (3) in the Book of Revelation. The Tree of Life was in the Garden of Eden:

> And out of the ground the Lord God made every tree grow that is pleasant to the sight and good for food. The tree of life was also in the midst of the garden, and the tree of the knowledge of good and evil. (Genesis 2:9)

> Then the Lord God said, "Behold, the man has become like one of Us, to know good and evil. And now, lest he put out his hand and take also of the tree of life, and eat, and live forever"... So He drove out the man; and He placed cherubim at the east of the Garden of Eden, and a flaming sword which turned every way, to guard the way to the tree of life. (Genesis 3:22, 24)

The Tree conferred continuing life. Before Adam and Eve sinned, they had free access to the tree of life, but after their act of rebellion, two cherubim guarded the way to the tree's fruit. Adam and Eve's inability to eat from this tree after their sin showed that they failed to gain immortality or eternal life. Because of their sin, they were subject to death and dying. This condition lasted until the coming of Jesus Christ who offers eternal life to all who believe in Him (1 John 5:11-12). Isn't it interesting that both Christians and evolutionary biologists have a Tree of Life — very different trees and very different interpretations!

Back to our bicycle ride. We joined the main road running down the Jordan Valley. The road had a good, flat surface, the weather was beautiful, and the four of us were having a jolly good time. Every few minutes we had to stop to adjust something on someone's bicycle, but, with the Mountain of Temptation[29] as a backdrop, we made happy progress. Within twenty minutes, we arrived at the

---

[28] Maddison, D. R. and K.-S. Schulz (eds.) 1996-2006. The Tree of Life Web Project. Internet address: http://tolweb.org

[29] The traditional site where Satan tempted Jesus. Scripture says that "...the devil took Him up on an exceedingly high mountain, and showed Him all the kingdoms of the world and their glory. And he said to Him, "All these things I will give You if You will fall down and worship me" (Matthew 4:8-9).

mound of ancient Jericho. This is perhaps one of the more disappointing sites in Israel. Our high expectations weren't met, and the mound is disorganized and isn't well maintained. It has a number of signs and information boards but most of these have been knocked over and are lying flat on the ground and often tangled up with broken fences. Besides, there is little to see: the oldest remains are dated at 6,000–8,000 BC thus making Jericho the world's oldest city. In spite of this, we admit there was a certain thrill to just being here. This is where Rahab the harlot lived, and this was the location of one of the great events in history:

> *And the Lord said to Joshua: "See! I have given Jericho into your hand, its king, and the mighty men of valor. You shall march around the city, all you men of war; you shall go all around the city once. This you shall do six days. And seven priests shall bear seven trumpets of rams' horns before the ark. But the seventh day you shall march around the city seven times, and the priests shall blow the trumpets. It shall come to pass, when they make a long blast with the ram's horn, and when you hear the sound of the trumpet, that all the people shall shout with a great shout; then the wall of the city will fall down flat. And the people shall go up every man straight before him." ... And Joshua rose early in the morning, and the priests took up the ark of the Lord. Then seven priests bearing seven trumpets of rams' horns before the ark of the Lord went on continually and blew with the trumpets. And the armed men went before them. But the rear guard came after the ark of the Lord, while the priests continued blowing the trumpets. And the second day they marched around the city once and returned to the camp. So they did six days. But it came to pass on the seventh day that they rose early, about the dawning of the day, and marched around the city seven times in the same manner. On that day only they marched around the city seven times. And the seventh time it happened, when the priests blew the trumpets, that Joshua said to the people: "Shout, for the Lord has given you the city! ... So the people shouted when the priests blew the trumpets. And it happened when the people heard the sound of the trumpet, and the people shouted with a great shout, that the wall fell down flat. Then the people went up into the city, every man straight before him, and they took the city.* (Joshua 6:2-5, 12-16, 20)

After strolling around the ruins, we returned to our bicycles and wheeled them across the road to another biblical (traditional) site — the Spring of Elisha. Miraculously, after 2,800 years, in the early 2000s, the Spring of Elisha disappeared from its ancient location and reappeared one hundred meters away in the coach/car park in front of a major restaurant, near the entrance to the ancient mound of Jericho! How convenient is that?

> *Then the men of the city [Jericho] said to Elisha, "Please notice, the situation of this city is pleasant, as my lord sees; but the water is bad, and the ground barren." And he said, "Bring me a new bowl, and put salt in it." So they brought it to him. Then*

he went out to the source of the water, and cast in the salt there, and said, "Thus says the Lord: 'I have healed this water; from it there shall be no more death or barrenness.'" (2 Kings 2:19-21)

We ventured back on the road again, made a short stop to buy some freshly squeezed lemon juice, and in a short time we arrived at the edge of the modern town. We saw a large tree behind a fence to the left of the road and were informed that this is the tree that Zacchaeus climbed when he wanted to see Jesus:

Then Jesus entered and passed through Jericho. Now behold, there was a man named Zacchaeus who was a chief tax collector, and he was rich. And he sought to see who Jesus was, but could not because of the crowd, for he was of short stature. So he ran ahead and climbed up into a sycamore tree to see Him, for He was going to pass that way... And Jesus said to him, "Today salvation has come to this house, because he also is a son of Abraham; for the Son of Man has come to seek and to save that which was lost." (Luke 19:1-5, 9-10)

Zacchaeus climbed into a sycamore tree. This was most likely a type of fig tree because in several translations of the Bible there is a species of fig called sycamore — the sycamore fig. While we totally believe that Zacchaeus climbed into a tree, we don't believe for one minute that it was this one.

The next stage in our journey was the most difficult. There weren't any signposts to New Testament Jericho although we had a reasonable idea where it was. The difficulty was that the ride was only a few kilometers, but it was mostly gently sloping uphill — and on these bicycles, a gentle slope was a major challenge. After pushing hard for twenty minutes, our road seemed to be veering away from the site we were trying to reach. We turned through a gap in a hedge, entered a banana plantation, wheeled our bicycles for five minutes, and bingo, we emerged exactly at the site of New Testament Jericho — it was occupied by a Bedouin encampment!

The site is largely dominated by the ruins of one of Herod's winter palaces, and it was here that Herod died and was transported to Herodian for burial. The palaces were situated below the cliffs of the Judean Desert at the entrance to Wadi Qelt, west of today's Jericho. The remains of the palaces, including the two artificial mounds, are on both sides of Wadi Qelt. Excavations have revealed a series of royal palaces with banquet halls and baths.

We were impressed by three things. First, the nature of the ruins themselves, second the setting in this barren landscape with high cliffs as a backdrop, and third that Bedouins were camped on the floor of the banquet hall of King Herod's Palace — I'm thinking the king wouldn't have approved. Perhaps the most exciting thing for us was that we could see the road that comes from Jericho and passes to the south of the site. It winds its way uphill and enters the Wadi Qelt and from there goes on in the direction of Jerusalem. This is important because of the Scripture that says:

> ...As He [Jesus] went out of Jericho with His disciples and a great multitude, blind Bartimaeus, the son of Timaeus, sat by the road begging. And when he heard that it was Jesus of Nazareth, he began to cry out and say, "Jesus, Son of David, have mercy on me!"... So Jesus answered and said to him, "What do you want Me to do for you?" The blind man said to Him, "Rabboni, that I may receive my sight." Then Jesus said to him, "Go your way; your faith has made you well." And immediately he received his sight and followed Jesus on the road. (Mark 10:46-47, 51-52)

This event occurred as Jesus was leaving Jericho on his way to Jerusalem, which means it happened somewhere along this stretch of road. It is difficult to precisely identify the location of many New Testament events, but this one we can pinpoint to within a few hundred meters —exciting! We plundered around the ruins, and it was a long, gentle ride back into Jericho. Our visit lasted almost six hours. What a wonderful way to experience Jericho.

Joshua had his orders from God to begin the conquest of the Promised Land. The people had been delivered from slavery in Egypt some forty years earlier, and now they were prepared for conquest. From Jericho, Joshua sent men to spy out the country around the city of Ai, which is about forty kilometers to the west. They returned to Joshua and reported that this would be an easy attack and that Joshua should only send about two thousand or three thousand men to Ai.

> So about three thousand men went up there from the people, but they fled before the men of Ai. And the men of Ai struck down about thirty-six men, for they chased them from before the gate as far as Shebarim, and struck them down on the descent; therefore the hearts of the people melted and became like water. (Joshua 7:4-5)

Joshua was so upset at the defeat that Scripture tells us that he tore his clothes and fell to the earth on his face before the Ark of the Lord and said:

> Alas, Lord God, why have You brought this people over the Jordan at all—to deliver us into the hand of the Amorites, to destroy us?... (Joshua 7:7)

And God's answer was simple — Israel had sinned, goods had been stolen during the attack on Jericho, and He wasn't going to help them anymore until the thief had been identified and destroyed. The thief was identified as Achan, and he and his family were brought to the Valley of Achor, and:

... all Israel stoned him with stones; and they burned them with fire after they had stoned them with stones. Then they raised over him a great heap of stones, still there to this day. So the Lord turned from the fierceness of His anger. Therefore the name of that place has been called the Valley of Achor to this day. (Joshua 7:25-26)

The Valley of Achor is usually identified with the Wadi Qelt, which descends through a deep ravine from the Judean hills and runs between steep banks west of Jericho. The Wadi Qelt today offers a stunning four-hour walk through the Judean wilderness; it's probably one of the most spectacular hikes in Israel, a walk we've done more than once.

The hike began from the Jerusalem to Jericho Road, and then, with great caution, we negotiated a steep track down to the Wadi. To our left, we saw a bridge, and it supports an ancient aqueduct, an aqueduct that's been renovated and carries water from the wadi's springs all the way to Jericho. When we finally reached the wadi, we were greeted by a natural spring and a sizeable pool with local Bedouin children bathing. This area is semi-arid in the winter and totally barren in summer except for the few small patches of vegetation huddled around the spring and the aqueduct that runs from it. It is this aqueduct that we follow for at least the first two hours of our hike to the sixth century AD monastery of St George. During most of this time, we are in the Nahal Prat Nature Reserve. We walked along at quite a good pace, variously following the marked trail or the aqueduct itself.

The landscape was stunning in its barrenness, with undulating ridges of pure-white chalk, and the sometimes steep, limestone cliffs that marked the edges of the canyon through which we were walking. There was little sign of life other than the occasional Bedouin sitting on a rock and staring aimlessly at a few goats under his care. There were endless opportunities for photographs, and after about an hour, we met three small but bedraggled and smiling children with their donkeys. We were surprised to meet them at all because we thought we were in the middle of nowhere — evidently not. I raised my hands as though to reach for my camera, and like a flash, the children jumped from their donkeys, and with outstretched dirty little hands asked for money. Photographing people is seldom free of charge in the West Bank! We paid the fee. The children were beautiful with their dark eyes and curly black hair, and they were as cute as buttons. Obviously, we couldn't communicate effectively, but I would love to have known where they came from and where they were going.

It took about two hours to reach St. George's Monastery. We knew we were getting close to the monastery when we met a monk with two Arab workers on the trail. The Arab men were installing a pipe to carry water from a spring to the monastery. Evidently the monk wasn't happy with their work, and his language wasn't exactly befitting his clerical robes. He mellowed a little as we approached, but we had already seen his true colors — and they didn't include white.

When the monastery first comes into view, it is a wonderful sight, dating from the fifth or sixth century. It was built at the cave where the prophet Elijah is said to have hidden to escape the wrath of Jezebel. There are some vague claims that the site commemorates the location of the attack in the story of the Good Samaritan. It is quite a large structure, literally hanging off the side of a cliff and marvellously camouflaged against the native color of the cliff. On our first hike along the wadi, we weren't able to enter the monastery because we were wearing shorts. No exposed flesh in here, but a monk did come to the door and gave us a very much appreciated and refreshing jug of grapefruit juice, which was badly needed after the 39C hike. All appropriately attired visitors are invited in and for a donation can drink all the juice required. Appropriately attired includes not carrying a weapon, and we were amused to see about thirty M-16s leaning against the wall outside the main door; there was a group of Israeli soldiers inside! The cool and shade of the monastery is a very welcome break from the relentless and scorching heat of the unshaded wadi. On our second visit we were acceptably attired and entered the monastery where we spent an hour looking around and speaking with the monk on duty.

After lots of Kool-Aid and rest, we continued our journey to Jericho. This next hour is the most spectacular portion of the entire walk: the path narrows, the canyon deepens, the walls are steeper, and the path follows a serpentine route, finally emerging in the plains to the west of Jericho. Except for some remarkable remains from one of King Herod's winter palaces on the site of New Testament Jericho, it is a tedious forty-five-minute hike along the flat and into Jericho — where we walked into a restaurant and almost fell flat from heat exhaustion.

Okay, so Achan and his family met their end somewhere along the Wadi Qelt, but now we continue with our story of Joshua. Achan's sin had been dealt with and it was time to attack Ai again. This attack is described in more detail (Joshua 8:1-28) than almost any other similar event in the Scriptures, and ends with this decisive statement:

So Joshua burned Ai and made it a heap forever, a desolation to this day. (Joshua 8:28)

For this trip to Ai, we rented a car from a West Bank Company operating out of east Jerusalem. We put a couple of traditional Arab headscarves called keffiyeh on the dashboard of the car, and stuck a few small Canadian flags to our windows, all attempts to indicate to the natives that we were friendly, we were harmless (perhaps a little naive) tourists, we weren't Americans, and we weren't Jewish. As we drove north from Jerusalem, we were constantly aware that we were tense and nervous even though the worst that can happen is that the car gets hit with stones. We drove through Ramallah and on to the vicinity of Ai. We first came to Bethel, where we were swarmed by uniformed schoolgirls all wanting to talk to us, to touch us, and wanting their photographs taken. They were beautiful young girls and yet our minds couldn't help but jump to the conclusion that the current pattern of history wasn't going to give them much hope of a better tomorrow.

We left the raucous and drove the short distance, about 3.5 kilometers to the village of Deir Dibwan. We knew that Ai was close to this village. When we were on this type of 'adventure travel,' Evelyn would drive, and I would read maps. We were nervous, very nervous, as we approached a small turning circle in the village. There weren't many other vehicles other than a few dilapidated Peugeots 405s and Toyota pick-up trucks. I don't know if it was the rather new-looking rental car or the four white people in the rental car, but either way, we were drawing attention, and we didn't like it. Almost instinctively, Evelyn stopped the car and I jumped out as if to talk to someone and ask directions. We had done this many times before in similar circumstances, and it seems to work because Arab youth will throw stones at cars, but usually not at people! I hope this works for adults. I spoke with about four or five men for a few minutes just to establish my fake naivety! I spoke, they spoke, and we laughed because none of us spoke a word that the other could understand. However, this maneuver worked, and now that we were guests in their village they pointed us in the direction of the enormous pile of rubble that is Ai. In a few moments, we arrived and climbed to the top of the ruins which are topped by a one-meter-high wall that is a remnant of an old Canaanite palace dating back perhaps more than 4,500 years.

Few narratives in the Bible are described in as much detail as Joshua's second attempt to capture Ai. While standing on the ruins facing east down the valley toward Jericho, we could easily see the whole story of Joshua chapter 8 unfold. First, there were the ambush forces who came from the east and crept past the city under darkness and hid to the west of the city (vs. 4, 9, 12). Then Joshua led his 'decoy forces,' approached the city from the east, and finally set up camp across the valley to the north of Ai (vs. 10, 11). Verses 14–17 describe how the King of Ai and the people of Ai were lured by Joshua. When Joshua saw the people of Ai coming out to fight, he ordered a retreat, and they were pursued by the unsuspecting Ai-ites. When the city was empty, Joshua raised his javelin (v.18) as a signal to the ambush force to enter and destroy the deserted city. The people of Ai realized that they were literally between a rock and a hard place — they were in a valley between ambush forces to the west and decoy forces to the east, and they were about to be annihilated — it's a beautiful thing to re-enact the entire story while standing right on site. Unfortunately, subsequent archaeological research seems to be trending towards changing the identification of Ai to a location about one kilometer to the southwest, but the details still fit.

We said our farewell to the site and returned to our rental car. As we were about to get back into the car, we noticed a group of youths waiting about one hundred meters down the road. This was a dead-end road, so the kids knew we would have to return past them. We had a strong suspicion that the kids would have stones. Evelyn was driving. I believed that if I walked down the road to the kids that they wouldn't throw. It is 'safe' for kids to throw stones at a car but not at pedestrians — at least this way they wouldn't stone us. I asked Evelyn to wait with the car until I indicated that it was safe for her to approach. I started off downhill and walked down to the kids who were all armed with handfuls of stones. They didn't know a word of English nor me a word of Arabic, but we 'talked.' After a few moments, a middle-aged woman appeared from one of the homes. She spoke good English, and she had lived in California for a number of years. Now that I knew that we were 'safe,' I turned around and signaled Evelyn. The lady said something to the kids that sounded like an Arabic scolding and they dropped their stones — one kid was standing with a stone the size of a discus! It seems that all of our attempts to 'signal' that we were friendly didn't really work. Somehow our visit to Ai was enhanced, rather than marred, by this little incident.

On our way back to Jerusalem we also visited Michmash where we had another experience of nervous excitement. It was near here that the Philistines camped before battling Saul and where Jonathan and his armor bearer came after leaving camp and invading the Philistine camp. 1 Samuel 14 describes how Jonathan climbed down a cliff, crossed a wadi, and climbed up the other side before invading the Philistines encamped at Michmash. This is what we had come to visit, but to get to the wadi we had to drive through the village and, unfortunately, like Ai, we were forced to return by the same route as we entered.

Michmash can be a troublesome area, and as we made our way through the village, we were acutely aware that we were being noticed. After an amazing visit to the wadi, we returned to the village. We were aware of the potential threat, so we drove cautiously but kept moving. Evelyn was driving, and I was keeping my eyes alert for signs of trouble. The road drops quite steeply through the village and makes a couple of fairly sharp turns. We negotiated one of these turns and there they were —three or four children, mere boys, standing high up on a ledge waiting to ambush us. Despite our friendly signs, they began chucking stones at the car. Instinctively Evelyn hit the accelerator, and thankfully the stones flew over the top of the car, and we weren't hit. I guess if Jonathan had trouble here three thousand years ago, why should we be exempt today?

I was back in Michmash a few years later with two graduate students because I wanted to show them the wadi. As we stopped at an intersection in the middle of the village, I noticed steam rising from the engine of our Fiat Uno. One of the graduate students was driving. He switched off the engine and we pushed the car across the intersection onto a grassy shoulder. We raised the hood and watched the steam bellow from our radiator. It wasn't so dangerous this time, and there was no sense of trouble because the level of trouble and political instability had declined quite markedly during the 1990s. A wonderful, older Arab woman came to us with two 7-UP bottles. Initially, we thought she was bringing us a drink, but the bottles were filled with water for the car! We let the engine cool for thirty minutes, topped up the radiator with water, and continued on our way. This was a lot less exciting, but much more comfortable, than our first visit to Michmash.

The story of Joshua now takes an unexpected turn. In Joshua 8:29, Joshua is cleaning up after Ai, and in the next verse he is forty-five kilometers north on a mountain overlooking the biblical city of Shechem, today's Arab city of Nablus:

Now Joshua built an altar to the Lord God of Israel in Mount Ebal, (Joshua 8:30)

We will describe our visit to Mount Ebal in more detail in the chapter describing the journey of the Ark of God, but a few details are necessary here. In Moses's farewell speech to the people he issued the following commandment:

Therefore it shall be, when you have crossed over the Jordan, that on Mount Ebal you shall set up these stones, which I command you today, and you shall whitewash them with lime. And there you shall build an altar to the Lord your God, an altar of stones; you shall not use an iron tool on them. You shall build with whole stones the altar of the Lord your God, and offer burnt offerings on it to the Lord your God. You shall offer peace offerings, and shall eat there, and rejoice before the Lord your God. And you shall write very plainly on the stones all the words of this law. (Deuteronomy 27:4-8)

And again in the book of Joshua we read:

as Moses the servant of the Lord had commanded the children of Israel, as it is written in the Book of the Law of Moses: "an altar of whole stones over which no man has wielded an iron tool." And they offered on it burnt offerings to the Lord, and sacrificed peace offerings. (Joshua 8:31)

The people were commanded to go to Mount Ebal and build an altar. Adam Zertal[30] of Haifa University was very confident that he had found the altar built by Joshua, and not without good reason. From these verses, we see that there should be an altar on Mount Ebal, made of uncut stones, and on it were sacrificed both burnt and peace offerings. Given that this was the Israelites invading a Canaanite culture, we might expect to find artifacts of both cultures at this altar. The Israelites settled this area during the Early Iron Age, 1,200–1,000 BC. From Zertal's work, he has been able to determine that this altar is the only Early Iron Age structure on Mount Ebal. The altar has a ramp about one meter wide and seven meters long. The presence of a ramp is significant because in the book of Exodus we read:

Nor shall you go up by steps to My altar, that your nakedness may not be exposed on it. (Exodus 20:26)

Zertal states with considerable confidence that the pottery found on site is dated to the period of Israelite settlement of the area. The excavations also revealed bones that proved to be from young male bulls, sheep, goats, and fallow deer. This is in close agreement with:

He shall kill the bull before the Lord; and the priests, Aaron's sons, shall bring the blood and sprinkle the blood all around on the altar that is by the door of the tabernacle of meeting. … 'If his offering is of the flocks—of the sheep or of the goats— as a burnt sacrifice, he shall bring a male without blemish. (Leviticus 1:5, 10)

There seems little doubt that this was an Israelite cult center, an altar that was independent of a temple. But could it really be the actual altar that Joshua built? We aren't archaeologists, so we can't offer a professional opinion — but we are convinced. The story continues:

Then all Israel, with their elders and officers and judges, stood on either side of the ark before the priests, the Levites, who bore the ark of the covenant of the Lord, the stranger as well as he who was born among them. Half of them were in front of Mount Gerizim and half of them in front of Mount Ebal, as Moses the servant

---

[30] Zertal, A. (1985). Has Joshua's Altar Been Found on Mt. Ebal? *Biblical Archaeology Review*, (Jan/Feb), 26.

of the Lord had commanded before, that they should bless the people of Israel. And afterward he read all the words of the law, the blessings and the cursings, according to all that is written in the Book of the Law. (Joshua 8:33-34)

The view from Mount Gerizim is awesome. Obviously, you can see Mount Ebal across the valley although you can't see the altar. You can also see the Arab city of Nablus, the ruins of biblical Shechem, Jacob's Well, the tomb of Joseph (a Palestinian mob destroyed this site in 2000), the village of Sychar (you can imagine the whole story unfold of Jesus and the woman at the well (John 4:1-26)), and the village of Elon Moreh near where God promised Abram that he would inherit the land. This is a truly special site.

After the detour north to Mount Ebal and Mount Gerizim, Joshua returns to Gilgal and now meets with a group of people called the Gibeonites:

But when the inhabitants of Gibeon heard what Joshua had done to Jericho and Ai, they worked craftily, and went and pretended to be ambassadors. And they took old sacks on their donkeys, old wineskins torn and mended, old and patched sandals on their feet, and old garments on themselves; and all the bread of their provision was dry and moldy. And they went to Joshua, to the camp at Gilgal, and said to him and to the men of Israel, "We have come from a far country; now therefore, make a covenant with us."... So Joshua made peace with them, and made a covenant with them to let them live ... (Joshua 9:3-6, 15)

Gibeon is today's village of el-Jib, about ten kilometers northwest of Jerusalem. The most dramatic find at Gibeon is the giant 'pool' measuring eleven meters in diameter and ten meters in depth and cut into the solid bedrock. This cylindrical cutting has a circular staircase that led to a stepped tunnel that continued downward another thirteen meters below the pool's floor to a water chamber. This pool was the exact location of a battle between the army of Ishbosheth under Abner and that of David led by Joab. Instead of having an all-out bloody battle, it was decided to choose twelve men from each side to determine the victory. The outcome was unexpected and indecisive because each of the men killed his fellow, so they all perished.

Now Abner the son of Ner, and the servants of Ishbosheth the son of Saul, went out from Mahanaim to Gibeon. And Joab the son of Zeruiah, and the servants of David, went out and met them by the pool of Gibeon. So they sat down, one on one side of the pool and the other on the other side of the pool. Then Abner said to Joab, "Let the young men now arise and compete before us." And Joab said, "Let them arise." So they arose and went over by number, twelve from Benjamin, followers of Ishbosheth the son of Saul, and twelve from the servants of David. And each one grasped his opponent by the head and thrust his sword in his opponent's side; so they fell down together. Therefore that place was called the Field of Sharp Swords, which is in Gibeon. (2 Samuel 2:12-16)

The village of el-Jib is not difficult to find, but finding the giant cistern is another matter. We turned off the main road into the village and traced the road to the top of the hill. We stopped with a group of middle-aged women having a chit-chat at the village well. This was an obvious place to ask for directions to the pool. Ten minutes later desperation was beginning to set in; the ladies did understand even the odd word of English. Then they found another woman and they brought her to us because she could apparently speak English — she couldn't! The ladies laughed and chuckled as I said, "well, cistern, tank, reservoir," gesticulating with my arms as I tried to 'draw' the cistern in mid-air, and I even tried to sketch a diagram in the soft soil. All to no avail and out of desperation I said, "It looks like a big hole." For some inexplicable reason, this did the trick and three or more of the ladies laughed and in unison said "Ah, the big hole," in such a way as to imply "why didn't you say that before?"

Almost instantly, we had our directions and ironically they were able to point to the 'big hole' among the olive trees, and it was no more than one hundred meters from where we had been standing. We were so excited to see this archaeological wonder, that we almost jogged over the rough soil to get to the cistern. At once, it was both spectacular and disappointing. It was spectacular because of its size and structure, and because of its biblical significance, but it was disappointing because it was an ill-kept mess and very dangerous. The coiled barbed wire fence surrounding the cistern was broken and rusted, and clearly, it had been used occasionally as a garbage dump. We were able to stand at the edge of the cistern and look straight in, which is straight down, and while doing so, we could relive in our minds the battle between Joab and Abner. It was perhaps a little foolish, but we decided to descend the spiral staircase to the bottom of the cistern. There was extra barbed wire at the top step, but it had clearly been breached many times before. The descent wasn't too bad even though the steps had been badly broken in a number of places.

Close to the cistern, about three meters away from the northern edge, we spotted a very small opening that apparently leads nowhere except into a dark hole. We knew from preparatory reading that there was another entrance to a separate water system, and we guessed that this must be it. We had a flashlight, and after spending four or five minutes removing the barbed wire blocking the entrance, we ventured inside. Even though we had a flashlight, it took a little time to adjust to the darkness.

Within a short time, we realized that we were standing at the top of a long, downward, slightly curving staircase. We didn't have to have a committee meeting to make a decision. We were here to see this place, and although it was quite apparent no one had been here in a very long time, we were going to break the pattern. We counted as we descended, and at step ninety-one we could see the pool of water reflecting our flashlight. Even though this source of water is perhaps no more than twenty meters from the bottom of the large cistern, it is apparently a separate source of water. It was sort of creepy being down here — what if someone blocked the entrance up above? After customary discussion of the site, we ascended in the blackness, and my heart rate jumped to almost lethal rates when I heard Evelyn scream — it took a few seconds for me to realize that she had broken a fingernail!

Gibeon figures quite prominently in the Scriptures. Soon after Solomon came to the throne, he paid a visit to Gibeon, and on this occasion, the Lord appeared to him in a memorable dream:

> *At Gibeon the Lord appeared to Solomon in a dream by night; and God said, "Ask! What shall I give you?" And Solomon said:… give to Your servant an understanding heart to judge Your people, that I may discern between good and evil. For who is able to judge this great people of Yours?" The speech pleased the Lord, that Solomon had asked this thing. Then God said to him: "Because you have asked this thing, and have not asked long life for yourself, nor have asked riches for yourself, nor have asked the life of your enemies, but have asked for yourself understanding to discern justice, behold, I have done according to your words; see, I have given you a wise and understanding heart, so that there has not been anyone like you before you, nor shall any like you arise after you. And I have also given you what you have not asked: both riches and honor, so that there shall not be anyone like you among the kings all your days. So if you walk in My ways, to keep My statutes and My commandments, as your father David walked, then I will lengthen your days." (1 Kings 3:5-6, 9–14)*

After the destruction of Nob by Saul, the Tabernacle was set up at Gibeon and remained until the building of the Temple. Other events in the history of Gibeon include the execution of the seven sons of Saul, and Amasa being put to death by Joab.

One of the most remarkable incidents connected with this city was the victory Joshua gained over the five Canaanite kings. Their armies were completely routed, and the five kings were taken prisoner and put to death. During this rout, we have one of the most controversial passages in Scripture — Joshua's 'long day' when, at the request of Joshua, the sun didn't set for a whole day. The next three sites are dictated to us by the chronology of this biblical narrative. Joshua was in the process of routing the Canaanite kings and he pursued them from Gibeon to Beth Horon and on to Azekah and Makkedah.

> So the Lord routed them before Israel, killed them with a great slaughter at Gibeon, chased them along the road that goes to Beth Horon, and struck them down as far as Azekah and Makkedah. And it happened, as they fled before Israel and were on the descent of Beth Horon, that the Lord cast down large hailstones from heaven on them as far as Azekah, and they died. There were more who died from the hailstones than the children of Israel killed with the sword. Then Joshua spoke to the Lord in the day when the Lord delivered up the Amorites before the children of Israel, and he said in the sight of Israel: "Sun, stand still over Gibeon; And Moon, in the Valley of Aijalon." So the sun stood still, And the moon stopped, Till the people had revenge upon their enemies. Is this not written in the Book of Jasher? So the sun stood still in the midst of heaven, and did not hasten to go down for about a whole day. (Joshua 10:10-13)

Interestingly, the sun stood still at Gibeon, the moon stood still over the Valley of Aijalon, and the pass of Beth Horon connects the two. The pass of Beth Horon gets its name from the villages in the pass. These are twin towns (today's Beit Ur el-Foka and Beit Ur et-Tahta) called Upper and Lower Beth Horon because of their difference in elevation (615 and 369 meters above sea level, respectively). The steep descent between them provided the best pass through the mountains from Jerusalem to Joppa (modern Jaffa) and the Mediterranean Sea. Today, this is a major four-lane divided highway leading from the coast up to Ramallah and Jerusalem in the hills. As we reached the bottom of the descent, we arrived in the northern end of the valley of Aijalon, and just like Joshua, we turned left, that is south along the valley where the moon stood still.

Our first task now was to track down the ruins of the city of Aijalon. We knew from our reading and our maps exactly where to go. It was identified, even on some recent maps, as the village of Yalo even though the village was abandoned in 1948. This was the first site that we used GPS to help us. We had the coordinates and blindly followed them, turning off the main road and following a track through fields for a few kilometers. Then, our track crossed over a rather shallow but quite muddy creek. Wary of becoming stuck, we drove steadily but determinedly into the creek, and with only a little spinning of wheels and slipping and sliding we got to the other side.

I hope we can get back again! A few hundred meters farther, we came to a broken barbed-wire fence with the emphasis being on the 'barbed' — these were big and nasty. We scoured the area for a number of good-sized stones, placed them over the wire, and took the mats out of the rental car, doubled them up, and placed them over the stones and barbs before driving over. Success. Our GPS told us we were close, but now we had run out of track. We merely drove across the rough scrubland, entered a wooded area, and suddenly found a road! How embarrassing. It was then that we remembered about the car mats and had to return to retrieve them. We had managed to find a backway into Canada Park, which is mostly a recreational and picnic area with trees planted by the Jewish National Fund. The mound of ancient Aijalon is totally uninspiring, but it offers a beautiful viewpoint over the Aijalon Valley. We left the park by the civilized route and continued along the valley of Aijalon towards Azekah.

Before proceeding to Azekah, we will detour briefly to the site of Gezer. From the Tel Aviv-Jerusalem highway, Gezer is rather unremarkable. It's only when you stand atop the Tel that you can appreciate its prominent view. Its chief attraction is the High Place, a row of ten monoliths dated to sixteen thousand BC, and standing up to three meters tall along with an underground water system dated to at least one thousand BC. In the spring of 1994, the ten standing monoliths were almost reduced to nine standing and one lying flat. I'd skidded and spun and drove my little rental car to the top of the mound. The wildflowers around the monoliths were extravagant. I stopped the car to get out and take some photographs. I forgot to engage the handbrake, and when I returned, my car had run off downhill about fifteen meters and rested up against one of the still-standing stones —only a scratch — on the stone that is!

Joshua's pursuit of the Canaanite kings from Gibeon to Azekah was about forty kilometers, and Joshua chapter 10 describes the entire conquest. While Aijalon to Azekah is only about fifteen kilometers, what a fascinating fifteen kilometers it is — we drove past (and of course visited) Zorah,[31] the Altar of Manoah,[32] the Brook Sorek,[33] Beth Shemesh,[34] Beit Jimal,[35] Jarmuth,[36] and the

---

[31] Birthplace of Samson (Judges 13:2-5,24)

[32] This is (or was) a rock altar built as the Hebrews would have built an altar in the time of the judges. Many believe that this could be the altar where Manoah, the father of Samson, presented his offering and the angel of the Lord appeared to him (Judges 13:15-23).

[33] This is the brook where Samson and Delilah romanced, and also where Samson had his eyes gouged out (Judges 16:4-21).

[34] The Ark of God came to Beth Shemesh and seventy men were killed for looking into it (1 Samuel 6:9-19).

[35] This was the site of the Jewish village of Gamla, birthplace of Rabban Gamaliel, head of the Sanhedrin. It is early Christian tradition that Gamaliel was Stephen's teacher. The site has a monastery and behind it is a pretty little church painted in mock Byzantine. Inside, the church has four beautiful murals depicting the commissioning, trial, stoning, and burial of Stephen.

[36] Joshua killed Piram the King of Jarmuth (Joshua 10:16-27).

Elah Valley. This is a very useful region to brush up on Bible quizzing skills! After many stops, we finally arrived at the great hill of Azekah which overlooks the Valley of Elah where, some two hundred years later, the Philistines under Goliath would fight the Israelites under David. We will cover that area in a later chapter. But the current story is quite bloody as well:

> ... the Lord cast down large hailstones from heaven on them as far as Azekah, and they died. There were more who died from the hailstones than the children of Israel killed with the sword. (Joshua 10:11)

From the Valley of Elah, the hill of Azekah looked rather daunting. It would be perhaps a one-kilometer walk across cultivated land and olive groves, followed by a rather challenging scramble to the top of the hill. But we had been around Israel long enough to know that there are tracks and roads to almost everywhere, and to the top of almost everything. We engaged in our usual pursuit of looking for some kind of access, and we were rewarded by finding a relatively good, but unpaved, road that ran behind the mound.

We drove along this for a short distance and, presto, managed to find another track wide enough to drive our rental car to the very top of the hill. It was a little bumpy; although we paid a price by slipping and skidding on the loose stones and gravel and hitting the undercarriage on a few occasions, the view from the top was magnificent. In the far distance to the east, we could see Bethlehem on the hilltops. In the near distance, we could see the site where the Philistines and the Israelites encamped before the battle between David and Goliath, and remarkably, we could trace the route along which the Israelites pursued the Philistines almost as far as Gath. The Scriptures tell us that the Philistines encamped between Azekah and Socoh, and from the top of Azekah, we could see Socoh, which was our next port of call.

There is nothing of any archaeological interest to see at Socoh, but the botany is amazing. In the springtime, this site has an amazing display of wildflowers, especially cyclamen and lupine, which cover virtually every square inch. This is perhaps the greatest wildflower show in Israel except for Galilee. We climbed to the top of the mound, found a beautifully pitted rock arrayed with cyclamen, sat down, and had a relaxing picnic. We decided to leave this site rather hurriedly when a one-meter-long black snake slithered by at too close a range.

One would imagine that the capture and killing of the kings of Jerusalem, Hebron, Jarmuth, Lachish, and Eglon would be a crucial episode in Joshua's campaign, yet the biblical narrative merely lists it as one of a long list of successful exploits. Joshua now continues his campaign, and this also seemed to be a rather bloody affair. Joshua chapter 10 continues with this story:

> *Then Joshua passed from Libnah, and all Israel with him, to Lachish...*
> *From Lachish Joshua passed to Eglon, and all Israel with him...*
> *So Joshua went up from Eglon, and all Israel with him, to Hebron...*
> *Then Joshua returned, and all Israel with him, to Debir...* (Joshua 10: 31, 34, 36, 38)

Lachish is one of the most important archaeological sites in Israel, yet it has not been developed for tourism. It was of immense strategic importance, dominating the ancient road from the highlands to the coast. Joshua destroyed the city, but five hundred years later, during the reign of King Hezekiah, Sennacherib the king of Assyria attacked Lachish.

> *After this Sennacherib king of Assyria sent his servants to Jerusalem (but he and all the forces with him laid siege against Lachish), to Hezekiah king of Judah, and to all Judah who were in Jerusalem, saying,* (2 Chronicles 32:9)

The Bible tells us no more about this siege of Lachish in 701 BC by Sennacherib. However, we know that Lachish fiercely resisted the siege but ultimately capitulated in 701 BC. Its capture was so important to Sennacherib that he memorialized it in a magnificent series of reliefs on the wall of his palace at Nineveh. The reliefs, engraved in stone, are today displayed in their own gallery in the British Museum in London. The reliefs, about sixteen meters long and more than two meters high, show the Assyrian troops advancing. The city is then attacked with wheeled-battering rams while the defenders of the city are throwing burning brands down on their attackers. The assault on the city was done by using a siege ramp. The reliefs then show prisoners being led away by Assyrian troops, some of whom are carrying incense stands. Finally, Sennacherib is shown sitting on his throne with an inscription over his head which states: "Sennacherib, king of the world, king of Assyria, on a seat he sat and the booty of Lachish before him it passed."

We visited Lachish on a number of occasions. As you approach the site, the height of the mound becomes apparent and impressive. You must stand on top of this mound to appreciate its commanding position. A rough road runs from the main road up to a crude parking lot on the southwest corner of the mound. This is where the Assyrian army concentrated its assault on the city, and there are still remains of the Assyrian siege platform, made of uncut stones and mortar. The ramp is up to fifty meters wide at its base and narrows towards the top. It is quite a spine-chilling experience to stand on this ramp and mentally re-enact the

Assyrian attack on the city—the sounds of the chariots and the battering rams can become quite realistic. About one hundred years later, Lachish was again a stronghold. This time it was Nebuchadnezzar, king of Babylon, who attacked and defeated the city when he took Judah into captivity in 586 BC. When the Jews returned from captivity in Babylon, the city of Lachish was once again inhabited.

The site today is unkempt and overgrown, yet still fascinating to explore — but be careful! On our first visit, as we waded through the chest-high grass, suddenly our sixth senses kicked in, and we had that strange nervous feeling demanding caution. Just two steps farther and we were at the edge of a great hole, perhaps fifteen meters square, and gaping down a great shaft almost twenty-five meters deep. This frightened us a little because we had no idea what other dangers might be lurking in the long grass. We didn't know that there was a forty-meter-deep well on another part of the site.

The most notable features at the site are the ramp leading up to the gateway, the gateway itself where important and inscribed pottery fragments were found in 1935, and the palace area in the middle of the site. The palace area is a huge platform about thirty-five by seventy meters, and this probably served as a foundation for a number of great buildings. A lasting memory for us occurred as we left the palace area: we heard rustling grass, and immediately we thought snakes, but this time it was a mother tortoise with her young, quite beautiful and perhaps no larger than a silver dollar.

The people in the city of Eglon must have been having a panic attack. Their king had already been killed by Joshua, and if they were reading their newspapers, they could easily trace Joshua's relentless campaign through their country. And for the people of Eglon, a pattern was emerging with a single inevitable result — Joshua had gone on a relentless march taking Jericho, Ai, Gibeon, Beth Horon, Aijalon, Azekah, Libnah, and Lachish — and Eglon was probably going to be next — and it was!

Eglon is probably Tel Hasi, which is about ten kilometers west of Lachish. This was a daunting one to find, but having found it, quite easily accessible. We drove south of Qiryat Gat for only a few kilometers until coming to a rather inconspicuous dirt road that took off at right angles to the west. This dirt road is used as access to the vast orange groves in this area. On our first attempt to find Eglon we were turned back because the road had been washed out after some heavy rains in the early springtime. A few weeks later, we tried again, and this time with almost no difficulty we reached Nahal Shiqma, which is only a few hundred meters from the site. This is a perennial stream, about six meters wide, yet the road cuts straight across this barrier, dipping gently in at one side and climbing out a little more abruptly at the other. We drove our rental car to the edge of the stream but had second and third and fourth thoughts about entering and trying to drive across; it looked muddy, and we could possibly get stuck.

As we stood there assessing the risk, a small truck full of Bedouin farmworkers approached the river and without hesitation drove across. They'd obviously done this many times before. We still weren't convinced, and we conjured up all sorts of reasons why a truck could go across and a car might not. Then, coming from the other direction, there was a Mercedes and a Peugeot 405. They both went through but slithered and slipped a little as they came out of the water. I was now convinced we shouldn't do it, and we finally made the decision we should have made twenty minutes earlier. We parked the car, took off our shoes and socks, rolled up our pant legs, and waded in. It wasn't comfortable, the mud squished between our toes, but we were soon across. Within minutes, we were exploring a rather uninteresting mound that Joshua had attacked more than three thousand years earlier.

Joshua's next target was the city of Hebron even though Hoham the king of Hebron had already been killed. Like most of these cities, Scripture tells us almost nothing about the battle other than Joshua destroyed the place and all its people.

Hebron's primary claim to fame biblically is as the city of the patriarchs, described in detail in an earlier chapter, but many other significant events occurred here. This city is the burial site of Abraham, Sarah, Isaac, Rebecca, Jacob, Leah, Joseph, Ruth, Jesse, and Abner. David was crowned king in Hebron and he ruled here for seven years, and six of his sons were born here. So given this context, the sacking of the city by Joshua becomes a relatively minor affair.

Joshua's final battle was against the city of Debir. The location is not certain but most likely is Tel Rabud, twelve kilometers south of Hebron. Our visit was uneventful except for a nervous moment on our return trip. We had just entered a village, turned a corner, and immediately were confronted by a Palestinian protest meeting. We couldn't turn back because this was our only route back to Hebron. Also, we had no idea what the Palestinians were protesting, but there were lots of flags, lots of screaming through megaphones, and lots of angry people. Why were we nervous? We were driving an Avis rental car with those conspicuous yellow license plates. We can only surmise that either the Lord was watching over us, or that the Palestinians were so absorbed in their protest that they had no time to be distracted by a few delinquent, wayward, naive tourists.

And so Joshua's conquest of the central and southern parts of the Promised Land was complete, and the summary is compactly described:

So Joshua conquered all the land: the mountain country and the South and the lowland and the wilderness slopes, and all their kings; he left none remaining, but utterly destroyed all that breathed, as the Lord God of Israel had commanded. And Joshua conquered them from Kadesh Barnea as far as Gaza, and all the country of Goshen, even as far as Gibeon. All these kings and their land Joshua took at one time, because the Lord God of Israel fought for Israel. Then Joshua returned, and all Israel with him, to the camp at Gilgal. (Joshua 10:40-43)

VI.
ISRAEL'S JUDGES

The Judges were military heroes or deliverers who presided over the affairs of the Children of Israel between the death of Joshua and the accession of Saul, from about 1380-1050 BC. Their exploits are documented in the Book of Judges. During this period, the government of Israel was a loose confederation of tribes. The nation didn't have a central human figure to guide them, so they tended to rebel and fall into worship of false gods time and time again. The Book of Judges describes these chaotic times:

In those days there was no king in Israel; everyone did what was right in his own eyes. (Judges 17:6)

These words are frequently repeated in the book and gives us the over-arching keynote: a pattern is repeated throughout Judges — a cycle of rebellion, discipline, petitioning for help, the Judges aiding, and God delivering. The children of Israel rebelled against God even though He had shown special favor to them. To punish the people, God sent foreign nations or tribes to oppress them; they then cried to Him in their trouble; the Judges then rallied the people to defeat the enemy. As God's agents for deliverance, the Judges acted to free the nation from oppression. The land then had a period of rest, but the Judges themselves were often weak, and their work was short-lived. The people would then enter another stage of rebellion and idolatry, only to see the cycle of oppression and deliverance repeated all over again.

The Judges were a diverse group, and some of them only receive a brief mention —Shamgar, Tola, Jair, Ibzan, Elon, and Abdon. The careers of other Judges are described in greater detail. Othniel, a nephew of Caleb, was a warrior-deliverer who led the Israelites against the king of Mesopotamia. Ehud was distinguished by left-handedness and his deftness with the dagger. Jephthah was a harlot's son whose devotion to God was matched only by his rashness. Gideon heeded many encouragements to act upon God's call, and he finally led three hundred Israelites to defeat the Midianites. The most interesting of the Judges, was perhaps Samson, whose weaknesses led to his capture by the hated Philistines. The most courageous of the Judges was Deborah, a woman who prevailed upon Barak to attack the Canaanite army. The stories of the Judges make interesting reading because of their rugged personalities and the nature of the times in which they lived. The open, honest, and candid way they are portrayed, including their weaknesses, is one mark of the integrity of the Scriptures.

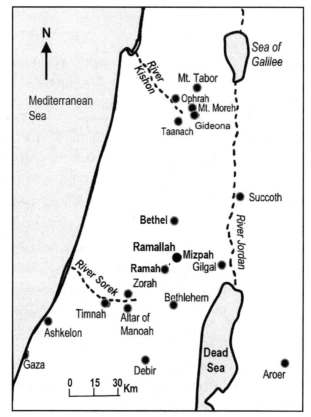

Birthplaces of some of Israel's Judges and other important locations in their rule.

As we traveled through the Bible lands, we were constantly on the lookout for sites associated with the Judges; we will 'visit' these in the order they appear in the Bible beginning with Othniel, then Ehud, Deborah, Gideon, Ibzan, Jephthah, and ending with Samson and Samuel.

OTHNIEL

Othniel was the younger brother of Caleb. The only real story featuring Othniel was when Joshua went to fight at Debir. We were introduced to Debir at the end of the previous chapter.

It is a large hill, and the climb to the top is tough and unnecessary. We parked our car beside a little store on the edge of a small unnamed village. The owner of the store was called Salim. He was also a school teacher and spoke fluent English. He was kind, gave us Coca-Cola, and acted as interpreter as we chatted to about a million children who swarmed around us, wanting their photographs taken. He then left us with a lasting memory. Surprisingly, this Muslim man quoted a few verses from the Old Testament to us. He didn't actually recite the verses, but he paraphrased the story:

> And Caleb said, "He who attacks Kirjath Sepher [Debir] and takes it, to him I will give Achsah my daughter as wife." So Othniel the son of Kenaz, the brother of Caleb, took it; and he gave him Achsah his daughter as wife. Now it was so, when she came to him, that she persuaded him to ask her father for a field. So she dismounted from her donkey, and Caleb said to her, "What do you wish?" She answered, "Give me a blessing; since you have given me land in the South, give me also springs of water." So he gave her the upper springs and the lower springs. (Joshua 15:16-19)

These verses tell us that Caleb's daughter asked her father for two springs of water. Salim explained to us that local tradition identifies the two wells. There are many wells in the Rabud area, but only two of them are old, and both are in the village. These could well be the upper and lower wells that Caleb gave to his daughter when she complained about the aridity of the land she had been given. And perhaps not, it doesn't really matter, they still serve as beautiful object lessons and reminders that biblical stories describe real people and real places.

EHUD

Judges 3:12-19 describes how the Children of Israel were oppressed by Eglon king of Moab. The Lord raised up Ehud, a left-handed judge. Ehud made himself a double-edged dagger that was almost half a meter long. The Scriptures describe how Eglon was a very fat man, and:

> Then Ehud reached with his left hand, took the dagger from his right thigh, and thrust it into his [King Eglon's] belly. Even the hilt went in after the blade, and the fat closed over the blade, for he did not draw the dagger out of his belly; and his entrails came out. (Judges 3:21-22)

This happened "near Gilgal" as did many other biblical events. Except for Jerusalem, Gilgal may have had more significant biblical events than any other location. Gilgal is about 2–3 kilometers from the River Jordan and about midway between the Jordan and Jericho. The Children of Israel camped here when they first entered the Promised Land. From there, they walked around Jericho until the walls fell down. It was here that Joshua encountered the Angelic Captain of the Lord's Host, the Ark of the Covenant was placed for fourteen years, and Israel made a treaty with the Gibeonites. Gilgal was also on Samuel's circuit as a judge of Israel, and Gilgal is where Saul was confirmed as king, Samuel killed Agag the king of the Amalekites, and Elisha cured death in the pot. It was also near here that Jesus Christ was baptized and that Elijah was swooped off to heaven in a chariot of fire. Important? I think so! Nevertheless, the site of Gilgal itself is rather uninspiring and is located just off to the side of the Jericho bypass road. The discovery of Gilgal is interesting, but we will deal with this in a later chapter when we follow the journey of the Ark of the Covenant.

DEBORAH AND BARAK

The exploits of Deborah and Barak are limited to three locations: Mount Tabor, the Kishon River, and Taanach. While these are close, they are located in a very special region with a high concentration of biblical sites, perhaps more than any other area, except Jerusalem. A circle with a diameter of about 15–20 kilometers encompasses Mount Tabor, Nazareth, Armageddon, Megiddo, Mount Carmel, Mount Gilboa, Mount Moreh, Jezreel, Taanach, Kishon River, the villages of Shunem and Nain, Ophrah, Endor, and Gideon's Spring — and the wonderful McDonald's Drive-Thru at Golani Junction! This is a fascinating region to spend a few days.

The first biblical narrative with Deborah and Barak describes their victory over Sisera:

> *Then she [Deborah] sent and called for Barak... and said to him, "Has not the Lord God of Israel commanded, 'Go and deploy troops at Mount Tabor; take with you ten thousand men...; and against you I will deploy Sisera, the commander of Jabin's army, with his chariots and his multitude at the River Kishon; and I will deliver him into your hand'?"... So Sisera gathered together all his chariots, nine hundred chariots of iron, and all the people who were with him, from Harosheth Hagoyim to the River Kishon. Then Deborah said to Barak, "Up! For this is the day in which the Lord has delivered Sisera into your hand. Has not the Lord gone out before you?" So Barak went down from Mount Tabor with ten thousand men following him. And the Lord routed Sisera and all his chariots and all his army with the edge of the sword before Barak;.. and all the army of Sisera fell by the edge of the sword; not a man was left.* (Judges 4:6-7, 13-16)

Ironically, we visited most biblical sites in Israel on multiple occasions, but we only returned to Mount Tabor once, some twenty-five years after our initial visit. Mount Tabor is a five hundred meter steep-sided mountain rising from the Plain of Jezreel. This is the traditional site of the Transfiguration of Jesus Christ as recorded in Matthew 16:13-20, but we will tell you all about that later. We visited Mount Tabor on the first day of our biblical travels.

It was an unusually clear day, and the view was spectacular, especially with Nazareth perched delicately on the top of the hill to the west and the plains of Armageddon spread out before us to the south, running in a vast sweep from east to west. This part of the plains, known as the Valley of Jezreel, was the crossroads of two ancient trade routes and thus was a strategic military site. We mused about the turmoil that had already happened within our field of vision. The low hills and the plains around this area have perhaps witnessed a greater number of bloody encounters than any other similar-sized area of the world's surface — this was the great battlefield of Palestine.

First is our story of how Deborah and Barak defeated the armies of Sisera. The fatal struggle between Josiah and Pharaoh Necho (2 Kings 23:29) took place here. Just off to the left (the east), Gideon defeated the Midianites, and just beyond, Saul was killed on Mount Gilboa (1 Samuel 31:8). Directly west across the valley is the traditional cliff where the natives of Nazareth tried to kill Jesus, and directly opposite (but out of view) is Taanach, which was on the front lines of the War of Independence in 1948. Megiddo has become a symbol of the final conflict between God and the forces of evil. According to the Book of Revelation, Armageddon will be the site of the final end-times battle.

Just below Mount Tabor, to the southeast, is Endor. This is a tough one to find, but the giveaway is the name itself — Endor, a fountain, or spring, of habitation. We could easily find kibbutz Endor because it is signposted, but finding the "Spring of Dor" was another matter. The folk at the kibbutz gave us instructions. We left the main road and drove for about one kilometer, then found an open gate that led us onto a very well-traveled track that twisted and turned through the fields for about another kilometer until it arrived at a very definite destination: nine large palm trees[37] growing by a spring. It was probably at this precise spot that Saul declined to his lowest when he went to visit the witch or medium:

> Then Saul said to his servants, "Find me a woman who is a medium, that I may go to her and inquire of her." And his servants said to him, "In fact, there is a woman who is a medium at En Dor." So Saul disguised himself and put on other clothes, and he went, and two men with him; and they came to the woman by night. And he said, "Please conduct a seance for me, and bring up for me the one I shall name to you." (1 Samuel 28:7-8)

---

[37] Sadly, when we visited the region in 2018, the palm trees had been removed.

With a keen eye on a clear day, you can see in the distance the thin outline of the Kishon River with Mount Carmel as its backdrop. The Kishon is a rather unremarkable river with a more remarkable history. It rises near Mount Tabor and is perennial for no more than about fifteen kilometers of its length. It is mostly less than ten meters wide, and except after heavy rains, it isn't very deep. It was at the Kishon that Elisha killed the 450 prophets of Baal, and it was also here that Deborah and Barak were victorious over the armies of Sisera — Sisera certainly met one of the most ignominious deaths recorded in Scripture:

> *Then Jael, Heber's wife, took a tent peg and took a hammer in her hand, and went softly to him [Sisera] and drove the peg into his temple, and it went down into the ground; for he was fast asleep and weary. So he died. And then, as Barak pursued Sisera, Jael came out to meet him, and said to him, "Come, I will show you the man whom you seek." And when he went into her tent, there lay Sisera, dead with the peg in his temple.* (Judges 4:21-22)

In the following chapter of Judges, we have what is commonly referred to as Deborah's Song in which we get an even more graphic description of Sisera's demise:

> *She [Jael] stretched her hand to the tent peg,*
> *Her right hand to the workmen's hammer;*
> *She pounded Sisera, she pierced his head,*
> *She split and struck through his temple.*
> *At her feet he sank, he fell, he lay still;*
> *At her feet he sank, he fell;*
> *Where he sank, there he fell dead.* (Judges 5:26-27)

In the great struggle of the Canaanites under Sisera against Deborah and Barak, it appears that Taanach was the headquarters of the Canaanite army.

> *The kings came and fought, then the kings of Canaan fought in Taanach, by the waters of Megiddo; they took no spoils of silver.* (Judges 5:19)

Taanach is only a short distance from Megiddo, and the two are joined by a major road artery both currently and historically. But getting from here to there is not necessarily easy. During most of the 1990s, there were informal security checkpoints on many of the roads leading from Israel (proper) to the West Bank. I was traveling alone in 1995 trying to track down a few biblical sites that we hadn't yet visited. One site, in particular, was Taanach, which has only four references in Scripture. The ruins of Taanach are on the southwestern edge of the Valley of Jezreel near Megiddo — Taanach is in the West Bank, Megiddo is not, and to get to Taanach means passing an Israeli security point. Strangely, this was a police checkpoint going east, whereas it was a military checkpoint on the other side of the road on the outward journey! Vehicles passing through this checkpoint were typically Palestinian, typically trucks with produce, and had West Bank plates. Yellow plates in the West Bank indicated a 'Jewish car' and attracted unwanted attention — and my rental car had yellow plates. I cautiously approached the checkpoint, and I had to wait for the vehicles in front of me — all with West Bank plates. The road was in very bad repair with enormous waves and ruts indicating years of neglect.

About one kilometer beyond the checkpoint, on the right side of the road, I could see my destination: the huge mound of Tel Taanach. But I wasn't going to visit Taanach on this day. The police officer quizzed me, excruciatingly thoroughly, even though he spoke very little English. This was often a problem in Israel — police seemed to speak little English whereas soldiers were typically quite fluent. In the officer's gruff, Israeli, half-English, he indicated that I wasn't getting through. I tried to reason that "I am only going to that mound," as I pointed to my destination just a short distance ahead. I couldn't get a clear answer from him if he was saying that I couldn't go through, or that I shouldn't go through. He didn't respond and simply nodded in disapproval and waved me to turn around. So I turned around and spoke with a soldier. He was fluent in English, and we had a long chat. He indicated that I could go through, but shouldn't, and surmised that the police officer didn't understand. "Would you shout across to the police officer for me?" All I received was a defensive smile and a shrug of the shoulders meaning 'no.'

A year later I was back. Same checkpoint, same absurdly awful road conditions, but this time with Evelyn. We joined the end of the long lineup, at least three hundred meters, and we guessed at least one hour, but we had a new trick up our sleeve. Someone had told us that we didn't need to wait in the long line of Palestinian vehicles entering the West Bank. Having yellow license plates was like having a place of privilege. Never opting to turn our backs on a good idea, we pulled out of the lineup and sheepishly drove past all the other vehicles to the head of the lineup. No one blinked, and with a few short questions, and a quick wave of the hand, (from a soldier this time!) and we were on our way to see Taanach.

Our visit was more nervous than exciting. The village at the foot of the mound is only a few homes. As we drove into the village, we were immediately surrounded by a group of children and young people. They were all happy and smiling, but it meant we had already drawn attention to ourselves. We got out of the car and spoke with the children. To our surprise, two or three fellows emerged from the group with good, conversational English. They indicated where we could park our car, and we told them we would like to visit the mound. So, we rather sheepishly and perhaps naïvely left our car, and six young fellows escorted us. They were very keen to show us every little hole, mostly left behind from earlier excavations, but there was nothing too exciting to see, except the foxhole where King Hussein of Jordan was on the frontlines of battle during the Six-Day War of 1967.

All the time that we were walking the mound, we were very fearful for the fate of our car. And yet, we reasoned that because we were with these teenagers, it would be against their honor to allow anything bad to happen to their guests. We also had to be cautious because they didn't know who we were. We were asked repeatedly, "Do you speak Hebrew?" which really means, "Are you Jewish?" "Where do you live, why are you visiting Israel, why did you come to our village (because no one else comes here!), where are you staying, where will you visit tomorrow, where did you visit yesterday?" These kids meant no harm but were curious to know why two Canadians would want to visit Taanach. We survived, had an enjoyable time, took the mandatory photographs of the children, and gave them our address in Canada. When we returned to Canada we sent them copies of the photographs and they wrote back to us. Their letter was postmarked in Jenin, a hotbed of Palestinian hostilities. We often wondered if Israeli authorities were keeping an eye on us because we had in our possession, in Canada, letters that had been stamp-marked in Hebron, Bethlehem, Ramallah, Nablus, and now Jenin — these are all the Palestinian hotspot cities in the West Bank.

We said our goodbyes and returned to the checkpoint. As we passed, we were amused to read a sign that we had missed on our way in; I think we missed it because we were so engrossed with avoiding the potholes. The sign read:

> Individual Tourists Not Admitted.
> Groups Allowed With Prior
> Permission of I.D.F.[38] Authorities.

GIDEON

Gideon, also called Jerubbaal, is one of the heroes of the Old Testament, and his history is substantially documented (Judges 6-8). Deborah and Barak had been victorious over Jabin, but Israel once more sank into idolatry, and the Midianites and Amalekites began to plunder and desolate the land. Gideon became God's man to undertake the task of delivering the land from these invaders.

---

[38] Israeli Defense Forces

Gideon was from the village of Ophrah (Judges 6:11). Although the identity of this site is uncertain, many commentators identify Ophrah as today's a-Tayibe, which is about halfway between Afula and Beth Shean. The early stories happened in his hometown. His first assignment was to build an altar to the Lord, then destroy his father's altar of Baal in the family's backyard:

So Gideon built an altar there to the Lord, and called it The-Lord-Is-Peace. To this day it is still in Ophrah of the Abiezrites. Now it came to pass the same night that the Lord said to him, "Take your father's young bull, the second bull of seven years old, and tear down the altar of Baal that your father has, and cut down the wooden image that is beside it; and build an altar to the Lord your God on top of this rock in the proper arrangement, and take the second bull and offer a burnt sacrifice with the wood of the image which you shall cut down." (Judges 6:24-26)

Next, we have the sign of the fleece, which also occurred at Ophrah:

So Gideon said to God, "If You will save Israel by my hand as You have said—look, I shall put a fleece of wool on the threshing floor; if there is dew on the fleece only, and it is dry on all the ground, then I shall know that You will save Israel by my hand, as You have said." And it was so. When he rose early the next morning and squeezed the fleece together, he wrung the dew out of the fleece, a bowlful of water. Then Gideon said to God, "Do not be angry with me, but let me speak just once more: Let me test, I pray, just once more with the fleece; let it now be dry only on the fleece, but on all the ground let there be dew." And God did so that night. It was dry on the fleece only, but there was dew on all the ground. (Judges 6:36-40)

From a-Tayibe it is about ten kilometers to the well of Harod:

Then Jerubbaal (that is, Gideon) and all the people who were with him rose early and encamped beside the well of Harod, so that the camp of the Midianites was on the north side of them by the hill of Moreh in the valley. (Judges 7:1)

There was no real excitement to finding a-Tayibe except that we were nervous about entering the village; there are no actual ruins or excavations to observe, so we decided to view the village from a distance. On the journey to a-Tayibe we drove across a famous battlefield —the general location of where Gideon's men routed the Midianites on the lower slopes of Mount Moreh. A few minutes later, we rounded a corner to be met with a view of the village of a-Tayibe nestled in a wonderful pastoral setting. It looked so calm, peaceful, and inviting, that we decided to continue driving. However, as we approached the edge of the village, the large, spray-painted sign telling Jews to stay out caused us some concern. Strangely, the sign was in English! We aren't Jewish but the locals wouldn't know that, so we decided to stay out, performed a quick U-turn, and went back in the direction of the well, or the spring, of Harod.

The spring at Harod is a delightful spot directly across the valley of Esdraelon from Mount Moreh and a-Tayibe. It's at the base of Mount Gilboa, inside a park and picnic area. We arrived at the park later in the afternoon as most others were leaving. The attendant at the gate was intent in charging us the full entry cost, and we were equally intent in not paying it! I suspect he had no idea what we were talking about — which is often useful in Israel — and he may have raised the barrier just to get rid of us. The park is much more developed than it was twelve years earlier. Today the park has many amenities: there is a very large, blue-painted pool for children to splash in, many picnic tables and barbeque spots, a few planted shrubs and flower gardens, the ubiquitous eucalyptus, and a too-well manicured stream that runs in a constructed brick-lined channel from the spring and through the recreational area. The spring itself is pleasantly delightful and had a few young children splashing around even though there is a low fence designed to keep people out.

It was at the spring of Harod that one of the great stories from Scripture occurred. Gideon had more than thirty thousand men ready to fight the Midianites, but the Lord told Gideon to reduce the size of his army. First, he invited any who were afraid to fight, to leave, and over twenty thousand did so! This was still too many, so the Lord instructed Gideon to take his people to the spring at Harod and to test them... And the rest of the story we know very well:

> "So he brought the people down to the water. And the Lord said to Gideon, "Everyone who laps from the water with his tongue, as a dog laps, you shall set apart by himself; likewise everyone who gets down on his knees to drink." And the number of those who lapped, putting their hand to their mouth, was three hundred men; but all the rest of the people got down on their knees to drink water. Then the Lord said to Gideon, "By the three hundred men who lapped I will save you, and deliver the Midianites into your hand. Let all the other people go, every man to his place."
> (Judges 7:5-7)

Gideon defeated the Midianites and pursued them east along the valley of Esdraelon in the direction of Beth Shean. When they reached the Jordan valley, they turned south and came to Abel Mehola.

> When the three hundred blew the trumpets, the Lord set every man's sword against his companion throughout the whole camp; and the army fled to Beth Acacia, toward Zererah, as far as the border of Abel Meholah, by Tabbath. (Judges 7:22)

Gideon continued his pursuit of the Midianites to Succoth. His men were exhausted, and when they came to Succoth and to Penuel, the leaders of neither city would provide bread or supplies. Gideon promised revenge! On his return from battle Gideon killed the seventy-seven elders of Succoth, and:

... he tore down the tower of Penuel and killed the men of the city. (Judges 8:17)

After Gideon's victory over the Midianites, the Israelites wanted him to rule over them. He refused, but asked that:

... each of you would give me the earrings from his plunder." For they had golden earrings, because they were Ishmaelites. So they answered, "We will gladly give them." And they spread out a garment, and each man threw into it the earrings from his plunder. Now the weight of the gold earrings that he requested was one thousand seven hundred shekels of gold, besides the crescent ornaments, pendants, and purple robes which were on the kings of Midian, and besides the chains that were around their camels' necks. Then Gideon made it into an ephod and set it up in his city, Ophrah. And all Israel played the harlot with it there. It became a snare to Gideon and to his house. (Judges 8:24-27)

Our journey with Gideon comes back to the village of his birth, Ophrah. It was here that Gideon set up the ephod, part of the sacred dress of the Levitical priesthood, and it was here that he was buried:

Now Gideon the son of Joash died at a good old age, and was buried in the tomb of Joash his father, in Ophrah of the Abiezrites. (Judges 8:32)

SAMSON
Samson is introduced to the biblical narrative as follows:

Now there was a certain man from Zorah, of the family of the Danites, whose name was Manoah; and his wife was barren and had no children. And the Angel of the Lord appeared to the woman and said to her, "Indeed now, you are barren and have borne no children, but you shall conceive and bear a son... Then Manoah said to the Angel of the Lord, "Please let us detain You, and we will prepare a young goat for You."... So Manoah took the young goat with the grain offering, and offered it upon the rock to the Lord. And He did a wondrous thing while Manoah and his wife looked on—it happened as the flame went up toward heaven from the altar—the Angel of the Lord ascended in the flame of the altar! When Manoah and his wife saw this, they fell on their faces to the ground. When the Angel of the Lord appeared no more to Manoah and his wife, then Manoah knew that He was the Angel of the Lord... So the woman bore a son and called his name Samson; and the child grew, and the Lord blessed him. (Judges 13:2-3, 15, 19-21, 24)

These verses refer to Manoah making an offering to the Lord on a rock. It's possible that this rock still exists. We came across an old book by Zev Vilnay. This book was relatively unique in having a black-and-white photograph of an altar "near to Beth Shemesh," and Vilnay believed it might be the Altar of Manoah.

We went to Beth Shemesh and stopped with a group of about half a dozen soldiers standing at a bus stop. Soldiers are often a good bet; they usually speak relatively good English and often have a deep knowledge of the land — these did not! Next, we asked some locals, but no one had a clue what we were talking about — even when we showed them the black-and-white photograph. We then went to the local police station and spoke with some officers and more soldiers, and, again, no luck. After the police station, we went to the local Kibbutz Zorah. After speaking to various people, one guy strolling past casually quipped, "Oh, I know where that is." He gave us directions, and we headed off. After sorting through a virtual debris field we found the altar exactly where this guy said we would — about a two-minute drive from the police station.

This is a rock altar as the Hebrews would have built an altar in the time of the Judges. It is a large, irregular single block of rock, perhaps three meters long, 1.5 meters wide, and 1.5 meters high. It had two layers towards the top, much like a wedding cake or a step pyramid. The topmost layer had cup holders. This could have been the altar where the angel of the Lord appeared to Manoah and his wife, and where Manoah presented his offering. This first visit was in 1993, and the altar was recognizable by having a small tree growing from a crack in the large stone. On a return visit in 1994, some delinquent had cut the tree down, and the altar had some graffiti. A subsequent visit in 1997 revealed an increasing mess; a new road was being constructed through the area, and the altar had been unceremonially dumped (still the correct way up!) among all the other debris resulting from the road clearing activities. Unfortunately, the altar was moved, or dumped, during road construction, and in 1998 we couldn't find it. In 2015, on a whim, we were in the area and dropped by to have a look — it was back again within ten meters of its original location in 1993. Think about this. This altar might have been sitting on this spot for over three thousand years, and then someone, perhaps unknowingly, dumped it then replaced it. Surely someone on the management and planning of the road construction must have known about this piece of Israeli history.

The first recorded event in the life of Samson was his marriage to a Philistine woman from Timnah. This is recorded in Judges Chapter 14, and this, along with chapters 15 and 16, contains some of the most grotesque yet captivating reading in all of Scripture. There is the story of a messed-up marriage, revenge, counter revenge, and counter-counter revenge. Samson kills a lion and thirty Philistines, visits a prostitute, rips the gates of the city of Gaza, gets a second wife, and finally has his eyes gouged out in prison — and then there's the great finale when he pushes over the pillars of the Temple of Dagon in Gaza and kills over three thousand Philistines. I feel a sermon coming on. Remember, this man Samson was a rough, immoral character, and yet he was chosen by God to lead Israel, and Hebrews chapter 11 praises Samson for his faith.

> *"For behold, you shall conceive and bear a son. And no razor shall come upon his head, for the child shall be a Nazirite to God from the womb; and he shall begin to deliver Israel out of the hand of the Philistines."* ... *and the child grew, and the Lord blessed him* (Judges 13:5, 24)

> *And what more shall I say? For the time would fail me to tell of Gideon and Barak and Samson and Jephthah, also of David and Samuel and the prophets: who through faith subdued kingdoms, worked righteousness, obtained promises, stopped the mouths of lions, quenched the violence of fire, escaped the edge of the sword, out of weakness were made strong, became valiant in battle, turned to flight the armies of the aliens.* (Hebrews 11:32-34)

The exploits of Samson center on three locations: Timnah, which is in the Valley of the River Sorek, Ashkelon, and Gaza. Our travels begin at Timnah, where Samson got his Philistine wife.

> *Now Samson went down to Timnah, and saw a woman in Timnah of the daughters of the Philistines.* (Judges 14:1)

Since his second wife, Delilah, came from the valley of the Sorek, she may also have come from this area because the Sorek runs right past Timnah. Today, the old railway from Jerusalem to Tel Aviv enters the valley of the Sorek close to Beth Shemesh and more or less follows the Sorek valley to Tel Aviv. It was along this valley that the Ark was taken from Ekron to Beth Shemesh, and in doing so came past Timnah. It was in this area that Samson killed a young lion:

> *So Samson went down to Timnah with his father and mother, and came to the vineyards of Timnah. Now to his surprise, a young lion came roaring against him. And the Spirit of the Lord came mightily upon him, and he tore the lion apart as one would have torn apart a young goat, though he had nothing in his hand...* (Judges 14:5-6)

Finding Timnah was easy, but getting to it was another matter. We left Beth Shemesh, following a secondary road along the Sorek valley. As this road began to veer away from the river, we happened upon a farm trail that followed the river, winding its way through vineyards and grain fields. Interestingly, Judges 14:5 refers to vineyards, and Judges 15:5 refers to grain fields.

> *Then Samson went and caught three hundred foxes; and he took torches, turned the foxes tail to tail, and put a torch between each pair of tails. When he had set the torches on fire, he let the foxes go into the standing grain of the Philistines, and burned up both the shocks and the standing grain, as well as the vineyards and olive groves.* (Judges 15:4-5)

Timnah was a difficult site to access, and we tried various roads and tracks to no avail. Then we got lucky. We were on the train from Jerusalem to Tel Aviv. As we approached Timnah, we eagerly looked out the window — and bingo — we could see a very drivable track to the mound coming down from the kibbutz at Tal Sharar. A week later we were there. We parked, climbed out of the car, and were startled when two Israeli soldiers, with the customary M-16s slung over their shoulders, suddenly emerged from the cover of a field of corn. Even more surprising, they walked right past us as if they didn't see us — and there was no one else or nothing else within eyesight — weird! After all the bother we endured to find Timnah, there was absolutely nothing to see. This time, the journey was much more interesting than the destination.

Our journey to Ashkelon was uninspiring and certainly had a lot less activity than occurred with Samson:

> *Then the Spirit of the Lord came upon him mightily, and he went down to Ashkelon and killed thirty of their men...* (Judges 14:19)

Ancient Ashkelon was the capital of the Canaanite kings, one of the five key Philistine cities along the coast, a harbor of the Philistines, and today it is in a beautiful national park and resort. When we visited, there were just too many people, footballs, and picnics, so after a quick visit we kept moving to Gaza, the third great location in the life of Samson. It was in Gaza that Samson became intimate with a prostitute. The men of Gaza closed the city gates intending to kill him in the morning as he was leaving the prostitute's house. But at midnight Samson arose and, breaking away bolts, bars, and hinges, he carried the city gates to the top of a hill looking toward Hebron.

> *Now Samson went to Gaza and saw a harlot there, and went in to her. When the Gazites were told, "Samson has come here!" they surrounded the place and lay in wait for him all night at the gate of the city. They were quiet all night, saying, "In the morning, when it is daylight, we will kill him." And Samson lay low till midnight; then he arose at midnight, took hold of the doors of the gate of the city and the two*

gateposts, pulled them up, bar and all, put them on his shoulders, and carried them to the top of the hill that faces Hebron. (Judges 16:1-3)

After this, Samson met Delilah:

Afterward it happened that he loved a woman in the Valley of Sorek, whose name was Delilah. And the lords of the Philistines came up to her and said to her, "Entice him, and find out where his great strength lies, and by what means we may overpower him, that we may bind him to afflict him; and every one of us will give you eleven hundred pieces of silver." So Delilah said to Samson, "Please tell me where your great strength lies..." (Judges 16:4-6)

Samson repeatedly lied to Delilah in his answers to her question. He variously told her to "bind me with seven fresh bowstrings... bind me securely with new ropes... and weave the seven locks of my head into the web of the loom" (Joshua 16:7, 11, 13). None of these worked, but:

...when she pestered him daily with her words and pressed him, so that his soul was vexed to death, that he told her all his heart, and said to her, "No razor has ever come upon my head, for I have been a Nazirite to God from my mother's womb. If I am shaven, then my strength will leave me, and I shall become weak, and be like any other man. (Judges 16:16-17)

Then we read the horrible consequences of Samson's failure as he ground grain as a blinded prisoner:

Then the Philistines took him and put out his eyes, and brought him down to Gaza. They bound him with bronze fetters, and he became a grinder in the prison. (Judges 16:21)

The book of Judges records how the lords of the Philistines gathered to offer a great sacrifice to Dagon their god, and to rejoice over the capture of Samson. In an ultimate attempt at humiliating and defeat the Philistines, they brought Samson before the crowd to make fun of him. But they made a terrible mistake, standing him between two pillars in the Temple of Dagon:

Then Samson said to the lad who held him by the hand, "Let me feel the pillars which support the temple, so that I can lean on them." Now the temple was full of men and women. All the lords of the Philistines were there - about three thousand men and women on the roof watching while Samson performed. Then Samson called to the Lord, saying, "O Lord God, remember me, I pray! Strengthen me, I pray, just this once, O God, that I may with one blow take vengeance on the Philistines for my two eyes!" And Samson took hold of the two middle pillars which supported the temple, and he braced himself against them, one on his right and the other on his left. Then Samson said, "Let me die with the Philistines!" And he pushed with all his might, and the temple fell on the lords and all the people who were in it. So the dead that he killed at his death were more than he had killed in his life. (Judges 16:26-30)

Gaza was the most southerly of the five federated cities of the Philistines. It was a troublesome piece of real estate then, and it is so today. So much so that we made four attempts to enter it before being successful. There is endless fighting, stoning, stabbing and shootings in Gaza, and it seems that someone is killed almost daily. The first attempt was easy. We were near Yad Mordechai about five kilometers from the Erez border crossing into Gaza when we approached an army checkpoint. That was it; no way; not a chance; not even going to get close. The second attempt was similar, but we at least got as far as the large parking lot at the Erez crossing. I parked, walked to the border checkpoint and that was it; no way; not a chance; go away. The third attempt was in 1997, and we got as far as the barrier at the crossing. I walked a few steps to a soldier sentry point. I told him what I wanted to do. He gave me that irritating and typically Israeli shrug of the shoulders while showing you the palms of their hands that in body language means *"Okay, I will if I have to, but I don't want to do this."* The soldier disappeared into a cinder-block office and reappeared about two minutes later. I assume he was asking permission from someone in authority — but, he may have been having a cup of coffee! He sauntered back towards me looking totally bored with his lot in life, lazily said "no," and waved me away with a dismissive sweep of his hand. No explanation, no appeal, just a plain and lazy "no." I guess this was no!

Finally, in the spring of 1999, I was traveling on a day trip with one of my graduate students. We parked in the Erez parking lot, walked to the border, passed through extremely tight security procedures, were frisked, checked and double-checked, frisked again, had passports thoroughly checked, and with a wave of the hand, we were in Gaza. We waved down a taxi, and we told the driver that we wanted to go to the remains of the ancient city of Gaza and that we wanted to see an ornate mosaic tile floor that was somewhere near to the beach not too far from city canter. We had photographs of the ruins and of the mosaic floor. The driver spoke very good English and led us to believe that he knew exactly where we wanted to go. When we tried to barter for a price for the rental he just kept saying "not much, you decide when we come back." I can't believe we were so stupid. We knew enough about this country, and its inhabitants, that it's always necessary to set a firm price for everything beforehand. But in hindsight, this was all very intimidating. The first part was easy. What remains of ancient Gaza is about five kilometers along the main road between the border crossing and Gaza City in the northeastern part of the present city.

We soon spotted the relatively scant ruins on the east side of the road beside a school. The driver agreed to wait for us, and we walked around, took a few photographs, and mostly tried to avoid the thirty or forty young children that gathered around to smile at us —there are always lots of children! After photographing each of the kids at least twenty times with no film in the camera (deliberately!) we returned to the taxi.

By this point, our feeling of intimidation was declining, and we demanded a fixed price from our driver. "Oh, not much, you decide." I hate that answer! An hour later we were having absolutely no luck, and we asked the driver to take us back to the border crossing. He was having none of that, and two hours later we had had no lunch, and still no mosaic, although we had reluctantly seen most of Gaza city. We were in and out of offices and security offices, and we assume that our driver was asking about the mosaic, but who knows. But no mosaic. Finally, someone was able to describe to us where the mosaic had been found and explained that it had been moved (they said stolen) to a museum in Israel.[39] This ended our adventure and the driver brought us back to the Erez crossing. "How much?" I asked. "Oh, you decide." I was beginning to dislike this guy. I calculated that $75 USD was enough for five hours of time (three of which were wasted), with probably no more than twenty-five kilometers of actual driving. When we gave him the $75 USD he was quite upset and "not enough." What happened to "not much, you decide?" He was turning nasty, and we were becoming upset, so we left $50 USD, yep $50 USD, on the front passenger seat, jumped out of the taxi, briskly moved towards the security checkpoint, and escaped back into Israel! It would probably have been easier to have ripped the gates of the city and carry them to the hill overlooking Hebron — but I can guarantee we left behind one steaming mad taxi driver wondering how he had been out-maneuvered by two naïve tourists!

The story of Samson ends with:

> *And his brothers and all his father's household came down and took him, and brought him up and buried him between Zorah and Eshtaol in the tomb of his father Manoah. He had judged Israel twenty years.* (Judges 16:31)

After his death, Samson's family recovered his body from the rubble and buried him near the tomb of his father Manoah. A tomb structure that some

---

[39] We accidentally stumbled across this mosaic almost eighteen years later when traveling with Fergus. We were traveling to Jerusalem from the Dead Sea and saw an advert for the Inn of the Good Samaritan. This "Inn" is now a museum with several mosaics on display. We were ahead of schedule so decided to pay a quick visit, and voila, the mosaic from Gaza that we had been searching for some eighteen years earlier.

attribute to Samson and his father stands on the top of the mountain in Tel Tzora. The white tomb is visible from the stone altar where the angel first met with Samson's parents.

SAMUEL

Samuel was born at Ramah and spent his childhood at Shiloh. Although Samuel is typically considered to be a prophet, nevertheless, Scripture also calls him a judge:

> And Samuel judged Israel all the days of his life. He went from year to year on a circuit to Bethel, Gilgal, and Mizpah, and judged Israel in all those places. But he always returned to Ramah, for his home was there… (1 Samuel 7:15-17)

This verse identifies some of the major sites in Samuel's life: Ramah, Bethel, Gilgal, and Mizpah. We will visit Bethel, Gilgal, and Shiloh later in our journey with the Ark of God; here we will deal only with Ramah and Mizpah:

> Then Samuel died; and the Israelites gathered together and lamented for him, and buried him at his home in Ramah… (1 Samuel 25:1)

There is some debate as to the identity of Ramah. We didn't mind these disagreements over locations because it gave us an excuse to visit all of the proposed sites. The consensus seems to be that Ramah is on the hill overlooking Ramot Allon in the northwestern suburbs of Jerusalem. The site is easily identified by a prominent mosque perched on top. There was no particular excitement involved in going to this site, and even when you arrive, the ruins don't offer a lot.

However, there are three things worth doing. First and second are to visit the two cenotaphs commemorating the burial of Samuel. The Muslim burial site is in a dark, glum, and uninspiring alcove, behind a tightly-meshed grill in the main hall of the mosque. The Jewish site is downstairs, and it is bright, untidy, and exciting as young Jewish men bob as they pray. The third thing is to climb the long, narrow staircase to the roof of the mosque. From the roof, you can relive a few well-known bible stories, which we will describe in a later chapter on Grave Matters.

But where is Ramah? Some argue that Ramah was located at today's city of Ramallah. The name Ramallah is an Arabic name meaning 'Height of God' [Ram-Allah] and probably the 'Hill of God.' Others argue that Ramah is Er-Ram midway between Jerusalem and Ramallah. Like so many sites, we don't know for sure.

On the southern outskirts of Ramallah, on the main road to Jerusalem, is the mound of Mizpah, a significant site in the life of Samuel. It is large but mostly rubble-covered with few discernable ruins except for a prominent wall on the northeastern corner that was built by King Asa (1 Kings 15:22). Nevertheless, this location is important because it was here that Samuel gathered all of Israel together and where Saul was chosen as Israel's first king:

> *When he [Samuel] had caused the tribe of Benjamin to come near by their families, the family of Matri was chosen. And Saul the son of Kish was chosen. But when they sought him, he could not be found. Therefore they inquired of the Lord further, "Has the man come here yet?" And the Lord answered, "There he is, hidden among the equipment." So they ran and brought him from there; and when he stood among the people, he was taller than any of the people from his shoulders upward. And Samuel said to all the people, "Do you see him whom the Lord has chosen, that there is no one like him among all the people?" So all the people shouted and said, "Long live the king!"* (1 Samuel 10:21-24)

Along the eastern base of the mound is the main road connecting Jerusalem and Ramallah. There are a few stores and businesses, and it was here in 1993 that a Jewish woman was shot dead by Palestinians as she was changing a flat tire. As the road continued to the north and widened into a divided boulevard, we realized that we were looking at a view that we'd seen many times on newscasts. Evidently, Mizpah, or somewhere very close by, is a TV vantage point for capturing footage of the troubles that frequent this piece of roadway on the southern outskirts of Ramallah. As we stood on the mound, an interesting thought entered our minds. We were able to identify with these recent troubles and disturbances, and yet, three thousand years ago it was just the same:

> *And Samuel said, "Gather all Israel to Mizpah, and I will pray to the Lord for you."... Now when the Philistines heard that the children of Israel had gathered together at Mizpah, the lords of the Philistines went up against Israel. And when the children of Israel heard of it, they were afraid of the Philistines... Now as Samuel was offering up the burnt offering, the Philistines drew near to battle against Israel. But the Lord thundered with a loud thunder upon the Philistines that day, and so confused them that they were overcome before Israel... So the Philistines were subdued, and they did not come anymore into the territory of Israel...* (1 Samuel 7:5, 7, 10, 13)

The more things change, the more they stay the same.

DETOUR SEVEN:
MINISTRY IN RAMALLAH

We made our first contact with a Baptist church in Ramallah shortly after arriving in Jerusalem in 1992. This church was of interest to us because it had the only AWANA ministry in Israel. Ramallah is about sixteen kilometers north of Jerusalem in the West Bank, and we got there by bus and shared taxi. This journey and visit became an almost weekly event for most of the months we lived in Jerusalem. The church is only a five-minute walk from Ramallah city center. On our first visit we had arranged for the pastor of the church, Pastor Musa, to meet us in the city center where the sherut from Jerusalem arrived.

Ramallah city center was abysmal. Buildings were defaced, dilapidated, and covered with Arabic graffiti. It was hot, and the place smelled from the meat, vegetable, and fruit vendors in the area. The popular Arab uprising, the Intifada, made everything tense. Most streets were quite deserted, and some streets had been barricaded by the Israeli army. About fifty years earlier, Ramallah was almost 100% 'Christian,' but now was almost 100% Muslim. The First Baptist Bible Church had been there for quite some time, and the current building was completed in 1978 — they hadn't been able to afford to paint it once since it was built. They couldn't even afford to erase the Arabic graffiti sprayed over the front of the church, which said, "Palestine is for Muslims only," and, "Death to Jews." The building seated about two hundred. In the early 1980s, the church had about 150 in regular attendance, but by 1995 this had dwindled to about fifty. The decline had been due to the Intifada, and other factors, forcing many families to leave Ramallah and move to the US.

And in the middle of all of this was an AWANA club. On our first visit, there were about twelve children ranging from 3–12 years old. We were there to help with games and activities. This poor club didn't even have a balloon, a ping-pong ball, or any type of ball to play kids' games. Evelyn and Andrea made bean bags, we bought a few balloons, and we played a lot of games with these basics. This church reminded us strongly of the so-called rich little poor church at Smyrna of which Jesus said: "I know your works, tribulation, and poverty (but you are rich)…" (Revelation 2:9)

On a few occasions, Pastor Musa called us and said they were canceling club for that day because the situation in Ramallah was too dangerous. There had been a lot of trouble in the West Bank with Palestinian hunger strikes in the prisons, workers' strikes, and protests. Israeli troops had shot dead a few protesters in Gaza and Ramallah. Palestinians set a booby-trapped bomb in Ramallah, which killed a Russian immigrant and wounded a number of others. Israeli soldiers responded, and there were a number of deaths. On three occasions we were turned back. This occurred when the Israeli army sealed off the West Bank, usually in response to Palestinian rioting or other troubles. Movement in and out of Ramallah was difficult, and at times wasn't safe. On another occasion, we were delayed leaving Jerusalem. When we arrived in Ramallah there was a strong army presence and barbed wire blocked off a few of the main streets; a couple of terrorists had been shot about fifteen minutes before we arrived. These incidences had a tremendous impact on each of us. A difficult situation, yet the life of the church and the ministry to the children continued.

VII.
DAVID AND GOLIATH

We were in this area in an earlier chapter when Joshua was pursuing the Canaanite kings past Azekah. From the top of the mound of Azekah, the Valley of Elah below extends to the east. This is the famed battleground of David and Goliath. Scripture describes the layout of the battlefield:

> *Now the Philistines gathered their armies together to battle, and were gathered at Sochoh, which belongs to Judah; they encamped between Sochoh and Azekah, in Ephes Dammim. And Saul and the men of Israel were gathered together, and they encamped in the Valley of Elah, and drew up in battle array against the Philistines. The Philistines stood on a mountain on one side, and Israel stood on a mountain on the other side, with a valley between them. And a champion went out from the camp of the Philistines, named Goliath, from Gath, whose height was six cubits and a span.* (1 Samuel 17:1-4)

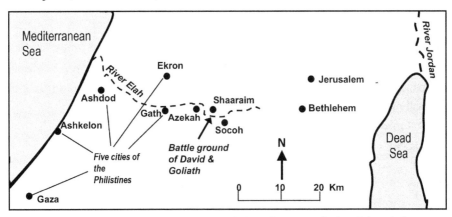

The battlefield of David and Goliath and the subsequent flight of the Philistines.

Given this description, the site of David and Goliath's encounter is probably a few hundred meters upstream from the main road towards Netiv Halamed-Heh Kibbutz. One can easily envision the entire battle site. The brook from which David gathered his five stones is running towards us.[40] The Philistines

---

[40] Until the mid-90s the stream was running, but with upstream development by about 1998 the brook was dry and by 2010 it was used as a track for farm vehicles. So tragic that such a site was not preserved.

were lined up along the right (south) side of the stream from Azekah to Socoh in the distance, and the Israelites lined up on the opposite side of the brook. When the battle was over, with Goliath dead and the Philistines defeated, the remaining Philistines ran downstream, meandered around Azekah and off into the distance to Gath and Ekron. Gath can be seen eight kilometers away, but not Ekron.

The story of David and Goliath is both interesting and important, and within the story is an important city that mostly goes unnoticed — Shaaraim. This city is mentioned only three times in scripture. When the Philistines realized that their champion was dead, we read:

> Now the men of Israel and Judah arose and shouted, and pursued the Philistines as far as the entrance of the valley and to the gates of Ekron. And the wounded of the Philistines fell along the road to Shaaraim, even as far as Gath and Ekron. (1 Samuel 17:52)

Shaaraim literally means "two gates" or "two-gated city." Shaaraim was a key strategic location on the main route from the Coastal Plain to the hill country. It has massive fortifications,[41] and two gates: one to the south and one to the west. This is Khirbet Qeiyafa, and it is located on the top of a hill that borders the Elah Valley on the north, about one kilometer from where David fought Goliath. The Qeiyafa ostracon[42] was found here; this is possibly the oldest known Hebrew inscription and refers to the "establishment of a monarchy," a "king," and "delivering justice in a manner different from that of the judge." Given that the city has been dated to the tenth century BC, this ostracon is probably referring to King Saul and to the prophet Samuel and deals a severe blow to biblical minimalism.[43]

From the early 1980s many scholars, labeled minimalists, argued that the Old Testament was mostly written down in the Hellenistic period, and therefore cannot be used to write or contribute to the history of ancient Israel. The loudest voices among these minimalists argued that David, Solomon, and most of the figures and events recorded in the Bible, were imaginary creations with doubtful

---

[41] Shanks, H. (2009). A fortified city from King David's time Khirbet Qeiyafa. *Biblical Archaeology Review*. (Jan/Feb, 35:1), 38.

[42] Shanks, H. (2010). Oldest Hebrew inscription discovered in Israelite fort on Philistine border. *Biblical Archaeology Review* (Mar/Apr, 36:2), 51.

[43] Lawrence Mykytiuk has presented evidence from archaeology and ancient texts for the existence of fifty-three people in the Old Testament (Biblical Archaeology Review, 2014, 40 (2) pp. 46-47; *biblicalarchaeology.org/biblepeople*), twenty-three political figures in the New Testament (Biblical Archaeology Review 2017, 43 (5) pp. 56-57) and seven New Testament religious figures (Biblical Archaeology Review, 2021, 47 (2), pp 38-47; *biblicalarchaeology.org/ntpeople*).

basis in historical or archaeological fact. Until the 1993 discovery of the ninth-century BC pottery inscribed with "House of David" at the northern city of Dan, there wasn't any nonbiblical evidence that David actually existed. Few dispute it now.

Accessing Shaaraim is now relatively easy because the Israel National Walking Trail passes right by. There is also an access track from route 38, but this is in terrible condition and generally limited to four-wheel-drive vehicles. When we first tried to find the site in 2015 it was, to say the least, extremely frustrating. Given that we had a regular rental car, we knew we had to find another entry route, and this could only be via Netiv HaLamed-Heh Kibbutz. We entered the Kibbutz and called into the reception kiosk which doubled as an information center. We shared photographs and descriptions to no avail. It was unfathomable to think that such an important archaeological find, perhaps abutting kibbutz land no more than three kilometers away, would be unknown; and yet, no one had any idea, and some even suggested we were in the wrong valley.

We decided to go it alone. We drove through the kibbutz in a generally western direction past a few residential units, farming equipment, and storage warehouses, finally emerging on a well-used track running through the kibbutz's fruit orchards. We drove to the far end of the orchards and spotted a rough track running uphill to Shaaraim. We drove up the track for perhaps one hundred meters until the spinning wheels of our rental car couldn't gain traction on the steep, gravelly track.

We tightly pulled the hand brake, placed rocks behind all four wheels, and walked the final five minutes up to the ruins. Impressive! We spent quite a bit of time wandering around, taking photographs, and marveling at the double casemate wall, the two city gates, and other structures. We were particularly excited to find the location where the ostracon had been found. We returned to our car, and, after removing rocks from the wheels, we reversed to the bottom of the hill, which by the way was only two hundred meters from the fruit orchards. We retraced our steps and stopped at the reception kiosk. Surprise! On the wall of this room was a large, schematic map of the Valley which we had missed earlier with Shaaraim marked on it! We pointed this out to those at the desk — blank!

We returned a few years later with Fergus, and this time it was a lot easier. We simply drove through the kibbutz, totally ignoring reception, until we reached the end of the buildings and storage warehouses. We couldn't believe our eyes. We were faced with a newly constructed road that ran right across our route, and many workers with heavy equipment were still on site. Fergus and I decided to avoid any potential problems associated with talking to workers in a construction zone, so we just kept driving, found an opening ("bridge-tunnel") under the new road, and picked up our same track through the fruit orchards. Our biggest challenge this time was to get our rental car farther up the hill than previously; we did, by about fifty meters, but not without a lot of tire wear.

VIII.
JOURNEY OF THE ARK

Perhaps nothing else in Scripture has sparked as much interest as the Ark, variously called the Ark of the Lord, the Ark of God, the Ark of the Covenant and the Ark of the Testimony. It has been the focus of movies such as "*Raiders of the Lost Ark*" and the subject of much speculation.

The sacred Ark, designed to be a symbol of the presence of God among His people, was built at Mount Sinai and was taken by the Israelites to Canaan. It was the most important sacred object of the Israelites during the wilderness period.

The Ark was portable chest made of acacia wood and overlaid with gold both inside and out. It had a gold cover known as the mercy seat because the Israelites believed the Ark to be God's throne. Joined as one piece with the mercy seat were two angelic statues called cherubim. They stood at opposite ends, facing each other with wings outstretched above and their faces bowed toward the mercy seat. They marked the place where the Lord dwelled and communicated with Moses.

The Ark also had four rings of gold through which carrying poles were inserted. These poles were never removed from the rings, apparently to show that the Ark was a portable sanctuary. The Ark was the only article of furniture in the innermost room, or Holy of Holies, of Moses's tabernacle and Solomon's Temple. Within the Ark were the two stone tablets containing the Ten Commandments, a golden pot of manna, and Aaron's rod that budded. For these next few pages, we will follow the route of this sacred chest as it entered the Promised Land.

After Moses died, Joshua assumed command of the people, and his first task was to lead them over the River Jordan and into the Promised Land. The Ark moved from site to site before it was finally placed in the Holy of Holies in the new temple in Jerusalem.

Our journey begins at the River Jordan.

So it was, when the people set out from their camp to cross over the Jordan, with the priests bearing the ark of the covenant before the people, and as those who bore the ark came to the Jordan, and the feet of the priests who bore the ark dipped in the edge of the water (for the Jordan overflows all its banks during the whole time of harvest), that the waters which came down from upstream stood still, and rose in a heap very far away at Adam, the city that is beside Zaretan. So the waters that went down into the Sea of the Arabah, the Salt Sea, failed, and were cut off; and the people crossed over opposite Jericho. Then the priests who bore the ark of the covenant of the Lord stood firm on dry ground in the midst of the Jordan; and all Israel crossed over on dry ground, until all the people had crossed completely over the Jordan. (Joshua 3:14-17)

This location[44] is exciting, and we described it earlier as the location where Joshua led the people of Israel into the Promised Land. We will also visit it later as the site of Christ's baptism and as a description of one of the more exciting border crossings we made. After crossing the Jordan, it is no more than 2–3 kilometers to Gilgal where Israel camped for about fourteen years. Israel's beginning was here at Gilgal. When Joshua arrived at Gilgal, the Angelic Captain of the Lord's Host commanded Joshua to "Take your sandal off your foot, for the place where you stand is holy" (Joshua 5:15).

Then the Lord said to Joshua, "This day I have rolled away the reproach of Egypt from you." Therefore the name of the place is called Gilgal to this day. Now the children of Israel camped in Gilgal, and kept the Passover on the fourteenth day of the month at twilight on the plains of Jericho. (Joshua 5:9-10)

Despite the tremendous importance of Gilgal to the Jewish people, its location had long been lost and was rediscovered relatively recently. The honor of 'finding' Gilgal fell to Vendyl Jones whom we met in an earlier chapter as we circled the Dead Sea region. Jones believed that the location of Joshua's Gilgal was east and south of Jericho instead of being north as shown on present-day maps. He therefore undertook an ambitious state-of-the-art, infrared (thermal), remote sensing project in 1994, intended to uncover the location of Gilgal.[45] Thermal remote sensing is a method for sensing temperature differentials in the ground for the purpose of locating specific objects or anomalies. This is accomplished through a special type of infrared aerial photography. Soil that has been used for roads or that has been compacted in any way becomes denser than the surrounding soil, and these differentials can be easily isolated.

Investigators from the Ben Gurion University in the Negev, the Israeli Institute of Geology, and from Lockheed, Mobil Oil, NASA, and the Army

---

[44] We will return to this location later, but the place of crossing the River Jordan is very close to the Allenby Bridge border crossing, the place where Elijah ascended to heaven in a chariot of fire, and the place of Jesus's baptism.

[45] The description that follows comes primarily from:
http://www.geocities.com/Athens/Crete/9923/ark.html
http://rense.com/general2/ark.htm
http://www.vendyljones.org.il/Gilgal.htm

Corps of Engineers reviewed remote sensing data of Joshua's suspected Gilgal area from the American Landsat, the French Spot, and Russian Radar satellites. It was here that they saw for the first time the suspected location of Gilgal. Subsequent filter and enhancement techniques were applied to the imagery to produce the detail necessary to ultimately identify and map the exact location for on-site exploration.

Gilgal today is uninspiring, sitting as it does on a barren plane west of the River Jordan. It is located just off the side of the Jericho bypass road. Uninspiring it may be, but it has a rich history. This is where Israel first camped after entering the Promised Land; this is where the Passover was first celebrated; and this was the staging post for one of most famous battles in history — the battle of Jericho — and of course the Ark of God was central to the battle plan. I can only imagine what the residents of Jericho must have been thinking. Here was a strange procession coming from Gilgal towards the city led by a group of priests blowing trumpets, followed by the Ark, followed by the fighting men. This strange procession encircled the city of Jericho and returned to Gilgal! Now what was that all about? Even more strange, they repeated the strange procession for five more days!

You shall march around the city, all you men of war; you shall go all around the city once. This you shall do six days. And seven priests shall bear seven trumpets of rams' horns before the ark. But the seventh day you shall march around the city seven times, and the priests shall blow the trumpets. It shall come to pass, when they make a long blast with the ram's horn, and when you hear the sound of the trumpet, that all the people shall shout with a great shout; then the wall of the city will fall down flat. And the people shall go up every man straight before him." (Joshua 6:3-5)

At this point, there is a strange twist in the biblical narrative. Although the Ark of God was encamped at Gilgal, and was being paraded around Jericho in chapter 6, suddenly in Joshua chapter 8, the Ark is forty-five kilometers north on Mount Ebal.

Now Joshua built an altar to the Lord God of Israel in Mount Ebal, as Moses the servant of the Lord had commanded the children of Israel, as it is written in the Book of the Law of Moses: "an altar of whole stones over which no man has wielded an iron tool." And they offered on it burnt offerings to the Lord, and sacrificed peace offerings. And there, in the presence of the children of Israel, he wrote on the stones a copy of the law of Moses, which he had written. Then all Israel, with their elders and officers and judges, stood on either side of the ark before the priests, the Levites, who bore the ark of the covenant of the Lord, the stranger as well as he who was born among them. Half of them were in front of Mount Gerizim and half of them

in front of Mount Ebal, as Moses the servant of the Lord had commanded before,
that they should bless the people of Israel. (Joshua 8:30-33)

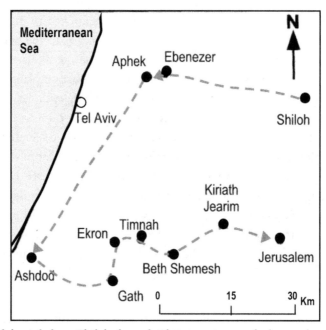

Journey of the Ark from Shiloh through Phiistine cities and ultimately to Jerusalem.

I had read in the Bible Archaeology Review (BAR) that Professor Adam
Zertal[46] at the University of Haifa had uncovered what he proposed to be the
altar that Joshua built on Mount Ebal. Mt. Ebal is immediately to the north,
and overlooking the city of Nablus, the site of biblical Shechem. Armed with my
copy of BAR, which had many photographs of the site, one of my PhD graduate
students and I headed to Nablus from Jerusalem. The journey to Nablus is a
cautious trip because this in an intensely anti-Israeli and anti-Jewish region. In
Nablus we asked numerous people about the altar, but we met consistently with
blank stares. Even with the color photographs, we were getting no idea of the
location of this altar on Mt Ebal. No one we spoke to knew anything.

Finally, we met a doctor in Sychar, a suburb of Nablus, who spoke good
English and seemed to recognize some of our panoramic photographs. He pointed
us in a reasonable direction, which brought us a little way up the mountain. Here
we met another young man who excitedly affirmed that he knew the site and
would take us there.

---

[46] Zertal, A. (1985). Has Joshua's altar been found on Mt. Ebal? *Biblical Archaeology Review.* (Jan/
Feb ,11:1), 26.

After bumping our rental car along a rough track for about five kilometers, we parked and got out to walk. This young man and my student were younger and fitter, and they charged up the hill with me dragging behind. After about thirty minutes, we arrived — but it was the wrong site! Many Palestinians have a character trait that is amusing. If asked for directions, and they don't know, they are too embarrassed to admit it; they panic, and they'll tell you anything and send you to the wrong place rather than say, "I don't know!" Honor is much more important than facts.

We finally shook ourselves free from our Arab guides and decided that we would try another tact. It seemed from one of the photographs that there was a drivable track close to the altar. We reasoned that if we started to drive around the mountain and kept turning on any road or track that led farther up, then we might luck out. We drove completely around the mountain and found nothing! On our circuit we ended up in a little village, Asira ash-Shamaliya, to the north-east of the mountain.

We stopped and showed an elderly man our photographs. He seemed to act rather strangely and indicated that we should follow him. We went around the corner and parked the car as he indicated, and we followed him into a building where about seven or eight men were sitting. Now we were getting nervous; whatever possessed us to agree to follow this man and enter this building? This was apparently a 'town hall' meeting, but they were clearly very suspicious of us and asked many questions. We got particularly nervous because, although they understood us when we gave some answers, they claimed not to understand at all the important times. Who are you? Why are you here? Do you speak Hebrew? Why are you driving an Israeli (yellow license plates) car? Where do you live? Where are you staying? After fifteen minutes, we excused ourselves, but we had still no idea where the altar was located. A year later I discovered that the altar could almost certainly be seen from this same village and was probably less than a ten-minute drive! We finally gave up because we had to return to Jerusalem before dark.

I wrote to Professor Zertal a few weeks later who kindly sent me a rough, hand-drawn map. A year later, we went hunting for the altar once again. It took us some time, but after we followed the map and made a few approximate judgments, we finally spotted the altar after about 1½ hours. It was exhilarating to find, to see, and to actually stand on this altar and ponder about the events that happened here. There is a strong possibility that this is the location where Joshua gathered half of the Children of Israel and pronounced the judgments that God would administer to them if they were disobedient to His commandments. And straight across the valley to the east, perhaps no more than five kilometers, we could see a bump on top of a high hill, the oak at Moreh, the place where Abram first camped when he entered the land of Canaan.

I wanted to show Joshua's altar to my friend and colleague, so yet another year later we were to make the trip again. However, my colleague was a government employee with the Nature Reserves Authority. To avoid risk, unknown to me, she arranged an escort for us of two jeeps and eight, armed Israeli soldiers! I asked one of the soldiers if I could have a photograph taken with his gun. He reluctantly agreed but all the other soldiers hid out of camera-shot while I held the gun.

DETOUR EIGHT:
JOSHUA'S ALTAR ON MOUNT EBAL

I returned to the altar again in 2018 with our son-in-law Fergus. We approached from our usual direction which is up a very long steep hill on the Western slope of Mount Ebal. We had rented a rickety old car with a manual gearshift from an Arab rental agency in Jerusalem, and we weren't certain that this car would make it to the top — it struggled and more than once jumped out of gear. This is the only paved road on the mountain, and it's also the access route to the Israeli military post on the summit of Mount Ebal. About one hundred meters before the military camp a rough track turns off to the right and we bumped along for about two kilometers, circling around the military base to a point where the track takes a sharp right and a steep downhill.

Fergus had the car in low gear and relied heavily on the brakes as the car went downhill doing more skidding than driving on the loose surface. We looked at each other and simultaneously thought, *"this is not a good idea,"* especially as we were about to navigate a deep rut that ran diagonally across the track, presumably created by heavy rainfall. We knew if our wheels got into this rut we were in deep trouble! With the plan to go back uphill, I got out of the car, Fergus put the car in reverse, released the handbrake, and with all the engine speed he could muster this car wasn't going uphill but insisted on lots of skidding on the steep stony track. Given that Fergus is heavier and a lot stronger, we switched positions so that he pushed while I was driving. It worked! We managed to reverse about fifty meters up hill, parked the car, and walked the last kilometer to the altar.

On our return journey, we were back on the steep hill on the Western slope when Fergus said, "I think the army is following us." Sure enough, a military vehicle pulled alongside and questioned us. They were only young lads, spoke good English, and were courteous and chatted to us through an open window in their vehicle. We explained to them that we had been to Joshua's altar and were next going to visit the site of ancient Shechem which happens to be in Nablus. They made it clear that we weren't going to Nablus today because: "This is a dangerous area." But we had a plan up our sleeve. We left the soldiers and continued along our road with the intent of taking the next left towards Nablus. This didn't work because the soldiers were driving about one hundred meters behind us. The next several left turns also didn't work because the soldiers continued to follow us — this continued for about fifteen kilometers until we were on the main road to Jerusalem and well past Nablus. Drat! Foiled! The reason for the soldiers' insistence was because trouble had been brewing in the Gaza Strip with threats of thousands of Gazans charging at the security fence in an attempt to breach it. Unrest of this nature can quickly spread through Hebron, Ramallah, and Nablus, and it wouldn't have been a good idea for us to be there.

About fourteen years after Joshua arrived at Gilgal, the land was redeemed, and the tribes received their inheritance and moved from Gilgal into their designated territories. The Tabernacle was moved to the center of the land at Shiloh, which is about thirty kilometers north of Jericho. The Scriptures tell us that Shiloh is "north of Bethel, on the east side of the highway that goes up from Bethel to Shechem, and south of Lebonah" (Judges 21:19), and that is exactly where it still is!

> *Then all the children of Israel, that is, all the people, went up and came to the house of God and wept. They sat there before the Lord and fasted that day until evening; and they offered burnt offerings and peace offerings before the Lord. So the children of Israel inquired of the Lord (the ark of the covenant of God was there [in Shiloh] in those days, ...* (Judges 20:26-27)

Our first attempt to find Shiloh was in February 1993. We had been living in Jerusalem for about six months, and because the West Bank had been restless, we had little opportunity to visit this region. We made arrangements with Pastor Musa to take us for a day trip north of Jerusalem. Musa arranged for a taxi to pick us up in Jerusalem, and during the next seven hours, we visited or at least tried to find Ai, Bethel, Shiloh, Shechem, Jacob's well, Nablus, Jenin, Dothan, and Samaria.

This was a wonderful day during which we had no food because it was Ramadan. Our taxi broke down in Nablus, Israeli jets frightened the life out of us as they broke the sound barrier over Shechem, and we were stopped by military police at Dothan for taking video. Not bad for a single day!

As we headed north from Jerusalem, the first city we passed through was Ramallah. Later, we arrived at Shiloh, which hadn't been developed yet for tourists, so finding it wasn't easy. We came to the approximate location as indicated on our maps, but after driving around local roadways and tracks for more than half an hour we finally gave up. Overlooking the site is the modern Jewish community of Shiloh, but it was barricaded like Fort Knox, so there was no way to ask anyone for directions. It was only upon our return to Jerusalem and being able to see more detailed military maps that we realized we had literally driven completely around the mound of ancient Shiloh but failed to see it — probably because there was nothing to see!

Later, we rented a car from Jerusalem and our whole family headed north once again in search of Shiloh. In hindsight, this was a rather silly thing to do. The natives were quite restless during this Intifada, we had a rental car whose insurance coverage didn't extend to the West Bank, and no one knew where we were (we never told anyone when we were going on such trips because of the inevitable attempts to prevent us). Like our previous trip into this region with Pastor Musa, this was also an exciting day — we had stones thrown at us at Michmash, ran a gauntlet of stones at Ai, and we were quite frightened when we got into a little village and the road came to a dead end. This little village seemed to have a lot of children, a lot of Palestinian flags painted on gable walls, and a lot of unprintable anti-Israeli slogans that were strangely printed in English.

We learned one survival tactic very quickly while traveling in troublesome areas. If we weren't sure where we were, or a particular direction to take, the best tactic was to stop the car, get out, and attempt to talk to the local people even though we didn't know a word of Arabic. This would inevitably and rapidly draw a crowd, all of whom either wanted to help or wanted to know what was going on. In a matter of moments, a threatening environment is diffused. On most occasions, someone emerges from the crowd who can speak English, and all is saved. It was always amusing to us, and even more amusing to the local people, that anyone would be interested in finding these heaps of rubble and piles of rocks that are a vestige of some ancient glory.

Finally we reached the area of Shiloh, and now we knew exactly where to go. Unfortunately, the road had been blocked! So, not to be deterred, we simply drove along another tack, but this one had been closed by an enormous yellow metal gate as part of the safety barrier surrounding the Jewish Community. One more possibility was available, and we drove in a clockwise direction along a rough track that led to the backside of the mound. This too was blocked but only half-heartedly. Someone had placed a small pile of dirt and stones, about thirty centimeters high, right across the track. This was clearly meant to send a small message but not a strong warning! We looked at each other, and we all knew what was required. We maneuvered over the little ridge and drove a few hundred meters to our spot. Ironically, there was virtually nothing to see at Shiloh, just a few virtually unrecognizable ruins scattered sporadically over this quite small hill. But forget the stuff to see — this was the site of Shiloh; this is where the Ark of God sat in the tabernacle for between 350–400 years; this is where Hannah brought her son Samuel to be under the watchful eye of Eli the High Priest, and this is where Samuel was commissioned to the service of God:

> And it came to pass at that time, while Eli was lying down in his place, and when his eyes had begun to grow so dim that he could not see, and before the lamp of God went out in the tabernacle of the Lord where the ark of God was, and while Samuel was lying down, that the Lord called Samuel. And he answered, "Here I am!" (1 Samuel 3:2-4)

But we can't leave Shiloh without a description of our next visit in 1997. We had been part of a tour group visiting Israel and Jordan for two weeks. It was our last full day, and while many of the group wanted to go shopping in the old city of Jerusalem, about six others wanted to go into the region of Samaria. I went to the Damascus Gate and arranged a mini-van taxi for the following day. This was an Arab taxi driven by a Palestinian, so we knew that we would be safe in the Palestinian areas that we wanted to visit. We went to Gibeah, Gibeon, Michmash, Bethel, and Ai, and were now heading north to Shiloh. Our driver was going quite fast. In fact, he was going very fast, and ahead of us we could see an Israeli police vehicle.

Not surprisingly, we were pulled over to the side of the road. Our driver jumped out and walked back about thirty meters to the police vehicle. They seemed to talk for a long time. As leader of the group, I decided to get out and go join the conversation. It was getting intense, and our driver and the police officer were exchanging some very heated and loud words. Most of this was either in Arabic or Hebrew, with a few English words thrown in, but it was turning nasty. It turned out that our driver wasn't licensed to carry passengers, and the officer was imposing an on-the-spot fine of $100 USD — we were paying the driver

$120 USD for the day. The exchange continued to intensify, and at one stage the officer grabbed our driver; without thinking, I jumped in to separate them. Clearly, the officer wished that I hadn't been there. Anyway, when I explained to the officer that we were a Christian group visiting Jewish holy sites, he settled down. Often, Christian groups traveling in the West Bank are viewed with suspicion because they often have a pro-Palestinian political agenda. The fine was paid, we were on our way, and within ten minutes we arrived at Shiloh.

Shiloh had now been changed and actually had constructed pathways and explanatory signboards for tourists! It was particularly special to stand on a flat area at the bottom of the mound. Archaeologists believe this was probably the location where the Ark sat in the tabernacle for the 350-plus years that it remained at Shiloh. What a thrill! Likely, the old priest Eli stood on this spot, as did Hannah, and Samuel — exciting! It was also in this town where old Eli fell from his chair and died when he received the news about the death of his two sons.

The early chapters of 1 Samuel talk about the early childhood of Samuel and the not-so-flattering account of Eli the priest and his family. The Ark of the Covenant was housed at the tabernacle in Shiloh under the care of Eli the priest. The Philistines were fighting against the Israelites, and Israel was being defeated. In an effort to turn their fortunes, and trusting in the 'magic power' of the Ark rather than God, the Ark was brought from Shiloh to the Israelites encamped at Ebenezer; the Philistines were camped at Aphek. The Ark was taken into battle against the Philistines, the Israelites suffered a crushing defeat, and during the subsequent fighting the Philistines captured the Ark. This story of the Ark's journey is recorded in 1 Samuel 4-6.

> *...Now Israel went out to battle against the Philistines, and encamped beside Ebenezer; and the Philistines encamped in Aphek. Then the Philistines put themselves in battle array against Israel. And when they joined battle, Israel was defeated by the Philistines, who killed about four thousand men of the army in the field. And when the people had come into the camp, the elders of Israel said, "Why has the Lord defeated us today before the Philistines? Let us bring the ark of the covenant of the Lord from Shiloh to us, that when it comes among us it may save us from the hand of our enemies." So the people sent to Shiloh, that they might bring from there the ark of the covenant of the Lord of hosts, who dwells between the cherubim...* (1 Samuel 4:1-4)

The capture of the Ark of the Covenant, and the subsequent death of Eli's two sons, Hophni and Phinehas, is one of the saddest, darkest days in Israel's history.

... and Israel was defeated... There was a very great slaughter, and there fell of Israel thirty thousand foot soldiers. Also the ark of God was captured; and the two sons of Eli, Hophni and Phinehas, died. (1 Samuel 4:10-11)

Ebenezer and Aphek are only about 2–3 kilometers apart, and they lie where the Plain of Sharon begins to rise into the foothills — Aphek on the plains, Ebenezer in the foothills. The ruins of Ebenezer are in an open area in the community of Rosh Ha'Ayin, and from here the skyline of Tel Aviv can be seen clearly in the distance. Aphek was renamed Antipatris by Herod the Great after his father Antipater. The large mound is occupied by the remains of a large Turkish citadel built on the remains of a Crusader castle; here we are only about ten kilometers from the city center of Tel Aviv.

Then the Philistines took the ark of God and brought it from Ebenezer to Ashdod. When the Philistines took the ark of God, they brought it into the house of Dagon and set it by Dagon. And when the people of Ashdod arose early in the morning, there was Dagon, fallen on its face to the earth before the ark of the Lord... (1 Samuel 5:1-3)

The journey from Aphek to Ashdod drives through the coastal plain. The coastal plain is low, open, fertile, and is one of the most highly cultivated regions in Israel. We can only guess what the original vegetation of this area looked like because it's been cultivated since biblical times. As we followed the journey of the Ark to Ashdod, and ultimately back to Jerusalem, there was little by way of excitement.

Today, most of these sites are little more than large mounds sitting in the middle of a field. Ancient Ashdod is only a few kilometers south of modern Ashdod. It was a little difficult to find, but when we did all we had to do was to park the car in the middle of a few bushes, squeeze through a hole in a rather rickety fence, and go through an orchard strung with danger signs. It was rather sad to see Ashdod in its current state. This was one of the major Philistines cities and was the site of major excavations. Unfortunately, the excavators did what they had to do and simply walked off and left the site to crumble. Today it is little more than an overgrown series of mounds and hollows. More modern excavations require that sites be backfilled after archaeologists have done their work to preserve the original.

Therefore they sent and gathered to themselves all the lords of the Philistines, and said, "What shall we do with the ark of the God of Israel?" And they answered, "Let the ark of the God of Israel be carried away to Gath." (1 Samuel 5:8)

It was a challenge finding Gath because archaeologists have changed their minds on a few occasions about its location. On one occasion, we had driven our rental car almost to the top of Tel Erani, which is close to the city of Qiryat Gat. Tel Erani was formerly proposed to be the site of Gath. We returned to the car, drove back to the main road, and failed to stop at a railroad crossing. Almost immediately, we were flagged down by a police car. Of course, the children were excited, and Evelyn and I smiled at each other because we had a reasonable idea of what would happen next — we could speak no Hebrew, the officer could probably speak no English, he would probably then raise his voice and shout at us in Hebrew, thinking this might help us to understand him, frantically try to explain what we had done using sign language, while we would smile at him and pretend that we had absolutely no idea what he was trying to communicate. Then, probably after three or four minutes of communication-in-ignorance, the officer would probably realize the hopelessness of the situation and wave us along. And that is exactly what happened, as we guessed it would, because we had been there before — and done that before!

All one has to do is to be polite, smile lots, pretend to be totally bewildered, keep tossing in words like Jerusalem, or Beersheba, or Sede Boqer, or Canada, and finally your persistence will win out. Previously, we had been stopped by the police for passing a slow-moving Arab produce truck on a solid white line, at the Good Samaritan's Inn on the road from Jerusalem to Jericho. We had also been stopped by the army for traveling without identification on the road to Jerusalem from Jericho. And just a few days earlier we were stopped by the army for straying into a sensitive military zone on the Egyptian border near Nizzana. We had lots of exciting times driving in Israel, which will be related in appropriate chapters.

Anyway, in our story, we will next visit Gath. This was the home of the famous Goliath. One day while we were visiting the site of Goliath's famous battle with David, we tried to trace the road of the fleeing Philistines from the battlefield back to the city of Gath. According to our maps, there was a disused road most of the way. We followed this route along tracks, through grain fields, and on many occasions, the road was so overgrown that there was barely enough room for our car to fit between the shrubby edges. But after about thirty-five minutes we could see our destination in the distance, and ironically we emerged on to a brand new road near the site. This new road was a recent construction to a major power plant and hadn't been marked yet on maps. So although Gath is much more accessible than we had made it, nevertheless, it was interesting to follow the route of the fleeing Philistines. More recently, Gath has been upgraded with signage and explanation boards, and a nature trail winds its way around the mound, up to the top, and back to the parking lot.

> *So it was, after they had carried it away, that the hand of the Lord was against the city [of Gath] with a very great destruction; and He struck the men of the city, both small and great, and tumors broke out on them. Therefore they sent the ark of God to Ekron... there was a deadly destruction throughout all the city; the hand of God was very heavy there. And the men who did not die were stricken with the tumors...* (1 Samuel 5:9-12)

In 1993 Ekron was easy to access. All one has to do is to go to the kibbutz Rivadim and drive a kilometer or so through agricultural fields to the ruins of the Philistine city. Many years later, with the construction of the new Highway 6, Ekron isn't so accessible, and unless you are desperate for something to do, go somewhere else — Ekron has very little to offer and is a mess.

> *Now therefore, make a new cart, take two milk cows which have never been yoked, and hitch the cows to the cart; and take their calves home, away from them. Then take the ark of the Lord and set it on the cart; and put the articles of gold which you are returning to Him as a trespass offering in a chest by its side. Then send it away, and let it go. And watch: if it goes up the road to its own territory, to Beth Shemesh, then He has done us this great evil... Then the cows headed straight for the road to Beth Shemesh...* (1 Samuel 6:7-9, 12)

The journey of the Ark from Ekron to Beth Shemesh inevitably passed by Timnah even though the city is not mentioned in the bible in the context of this story. This city and the surrounding area is where Samson met his first wife, killed the young lion, romanced with Delilah, and had his eyes gouged out. It was also in this area that he pulled off one of his more miraculous stunts:

> *Then Samson went and caught three hundred foxes; and he took torches, turned the foxes tail to tail, and put a torch between each pair of tails. When he had set the torches on fire, he let the foxes go into the standing grain of the Philistines, and burned up both the shocks and the standing grain, as well as the vineyards and olive groves.* (Judges 15:4-5)

Interestingly, today the major crops in the valley today are still grain, vineyards, and olives — but we didn't notice any young lions lurking in the bushes! From Timnah, it is a mere six kilometers to Beth Shemesh along the valley of the River Sorek. Beth Shemesh is one of our favorite sites. The ruins of the ancient city lie on both sides of the main road beside today's modern city with the same name, on a raised spur of land overlooking the Sorek valley. From this vantage point, you can see Zorah the birthplace of Samson, the Brook Sorek, and in the distance is Timnah.

As we stood there looking west down the broad Sorek valley, we could imagine the Ark of God coming towards us from Timnah, on a cart being pulled by two young cows. We could also imagine the people in their fields harvesting their wheat and rejoicing at the return of the Ark (1 Samuel 6:10-13). Having reached Beth Shemesh, the Ark was now back in Israelite territory. Archaeologists have discovered a structure at Beth Shemesh that resembles a temple from nearly three thousand years ago. Inside the building they discovered a large stone slab which the excavators believe may have been the table used as a resting spot for the Ark:

> *Then the cart came into the field of Joshua of Beth Shemesh, and stood there; a large stone was there. So they split the wood of the cart and offered the cows as a burnt offering to the Lord. The Levites took down the ark of the Lord and the chest that was with it, in which were the articles of gold, and put them on the large stone. Then the men of Beth Shemesh offered burnt offerings and made sacrifices the same day to the Lord.* (1 Samuel 6:14-15)

Emotionally, this is near the top of the list. We sat down on this great stone and realized that we were possibly sitting on the stone upon which the Ark of God rested three thousand years earlier. But that is the romantic image. Unfortunately, there is another not-so-romantic ending to the story at Beth Shemesh. Some men looked inside the Ark and by doing so made God very unhappy:

> *Then He struck the men of Beth Shemesh, because they had looked into the ark of the Lord. He struck fifty thousand and seventy men of the people, and the people lamented because the Lord had struck the people with a great slaughter. And the men of Beth Shemesh said, "Who is able to stand before this holy Lord God? And to whom shall it go up from us?"* (1 Samuel 6:19-20)

This is one of the most poignant and enduring questions in all Scripture: "Who can stand in the presence of the Lord, this holy God?" (1 Samuel 6:20, NIV).

Samson was born three kilometers from Beth Shemesh at Zorah. In a field at the bottom of the hill of Zorah is a rock altar, just as the Hebrews would have built an altar in the time of the judges. Many believe that this could have been the altar where the angel of the Lord appeared to Manoah and promised him a son — Samson. We describe our frustrating and relentless efforts to locate this altar in a previous chapter on Israel's Judges.

So far, the Ark is five-for-five. It was brought to five cities and major trouble followed it each time: Ebenezer, Ashdod, Gath, Ekron and Beth Shemesh. Now it moved once again:

Then the men of Kirjath Jearim came and took the ark of the Lord, and brought it into the house of Abinadab on the hill, and consecrated Eleazar his son to keep the ark of the Lord. So it was that the ark remained in Kirjath Jearim a long time; it was there twenty years... (1 Samuel 7:1-2)

It's a short journey from Beth Shemesh to Kirjath Jearim, and the early part of the road is a pleasant journey mostly through pine forests planted by the Jewish National Fund. On meeting the main Tel Aviv-Jerusalem freeway we head east into the hills towards Kirjath Jearim. This is a narrow gorge, and it's been a major supply and transport route for centuries. Within a short distance, one sees burned and bent frames of many armored vehicles alongside the road. These have been left as a monument to the brave drivers and crews of convoys that were supplying besieged Jerusalem during the 1948 War of Independence. Soon we reach Kirjath Jearim thirteen kilometers west of Jerusalem. Today it is called Abu Gosh.

A large Roman Catholic monastery and church of Notre Dame de l'Arche de l'Alliance, which means the church of Our Lady of the Ark of the Covenant, is said to be built on the former site of the home of Abinadab. This church boasts one of the largest statues of the Virgin Mary and the infant Jesus anywhere in Israel, and it is easily visible from the main motorway. Inside, the church is quite plain, but the acoustics are amazing. Few tour groups visit this church, but those that do are rewarded by having an empty church and the opportunity to sing without pressure from other tourists waiting to get in. For any tour group, it is worth visiting the site just to sing in the church. The Ark remained at Kirjath Jearim until David brought it to Mount Zion in Jerusalem.

So they set the ark of God on a new cart, and brought it out of the house of Abinadab, which was on the hill; and Uzzah and Ahio, the sons of Abinadab, drove the new cart... And when they came to Nachon's threshing floor, Uzzah put out his hand to the ark of God and took hold of it, for the oxen stumbled. Then the anger of the Lord was aroused against Uzzah, and God struck him there for his error; and he died there by the ark of God. (2 Samuel 6:3, 6-7)

Now as the ark of the Lord came into the City of David, Michal, Saul's daughter, looked through a window and saw King David leaping and whirling before the Lord; and she despised him in her heart. So they brought the ark of the Lord, and set it in its place in the midst of the tabernacle that David had erected for it... (2 Samuel 6:16-17)

David placed the Ark in a tent prepared for it. David had intended to build a temple, in which the Ark was to find its place because before this it had always found its resting-place in a tent. But God would not allow this. David's son Solomon would ultimately build the temple and place the Ark of the Covenant in the Holy of Holies, where it was placed under the wings of two mighty cherubim images.

> *Now Solomon assembled the elders of Israel and all the heads of the tribes, the chief fathers of the children of Israel, to King Solomon in Jerusalem, that they might bring up the ark of the covenant of the Lord from the City of David, which is Zion... So all the elders of Israel came, and the priests took up the ark... Then the priests brought in the ark of the covenant of the Lord to its place, into the inner sanctuary of the temple, to the Most Holy Place, under the wings of the cherubim.* (1 Kings 8:1,3,6)

Nothing is known of what became of the Ark. It disappeared when Nebuchadnezzar's armies destroyed Jerusalem in 586 BC and wasn't available when the second and third temples were built. So what happened to the Ark? Many books, mostly unscholarly speculation, have been written in response to this question. Of the many theories that abound, the Ark is perhaps buried beneath the Temple Mount in Jerusalem, or was melted down and destroyed by the Babylonians, hidden in a cave near Qumran at the Dead Sea, or perhaps even sitting in a church in Ethiopia. It is an unsatisfactory way to end a wonderful story. The Ark was the very presence of God, the Shekinah glory, the throne of God, it led the people of Israel through the wilderness, it crossed the River Jordan on dry land, it encircled Jericho before Jericho fell to Joshua and his armies, it followed the route we described in this chapter, it was placed in the tabernacle and then finally in the Holy of Holies in Solomon's magnificent temple — and then it just disappeared!

DETOUR NINE:
IS GRACE REALLY ALL THAT AMAZING?

We sing Amazing Grace at many national events and special occasions but few really believe that grace is amazing. We tend to take grace for granted because this is God's usual; consequently, grace no longer amazes us. Because we expect grace, we are surprised when God takes action and punishes sin.

When the Ark of God entered Beth Shemesh many men (seventy – ESV, NIV; 50,070 – KJV, NKJV, NASB) were put to death for looking into the Ark. Later, David had organized a huge celebration for the whole country and he had a new cart made to carry the Ark. They were taking the Ark back to its rightful place; the Philistines had captured it, but now it was coming home. This was a jubilant procession with musicians and instruments.

This parade was moving along wonderfully until one of the oxen stumbled and the Ark began to slide, in danger of falling off the cart. Instinctively, Uzzah put his hand on the Ark to prevent it from falling, and he was instantly executed (2 Samuel 6:3, 6-7). Many have tried to explain the sudden execution of Uzzah as a flash of anger by God, and similar episodes in the Old Testament are seemingly incompatible with the New Testament portrait of the love of God revealed in Jesus Christ. But they haven't read Numbers 4 — the Ark had rings and poles so that the priests never came into direct contact with it. The Ark was holy, and under no circumstances should anyone touch the Ark. If anyone touched the Ark, they must die — and Uzzah touched the Ark.

In Leviticus 10:1–6 we have the account of two sons of Aaron, Nadab and Abihu, offering strange fire to the Lord. We aren't told specifically what this strange fire was, but whatever it was, it certainly didn't please God. These two young priests offered a new way of worship and a new way of doing things, and God killed them. The reason God did this is embedded in Moses' response to Aaron when he said, "This is what the Lord spoke, saying: By those who come near Me I must be regarded as holy; And before all the people I must be glorified" (Leviticus 10:3). Simple. "I must be regarded as holy and … I must be glorified." In Romans 6:14, Paul says, "you are not under law but under grace." This means that in Christ we are no longer relying on our own merits (under law) but relying totally on the merits of Christ (under grace). In fact, Paul is saying that the law condemns us because we cannot possibly attain its requirements. Amazing grace really is amazing!

———————

IX.
ISRAEL'S PROPHETS

Israel's prophets were a diverse group with little in common. Isaiah was an officer of the state, Elijah a political outcast, Jeremiah in office for decades, Haggai for only a few months, Elisha performed miracles, and Malachi and Jonah did not. Elijah was a true child of the desert. Elisha was a civilized man, preferring companionship, dwelling in cities, and often in close connection with kings. However, the prophets all had in common a distinct call of God to the office, and each of them declared the Word of God. They didn't all leave a geographic footprint in the land, and for some, we are only told where they were born or buried. But for those that did leave a trace, let's go on a journey.

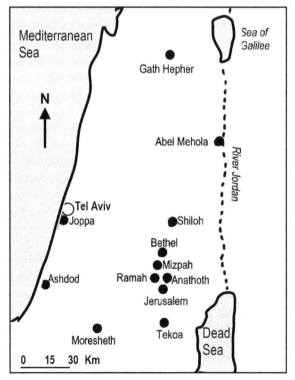

Some of the major locations of the ministry of Israel's Prophets.

SAMUEL

Samuel was the last judge of Israel and the earliest of the great Hebrew prophets. He led his people against their Philistine oppressors, and when he was an old man, Samuel anointed Saul as the first king of Israel. He later anointed David as Saul's successor, and he is recognized as one of the greatest leaders of Israel.

RAMAH

Samuel was born and buried at Ramah, which is only a short distance northwest of Jerusalem just beyond the Ramot Allon neighborhood.[47]

> *Then they rose early in the morning and worshiped before the Lord, and returned and came to their house at Ramah. And Elkanah knew Hannah his wife, and the Lord remembered her. So it came to pass in the process of time that Hannah conceived and bore a son, and called his name Samuel...* (1 Samuel 1:19-20)

The site is easily identified by a prominent mosque perched atop the hill. Although there are some recent excavations the site does not have much to offer archaeologically — but geography is another matter. On our many visits to Ramah, it always puzzled us that busloads of tourists would arrive, be disgorged close to the mosque, race inside, peer through a dimly-lit grill to get a not-very-good view of the Islamic cenotaph commemorating Samuel, then out the door, and away. What were these people doing? What were their tour guides doing? Didn't they know that there is a small, but brightly lit Jewish memorial tomb downstairs?

The most important thing that these rushing tourists miss is the view from the roof of the mosque. Immediately upon entering the rather dull cavernous mosque, there is a long staircase to the roof. To the southeast is an excellent view over some of Jerusalem's newer neighborhoods. To the southwest is the village of Qubeibeh, (a possible location of New Testament Emmaus). To the north and west, we overlook Gibeon (the site on many biblical events), and the Valley of Gibeon is the setting for the wonderful pursuit of the Amorite kings by Joshua. This is also where Joshua prayed that the sun would stand still until he defeated his enemies. And then there's the view to the east; in the distance, perhaps four or five kilometers away, we can see what remains of the ill-fated attempt by King Hussein of Jordan to build a palace on Gibeah, Saul's royal capital. It was here that Saul tried to kill David. The story picks up in 1 Samuel 19:11 and describes David's escape, how he came to visit Samuel at Ramah, and how he later went to the priests at Nob. Nob was quite likely located on the site of the Hebrew

---

[47] Other identifications of Ramah are today's city of Ramallah, and Er-Ram mid-way between Jerusalem and Ramallah.

University on Mount Scopus. From the top of the mosque at Ramah, we can visibly trace David's trek from Gibeah to Ramah to Nob — poor tourists!

SHILOH

Shiloh is twenty kilometers north of Ramallah on route 60, and sixteen kilometers "north of Bethel and east of the road that goes from Bethel to Shechem, and to the south of Lebonah" (Judges 21:19).

> *Now when she had weaned him, she took him up with her, with three bulls, one ephah of flour, and a skin of wine, and brought him to the house of the Lord in Shiloh. And the child was young. Then they slaughtered a bull, and brought the child to Eli.* (1 Samuel 1:24-25)

The first time we went searching for the site of Shiloh was with Pastor Musa in 1993. We were in a rented West Bank taxi with a Palestinian driver so we felt quite safe. The main road from Jerusalem, through Ramallah and on to Nablus (Biblical Shechem) was located a few kilometers to the west of Shiloh, just as the Scriptures describe. We turned off the main road and followed the signs to the Jewish community of Shiloh. From our maps, we knew that the ancient site was just north of the new community. We saw the small hill to the north of the community but didn't realize that the ruins were on the hill. Instead, we drove around the hill a few times and explored a few neighboring tracks, and of course, we found nothing. Our other visits to Shiloh were more successful and have been described earlier when we were following the Journey of the Ark. Today, it is totally set up for tourists including a multimedia theater on the summit of the mound and overlooking the likely location of the tabernacle.

BETHEL, GILGAL AND MIZPAH

These three cities were on Samuel's circuit as a judge of Israel.

> *He went from year to year on a circuit to Bethel, Gilgal, and Mizpah, and judged Israel in all those places. But he always returned to Ramah, for his home was there. There he judged Israel, and there he built an altar to the Lord.* (1 Samuel 7:16-17)

DETOUR TEN:
I KNEW THEY WERE GOING TO SHOOT YOU

Only three kilometers south of Mizpah on the main road going to Jerusalem from Ramallah, there is an Israeli checkpoint close to the former Jerusalem airport and the Qalandiya refugee camp. In 2017, we were in Jerusalem, and we hired a Palestinian driver to take us to various biblical sites in Samaria. At the end of the day, the driver was to drop us off at this Ramallah checkpoint from which we would catch the bus into Jerusalem. As we drove through Ramallah, passed Mizpah on our right, and made our way towards the checkpoint, it was a typically noisy and chaotic Middle Eastern city. The driver stopped about fifty meters from the checkpoint, and we all got out of his car.

Not too far from us there was a lot of screaming and shouting and someone seemed to have a major disagreement with a taxi driver. We took little notice because this type of chaos, noise, and general mayhem is quite normal. There were three or four lines of cars queued up at the border. George, our driver, walked between two of the rows towards the checkpoint and Evelyn followed behind him. I was also walking along, but I was between the other two rows of traffic; we both had small backpacks! Evelyn and I were quite amused at drivers opening their car doors and almost dragging us into their cars, shouting quite loudly at us. Our response was quite simple: "No thank you, we already have a driver and taxi."

Meanwhile, as we approached the checkpoint, now about fifteen meters away, we could see at least three or four Israeli soldiers waving their hands and arms and yelling, but we were initially unaware they were waving and yelling at us to back off. It was only when we both heard a booming voice, in English, from a watch-tower high above us that we realized that all this commotion and hand waving was directed at the three of us. Neither of us have any recollection of what the 'voice' said but there was a brief moment of panic, fear, and confusion — I'm not sure which, perhaps all three — but we instinctively knew we had to turn around and go back. We immediately turned around and walked back the way we had come between the cars, and even then, some drivers were urging us into their cars.

A few moments later, we were back near our own car. Everything had settled down, and we started to chat to a young woman. We suddenly realized the danger of our situation when she said, "I couldn't look because I knew they were going to shoot you. You were just about to make the headlines on tonight's news." After chatting with her for a few minutes, a bus came — this is the method pedestrians are supposed to cross the border. We paid our driver his money for the day, climbed on the bus, and drove for about fifty meters through the security border. An officer came on the bus and immediately looked at us sitting near the back of the bus — probably smirking inwardly and thinking "*stupid tourists*." Our passports were checked; we got off the bus and walked across the heavily militarized road and boarded the regular bus to Jerusalem. A narrow escape. We often wonder if our driver tells this story to anyone.

We have visited Bethel and Gilgal earlier, so now we visit Mizpeh where Saul was chosen to be king. Mizpeh is ten kilometers north of Jerusalem on the southern edge of Ramallah. This one is very easy to find. In fact, the main Jerusalem to Ramallah road veers from its fairly straight route to snake around this large mound. A prominent wall on the northeast corner of the mound was built by King Asa, but apart from that there are only enormous piles of rubble, perhaps a stark reminder of Israel's rejection of God:

> *Then Samuel called the people together to the Lord at Mizpah, and said to the children of Israel, "Thus says the Lord God of Israel: 'I brought up Israel out of Egypt, and delivered you from the hand of the Egyptians and from the hand of all kingdoms and from those who oppressed you.' But you have today rejected your God, who Himself saved you from all your adversities and your tribulations; and you have said to Him, 'No, set a king over us!' Now therefore, present yourselves before the Lord by your tribes and by your clans." And when Samuel had caused all the tribes of Israel to come near, the tribe of Benjamin was chosen. When he had caused the tribe of Benjamin to come near by their families, the family of Matri was chosen. And Saul the son of Kish was chosen...* (1 Samuel 10:17-21)

We had no real excitement or adventure finding or accessing the site on the numerous times we came here. However, for those addicted to television news, this is a strategic site for television cameras covering street fighting on the approach road to Ramallah.

JEREMIAH

Jeremiah is often called "the weeping prophet" because he wept about the sin of his countrymen. It seems that at times he was depressed about the futility of his message because his words of judgment went unheeded. Jeremiah was the major prophet during the decline and fall of the southern kingdom of Judah, and he prophesied during the reigns of the last five kings of Judah.

ANATHOTH

Jeremiah was born in the village of Anathoth.

> *The words of Jeremiah the son of Hilkiah, of the priests who were in Anathoth in the land of Benjamin,...* (Jeremiah 1:1)

The name survives in today's Arab village of Anata, about four kilometers northeast of Jerusalem, but a definitive site hasn't been identified. That didn't stop us from visiting the village of Anata. In the early 1990s, the roadway system to the north and east of Jerusalem was quite different than today.

We were driving east on the Jericho road, going downhill, following a cyclist at forty-five kilometers per hour. We were intrigued because bicycles were quite uncommon, and this fellow was on a well-equipped cycle going very fast. He was approaching the intersection where we would be turning left of the main road, and he was attempting the same turn. Oh, dear. Either he was traveling too fast or perhaps had a tire problem, but he came off the bike, and the rider and bicycle skidded across the road and both ended at the curbside. He seemed to be okay, hopped on his bike, and continued. Our two children were quite taken by the whole calamity.

In hindsight, our first journey to Anata was slightly embarrassing, but necessary! We were driving a new rental car with less than four thousand kilometers on the clock, and we were on our way up the enormous hill to Jerusalem. Near the top of the hill, there was a two hundred meter lineup of vehicles at an Israeli army checkpoint; it was quite common to have a checkpoint at this location. It was mid-afternoon, it was September, it was hot, the air conditioner was on, and we had just climbed the long hill from Jericho. The car was hot, and so were we.

Now this car had a manual gear shift and clutch, and as we edged towards the checkpoint, rather than putting the gear in neutral and applying the hand brake every ten meters, I was "riding the clutch." Then panic set in. About thirty meters before the checkpoint, the clutch began to slip, and I was getting very little engagement. If I applied the accelerator the only response was extra revs and more slippage on the clutch. Luckily, we were now moving at about 5-10 kilometers per hour and had some momentum, and we prayed fervently that the soldiers would signal us through without stopping.

We knew that if we stopped and lost our momentum, this little baby was going to go nowhere. Prayers answered, and we were waved through. We maintained what momentum we had, but we could only get the car up to about fifteen kilometers per hour. Meanwhile, it was an exercise in getting the car to keep moving without excessively revving the engine. I was in a sweat and a panic. How could I possibly explain to Avis that I had burned out the clutch in a new car? Then double panic; as we rounded the corner after the checkpoint, there was a lineup of traffic into Jerusalem which was at least six kilometers — and all uphill as far as the intersection with the Ramallah Road. There was no way to sit in this traffic because once we lost our forward momentum, this car would stop

— forever! I had only one option and that was to take the hard shoulder and pass all the other waiting vehicles. As we embarrassingly passed the other vehicles, we kept looking in the other direction to avoid any eye contact with those we were passing. But this really was an emergency. If we could only nurse and coax this car to the Ramallah Road, then it was mostly downhill from there directly to the car rental offices. We proceeded along at our fifteen kilometers per hour crawl, passing everyone, feeling both good and bad about what we were doing.

After a lot of nail-biting, we made it to the Ramallah Road and began heading in the direction of the rental outlet. But as we drove I seemed to be getting a lot more "catch" in the clutch, and within about ten minutes it seemed to be working perfectly well again. Apparently, if clutches overheat this will happen to them, and as they cool, they will be okay. But we didn't know that.

Akeldama

There is plenty of argument and debate about this one! But, let's pretend we know the answer! This name Akeldama means Field of Blood and is quite likely the location where Judas Iscariot committed suicide (Acts 1; 18, 19), and perhaps the tomb of Annas the High priest is here. The area is riddled with tombs, probably those of poor people,[48] leading some to suggest that Jeremiah went to the pauper's house rather than the potter's house — the potter was maybe a pauper, but he was a definitely a potter because he was making clay pots.

> *The word which came to Jeremiah from the Lord, saying: "Arise and go down to the potter's house, and there I will cause you to hear My words." Then I went down to the potter's house,…* (Jeremiah 18:1-3)

The Greek Orthodox monastery of St. Onuphrius today occupies much of the area known as Akeldama. It's situated on the southwest corner of the junction of the Hinnom and Kidron valleys about one kilometer south of the Old City of Jerusalem. A chapel in the monastery, called the Refuge of the Apostles, is in a cave which tradition identifies as the place where the apostles fled after Jesus's arrest (Mk 14:43-50). The monastery isn't generally open to the public, but we wanted in!

We went to the metal door of the monastery, put a hand through a grill in the door, and pushed a little red button. Bingo, a monk appeared and invited us in. He was from Chicago, extremely friendly, knowledgeable, and chatty. He

---

[48] It is unlikely that this was a graveyard for only the poor and for strangers because there are also several finely decorated burial caves. One of the tombs may be that of Annas, the High priest and father-in-law of Caiaphas the High priest.

provided us with drinks and gave us a grand tour of the monastery, including the chapels, the Apostles' Refuge, and all sorts of bones and skulls in burial niches. This is a fascinating site which, perhaps fortunately, is not open to the public. The public tend to ruin things! After the grand tour, we sat down and continued our chat … until I mentioned that our son was a student at the Moody Bible Institute in Chicago. He was still very polite, but clearly this visit was coming to an end. I trust that the potter treated Jeremiah as well as we were treated.

JEREMIAH'S GROTTO

At the eastern end of Skull Hill, there is a cave blocked from view by a Muslim mosque and the Arab bus station. In Jewish tradition, this cave is where Jeremiah may have written the book of Lamentations. In Lamentations chapter 1 Jerusalem was lonely (v. 1), its inhabitants weeping and mourning (v. 2), and the city has been taken into exile (v. 3). Because of the enormity of their sins, the people had been uprooted from their land (v.3, 5, 8). In verse 12 there is an appeal for help: Jerusalem is dejected and is calling on passers-by to consider whether her suffering did not concern them.

DETOUR ELEVEN:
JEREMIAH, JERUSALEM AND JESUS

Is it nothing to you, all you who pass by?
  Behold and see
  If there is any sorrow like my sorrow,
  Which has been brought on me,
  Which the Lord has inflicted
  In the day of His fierce anger. (Lamentations 1:12)

A few commentators interpret this verse in two different ways. Firstly, the immediate appeal for help, and second, a future fulfilment describing the scenes enacted (Christ's crucifixion) nearly 600 years afterward at a location perhaps not more than two hundred meters away. Following are a few examples of such commentaries:

1. Surely we may look beyond Jeremiah's days, and contemplate Christ as thus speaking, when he stood forth the Church's representative and surety in the days of his flesh. (Hawker's Poor Man's Commentary. Biblesoft Formatted Electronic Database Copyright © 2014 by Biblesoft, Inc.)

2. Can it be that any one reading these lines would reply to the heart rending question of the dying Lamb, and honestly confess, "It is nothing, all nothing to me?" Nothing to you that He was wounded for our transgressions and bruised for our iniquities! Nothing to you that God manifest in flesh so gave Himself to save guilty rebels against His outraged majesty! Nothing to you that the dreaded cup of wrath was pressed to His parched lips in order that the cup of salvation might be offered to you! Can it really be that it is nothing to you? (Ironside Commentaries, PC Study Bible formatted electronic database Copyright © 2012 by Biblesoft, Inc.)

3. This prefigures Christ, whom the language is prophetically made to suit, more than Jerusalem. Compare the use of the name "Israel" for Messiah, Isa 49:3. Compare with "pass by," Matt 27:39; Mark 15:29. As to Jerusalem, Dan 9:12. (Jamieson, Fausset, and Brown Commentary, Electronic Database. Copyright © 1997-2014 by Biblesoft, Inc.)

4. How extreme is the distress and humiliation here depicted is apparent from the fact that this language has been attributed to our Divine Savior when hanging upon the cross of Calvary. If a city never endured sorrow like that of Jerusalem, certainly no human being ever experienced agonies so piercing as those which the Captain of our salvation willingly bore for our sake when he gave his life a ransom for many. (The Pulpit Commentary, Electronic Database. Copyright © 2001, 2003, 2005, 2006, 2010 by Biblesoft, Inc.)

5. We can hear the voice of Jesus Christ here as He hung on the cross for the sins of the world. Remember how He wept over Jerusalem because He saw her day of judgment coming? (Wiersbe's Expository Outlines on the Old Testament © 1993 by Victor Books/SP Publications.)

AMOS

Amos is the shepherd-prophet who denounced the people of the northern kingdom of Israel for their idol worship, corruption, and oppression of the poor. Although he prophesied to the Northern Kingdom, Amos was a native of the southern kingdom of Judah. He came from the village of Tekoa, situated about ten kilometers south of Bethlehem.

TEKOA

The words of Amos, who was among the sheep breeders of Tekoa, which he saw concerning Israel in the days of Uzziah king of Judah, and in the days of Jeroboam the son of Joash, king of Israel, two years before the earthquake. (Amos 1:1)

Getting to Tekoa is relatively easy if not a little nervous. You simply drive from Jerusalem to Bethlehem then take the more easterly of the two roads that run to Hebron. This is a beautiful road and passes Herodium, the mountaintop fortress built by Herod the Great. After thirty-five years of searching, in 2007, a team of archaeologists led by Professor Ehud Netzer of the Hebrew University announced they had discovered the tomb of Herod the Great. The fortress was held by Jewish rebels during the Bar Kochba revolt against the Romans (AD 132-135).

Beyond Herodium the road crosses Wadi Khareitun. The road continues though a truly biblical landscape, and at the appropriate time of the year we see olive trees, large flocks of sheep and goats, and women gleaning in the fields, harvesting barley with sickles,. If Amos returned today, he'd probably see things similar to his day. We were a little nervous when we first arrived in Tekoa because we were, as usual, in a rental car with yellow license plates — to the Palestinians this is a "Jewish car." We then performed our usual stunt. We parked the car conspicuously in the village center, climbed out, and opened our maps. This always seemed to work for us and perhaps sent a message to the locals that we were helpless and totally stupid tourists that had lost our way — and we were outwitting them!

And then there's the usual response. Within minutes it seems that every child in the village is there, giggling, laughing, pointing, and trying to converse. Then a few adults arrive and by now the whole village is aware of the strangers in town who aren't Jewish, not American, and not British (which we are, but always travel in these areas using our Canadian passports). From the high ground on which the modern village stands, we could look down on the bare undulating desolate beauty of the hills of the Judean wilderness.

There is a route called the Ascent of Ziz, which leads from the western shore of the Dead Sea to Tekoa. This is likely the route taken by the band of Moabites and Ammonites who attacked Jehoshaphat. We've never actually explored this route because it's a hard walk and not able to be driven.

> *Tomorrow go down against them. They will surely come up by the Ascent of Ziz, and you will find them at the end of the brook before the Wilderness of Jeruel...So they rose early in the morning and went out into the Wilderness of Tekoa; and as they went out, Jehoshaphat stood and said, "Hear me, O Judah and you inhabitants of Jerusalem: Believe in the Lord your God, and you shall be established; believe His prophets, and you shall prosper."* (2 Chronicles 20:16, 20)

JONAH

Jonah is a sad and somewhat tragic figure. Before he finally went to preach repentance to the people of Nineveh, he was swallowed by a great fish and vomited back out on to dry land. It is a mark of the integrity of the Bible that a prophet like Jonah is described in such a candid manner. Our natural tendency would be to obscure and hide such a character, but God describes His heroes, warts and all, to illustrate truth. We don't know anything about Jonah after his preaching in Nineveh.

JOPPA

> But Jonah arose to flee to Tarshish from the presence of the Lord. He went down to Joppa, and found a ship going to Tarshish; so he paid the fare, and went down into it, to go with them to Tarshish from the presence of the Lord. (Jonah 1:3)

Joppa, or Jaffa, or Yafo, is an old suburb at the southern end of Tel Aviv. This was the ancient gateway of the region and it claims to be the oldest port in the world having been commissioned by Japheth the son of Noah. The archaeological mound of ancient Jaffa is located in Old Jaffa on the hill above the port. If you are lucky and have a window seat on your flight leaving Ben Gurion airport, you will see beautiful views of the port at Joppa only minutes after taking off. I often wonder what God would have used instead of a great fish if Jonah would have fled in an airplane! We had a lot less excitement at Joppa than Jonah did. Jonah must have been filled with nervous excitement, or fear, as he tried to run away from God. All we had to contend with was the horrible stench from the fish vendors lining the dockside and the obligatory photograph of the ugly bronze whale that has been erected near the harbor.

ASHDOD (GIVAT YONAH, OR THE HILL OF JONAH)

Just north of the residential area of modern Ashdod, south of the port and overlooking it, there is a park on top of a hill called Givat Yonah, or the Hill of Jonah. Both Jewish and Muslim traditions believe that Jonah was cast ashore, i.e. vomited, on the beach below this park, and from this hill he began his journey to Nineveh (Jonah 3:1-4).

> Now the Lord had prepared a great fish to swallow Jonah. And Jonah was in the belly of the fish three days and three nights. (Jonah 1:17)

> So the Lord spoke to the fish, and it vomited Jonah onto dry land. (Jonah 2:10)

The park overlooking the beach is a beautiful place for a picnic, provided you spread your blanket to look over the Mediterranean Sea and turn your back on the large ugly port of Ashdod, along with all its railway tracks. It is a shame that such a beautiful site has to be associated with vomiting!

NINEVEH

Assyria was a kingdom between the Tigris and Euphrates Rivers that dominated the ancient world from the ninth to the seventh century BC. Nineveh was its principal city and its third and last capital. The Assyrians defeated the northern kingdom of Israel in 722 BC. In modern geography, the ancient kingdom of Assyria is a region north of Baghdad, cantered on the city of Mosul, ancient Nineveh, and bordered to its south by Babylonia.

On our journey to ancient Nineveh, we probably had much more excitement than Abraham did. As for Ur and Babylon, our point of origin for this journey was Baghdad. We calculated that our return journey to the northern city of Mosul would take 10–11 hours. This looked rather daunting even if the temperature did plummet to a balmy 47C. We expressed our concern to Davir, the hotel clerk, and he promptly replied, "Why don't you fly?" We were initially puzzled by this suggestion because we didn't think there were any internal flights in Iraq, especially because of the UN-imposed no-fly zones in both the north and south of the country. Davir explained that the UN had given Iraqi Airlines permission to fly two flights per week. At 8:00 a.m. Thursday, two flights left Baghdad, one to the southern city of Basra and the second to Mosul. Each flight had about one hour on the ground to disembark passengers, take on new passengers, and then return to Baghdad. And tomorrow happened to be Thursday. We expressed concern at the possible cost, but Davir explained that it wouldn't cost much. The phrase, "it doesn't cost much," always worries us, but this time it was actually true. When Davir found out that a one-way ticket to Mosul cost $6.50 USD, we invited him to accompany us on our journey as our guide and translator — it's not often we have the opportunity, or the means, to buy someone an airline ticket.

We were up early the next morning, and after no breakfast for the third morning, we got a taxi to Baghdad airport. We were surprised by the beautiful condition of the airport. Although it was almost ten years old, with the UN embargo it had barely been used. Davir was so excited by the trip, and his first time flying, that he had us at the airport two hours early; we were the first passengers to arrive. We sat around and watched cleaners clean what seemed to be perfectly clear floors, and read with some interest the large handwritten paper sign that had the words "US go home." This struck us as strange because Americans were never in this place — especially since there were only two local flights once per week. We couldn't help but wonder if someone had seen us, concluded incorrectly that we were Americans, and put up the poster.

Check-in was easy, but security was incredibly tight, to the extent that the batteries were removed from our cameras. We walked from the terminal, across the pavement, climbed the steps into an old Boeing 707, and took our seats close to the front. The plane had almost filled when a bride arrived fully dressed in all her bridal wear, accompanied by a few chaperones. The plane had shelves instead of overhead bins, and this made our minds skip back thirty years to when we first flew the Atlantic on Boeing 707s.

We fastened seat belts, the flight attendant pushed everything back on the overhead shelves, and we were soon taking off. As we lifted off from Baghdad airport, it was the strangest sight to see a major international airport with only three aircraft at the terminal. The flight was uneventful, we could only vaguely see a barren landscape through a hazy atmosphere, and about fifty minutes later we arrived at Mosul.

After picking up our camera batteries, we boarded a bus and went into Mosul. This is the city where Saddam Hussein's two sons, Uday and Qusay, were shot by American soldiers in 2003. No one spoke English, and we were very appreciative to have Davir with us. We arrived at a taxi rank, and Davir was able to explain our travel itinerary: we wanted to see the ruins of Nineveh, then on to the ruins of Calah, ancient Nimrud, and then travel the entire 450 kilometers back to Baghdad, with a brief stopover at the revered mosque in the city of Samara. A deal was struck for $30 USD, and we were on our way. We arrived at the ruins of the ancient city in a matter of moments.

Nineveh was the principal city and the third, and last, capital of Assyria. As a major city, it dates from the time of Sennacherib (704-618 BC). It was one of the most powerful cites of the Middle East until its downfall in 612 BC, when it was sacked by the Medes of northern Persia. The ancient site is marked by the ruins of two mounds on the eastern edge of modern Mosul. The ruins are enormous, and the site will probably never be completely excavated. The walls of Nineveh were twelve kilometers in circumference, and there were fifteen gates; many of these gates, and much of the wall, was being subjected to rather questionable reconstruction under Saddam Hussein.

It was here that the Gilgamesh Epic Tablet and Siege of Lachish Reliefs were excavated, and these are now on display in the British Museum in London. Unfortunately, apart from the walls and gates, there is little else to see at Nineveh. Nevertheless, we asked our taxi driver to let us loose for half an hour so that we could simply wander over the site and contemplate. This was the city of the great Assyrian King Sennacherib who took the northern kingdom of Israel captive. And it was to Nineveh that God sent Jonah to preach:

> "Arise, go to Nineveh, that great city, and preach to it the message that I tell you." So Jonah arose and went to Nineveh, according to the word of the Lord. Now Nineveh was an exceedingly great city, a three-day journey in extent. And Jonah began to enter the city on the first day's walk. Then he cried out and said, "Yet forty days, and Nineveh shall be overthrown!" So the people of Nineveh believed God, proclaimed a fast, and put on sackcloth, from the greatest to the least of them. (Jonah 3:2-5)

About twenty-five kilometers southeast of Mosul is modern Nimrud, the site of biblical Calah. The first thing we saw as we approached the site were the remains of a huge, ancient 'temple tower' or ziggurat. Sadly, this towering sacred structure built nearly 2,900 years ago was totally destroyed by ISIS[49] in 2015. It has been reported that ISIS destroyed about 90% of the excavated ancient city. Once Assyria's second capital, it was first designated as the Assyrian capital by Ashurnasirpal II in 879 BC. It is an ancient Assyrian city founded by Nimrod:

> From that land he [Nimrod] went to Assyria and built Nineveh, Rehoboth Ir, Calah, and Resen between Nineveh and Calah... (Genesis 10:11-12)

The four cities formed one, great, complex city, to which the name Nineveh was given. It was from Calah that Shalmaneser attacked Syria, and the Black Obelisk (in the British Museum, London) describing his victory was originally set up in the main square. One of the most impressive discoveries is the palace of King Ashurnasirpal II, the city's founding monarch. At the entrance to the palace there are two impressive hawk-winged lions with human heads. As with all other sites in Iraq, it was hot in Calah, very hot, so our visit was relatively fast. We escaped into the relative cool of the taxi and began our 425-kilometer journey south to Baghdad.

Iraqi drivers have a strange habit of driving in the outside (fast) lane along motorways. When faster vehicles catch up, the slower vehicle moves to the inside (slow) lane, thereby allowing the faster vehicles to pass in the fast lane. As soon as the faster vehicles pass, the slower vehicles return to the outer fast lane. Weird!

---

[49] ISIS is an acronym for Islamic State of Iraq and Syria. It is a Sunni jihadist group with an especially violent ideology and claims religious authority over all Muslims.

Our taxi from Calah to Baghdad was cruising along at a steady 110–120 kph (in the fast lane) and because of his speed, we were regularly catching up on slower traffic, watching with amusement at their switching back and forth across lanes. About an hour south of Calah, we could see our driver take an extra-long look into his rear-view mirror, promptly and quickly moved to the slow lane while five black cars roared past in the fast lane, doing at least 150–160 kph. The consensus from the driver and Davir is that it must have been Saddam Hussein or his sons or some other high dignitaries of the Hussein family. Slightly unnerving. This is all the more likely because Saddam's sons, Qusay and Uday, lived in Mosul; they were shot dead by an American task force in Mosul two years later in 2003.

MICAH

Micah was a younger contemporary of the prophet Isaiah, and he spoke out fervently against those who claimed to be prophets of the Lord but who led the people of Judah into false hope. Little is known about Micah except that he was from Moresheth Gath, a town in southern Judah.

MORESHETH

The word of the Lord that came to Micah of Moresheth in the days of Jotham, Ahaz, and Hezekiah, kings of Judah, which he saw concerning Samaria and Jerusalem. (Micah 1:1)

Moresheth is easy to find but not worth the effort unless you are close by. It is a challenge to scramble to the top of the mound where you have every probability of being hit by an ATV because young hormone-charged teenagers have put their brains into neutral, and their ATVs into top gear. However, if you do reach the top of the mound unscathed, you are afforded quite a good view over southern Judah and the Shephalah.

ELIJAH AND ELISHA

These are two of the most exciting characters in the Old Testament. Their lives pepper us with examples of life experiences — depression, excitement, loyalty, and a life of prayer and trust in God — and of course, there were the miracles. Because many of the events in their lives overlap, we will consider them together.

Elijah was an influential prophet who shaped the history of his day. He was opposed to the accepted standards of his day, when belief in many gods was normal, and many of his miracles occurred during a period of struggle between the religion of Jehovah and Baal worship. His strange dress and appearance, his fleetness of foot, his rugged constitution, and his cave-dwelling habits all suggest that he had a robust, outdoors-type personality.

Elisha was an early prophet who succeeded Elijah. He ministered for about fifty years in the northern kingdom of Israel. Elisha's work consisted of presenting the Word of God through prophecy, advising and anointing kings, helping the needy, and performing miracles.

We will begin our journey with these two great men of God with Elijah when he predicted that a drought would grip the land. He did this as punishment against King Ahab for building a temple for Baal worship at Samaria. Elijah fled to the eastern side of the Jordan River and later to Zarephath on the Mediterranean coast to escape Ahab's wrath. At both locations he was kept alive through miraculous means. While staying at a widow's home, he performed a miracle by bringing her son back to life (1 Kings 17).

CHERITH BROOK

> "Get away from here and turn eastward, and hide by the Brook Cherith, which flows into the Jordan. And it will be that you shall drink from the brook, and I have commanded the ravens to feed you there."... The ravens brought him bread and meat in the morning, and bread and meat in the evening; and he drank from the brook.
> (1 Kings 17:3-4, 6)

The problem in finding the Cherith Brook is in knowing where to look. In 1 Kings 17:3, the KJV and ASV say that the Brook is "before Jordan," the NKJV says, "flows into the Jordan," while the NIV, NASB, and RSV say, "east of Jordan." Consequently, we have two potential brooks. The first site we've already visited with Joshua as he entered the Promised Land. This is the Valley of Achor, or Wadi Qelt, where Joshua dealt with Achan and his family. The four-hour trek through the Judean wilderness along this wadi is awesome.

After about two hours, we reached the sixth-century monastery of St. George's which has a spectacular setting hanging off the edge of a cliff — literally — marvellously camouflaged against the native color of the cliff. It was built at the cave where the prophet Elijah is said to have hidden to escape the wrath of Jezebel the Queen of Samaria. On our first visit, we were dismayed to be greeted by about three busloads of tourists who took the easy way in!

Our second visit was much more tranquil — just us, and nobody else. The cool of the monastery was a refreshing break from the relentless heat outside, although we have trouble dealing with all the icons and imagery. Because there were no tourists, the priest, from Montreal, seemed very relaxed and had time to sit and chat and show us around. He kindly provided us with a detailed description of the daily routine at the monastery, brought us to the bell tower, and pointed out the old caves and "habitations" used centuries ago by ascetics who practiced strict self-denial and abstinence from worldly pleasures as a measure of discipline.

The priest then took us to the Chapel of Elijah. It seems that this is not generally open to the public and may be more for private use by priests. We went through a few doors to get there, and the final door into the chapel had to be unlocked. We entered a small cave that had been effectively converted into a chapel with a tiled floor. It had kneeling pads, high chairs, an altar, candlesticks and candles, a nice chandelier, a number of icons and paintings, and a striking painting on the wall depicting the reason we were here — Elijah being fed by a raven. Elijah looks quite forlorn, and the raven is perched by his shoulder holding what looks like a single large cherry in its beak. The surroundings almost made us want to believe that this is where Elijah hid — but it probably wasn't.

Most authorities identify the Brook Cherith as Wadi Yabis, east of the River Jordan at the north end of the town of Wadi Yabis. We drove to the brook, which was completely dried up. This is a rather non-descript place, barren, and quite desolate. It certainly seemed to fit the ambiance of the story of Elijah. But of course, if this is the brook, we have no idea where along the brook's course that Elijah may have hung out.

ZAREPHATH

God then instructed Elijah to go to Zarephath and to lodge with a widow. It was while he was with the widow that he performed the miracle of the flour and the oil and that he raised the widow's son from the dead.

> *"Arise, go to Zarephath, which belongs to Sidon, and dwell there. See, I have commanded a widow there to provide for you." So he arose and went to Zarephath. And when he came to the gate of the city, indeed a widow was there gathering sticks...* (1 Kings 17:9-10)

> *The bin of flour was not used up, nor did the jar of oil run dry, according to the word of the Lord which He spoke by Elijah.* (1 Kings 17:16)

> *Now it happened after these things that the son of the woman who owned the house became sick. And his sickness was so serious that there was no breath left in him ... And he said to her, "Give me your son." So he took him out of her arms and carried him to the upper room where he was staying, and laid him on his own bed... Then the Lord heard the voice of Elijah; and the soul of the child came back to him, and he revived. And Elijah took the child and brought him down from the upper room*

into the house, and gave him to his mother. And Elijah said, "See, your son lives!"
(1 Kings 17:17, 19, 22-23)

Visiting biblical sites has many advantages for both the casual traveler and the serious Bible student. But there is one disadvantage; our preconceived-rosy images may be shattered. For example, most people envisage the Mount of Olives as a beautiful hill covered with olive trees. Many are quite disappointed to find that more than 60% of the mountain is either an Arab village or a Jewish cemetery.

Zarephath was another example of having an image shattered. When we heard or read this story our imaginations were carried away to some small village high in some remote, hilly region. We envision a little rocky terrain and sparse vegetation with some sheep and goats. Imagine our surprise to find that the widow of Zarephath probably had a waterfront or water view property on the Mediterranean Sea! Zarephath is quite likely the modern town of Sarafend, on the Mediterranean coast about twenty kilometers north of Tyre. I wonder when Elijah was raising the child from the dead, or miraculously providing an endless supply of oil and flour, if it crossed his mind that 2,800 years later, this peaceful little place would be flattened in war. During the 1982 war with Israel, the site was used as a Lebanese gunning position. This area is on the coast near the center of the current town, but absolutely nothing remains of the ancient town.

MOUNT CARMEL
Elijah challenged the prophets of Baal:

> *Now therefore, send and gather all Israel to me on Mount Carmel, the four hundred and fifty prophets of Baal, and the four hundred prophets of Asherah, who eat at Jezebel's table.* (1 Kings 18:19)

This summons to gather on Carmel is followed by one of the most powerful and amusing stories in the Bible. Each side would offer sacrifices to their god or God without building a fire. The god or God who could ignite the fire would be declared the strongest and would thereby reveal himself as the true God. Elijah mocked the prophets of Baal by saying that their god was either meditating, or busy, or on a journey, or perhaps even sleeping and must be awakened. Despite all their crying and hollering, and cutting themselves with knives and lances, Baal didn't show up. When it was Elijah's turn, he prayed to God and poured water over his sacrifice — to remove any possibility of fraud or misunderstanding about the offering. When God responded, and Elijah's sacrifice was consumed by fire from heaven, the people of Israel responded strongly in favor of God. The prophets of Baal and Asheroth were then slaughtered at Elijah's command, and God sent rain to end the drought.

> *Then the fire of the Lord fell and consumed the burnt sacrifice, and the wood and the stones and the dust, and it licked up the water that was in the trench. Now when all the people saw it, they fell on their faces; and they said, "The Lord, He is God! The Lord, He is God!" And Elijah said to them, "Seize the prophets of Baal! Do not let one of them escape!" So they seized them; and Elijah brought them down to the Brook Kishon and executed them there.* (1 Kings 18:38-40)

There is no problem finding Mount Carmel — just follow the tourist buses, and you will arrive at a beautiful little chapel, along with the customary souvenir stall and bookstore. In the courtyard in front of the chapel is a larger-than-life statue of Elijah, standing with his boot (I guess it's a sandal) on the neck of one of the prophets of Baal, and a knife in his uplifted hand. It is actually quite graphic but true to life — well, almost.

Elijah didn't kill the prophets here, rather this was the site of Elijah's challenge to the prophets. He had the false prophets killed about 2–3 kilometers away at the River Kishon, which flows near the bottom of the hill upon which we're standing. But before visiting the river we must climb the set of stairs to the flat roof of the souvenir shop and take in the marvelous view. The roof has direction pointers identifying the locations of many of the surrounding sites, chief of which is the great plain of Armageddon that spreads endlessly below us, and, in the distance, the little Arab village of Solem, biblical Shunem. On his travels between Mount Carmel and the Jordan Valley Elisha called at Shunem. Here he was hospitably entertained by a rich and godly woman.

> *Now it happened one day that Elisha went to Shunem, … And she said to her husband, "Look now, I know that this is a holy man of God, who passes by us regularly. Please, let us make a small upper room on the wall; and let us put a bed for him there, and a table and a chair and a lampstand; so it will be, whenever he comes to us, he can turn in there."* (2 Kings 4:8-10)

In appreciation, Elisha repaid the childless couple by promising them a son. In due time the couple had a son, then tragedy struck the child, but Elisha raised him from the dead.

> *And the child grew. Now it happened one day that he went out to his father, to the reapers. And he said to his father, "My head, my head!" So he said to a servant, "Carry him to his mother." When he had taken him and brought him to his mother, he sat on her knees till noon, and then died. And she went up and laid him on the bed of the man of God, shut the door upon him, and went out… Then she saddled a*

donkey, and said to her servant, "Drive, and go forward; do not slacken the pace for me unless I tell you." And so she departed, and went to the man of God at Mount Carmel... (2 Kings 4:18-21, 24-25)

When Elisha came into the house, there was the child, lying dead on his bed. He went in therefore, shut the door behind the two of them, and prayed to the Lord. And he went up and lay on the child, and put his mouth on his mouth, his eyes on his eyes, and his hands on his hands; and he stretched himself out on the child, and the flesh of the child became warm. He returned and walked back and forth in the house, and again went up and stretched himself out on him; then the child sneezed seven times, and the child opened his eyes. And he called Gehazi and said, "Call this Shunammite woman." So he called her. And when she came in to him, he said, "Pick up your son." (2 Kings 4:32-36)

We should jog our memories and recall that we are standing on the roof of the souvenir shop on Mount Carmel. As we stand here, it is easy to get lost in our own imaginations as we recall the story, and we can see very clearly the journey that the Shunammite woman made on her donkey from Shunem to Mount Carmel, and the return journey made by Gehazi and Elijah. It's also impossible not to think of the biblical account of future events that will unfold in the vale of Armageddon immediately below us.

Beersheva and Mount Sinai

Queen Jezebel was furious over the defeat and slaughter of the prophets of Baal and vowed revenge on Elijah. Elijah took refuge and fled to the desert south of Beersheva, eventually arriving at Mount Horeb, another name for Mount Sinai.

And Ahab told Jezebel all that Elijah had done, also how he had executed all the prophets with the sword. Then Jezebel sent a messenger to Elijah, saying, "So let the gods do to me, and more also, if I do not make your life as the life of one of them by tomorrow about this time." And when he saw that, he arose and ran for his life, and went to Beersheba, which belongs to Judah, and left his servant there. (1 Kings 19:1-3)

So he arose, and ate and drank; and he went in the strength of that food forty days and forty nights as far as Horeb, the mountain of God. (1 Kings 19:8)

While Elijah was at Mount Horeb, the Lord revealed Himself. Elijah received a revelation of the coming doom on Ahab and the northern kingdom of Israel (1 Kings 19:14). He was then instructed to anoint Hazael as king of Syria, Jehu as the future king of Israel, and Elisha as the prophet who would take his place (1 Kings 19:16). These changes would bring to power those who would later reform

Israel. You may have already guessed, someone, no doubt very well-meaning, has identified the cave in which Elijah took refuge at Mount Horeb. As indicated earlier, there is speculation over the location of Mount Horeb, so the identity of Elijah's cave is problematic. Regardless, if Elijah was in this area he was fortunate because this is a beautiful location.

A number of chapters earlier we brought you to the summit of Mount Sinai with Moses. We descended from the summit of Sinai by a different route than the camel path by which we ascended. This route is called the Steps of Repentance because it was built by monks from St. Catherine's monastery. It is a series of 3,750 steps between the monastery and the summit. It is shorter than the camel path but much more arduous if you are going up, yet fairly nice for coming down (although quite tricky in places especially where there was snow). This route passes through Elijah's hollow where tradition claims he hid from King Ahab and Queen Jezebel:

> And there he [Elijah] went into a cave, and spent the night in that place... Then He said, "Go out, and stand on the mountain before the Lord." And behold, the Lord passed by, and a great and strong wind tore into the mountains and broke the rocks in pieces before the Lord, but the Lord was not in the wind; and after the wind an earthquake, but the Lord was not in the earthquake; and after the earthquake a fire, but the Lord was not in the fire; and after the fire a still small voice. (1 Kings 19:9, 11-12)

Elijah would not be amused to learn that his cave is now occupied and used to sell Coca-Cola and Mars bars. We had the obligatory quick peek inside to confirm that there was nothing to see inside, and then we walked a few paces away from the cave, turned around, and it was almost as though our feet were glued to the ground as we stood and stared at the summit of Sinai. God was here, Moses was here, Elijah was here…

JEZREEL

It was either King Omri or King Ahab and his wife Jezebel that built Jezreel as the second capital of the northern kingdom of Israel. Jezreel was the site of Naboth's vineyard, and Elijah appears on the scene after Jezebel acquired Naboth's family-owned vineyard for Ahab by having Naboth stoned to death.

> And it came to pass after these things that Naboth the Jezreelite had a vineyard which was in Jezreel, next to the palace of Ahab king of Samaria. (1 Kings 21:1)

Perhaps fittingly, Queen Jezebel was later killed here, and the account of her death is one of the most grotesque descriptions in all Scripture. A short time after her death, another grizzly scene is described when the heads of the seventy sons of Ahab were sent to Jezreel in baskets —what a bloody place!

So it was, when the letter came to them, that they took the king's sons and slaughtered seventy persons, put their heads in baskets and sent them to him at Jezreel. Then a messenger came and told him, saying, "They have brought the heads of the king's sons." And he said, "Lay them in two heaps at the entrance of the gate until morning."...So Jehu killed all who remained of the house of Ahab in Jezreel, and all his great men and his close acquaintances and his priests, until he left him none remaining. (2 Kings 10:7-8, 11)

Once we found the site of ancient Jezreel, which is only a few kilometers east of Megiddo, it was easy to access. We parked, placed a foot on a sagging barbed wire fence, pressed it down, and climbed over the broken fence. That was the easy part. Next, we had to tramp a path through a jungle of weeds. Today's site displays none of its former glory, and there is no grave marker for Jezebel, or for Ahab's sons. The site has a few ruins and is totally overgrown by thistles and prickly pear cactus. Don't mention the prickly pear! While we were visiting, the prickly pear were in fruit. Evelyn was about to pick some fruit when we suggested, "Don't pick that because you will be pulling little spikes out of your fingers for weeks." For the next few weeks, Evelyn was plucking little spikes out of her fingers! Outside of Jerusalem, this location is unparalleled in terms of the number of biblical locations and events that are nearby. Within a short distance from west to east one can see (or almost see!) Megiddo, Valley of Armageddon, Ophrah, Nazareth, Mount Tabor, Shunem, Mount Moreh, the location of Gideon's battle against the Midianites, Gideon's spring, and Mount Gilboa.

We returned to Jezreel on a number of occasions, and each time there was some extra activity. In 2010, the title of an article in Biblical Archaeology Review caught my attention. The title was *"Jezreel: where Jezebel was thrown to the dogs."*[50] The article provided surveyors maps of the site, including the location of the city gates, the possible location of Jezebel's demise:

Now when Jehu had come to Jezreel, Jezebel heard of it; and she put paint on her eyes and adorned her head, and looked through a window. Then, as Jehu entered at the gate, she said, "Is it peace, Zimri, murderer of your master?" And he looked up at the window, and said, "Who is on my side? Who?" So two or three eunuchs looked out at him. Then he said, "Throw her down." So they threw her down, and some of her blood spattered on the wall and on the horses; and he trampled her underfoot. And when he had gone in, he ate and drank. Then he said, "Go now, see to this

---

[50] Ussishkin, D. (2010). Jezreel: Where Jezebel was thrown to the dogs. *Biblical Archaeology Review* (July/Aug 36:4), 32.

accursed woman, and bury her, for she was a king's daughter." So they went to bury her, but they found no more of her than the skull and the feet and the palms of her hands. Therefore they came back and told him. And he said, "This is the word of the Lord, which He spoke by His servant Elijah the Tishbite, saying, 'On the plot of ground at Jezreel dogs shall eat the flesh of Jezebel;... (2 Kings 9:30-36)

In a quirky sort of way, we find this to be one of the most interesting sites in Israel. We can climb over three barbed-wire fences, plod our way through hip-high weeds for twenty meters, and stand between the two major trenches that were dug to expose remains of the city gates. And as we stand very close to the exact spot of the demise of one of the most detestable women in Scripture, we can only marvel at the numerous tourist buses rushing past to reach their next site, with the occupants totally oblivious to what they are missing. It doesn't make matters any easier now that archaeologists have found evidence of an enormous vineyard[51] at the northeastern corner of Jezreel. Naboth's vineyard? Perhaps, we don't know, but it provides beautiful context for the story of King Ahab, Queen Jezebel, and Naboth's vineyard:

And it came to pass after these things that Naboth the Jezreelite had a vineyard which was in Jezreel, next to the palace of Ahab king of Samaria. So Ahab spoke to Naboth, saying, "Give me your vineyard, that I may have it for a vegetable garden, because it is near, next to my house; and for it I will give you a vineyard better than it. Or, if it seems good to you, I will give you its worth in money." But Naboth said to Ahab, "The Lord forbid that I should give the inheritance of my fathers to you!" So Ahab went into his house sullen and displeased because of the word which Naboth the Jezreelite had spoken to him... But Jezebel his wife came to him, and said to him, "Why is your spirit so sullen that you eat no food?" (1 Kings 21:1-5)

Then Jezebel his wife said to him, "You now exercise authority over Israel! Arise, eat food, and let your heart be cheerful; I will give you the vineyard of Naboth the Jezreelite." And she wrote letters in Ahab's name, sealed them with his seal, and sent the letters to the elders and the nobles who were dwelling in the city with Naboth. She wrote in the letters, saying, Proclaim a fast, and seat Naboth with high honor among the people; and seat two men, scoundrels, before him to bear witness against him, saying, You have blasphemed God and the king. Then take him out, and stone him, that he may die. (1 Kings 21:7-10)

And it came to pass, when Jezebel heard that Naboth had been stoned and was dead, that Jezebel said to Ahab, "Arise, take possession of the vineyard of Naboth the Jezreelite, which he refused to give you for money; for Naboth is not alive, but dead."... Then the word of the Lord came to Elijah the Tishbite, saying, "Arise, go down to meet Ahab

---

[51] Franklin, N., Ebeling, J., Guillaume, P., & Appler, D. (2017). Have we found Naboth's vineyard at Jezreel? *Biblical Archaeology Review* (Nov/Dec 2017, 43:6), 49.

king of Israel, … saying, 'Thus says the Lord: "In the place where dogs licked the blood of Naboth, dogs shall lick your blood, even yours."'" (1 Kings 21:15, 17-19)

And concerning Jezebel the Lord also spoke, saying, 'The dogs shall eat Jezebel by the wall of Jezreel.' The dogs shall eat whoever belongs to Ahab and dies in the city, and the birds of the air shall eat whoever dies in the field." (1 Kings 21:23-24)

On our most recent visit in 2018, we spent some time wading through the long grass and losing count of the number of winepresses that had been uncovered. Most of the remaining exploits of Elijah and Elisha have already been visited elsewhere in this book. Consequently, we will only provide a few brief comments on these sites.

ABEL MEHOLA

Elisha was the son of Shaphat from Abel Meholah, a town between the Sea of Galilee and the Dead Sea on the western side of the Jordan River. Elijah found Elisha plowing with a team of oxen. As Elijah walked past Elisha, he threw his mantle over the younger man's shoulders. Elisha immediately recognized this as a call to ministry, and he left his family to follow Elijah. The exact location is not certain, but the name is carried on by the Collective Farming village of Mehola twenty kilometers south of Beth Shean in the Jordan valley.

Also you [Elijah] shall anoint Jehu the son of Nimshi as king over Israel. And Elisha the son of Shaphat of Abel Meholah you shall anoint as prophet in your place... So he departed from there, and found Elisha the son of Shaphat, who was plowing with twelve yoke of oxen before him, and he was with the twelfth. Then Elijah passed by him and threw his mantle on him...So Elisha turned back from him, and took a yoke of oxen and slaughtered them and boiled their flesh, using the oxen's equipment, and gave it to the people, and they ate. Then he arose and followed Elijah, and became his servant. (1 Kings 19:16, 19, 21)

JERICHO

Then Elijah said to him, "Elisha, stay here, please, for the Lord has sent me on to Jericho." But he said, "As the Lord lives, and as your soul lives, I will not leave you!" So they came to Jericho. (2 Kings 2:4)

One of Elisha's early miracles was his purification of a spring near Jericho.

Then the men of the city said to Elisha, "Please notice, the situation of this city is pleasant, as my lord sees; but the water is bad, and the ground barren." And he said, "Bring me a new bowl, and put salt in it." So they brought it to him. Then he went out to the source of the water, and cast in the salt there, and said, "Thus says the

Lord: 'I have healed this water; from it there shall be no more death or barrenness.'"
So the water remains healed to this day, according to the word of Elisha which he
spoke. (2 Kings 2:19-22)

The location of this spring is quite certain, and it gushes from the base of an incredibly lush and magnificent bougainvillea, which seems to be in flower for at least eight months of the year. The spring is only a few meters from the main entrance to the ruins of ancient Jericho, and would most likely have been immediately outside the wall of the ancient city. It still gushes liberally today, but, despite the beautiful bougainvillea, someone really ought to pull the old bicycles, boxes, and other junk out of the spring, which is still used to supply some of the water for today's city of Jericho. As described earlier, rather than cleaning the spring, the spring miraculously relocated to the coach/car park in front of a major restaurant near the entrance to the ancient mound of Jericho!

BETHEL

Elisha went from Jericho to Bethel, no doubt following the same route that Joshua's armies followed when fighting against Ai and Bethel. As he approached the town, he was met by a number of children:

Then he went up from there to Bethel; and as he was going up the road, some youths came from the city and mocked him, and said to him, "Go up, you baldhead! Go up, you baldhead!" So he turned around and looked at them, and pronounced a curse on them in the name of the Lord. And two female bears came out of the woods and mauled forty-two of the youths. (2 Kings 2:23-24)

RIVER JORDAN

The Scriptures relate various events that took place in, or near, this lower section of the River Jordan about 7–8 kilometers before its entry to the Dead Sea. Elijah, and later Elisha, divided the waters of the Jordan, Elijah was taken up to heaven in a chariot of fire, and Elisha made an ax head float.[52]

Now Elijah took his mantle, rolled it up, and struck the water; and it was divided this way and that, so that the two of them crossed over on dry ground. And so it was, when they had crossed over, that Elijah said to Elisha, "Ask! What may I do for you, before I am taken away from you?" Elisha said, "Please let a double portion of your spirit be upon me." (2 Kings 2:8-9)

Then it happened, as they continued on and talked, that suddenly a chariot of fire appeared with horses of fire, and separated the two of them; and Elijah went up by a

---

[52] We will consider this section of the Jordan more fully when we describe the baptism of the Lord Jesus Christ.

whirlwind into heaven. And Elisha saw it, and he cried out, "My father, my father, the chariot of Israel and its horsemen!"... (2 Kings 2:11-12)

He also took up the mantle of Elijah that had fallen from him, and went back and stood by the bank of the Jordan. Then he took the mantle of Elijah that had fallen from him, and struck the water, and said, "Where is the Lord God of Elijah?" And when he also had struck the water, it was divided this way and that; and Elisha crossed over. (2 Kings 2:13-14)

...And when they came to the Jordan, they cut down trees. But as one was cutting down a tree, the iron ax head fell into the water; and he cried out and said, "Alas, master! For it was borrowed." So the man of God said, "Where did it fall?" And he showed him the place. So he cut off a stick, and threw it in there; and he made the iron float. (2 Kings 6:4-6)

GILGAL

It was a time of famine, and the food of the prophets was limited to any herbs that could be found.

And Elisha returned to Gilgal, and there was a famine in the land. Now the sons of the prophets were sitting before him; and he said to his servant, "Put on the large pot, and boil stew for the sons of the prophets." So one went out into the field to gather herbs, and found a wild vine, and gathered from it a lapful of wild gourds, and came and sliced them into the pot of stew, though they did not know what they were. Then they served it to the men to eat. Now it happened, as they were eating the stew, that they cried out and said, "Man of God, there is death in the pot!" And they could not eat it. So he said, "Then bring some flour." And he put it into the pot, and said, "Serve it to the people, that they may eat." And there was nothing harmful in the pot. (2 Kings 4:38-41)

DOTHAN

The Syrians warred against Israel, but their plans always seemed to be known to Elisha, who disclosed them to the king of Israel, and thereby saved the king several times. When the king of Syria discovered that Elisha was disclosing his plans, he sent a detachment of men to capture him. They came by night and surrounded Dothan, where Elisha lived.[53] His servant was the first to see the danger. At Elisha's request, the eyes of the young servant were opened to see the spiritual guards that protected them. This is the account of Elisha's great vision of heavenly horses and chariots (2 Kings 6:13-23). And in answer to Elisha's prayer, the Syrians were blinded.

---

[53] Recall that Dothan is where Joseph was put in the cistern by his brothers and subsequently sold to the Midianites.

*And Elisha prayed, and said, "Lord, I pray, open his eyes that he may see." Then the
Lord opened the eyes of the young man, and he saw. And behold, the mountain was
full of horses and chariots of fire all around Elisha.* (2 Kings 6:17)

SAMARIA

As we approached from the south, Samaria could clearly be seen in the distance,
perched on top of a high hill. This hill was situated on the major north-south
road through Palestine. It also commanded the east-west route to the Plain of
Sharon and the Mediterranean Sea. Because of its hilltop location, Samaria was
easily defended. It looks impregnable, but a three-year siege resulting in famine
can produce great results. As we turned off the main road, our secondary road
began to climb the hill, and we passed a number of tombs, a portion of the old
city wall, and then continued along an impressive colonnaded street through the
middle of a large olive grove — it looked surreal; it was springtime, and the olive
trees appeared to be emerging from a carpet of yellow wildflowers. As the row of
columns ends, the road curves left around the side of the mound and into the
little village of Sebastia and finally on to the parking lot.

It was sad when we first arrived. Clearly, this parking lot had been designed
to hold dozens of tour buses, but now, in the middle of the Intifada, we were
the solitary visitors at this marvelous site. And, would you believe it — a little
man appeared to sell us entrance tickets, and then a young woman appeared
inviting us to eat lunch in her restaurant! This made no economic sense. We
were at the city of Samaria, north of the very troubled city of Nablus, deep in
the West Bank, and not even on the main road. There was no one else to be
seen, indeed the ticket man told us that they don't get visitors anymore. With a
stretch of the imagination, I could understand why he was here because he was
probably picking olives a few minutes earlier, and we were extra revenue. But the
restaurant? Who was going to eat all that prepared food in there?

We have visited Samaria on at least six occasions. It is almost worth the
effort to travel from Jerusalem to Samaria just to see the scant remains of Ahab
and Jezebel's palace. The ruins at Samaria are precisely that: ruins. Archaeologists
have uncovered several different levels of occupation by the Israelites — parts
of a large outer wall 6–8 meters thick, a palace, some courtyards, and a pool
which may have been where the blood of Ahab was washed from his chariot
after he died in battle against the Syrians (1 Kings 22:38). There is also a series
of magnificent round towers, an aqueduct, a stadium, and an impressive theater
— but they are all in ruins. However, the view from the top is of a wonderful
biblical landscape dotted with limestone outcrops, stone walls, olive groves, and

villages. And as we looked to the north we could envisage the approaching Syrian army under Ben-Hadad and the Assyrian army under Shalmaneser, and their encampments and their siege — this is an inspiring place.

This was once the capital city of the northern kingdom of Israel. Samaria was built about 800 BC by King Omri, and most of Israel's kings reigned and were buried here. Samaria withstood an attack by Ben-Hadad, king of Syria, but it finally fell to the Assyrians in 722 BC, and its inhabitants were taken into captivity. There are over 120 Scripture references to either the city of Samaria or the region. It was here that Ahab married Jezebel, Ahab built a temple to Baal, and that Ahab was killed. But perhaps we know Samaria best for the ivory palace[54] built by Ahab, the famine during the siege by Ben-Hadad of Syria, and for the fall of the city and the northern kingdom to Shalmaneser of Assyria.

> *Now the rest of the acts of Ahab, and all that he did, the ivory house which he built and all the cities that he built, are they not written in the book of the chronicles of the kings of Israel?* (1 Kings 22:39)

When Ben-Hadad, the king of Syria besieged Samaria, there was a great famine in the city. Then Elisha came on the scene with an amazing promise that within twenty-four hours food would be plentiful. The next day the Syrian camp was found deserted because the night before God had caused the Syrians to hear the noise of horses and chariots, and they fled in panic and confusion. Thus God, according to the words of Elisha, delivered Samaria.

> *And it happened after this that Ben-Hadad king of Syria gathered all his army, and went up and besieged Samaria. And there was a great famine in Samaria; and indeed they besieged it until a donkey's head was sold for eighty shekels of silver, and one-fourth of a kab of dove droppings[55] for five shekels of silver.* (2 Kings 6:24-25)

> *Then Elisha said, "Hear the word of the Lord. Thus says the Lord: 'Tomorrow about this time a seah of fine flour shall be sold for a shekel, and two seahs of barley for a shekel, at the gate of Samaria.'"* (2 Kings 7:1)

---

[54] Several carved ivory pieces were uncovered from the royal palace at Samaria and are on display in the British Museum in London. They take the form of small decorated plates. The pieces were initially connected with Ahab's ivory palace but they have not been precisely dated and they could have been deposited in the palace at any time between its being built in the early ninth century BC, and its destruction in 722 BC.

[55] Although it makes a great (and humorous) sermon point, dove's dung refers to a plant, The Star-of-Bethlehem, *Ornithogalum narbonense*. The species often grows in such abundance that its white flowers resemble bird droppings, hence its biblical name of dove's dung. Bulbs of the plant were sold during the siege of Samaria.

Now the king of Assyria went throughout all the land, and went up to Samaria and besieged it for three years. In the Ninth year of Hoshea, the king of Assyria took Samaria and carried Israel away to Assyria... (2 Kings 17:5-6)

The adjacent village of Sebastia has a mosque/church which claims to have the tomb of Elisha. The context of this passage suggests that Elisha probably died and was buried in Samaria — but the power of the prophet didn't end with his death.

Then Elisha died, and they buried him. And the raiding bands from Moab invaded the land in the spring of the year. So it was, as they were burying a man, that suddenly they spied a band of raiders; and they put the man in the tomb of Elisha; and when the man was let down and touched the bones of Elisha, he revived and stood on his feet. (2 Kings 13:20-21)

X.
THE BOOK OF ESTHER

By the late summer of 2003, we had visited almost all known bible sites; however, the biblical sites of Iran and ancient Persia had so far eluded us. An opportunity presented itself when two Iranian ecologists at the University of Gorgon invited us to visit Iran. Each of them had spent a sabbatical year in my lab at the University of British Columbia. Despite having formal invitations from the university, including the university president, acquiring a visa proved to be difficult. In the Iranian government's eyes the nation of Israel doesn't exist. Therefore, Israeli citizens absolutely can't get a visa to visit Iran, nor can those with Israeli stamps in their passports get a visa. This was the first knock against us because our British passports had a number of Israeli stamps. However, having dual Canadian-British citizenship allows us the privilege of having two passports. So if our British passports are a problem we can simply use our Canadian passports. And this is knock number two. While Israeli's can never get a visa for Iran, and Americans can almost never get a visa, Canadians are very definitely on the "hard to get" list.

We applied for our visas through the Iranian embassy in Ottawa and after five weeks had no response. Over the next few days, there were many phone calls between Vancouver and my academic colleagues at the University of Gorgon, the Iranian embassy in Ottawa, and external affairs in Tehran. We later learned that the president of the University of Gorgon made an eight-hour journey to the Foreign Affairs offices in Tehran to plead our case. Meanwhile, we made our way to Israel and by this stage had virtually given up on getting entry visas for Iran. However, our daughter Andrea contacted us while we were in Israel to tell us that our visas had finally been issued after a full ten weeks, and she sent them by courier to catch us up. We never received a definitive explanation for all of the difficulties and delays, but it seems that Tehran was reluctant to permit independent travel —as we'll explain below.

We flew into Iran on a short one-hour flight from the city of Yerevan in Armenia. We boarded the plane and barely five minutes after takeoff the flight attendant announced: "Ladies, you will be entering the Islamic Republic of Iran, and according to Islamic custom, it is required that you have your head covered."

On hearing this, we knew we had arrived! Iran is a huge country with a diverse array of landscapes ranging from high mountains in the north and west, and in the center, south, and east is a large, sprawling desert and semi-desert occupying more than 50% of the country. The traveler sees mixed hardwood forests, oak woodlands, grasslands, and semi-desert scrub all within short distances.

We visited Iran in 2004, and our plans were simple — we had about three weeks, and we were going to spend the first four days at Gorgon University in the northeast of the country. We planned to travel independently for the remaining seventeen days and visit biblical sites, other major historic ruins at Persepolis and Pasargadae, and some of the beautiful cities that are bejeweled with brightly-colored mosques and palaces. The first four days went as planned and we were instantly struck by the warmth and hospitality of the people. The giving and the warmth were overwhelming and somewhat embarrassing because we were given no opportunity to reciprocate — and when we offered we were always told "not in my country." But during those four days it became clear that our following traveling days weren't going to go as planned. Rather than allowing us to move around as independent travelers, the university insisted that they provide us with a Nissan Patrol wagon and driver, and a graduate student as a guide and interpreter. We suspect that the Iranian government issued our visas on the condition that the university would not permit us to travel independently. This is a great country to travel in because costs are rock bottom. Gas was 14¢ per liter, meals in the best restaurants cost about $1 USD, a seven-hour bus journey typically $1 USD, and a city-to-city flight of one hour about $15 USD. The only payback was that I presented research seminars at universities in Shiraz, Yazd, and Esfahan. This accompaniment gave us security and safety, but we had to sacrifice independence and flexibility — but in Iran, it was definitely worth it.

The history of Iran, formerly Persia, is ancient and rich. In the last few years it seems to be finally recovering from the excesses of the Islamic Revolution that overthrew the Shah in 1979. There is some promotion of tourism, albeit strictly controlled, with a cautious and wary eye on the impact of an influx of rich westerners which, no doubt, would have an enormous impact on religious and cultural values. Although the west is the great bogey man, and the US the great Satan, nevertheless, the general populace craves what the west has to offer. In addition, the vehement anti-American, anti-Israeli, and anti-western government-sponsored propaganda, especially on television, is quite unsettling.

During our travels, we went to Tehran, which is a traffic-choked nightmare. Red lights and no entry signs seem to be little more than a good suggestion, most vehicles go around the roundabouts in the same direction, sidewalks are only a little less dangerous than the streets, you are advised to look right and left at least three times before crossing the road, but you should check behind your back as well. And then there are those countless, lawless, speeding, and weaving motorbikes — sidewalk beware. Tehran is worth avoiding except for a visit to the absolutely enormous complex around the tomb of the Emam Khomeine (believed to be the largest Islamic building in the world). There is also the incredible bazaar, which is without question the biggest and best in the middle east, the Golestan Palace complex, the National Jewels Museum, and the former US Embassy now referred to as the UN den of espionage.

We left Tehran and headed towards the first of our biblical destinations — Hamadan. The road to Hamadan brought us into the Zagros Mountains, and we would be close to this range for a few days as we journeyed in western Iran. The Zagros Mountains forest steppe runs northwest to southeast and is roughly parallel to the country's western border with Iraq. The Zagros have a semi-humid forest although many of the mountains' original oak forests are gone. The forests consist mainly of deciduous, broad-leaved trees dominated by oak, elm, pistachio, and walnut trees or shrubs, with a dense ground cover of steppe vegetation. An important aspect of the Zagros Mountains is its unique oak forests. Farther south along the range, the forest becomes more impoverished, and a richer steppe flora develops among the trees.

Upon arrival at Hamadan, we visited the tombs of Esther and Mordecai, which are only a short distance from the mound that was once Achmetha.[56] Achmetha was the site of the Royal archives where the decree of King Cyrus was recovered:

> *Then King Darius issued a decree, and a search was made in the archives, where the treasures were stored in Babylon. And at Achmetha, in the palace that is in the province of Media, a scroll was found, and in it a record was written thus: In the first year of King Cyrus, King Cyrus issued a decree … (Ezra 6:1-3)*

The tombs of Esther and Mordecai are located about two hundred meters southwest of the city center, and we will visit these tombs in a later chapter.

From Hamadan we went to Kermanshah and then drove south towards Shush. Although we were driving amid the beauty of the western slopes of the Zagros Mountains, it didn't take long to realize that Iran has the worst drivers anywhere in the world that we had visited. There was one particular two-hour segment of the journey that was candidly insane — plain insanity. We were on

---

[56] Achmetha is called Ecbatana in the ESV, NIV, and NASB.

part of the main road that joins the ports on the Persian Gulf to the interior of the country, and it is crowded with fully-laden Merc, Mack, and Volvo trucks. We counted from between fifteen to thirty trucks per minute, for two hours, as we drove this stretch of road, and thankfully (I think!) we were going in the opposite direction. Trucks were coming along in convoys of 10–20 vehicles, and they were so close to each other that, guaranteed, every truck driver could read the license plate of the truck three vehicles ahead. The real problem was that these trucks were always passing, and no one is going to argue with a fully laden truck, especially when going downhill at twice the speed limit on the wrong side of the road. Did I say speed limit —the speed limit is merely a suggestion.

Many of these trucks had slogans emblazoned in large letters across the top of their windshield — such things as "God only," "Mohammad," or "My God." Imagine the horror on our faces when, on one occasion, we drove around a corner and met a truck on the wrong side of the road, being driven by the devil himself, with the words "Oh My God" emblazoned across the windshield. On that single two-hour stretch we came across three major accidents, two of which involved over-turned trucks, and the third badly damaged. There was way too much testosterone on this road.

Eventually, we arrived at Shush, ancient Shushan, which is about 240 kilometers north of the Persian Gulf. When Cyrus the Great (550–529 BC) established the Persian Empire, he made Shushan its capital. At Shushan, Darius the Great (521–486 BC) built his magnificent royal palace. The site today is about two thousand hectares and is covered with ruins, and this is merely a fraction compared to the extent of ancient the city. However, most of it is indecipherable, and inaccessible, to the average traveler. Nevertheless, this is the setting for virtually the entire Book of Esther.

Esther is a historical book of the Old Testament that shows how God preserved His Chosen People — ironically, the book never mentions the name of God. Nevertheless, His sovereignty is 'seen' throughout the book. The Jewish historian Josephus claimed that the book was written by Mordecai, but this is open to much dispute. The book is named for its main personality, Queen Esther of Persia, whose courage and quick thinking saved the Jewish people from disaster. The book is written like a short story even though it reports on actual events. The main characters in this powerful drama are King Ahasuerus (identified with Xerxes I; 486-465 BC) of Persia; his wife, Vashti; his new Jewish wife, Queen Esther; his second in command, Haman; and Mordecai, a leader among the Jewish people scattered throughout the Persian Empire.

Esther's Jewish name was Hadassah, meaning myrtle. She saved the Jews from a plot to eliminate them. Esther was raised by Mordecai, her cousin, after her mother and father died. She was a member of a family carried into captivity about 600 BC that later chose to stay in Persia rather than return to Jerusalem.

The story of Esther's rise to become the queen of the mighty Persian Empire illustrates how God uses events and people as instruments to fulfill His promise to His People. Following several days of festivities, the drunken king Ahasuerus asked his queen, Vashti, to display herself to his guests. When Vashti refused, she was banished from the palace. Ahasuerus then had all the beautiful young virgins of his kingdom brought to his palace, so he could choose Vashti's replacement. Scripture records that the king appointed Esther as his new queen. At the time, Haman was the king's most trusted advisor. He was an egotistical man and demanded that people bow to him as he passed. Mordecai refused, and in a rage, Haman sought revenge on Mordecai and the entire Jewish population. Haman persuaded King Ahasuerus to issue a decree permitting him to kill all the Jews. Mordecai learned of Haman's plot and put pressure on Esther, and this is recorded as one of the key verses in the book:

For if you remain completely silent at this time, relief and deliverance will arise for the Jews from another place, but you and your father's house will perish. Yet who knows whether you have come to the kingdom for such a time as this?" (Mordecai to Esther in Esther 4:14)

Esther exposed Haman's plot and his true character to the king. As a result, Ahasuerus granted the Jews the right to defend themselves. With ironic justice, Haman and his ten sons were hanged on the gallows that he had prepared for Mordecai.

Now Harbonah, one of the eunuchs, said to the king, "Look! The gallows, fifty cubits high, which Haman made for Mordecai, who spoke good on the king's behalf, is standing at the house of Haman." Then the king said, "Hang him on it!" So they hanged Haman on the gallows that he had prepared for Mordecai... (Esther 7:9-10)

Then Esther said, "If it pleases the king, let it be granted to the Jews who are in Shushan to do again tomorrow according to today's decree, and let Haman's ten sons be hanged on the gallows." So the king commanded this to be done; the decree was issued in Shushan, and they hanged Haman's ten sons. (Esther 9:13-14)

Today, Jews celebrate their deliverance from this decree at the Feast of Purim, celebrated on the fourteenth and fifteenth days of the month of Adar, which is usually mid to late March.

So they called these days Purim, after the name Pur. Therefore, because of all the words of this letter, what they had seen concerning this matter, and what had happened to them, the Jews established and imposed it upon themselves and their descendants and all who would join them, that without fail they should celebrate these two days every year, according to the written instructions and according to the prescribed time, that these days should be remembered and kept throughout every generation, every family, every province, and every city, that these days of Purim should not fail to be observed among the Jews, and that the memory of them should not perish among their descendants. Then Queen Esther, the daughter of Abihail, with Mordecai the Jew, wrote with full authority to confirm this second letter about Purim. And Mordecai sent letters to all the Jews, to the one hundred and twenty-seven provinces of the kingdom of Ahasuerus, with words of peace and truth, to confirm these days of Purim at their appointed time, as Mordecai the Jew and Queen Esther had prescribed for them, and as they had decreed for themselves and their descendants concerning matters of their fasting and lamenting. So the decree of Esther confirmed these matters of Purim, and it was written in the book. (Esther 9:26-32)

The Shushan area is vast, but there is little to see except for the main part at the Royal City. The Royal City has the palace audience hall and the remains of the palace of Darius and his successors. It was hot upon arrival, probably 44° or 45°, although this is cool compared to the 53° which is recorded here in most summers. Evelyn was dressed in black from head to toe, and this alone probably raised the apparent temperature by a few degrees. We never understood or received a straight answer on why black was the typical color of choice rather than white or some other light color. In these temperatures, we clearly weren't going to spend too much time at the site, and yet this was one of our main reasons for coming to Iran.

Our driver, after some heated words with the gate attendant, drove beyond the parking lot, and we managed to avoid climbing the steep roadway to the top of the ancient mound. As we climbed out of our air-conditioned vehicle, the searing heat hit us like an open-oven door. We climbed onto a higher part of the ruins and looked down on the town from the heights of the ancient Acropolis. Over towards the northwest, rising from behind the corrugated-iron shop roofs of the main street, we could see a strange, white spiral resembling a large, elongated pine cone; this was the tomb of Daniel[57] the prophet, which we would visit later.

The site was sprawling and you'd need quite a vivid imagination to conjure up some vestige of Shushan's past grandeur. The palace walls and processional pathways remain for the visitor to walk around, and after some two

---

[57] Muslim traditional site.

and a half thousand years the baked brick wall footings still stand to waist height, outlining the building's ground plan. The apadana or audience hall is huge, perhaps at least seventy meters in both dimensions, and is a great hall of columns built by Darius the Great in 525 BC; it's now known as the throne-room of Artaxerxes. This throne room today is quite desolate and has the bases of about thirty of the once-enormous columns that were originally over twenty meters tall; these offer a tantalizing hint of what Shush must have been like before the place was plundered and all the glories destroyed or carted off as museum pieces. This magnificent room is the site of the great orgy of Esther chapter 1 resulting in the banishment of Vashti and the crowing of Esther as Queen of Persia.

> *The king loved Esther more than all the other women, and she obtained grace and favor in his sight more than all the virgins; so he set the royal crown upon her head and made her queen instead of Vashti.* (Esther 2:17)

We wandered around the ruins for perhaps half an hour. I was hot, Evelyn was hotter, and poor Abbas our guide probably wondered why we even wanted to spend time in this desolate place. There were many hints flying that we should get back to the truck, but there was still one more site I had to find. There were no maps and little by way of information. All I knew was that the ancient entry to the city was somewhere to the south of where we were standing. I walked off at a fairly brisk pace pretending that I knew exactly where I was going. Evelyn knew what I was doing but poor old Abbas just scratched his head — why would anyone want to wander aimlessly over these featureless bumps and hollows — especially in this searing heat?

But in a few moments, our grit was rewarded. We climbed up onto a low mound, and there on the other side were the gates of the city and the courtyard immediately inside the city gates. Physically it was unimpressive, but emotionally this was one of the most beautiful spots in all of Iran. All that remained was the lower fifty centimeters of the walls, and the courtyard, and the opening that was the gate. The area wasn't overgrown but certainly hadn't been tended for a while. In the middle of the courtyard was the base of what was once an enormous column. What we would dearly love would be to sit down on this large base, open the book of Esther, and read it in its entirety. It was precisely here at this spot that many events of the Book of Esther took place and possibly where Haman and his ten sons were hanged.

1. When virgins were gathered together a second time, Mordecai sat within the king's gate. (Esther 2:19)

2. In those days, while Mordecai sat within the king's gate, two of the king's eunuchs, Bigthan and Teresh, doorkeepers, became furious and sought to lay hands on King Ahasuerus. (Esther 2:21)

3. And all the king's servants who were within the king's gate bowed and paid homage to Haman, for so the king had commanded concerning him. But Mordecai would not bow or pay homage. Then the king's servants who were within the king's gate said to Mordecai, "Why do you transgress the king's command?" (Esther 3:2-3)

4. He went as far as the front of the king's gate, for no one might enter the king's gate clothed with sackcloth. (Esther 4:2)

5. So Hathach went out to Mordecai in the city square that was in front of the king's gate. (Esther 4:6)

6. So Haman went out that day joyful and with a glad heart; but when Haman saw Mordecai in the king's gate, and that he did not stand or tremble before him, he was filled with indignation against Mordecai. (Esther 5:9)

7. Yet all this avails me nothing, so long as I see Mordecai the Jew sitting at the king's gate. (Esther 5:13)

8. Then the king said to Haman, "Hurry, take the robe and the horse, as you have suggested, and do so for Mordecai the Jew who sits within the king's gate! Leave nothing undone of all that you have spoken." (Esther 6:10)

9. Afterward Mordecai went back to the king's gate. But Haman hurried to his house, mourning and with his head covered. (Esther 6:12)

While we would have had the time to read the Book of Esther, there is no doubt that our rapidly dehydrating bodies would not have permitted it. I paused to take a few more photographs, and when I turned around Evelyn and Abbas were already making a good distance back towards our vehicle. I jogged to catch up with them, and we continued to the comfort of our vehicle, climbed in, drove off, and contemplated the enormity of what we had just experienced.

XI.
GRAVE MATTERS

We suspect that the title of this chapter may induce a few readers to skip to the next chapter. But don't do that — you will be rewarded if you keep reading. To tell the stories of living heroes often stirs the soul, but so too does their memory. It has been said that "Life is a terminal illness curable only by death" — in visiting these tombs it wasn't to think about death, but about life. Every time we visit a tomb or gravesite, our minds wander back to the good times and the pleasant memories. Likewise, the tombs of the famous and infamous from the Bible evoke great recollections of some of the classic stories from Scripture — Abraham, Sarah, Isaac, Rebecca, Jacob, Rachel, Joshua, Caleb, Samuel, King David, Daniel, Esther, Mordecai, the Persian kings, Jesus Christ, Caiaphas[58] the High Priest, John, Peter, and Paul. Many of the more than fifty tombs that we visited had beautiful memorials and often provided us with some of the most serious challenges we've ever had in finding biblical locations. Ironically, some of our fondest memories and some of our more adventurous moments happened while searching for someone's burial place. So keep reading.

The first account of a burial in Scripture is that of Sarah, the wife of the patriarch Abraham:

> *And after this, Abraham buried Sarah his wife in the cave of the field of Machpelah, before Mamre (that is, Hebron) in the land of Canaan.* (Genesis 23:19)

And the first commercial transaction recorded in Scripture was the purchase of a burial place which Abraham purchased from Ephron:

> *And Ephron answered Abraham, saying to him, "My lord, listen to me; the land is worth four hundred shekels of silver. What is that between you and me? So bury*

---

[58] Caiaphas the High Priest is one of seven New Testament religious figures confirmed by archaeology and historical texts; the others are Jesus, Gamaliel the Elder, John the Baptist, James the brother of Jesus, Annas the High Priest, and Ananias the High Priest (see references at the bottom of p38 in Lawrence Mykytiuk 2021. New Testament religious figures confirmed. Biblical Archaeology Review, 47 (2), pp 38-47; *biblicalarchaeology.org/ntpeople*). Mykytiuk has also presented evidence for the existence of twenty-three political figures in the New Testament (BAR 2017, 43 (5) pp. 56-57) and fifty-three people in the Old Testament (BAR 2014, 40 (2) pp. 46-47; *biblicalarchaeology.org/biblepeople*).

your dead." And Abraham listened to Ephron; and Abraham weighed out the silver for Ephron... four hundred shekels of silver, currency of the merchants. (Genesis 23:14-16)

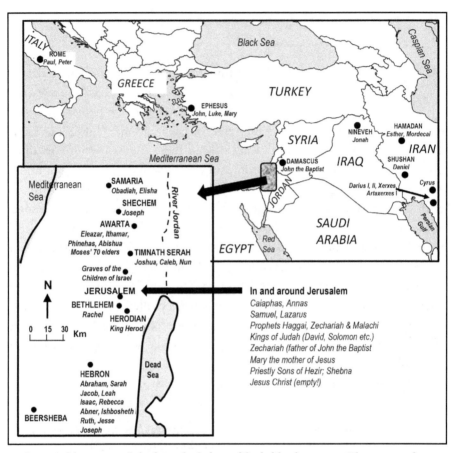

Proposed locations of the burial of about fifty bible characters. These range from being certain e.g. the Persian kings, Caiaphas to being possible e.g. Jonah, Joshua, Annas to extremely doubtful or don't know.

Interment in Bible times followed soon after death, as we see in the narratives of the burial of Sarah (Genesis 23), Rachel (Genesis 35:19-20), and Rebekah's nurse (Genesis 35:8). Cremation wasn't practiced except in unusual emergency cases, as in the case of Saul and his sons (1 Samuel 31:11-13). If possible, the Jews either entombed or interred their dead. Depending upon economic and social status, burial was either in a shallow grave covered with stones, or in a cave or tomb hewn out of stone, such as the tombs of the kings of Israel, Shebna, Annas the High Priest, or one of the purported tombs of Joshua. Tombs were often secured by rolling a circular stone over the entrance and sealing the tomb, for example, the tomb of Jesus. This was done to protect the body from scavenging wild animals.

Initially, it was customary for each family to have a family tomb: either a natural cave, prepared with stone shelves to receive the bodies, or else hewn out of rock in the hillside, each tomb having many niches in which a body could be placed (see Genesis 49:3).

> *There they buried Abraham and Sarah his wife, there they buried Isaac and Rebekah his wife, and there I buried Leah.* (Genesis 49:31)

Countless numbers of such tombs are to be found all over the Bible lands, with Machpelah being the best example, but also the tombs of the prophets on the Mount of Olives. Ordinary graves were marked by the heaping of crude stones. On occasion, hewn stones and sometimes costly pillars were set up as memorials. For example, King Josiah asked the question:

> ... *"What gravestone is this that I see?" So the men of the city told him, "It is the tomb of the man of God who came from Judah and proclaimed these things which you have done against the altar of Bethel."* (2 Kings 23:17)

This is a reference to a sepulchral pillar. Jacob also set up a pillar over Rachel's grave (Genesis 35:20). At the most extreme, we see the massive, and sometimes elaborate, edifices built over the graves of some royalty, such as the Persian kings. We'll first visit the tombs of Old Testament figures and generally travel from north to south through Samaria, Judea, then to Iran, and finish with tombs of a few New Testament characters.

OBADIAH AND ELISHA

Just below the ruins of ancient Samaria is the modern village of Sebastia. As we drove up the road to the site, we noticed many burial caves that were discovered during the construction of the road. When first found, many of these contained sarcophagi dating back to around 800 BC. In the village is an old Crusader church dating back to the twelfth century AD, and this has now been converted into a mosque with two tomb chambers. These are a mess. We entered one by climbing through a broken window, and the other by scrambling through a partially broken door with a twisted frame. Interestingly, there was a man at the site selling entrance tickets! Both tombs were littered with building materials. One is the reputed tomb of the prophet Elisha, the other is open to some question. Some allege that this is the burial place of John the Baptist, others that it is that of the prophet Obadiah, but the most popular view is that it is the resting place of another Obadiah, not the prophet:

And Ahab had called Obadiah, who was in charge of his house. (Now Obadiah feared the Lord greatly. For so it was, while Jezebel massacred the prophets of the Lord, that Obadiah had taken one hundred prophets and hidden them, fifty to a cave, and had fed them with bread and water.) (1 Kings 18:3-4)

Elisha means "God is my Salvation," or, "my God saves." Elisha was a true servant of God, and many miracles happened during his ministry. A rather interesting miracle occurred after his death. After Elisha's burial, some bandits raided Israel and the local men hastily threw the body of a friend into Elisha's tomb. As soon as the body touched Elisha's bones, the dead man was revived and jumped to his feet.

So it was, as they were burying a man, that suddenly they spied a band of raiders; and they put the man in the tomb of Elisha; and when the man was let down and touched the bones of Elisha, he revived and stood on his feet. (2 Kings 13:21)

This is one of the funniest funeral stories I've ever read. What a sight that must have been!

JOSEPH'S TOMB IN SHECHEM

Our visit to the tomb of Joseph in Shechem, modern Nablus, was uneventful. It was, nevertheless, part of an eventful day: we were evicted from the church over Jacob's well for taking photographs without permission, Israeli jets produced sonic booms over the ruins of ancient Shechem, police stopped us for taking video at Dothan, and our taxi broke down in Nablus. The parcel of land on which Joseph's tomb was situated is only a few meters east of the ruins of Shechem and perhaps a few hundred meters from Jacob's well. The land was purchased by Jacob:

The bones of Joseph, which the children of Israel had brought up out of Egypt, they buried at Shechem, in the plot of ground which Jacob had bought from the sons of Hamor the father of Shechem for one hundred pieces of silver, and which had become an inheritance of the children of Joseph. (Joshua 24:32)

The late Dr. Zvi Ilan described Joseph's Tomb as:

… one of the tombs whose location is known with the utmost degree of certainty and is based on continuous documentation since biblical times.[59].

---

[59] Zvi, I. (1997). *Tombs of the Righteous in the Land of Israel.* Carta Publ.

The tomb itself was situated in a room adjoining a Jewish school, a Yeshiva. It was a small building and Joseph's tomb was draped with a rich and vibrant purple material. A number of Jewish students were present and were oblivious to our presence as they engaged in their worship activities. They were also oblivious to, or totally ignored, the fact that our escort was a Palestinian Christian, who at that time was the pastor of the Bible Baptist Church in Ramallah.

Tragically, this cenotaph no longer exists. During September and early October 2000, the tomb was attacked with gunfire, stones, and firebombs. On the morning of October 7, 2000, Israel withdrew the small contingent of IDF border policemen who had been guarding the site. A group of Palestinian vandals entered the compound and systematically destroyed it. Within hours, Joseph's tomb was reduced to a smoldering heap of rubble festooned with Palestinian and Islamic flags. A new monument was built in 2010. We can't help but reflect on the reaction by the Muslim world if Jews (or anyone for that matter) would have razed the gravesite of one of the founders of Islam. The withdrawal of the IDF from Joseph's tomb was seen as a strategic error. Consequently, having learned from their error, in 2002 when fire bombings and gunfire occurred at Rachel's tomb on the northern outskirts of Bethlehem, the Israelis decided to include the site within the boundaries of a security zone to be constructed around Jerusalem.

ELEAZAR, ITHAMAR, PHINEHAS, ABISHUA, AND THE SEVENTY ELDERS

The Arab village of Awarta is only six kilometers southeast of Shechem. The village has tombs purportedly connected to the priestly family of Moses' brother, Aaron; these are Eleazar, Ithamar, Phinehas, Abishua, and the seventy elders who helped Moses bear the burden of caring for the people. As we approached the village, we passed though an Israeli army checkpoint. The soldiers were adorable. They were only youngsters, perhaps nineteen or twenty years old, going through a boring repetitive routine of "ID please, who are you, where are you going, and why?"

We added a bit of flavor to their monotony. "You are going where, to see what? Who in the name of God is Eleazar? If he was a son of Aaron, he's sure as hell not buried in Awarta." The young soldiers seemed unphased by the growing lineup of dilapidated vans and small trucks behind us and were intrigued by our search for tombs. And when a few impatient individuals behind us beeped their horns he gave them that wonderful uniquely Israeli hand gesture signaling, "*just one moment,*" and then carried on talking about Vancouver and Canada.

After receiving a fairly strong caution about being in the area, we nervously entered the village of Awarta. Almost instantly, we were swarmed by children, and we weren't sure if this was a good sign or a bad sign. With all of these children around our car, we couldn't drive more than about five kilometers per hour in case we hit one of them. Finally, we reached a little store, asked for directions, and in typical Palestinian fashion, the storekeeper closed his store, jumped into the car alongside us, and for the next hour brought us to all three of the tomb complexes. We don't have any way of knowing if these are authentic sites as they are held in deep Muslim tradition. We had a wonderful time visiting them anyway.

About halfway through the village we arrived at the first tomb. This was the tomb of Ithamar, a son of Aaron, and a brother of Eleazar. Aaron's first two sons, Nadab and Abihu, were killed for offering unholy fire to the Lord (Leviticus 10:1-7). Eleazar and his brother Ithamar were consecrated as priests in place of the two elder brothers. The setting for this tomb is fantastic. It was overgrown with the most magnificent show of wildflowers, and the backdrop, some six kilometers distant, was the twin peaks of Mount Gerizim and Mount Ebal, the sites of Joshua's famous speech to the children of Israel when he renewed the covenant with Israel. A little farther at the top of the village, and still surrounded by about twenty children, we were shown the tombs of Phinehas (a son of Eleazar the third high priest of Israel), his son Abishua (the fourth high priest of Israel), and the seventy elders who helped Moses bear the burden of caring for the people.

> So the Lord said to Moses: "Gather to Me seventy men of the elders of Israel, whom you know to be the elders of the people and officers over them; bring them to the tabernacle of meeting, that they may stand there with you. Then I will come down and talk with you there. I will take of the Spirit that is upon you and will put the same upon them; and they shall bear the burden of the people with you, that you may not bear it yourself alone. (Numbers 11:16-17)

From there, we were able to drive back downhill, finally leave the swarming children behind, and we came to the tomb of Eleazar, Aaron's the third son. This is a magnificent structure, and is enclosed within a sizeable, walled compound. We were enjoying the relative tranquility of this site, again with wildflowers, and again with Mount Ebal and Mount Gerizim, when all of the children arrived again. They had taken a shortcut through the fields to catch up with us, and we're still puzzled by how they knew where we were going. They began to sing to us and were only transiently distracted by the two supersonic booms that rattled overhead. Then, of course, the necessary photograph with all the adorable smiling children, and we were on our way. The only Scriptural support for any of these tombs comes from Joshua 24:33. The New International Version (and many other versions) state:

And Eleazar son of Aaron died and was buried at Gibeah, which had been allotted to his son Phinehas in the hill country of Ephraim. (Joshua 24:33, NIV)

The King James Version translates this verse as:

And Eleazar the son of Aaron died. They buried him in a hill belonging to Phinehas his son, which was given to him in the mountains of Ephraim. (Joshua 24:33, KJV)

Many versions state that Eleazar was buried at Gibeah. This is not to be confused with Gibeah, Saul's capital, on the northern outskirts of Jerusalem. All versions refer to the hill country or the mountains of Ephraim. The southern boundary of the territory of Ephraim had a border with Benjamin to the south (approximately at Ramallah), and the northern boundary was with Shechem, or modern Nablus. Here, in the village of Awarta, we are safely in the territory of Ephraim, and we are certainly in the hill country — maybe, just maybe, we are at the correct location.

JOSHUA

Now it came to pass after these things that Joshua the son of Nun, the servant of the Lord, died, being one hundred and ten years old. And they buried him within the border of his inheritance at Timnath Serah, which is in the mountains of Ephraim, on the north side of Mount Gaash. (Joshua 24:29-30)

As we read in this text, Joshua was buried at Timnath Serah; Judges 2:9 calls the place Timnath Hares but if you look closely 'Hares' is simply 'Serah' spelled in reverse! As you may expect, there is more than one traditional burial site for Joshua — both have good scholastic support.

There was nothing dangerous, nervous, or nail-biting about this site, just simply the thrill of being there. I am referring to the possible location of the burial place of Joshua at Khirbet Tibneh about twenty-five kilometers northwest of Ramallah. The tomb is one of many on the side of the hill. The one we sought had a large square-cut entrance, almost like a foyer. At the end of the foyer was a single entrance about fifty centimeters wide and perhaps seventy centimeters tall, but the entrance was half-buried with rocks and fairly well covered with weeds.

After five minutes of gardening and stone moving, the entrance was clear enough for us to slither through on our bellies. Luckily, we had a flashlight.

Inside, we entered a room with the entire floor covered with rocks, perhaps to a depth of fifty centimeters in places. The room itself was about three by four meters, and two meters high, and this had fifteen different burial niches. The central niche was the largest and ornate. We clambered into this larger niche, which opened into five or six more niches. Which one belonged to Joshua? Who knows? Did any of these belong to Joshua? We don't know — but it was sobering to think that bodies were placed in this rather remarkable tomb perhaps over three thousand years ago! As we sat in the tomb complex a horrible thought flashed through my mind — what would happen if something somehow went wrong and the entrance became blocked with us inside? No one knew where we were, and it's doubtful if anyone would be in here again for another three thousand years — I guess someone would see the car and start searching — just a horrible thought in the middle of a grand experience.

There is a second proposed burial location for the tomb of Joshua, this being at the village of Kifl Harit (also spelled Kifel Hares) which is only a short distance from the large Jewish Community of Ariel. This village also has the tombs of Caleb and Nun. Kifl Harit is a very small Arab village, but since 2003, the road leading into the village has been declared a Closed Military Zone.

Like similar villages, we drove in very slowly and cautiously because we have no way of predicting the type of reception: we could be welcomed with open arms or we could have stones thrown at us. We drove through the outskirts of the little village and soon arrived in the village square, which was strangely quiet. Little did we realize that we had parked our car right beside a sign indicating the tomb of Joshua. Unfortunately, the signs weren't easy to read because of graffiti and peeling posters of Yasser Arafat and other leaders of the Arab community. The sign read (in English, Arabic, and Hebrew) "Tomb of Joshua. Kindly show respect for the sanctity of this holy site," and the sign had the approval of the Israeli antiquities authority. On the outside, the structure was clean and freshly whitewashed, perhaps four meters wide and long, and about three meters high, and was located inside a pleasant courtyard. A few children approached us with bright, smiling, innocent faces and bouncing a dirty ball. It is good protocol to talk to the children even though we can't communicate a single syllable. A couple of the children beckoned us to go inside the structure. We entered a gate into a small courtyard and had to bend low to enter the little building. The inside was white and clean, but absolutely empty — a bit of a disappointment. About twenty years later, I returned to the tombs with my 2.04 meter tall son-in-law; Fergus had to do serious contortions to get through the low, narrow door.

CALEB AND NUN

When Caleb was eighty-five years old he came to Joshua at the camp at Gilgal and was reminded of the inheritance promised by Moses. Moses had given to Caleb a portion of the land of Kirjath-Arba as his inheritance. We have almost no other information pertaining to Caleb's life or death. And scripturally we have nothing on Nun except that he was the father of Joshua (Numbers 11:28). We know from Scripture that Joshua and Caleb both entered the Promised Land, and that all of the older people, including Nun, died before reaching the River Jordan. It is apparent that the remains of Nun were carried into the Promised Land for burial.

The purported tombs of Caleb and Nun are also in the village if Kifl Harit along with that of Joshua. We returned to our car, and by this time a few younger men had appeared, but they had a strong reluctance to speak to us. We asked about the tomb of Nun. One of the young men spoke to the children, and as they ran off it was clear that we were to follow them. This we did, rather nervously leaving our car behind, and within a few moments we arrived at a rather solid structure labeled as the tomb of Nun, located in the back garden of an apartment complex; there was no entrance. We returned to our car, and it was then that one of the young men told us that they couldn't really speak to us because they were "*being watched.*"

Unfortunately, we had this experience in other Arab villages where the local henchmen controlled who could speak and who could be spoken to. Evidently, we weren't on their list even though we did what we could to generate openness — we had a couple of small Canadian flags on the side windows of our car, and Arab head covering (keffiyeh) spread across the dashboard. It was a short distance to the tomb of Caleb, which was much more elaborate than the other two. It was clean both inside and out and even had a small flower garden outside with pomegranate in flower, but a short distance away was the dreadful smell and sight of burning rubbish.

We left the village and returned to the main highway. Just outside the entrance to Ariel we filled our car with gas — about three weeks later, Arab gunmen killed an Israeli soldier at this gas station.

SAMUEL

While driving the main motorway from Tel Aviv to Jerusalem, one finally reaches that long, final hill up to Jerusalem. Drivers with a rubber neck, and at least two sets of eyes, can see a white Muslim shrine with minaret in the distance, on the top of a hill to the northwest. This is the traditional burial place of Samuel the Prophet and is revered by both Jews and Muslims. The building is rather uninspiring, and on the ground floor Muslims have a cenotaph for Samuel, and on the lower floor, the Jews have a cenotaph for Samuel.

> *Then Samuel died; and the Israelites gathered together and lamented for him, and buried him at his home in Ramah....* (1 Samuel 25:1)

One thing is special about the mosque. It is a bit of a grind to climb the long stone staircase that leads to the roof of the building. The view in all directions is quite wonderful. However, if one looks carefully, about four to five kilometers to the east you can see the remains of a palace that was being built by King Hussein of Jordan until it was abruptly interrupted by the 1967 Six-Day War. This palace was being built on the site of Gibeah, which was King Saul's capital city. It was in Saul's Palace that the story unfolds of Saul throwing his spear at David while David was playing his harp (1 Samuel 19:9, 10). The rest of the story describes how David fled from Gibeah to find Samuel at Ramah and on to Nob, to Ahimelech the priest, and it was there that David ate the consecrated bread.

Although the location of Nob isn't certain, it is likely at the northern end of the Mount of Olives on a site now occupied by the Mount Scopus campus of the Hebrew University of Jerusalem. Standing on the roof of the mosque, we can vividly retrace the route most likely taken by David from Gibeah to Ramah and on to Nob. In addition, below us to the north is the site of the city of Gibeon where Joab and Abner's soldiers fought at the great pool (2 Samuel 2:12-17), and to the north and northwest is the valley where Joshua prayed that the sun would stand still:

> *Then Joshua spoke to the Lord in the day when the Lord delivered up the Amorites before the children of Israel, and he said in the sight of Israel: "Sun, stand still over Gibeon; And Moon, in the Valley of Aijalon." So the sun stood still, And the moon stopped, Till the people had revenge Upon their enemies. Is this not written in the Book of Jasher? So the sun stood still in the midst of heaven, and did not hasten to go down for about a whole day.* (Joshua 10:12-13)

All of this, and more, could be seen from the top of a simple and uninspiring little building on the northwestern outskirts of Jerusalem.

LAZARUS

> *Now a certain man was sick, Lazarus of Bethany, the town of Mary and her sister Martha... Then Jesus said to them plainly, "Lazarus is dead...Now when He [Jesus]*

had said these things, He cried with a loud voice, "Lazarus, come forth!" And he who had died came out bound hand and foot with grave clothes, and his face was wrapped with a cloth... (John 11:1, 14, 43-44)

This is one of the most familiar stories in the New Testament. Bethany is only a short distance from Jerusalem: about three kilometers east on the other side of the Mount of Olives. Bethany was the hometown of Mary, her sister Martha, and Lazarus. We jumped into a taxi at the Damascus Gate in Jerusalem and bartered for a price to take us to El-Azarieh,[60] which is the place of Lazarus in Arabic. The ten-minute taxi ride was uneventful, and we were dropped off at the Franciscan church of St. Lazarus.

Our first task was to purchase two bottles of water. Evelyn is always very quick to check that bottle seals are intact because it is common practice in these parts to refill plastic bottles with regular water, which in these areas guarantees stomach sickness to visitors. The seal of the first bottle was broken, and we were quite incensed that the vendor took the bottle back without question and replaced it on his little cart awaiting the next unsuspecting customer. We were also incensed that he would sell this stuff knowing the potential health consequences to the consumer. I felt like pulling a 'Jesus act' and over-turning his tables!

We visited the church and then walked uphill to the site that commemorates the tomb of Lazarus. The tomb is under a small mosque, but access is gained from the main road. The tomb has a low entrance and is monitored by a self-appointed guard. After we were assured that there was no cost for visiting the tomb, we entered and descended the twenty-four well-worn steps to the cave below. One had to be acrobatically nimble to bend low enough to enter the final vestibule while at the same time negotiating the final few very steep steps. The entire stairway and final resting vestibule were all well-lit with candles. As usual, we stood in the cave and relived the events that happened here.

As we emerged from the cave, the guard now decided that there was an exit fee! No way! We aren't sure what happened next, but in all our years of traveling, despite being cheated, stoned, lied to, and deceived, we always remained calm. But not this time. This man plainly ticked us off! After we told him what we thought, and after refusing to pay him, we walked off and made a memorable trek over the Mount of Olives, following the route of Christ on Palm Sunday, through the little village of Bethphage, over the Mount of Olives, and Jerusalem came in to view in the valley below us.

---

[60] This was in 1992 long before the security barrier was erected. The barrier runs north-south along the Mt. of Olives just a little to the east of the summit ridgeline. Bethany is on the other side of the barrier from Jerusalem, and it now takes about an hour by taxi to get to Bethany from Jerusalem.

THE TOMBS OF HAGGAI, ZECHARIAH AND MALACHI

We passed by the Russian Church of the Ascension and walked to a majestic viewpoint over Jerusalem. From this vantage, we could see almost everything of significance —the Old City, Gordon's Calvary, Rockefeller Museum, the Church of the Holy Sepulchre, Lions' Gate, the Eastern or Beautiful Gate, the Garden of Gethsemane, the Church of Dominus Flevit, the Temple Mount with the Dome of the Rock, the southern wall excavations, the Pinnacle of the Temple, the City of David, and the Kidron and Hinnom Valleys. Between us and these sites was the large Jewish cemetery with some seventy thousand graves which extends over the entire southern part of the Western slope of the Mount of Olives. And only three meters below where we were standing, at the base of the wall, is the tomb of Robert Maxwell. We have often wondered how many of the tens of thousands of tourists that have stood at this viewpoint were shown Maxwell's grave.

Just a short distance to the north of our viewpoint we came to a gate with a sign "Tombs of the Prophets – Haggai and Zechariah." We entered the gate into what seemed to be another world. There's a small house, which has a fairly pleasant but quite untidy courtyard, and a few hens running around add to the ambiance. It's hard to believe that we were in the middle of an enormous graveyard because from here it is mostly out of sight. We knocked on the door of the home rather loudly three or four times before the custodian appeared. She was a very pleasant woman and she provided us with oil lamps. She brought us the few meters to an inconspicuous opening, unlocked the black metal gate, and led us the twenty or thirty stone steps down to the burial chambers.

We entered a cavernous chamber with a hole in the roof that allows sunlight to filter through. From this chamber, there are three openings leading to semicircular tunnels and these tunnels are lined with perhaps as many as fifty burial niches. We lit our lamps, which poured out lots of black smoke, and the woman showed us the purported burial niches of Haggai, Zechariah, and Malachi. While we were bent over peering into the niche of Haggai and using our lamps to help us see, a potent smell came wafting by — I don't know what our son had for breakfast but we were sure it would raise Haggai from the dead!

DETOUR TWELVE:
I DUG HIS GRAVE; I PUT MAXWELL IN

Robert Maxwell was a British publishing baron in the 1980s and was one of the world's most prominent media moguls. He was born to poor Jewish parents in the Czech Republic, fought in the British Army in World War II, and then settled in Britain. In 1991 Maxwell drowned while yachting off the Canary Islands. Most of the thousands of tourists who visit the Old City of Jerusalem viewpoint on the Mount of Olives have no idea that Robert Maxwell's grave is right below them —we didn't know for at least the first ten times we visited. But that changed on Christmas Day 1992. My parents were visiting for Christmas, and we had Christmas dinner in the 7-arches hotel about fifty meters behind where we were standing. This was without question the most lavish and elaborate meal we've ever had in a restaurant — ever, and the view over the Old City just added to the occasion.

While having dinner, my dad mentioned Robert Maxwell, and that got the ball rolling. We knew he was buried on the Mount of Olives, and knew it was somewhere near the viewpoint, but that was the limit of our information. After dinner, we decided to go have a look. We entered the graveyard and in a bewildered sort of way, knowing we hadn't a chance of finding anything because of the enormity of the place. Besides, it was very cold, and we weren't in much of a mood for searching.

A middle-aged Arab man came by, and on the off chance that he might speak English, we asked him if he knew where Maxwell's grave was. He smiled knowingly and said, "I will show you." We took off to the south and walked and walked and then began circling towards the east. I began to think that we were searching for the lost Ark because this was definitely the wrong direction. We must have been getting close to Bethany (slight exaggeration!) when we did a fairly abrupt change in direction and came back around behind the 7-arches hotel and back around to the spot where we had first met this man. Then he brought us directly to the grave which was only twenty meters away. We were puzzled, really puzzled. Then he explained to us that he wanted to ensure that we weren't part of the Maxwell family — he smiled and with an emphatic voice and exaggerated hand gestures said, "I dug the grave, I put him in."

From here it is about a fifteen-minute walk down a steep narrow road to the garden of Gethsemane at the bottom of the Mount of Olives and then across the road to our next tombs.

ABSALOM'S MONUMENT AND THE CAVE OF JEHOSHAPHAT

The northern end of the Kidron valley is called the Valley of Jehoshaphat, where according to Scripture the last judgment will take place:

> *I will also gather all nations, And bring them down to the Valley of Jehoshaphat; And I will enter into judgment with them there On account of My people, My heritage Israel, Whom they have scattered among the nations; They have also divided up My land.* (Joel 3:2)

Here there are a series of Jewish tombs in the shadow of the eastern wall of the Temple Mount. First, there is the impressive twenty meters high Monument of Absalom behind which is the Cave of King Jehoshaphat. These two structures are burial monuments. Absalom was the rebellious son of King David who attempted to overthrow King David and take over the kingdom. The monument, however, dates to the early first century AD, so both Absalom and Jehoshaphat lived hundreds of years before the monument was built. While the identity of those buried in this funerary complex is not known, we know it wasn't King David's son or King Jehoshaphat.

> *And Jehoshaphat rested with his fathers, and was buried with his fathers in the City of David his father. Then Jehoram his son reigned in his place.* (1 Kings 22:50)

In 2003, an inscription was found on Absalom's monument: "This is the tomb of Zachariah, the martyr, the holy priest, the father of John," suggesting that this may be the burial place of Zechariah the father of John the Baptist. A few meters along the valley is the Tomb of the priestly Sons of Hezir;

> *There were more leaders found of the sons of Eleazar than of the sons of Ithamar, and thus they were divided. Among the sons of Eleazar were sixteen heads of their fathers' houses, and eight heads of their fathers' houses among the sons of Ithamar. Thus they were divided by lot, one group as another, for there were officials of the sanctuary and officials of the house of God, from the sons of Eleazar and from the sons of Ithamar...the seventeenth to Hezir, the eighteenth to Happizzez,* (1 Chronicles 24:4-5, 15)

And yet a few more meters away is the impressive Tomb of Zechariah. A fifteenth-century tradition connects the monument with the prophet Zechariah:

> *Then the Spirit of God came upon Zechariah the son of Jehoiada the priest, who stood above the people, and said to them, "Thus says God: 'Why do you transgress the commandments of the Lord, so that you cannot prosper? Because you have forsaken the Lord, He also has forsaken you.'" So they conspired against him, and at the command of the king they stoned him with stones in the court of the house of the Lord.* (2 Chronicles 24:20-21)

One can easily spend a few hours examining and exploring these tombs and monuments. However, it is not always friendly territory. On one occasion we were standing back and admiring the monument of Absalom when an Arab man, probably in his late twenties, approached us. It was hot and we had two bottles of water. The young man seemed friendly and asked us for a drink of water. Our two-liter bottle was half empty and our one-liter bottle was almost full. We poured half of the small bottle into the large and handed the young man a bottle with almost half a liter of water. He immediately became very upset. "Am I dirty that you will not share your bottle with me?" We attempted a brief explanation, but after about four words we were interrupted by the young man who was quite angry. We weren't sure what to do because this is not a friendly area. So we reached the bottle towards him and asked, "Do you want it?" We got our answer when he walked off in a rage. Unfortunately, we found this quite unsettling.

A few weeks later, while walking down this same part of the Kidron valley, we had stones thrown at us from the area of the Tomb of Pharaoh's daughter. And in a later year, we had stones thrown at us while we were at the Gihon Spring. Interesting place, yes —but also exciting!

THE TOMB OF SHEBNA, THE ROYAL STEWART.

Shebna is only mentioned twice in the Scriptures (Isaiah 22:15-19, Isaiah 36:30).

> *Thus says the Lord God of hosts: "Go, proceed to this steward, To Shebna, who is over the house, and say: 'What have you here, and whom have you here, That you have hewn a sepulchre here, As he who hews himself a sepulchre on high, Who carves a tomb for himself in a rock? Indeed, the Lord will throw you away violently, O mighty man, And will surely seize you. He will surely turn violently and toss you like a ball into a large country; There you shall die, and there your glorious chariots shall be the shame of your master's house. So I will drive you out of your office, And from your position he will pull you down.* (Isaiah 22:15-19)

Shebna was perhaps a steward in charge of King Hezekiah's palace. He built himself a tomb worthy of a king, was possibly pilfering the royal coffers and was demoted. I had read about this tomb being in the village of Silwan, an Arab village across the Kidron Valley from the City of David, and that the inscription from the tomb entrance was on display in the British Museum in London. Armed with my copy of Biblical Archaeological Review, I decided I was going to visit the tomb of Shebna. This isn't particularly advisable because the village of Silwan is notoriously anti-Israeli and kids often throw stones at people in the Kidron Valley below the village as I described in the previous paragraph.

I first tried to find this tomb in 1994, then in 1995, and both attempts ended in failure because I developed cold feet at the last moment — afraid to enter the main alleyway through the village. But, by 1997 we had learned from experience that kids only throw stones when they can hide, or run, or when they have a certain amount of protection. Otherwise, when you meet them up front and face-to-face, they are usually quite friendly and curious about why you want to visit their patch of real estate. So, in 1997 I tried again. This time, I went on a Thursday morning when the kids were all at school. I made my way for about 200–300 meters along the track that leads from Absalom's Pillar and Zechariah's Monument to the village.

Upon entering the village, I was stuck with an eerie feeling of 'being watched' or 'I shouldn't be here' and yet I didn't see a single person. I found myself, at first unconsciously, tip-toeing along the alley as though no one would hear me! This betrayed to me that I was actually quite anxious. I knew that I had to be within 10–20 meters of the tomb, but I couldn't identify anything specific. I didn't loiter around too long, no more than ten minutes, because what is a nice young man like you doing in a place like this? I followed along the alley which ultimately led down a broken set of steps to the Gihon Spring in the Kidron Valley. At this stage, I felt royally ticked off. After three attempts, I'd finally made it into the village, but couldn't find the tomb. I sat down near the Gihon Spring and looked all over my notes again — nothing new seemed to emerge. Then a group of three Israeli soldiers came by. I stopped them, started to chat, and asked them if they knew anything about this tomb. Often, soldiers are the best source of information for getting to hard-to-find places. They looked at me as if I were crazy.

"You want to go in the village?" one of them asked.

"Yes," I responded. "In fact, I have just come down from the village."

In a thick Israeli Hebrew accent one of them said, "You are not allowed into the village."

This surprised me because I certainly hadn't seen any "No entry" signs or any other types of warnings, so I asked: "Are you telling me that I can't go into the village, or that I shouldn't go into the village?"

"Oh, you can go if you wish to, but we strongly recommend against it because it is dangerous."

I thanked them and they moved off just a few meters to my side. I took another look at my notes, and then a light went on. I noticed in my notes that the tomb was "immediately beyond a set of stairs into a house." Bingo, I knew where this was, or so I thought. My first reaction was to race straight back up the steps I had come down just fifteen minutes earlier, but how to deal with these soldiers nearby?

I proceeded to walk up the Kidron away from the steps and back towards Absalom's Pillar, and from there I picked up my old path and came into the village again. And there it was, exactly where my notes said it was. But what a mess; it was a garbage dump. I had walked right past this just forty minutes earlier, and I didn't recognize it because someone decided to put a door on the tomb! Shebna would not have been impressed! You should have seen the look on the faces of the soldiers when I came back down the steps to the Gihon Spring. I almost persuaded myself to go over and tell them the location of the tomb (for the next tourist) but decided not to push my luck.

ROYAL TOMBS

The royal tombs of some of the kings of Judah were in the City of David, and perhaps in the palace garden. David's tomb apparently wasn't too far from The Pool of Siloam (Nehemiah 3:15, 16). In 2 Chronicles 32:33 King Hezekiah is said to have been buried "…on the hill where the tombs of David's descendants are" (2 Chronicles 32:33, NIV). The burial of later kings (Manasseh, Josiah, Amon, and Jehoiakim) is also recorded, but not located in the City of David. Two burial complexes have been located inside the grounds of St. Stephen's Basilica home to the French Bible and Archaeology School (École biblique et archéologique française de Jérusalem). The style of one of these complexes indicates they belonged to wealthy and important people and have led some to suggest, with much controversy, that this may be the burial place of later kings of Judah, from the time of Manasseh.

So David rested with his fathers, and was buried in the City of David. (1 Kings 2:10)

Then Solomon rested with his fathers, and was buried in the City of David his father. And Rehoboam his son reigned in his place. (1 Kings 11:43)

At the southern end of the City of David about sixty meters northeast of the Pool of Siloam, first-temple-period tombs have been excavated. These may have been the royal tombs of King David and other kings of Judah although this claim is disputed. When we first found out about these tombs we were very excited, but our only aid to finding them was a single photograph. The City of David is small, so we reasoned that these tombs would be easy to find — not true.

It was early June, and it was very hot and humid and no matter where you walk, it always seems to be uphill. We battled against the heat and humidity and tramped around for at least forty-five minutes, uphill and downhill, asking for help, but without any hint of luck. Then we bumped into an Israeli soldier. We love Israeli soldiers! We spoke to him briefly, explained what we were looking for, and showed him the photograph. He mumbled a few words but didn't say much, and we guessed that he wasn't going to be able to help. I believe he took pity on us because we probably looked something like hot and sweaty beetroots. He spoke into his walkie-talkie for a few moments in Hebrew and then turned to us and said, "They are waiting for you." We were actually puzzled as to his meaning. He then directed us down an alleyway, told us to walk for 2–3 minutes until we saw an Israeli flag on the left, and that someone would be at the gate to let us in.

So we dutifully trudged our sweating bodies off to the south, fairly quickly spotted the Israeli flag, and realized that this was a fenced enclosure that was an Israeli lookout position watching the Arab village of Silwan on the opposite side of the Kidron Valley. On arrival at the rather broken, but locked, gate to the enclosure, a young Israeli soldier jogged across to us. He unlocked the chains and invited us in.

We still didn't know why we were here. He then pointed over our shoulders and, although it took a few seconds, we realized that we were looking into the tombs for which we had been searching. We were slow to recognize the site because our photographs didn't show the multiple layers of garbage that had built up around and inside the tombs. For a number of years, the local Arab population had dumped their garbage over a wall and in so doing were either intentionally, or perhaps unintentionally, surrounding the tombs with garbage. The soldier then invited us to go over and visit the tombs and indicated that he "would spot us." My puzzled look obviously required an answer so he indicated that he would watch just in case some locals decided to chuck garbage over the wall while we were below.

We scrambled over the rotting and smelly garbage and made our way inside the main tomb. After walking in about ten meters, one is faced with a wall about 2.5 meters high, but with garbage piled up at least 1.5 meters, the remaining climb was easy! We climbed up onto a ledge, a flat platform with a depression perhaps just less than two meters long and fifty centimeters wide. If these were indeed the burial tombs of the kings of Judah, then this ledge was a place of special privilege and quite likely the resting place of King David or King Solomon. We experienced a strange mixture of emotions. We were possibly standing on the very resting place of King David, looking out over a pile of rotting and smelly garbage, looking at two Israeli flags, and two Israeli soldiers with machine guns — what would King David have thought of this scene?

ANNAS THE HIGH PRIEST

The first time we traveled down the Hinnom Valley was by car. We saw a beautiful little olive grove, the Greek Orthodox monastery of St. Onuphrius, and the so-called Field of Blood where Judas killed himself; isn't it interesting that Judas died in the Valley of Hell? The valley gets progressively dirtier with litter and rubbish scattered everywhere. At one point we had a beautiful view (in hell?) of the monastery framed by olive trees. We stopped the car, got out, and tried to position ourselves to get a beautiful photograph. It was just then that Evelyn had a few rocks land at her feet. "Where did those come from?" We had no idea because we couldn't see anyone, and everything was silent. Then more rocks landed close by, and we became very nervous. Evelyn decided that she and the children were getting into the car. After I took a very rapid video, we jumped into the car and got out of the Valley of the Hinnom (hell).

Only 50–100 meters beyond the monastery is a tomb which is probably that of Annas the High priest. A cover photo on a 1994 issue of Biblical Archaeological Review showed an elaborate entrance to another tomb nearby. Articles in that issue made a compelling case for the location of the Tomb of Annas[61]. From photographs in the article, it was easy to identify the tomb. It has the remains of the entrance, and the ceiling is finely decorated. However, what the BAR photos didn't show was an enclosure extending out from the entrance to the tomb to a distance of about fifteen meters. Inside the enclosure, and the tomb, were four Bedouins and about forty goats! I made a lot of noises and yo-ho's to catch the Bedouins' attention. Given their customary hospitality, they immediately invited me in. I threw my leg over the fence, shook hands with the men and was immediately offered tea in an extremely dirty glass! I couldn't offend them, so I just prayed that my stomach was lined with cast iron. I indicated to them that I would like to see inside, and they chased out most of the goats.

It was ironic that this may have been the tomb of Annas the High Priest, and I had to excuse the Bedouins and their goats before I entered. The Bedouins welcomed me in and they had a fire burning in a large barrel inside the tomb. Setting aside the Bedouins, goats, fire, smoke, and general filth, the tomb was actually quite nice with a highly ornate, albeit very smoky, ceiling. There were three niches in the main part of the tomb with the center one being the most elaborate — probably the resting place of Annas — and inside was a little bird

---

[61] Ritmeyer, K & L. (1994). Akeldama: Potter's field or High Priest's tomb? *Biblical Archaeology Review*. (Nov/Dec 20:6), 22.

Avni, G., & & Greenhut, Z. (1994). Akeldama: Resting place of the rich and famous. *Biblical Archaeology Review*. (Nov/Dec, 20:6), 36.

nestled in a bed of straw, unphased by the presence of people and goats. This is a strange irony — we were only a ten-minute walk from the Old City of Jerusalem, ten minutes from the Western Wall, and less than five minutes from what might be the Tomb of King David, in something that should be a highly prized antiquity site — and it is occupied by Bedouins and their flocks and filled with smoke.

CAIAPHAS

In 1990 archaeologists were working in southern Jerusalem when they found a 2,000-year-old tomb, from New Testament times; this tomb belonged to the Caiaphas family. It contained several ossuaries, one was magnificently decorated and inscribed with the name Joseph bar Caiaphas. The ossuary contained the bones of a man of about sixty years old, a woman, two children, and two infants. These are almost certainly the remains of the high priest, Joseph, surnamed Caiaphas, who was the Jewish high priest best known for his role during the trial of Jesus.

> ...*Again the high priest [Caiaphas] asked Him, saying to Him, "Are You the Christ, the Son of the Blessed?" Jesus said, "I am. And you will see the Son of Man sitting at the right hand of the Power, and coming with the clouds of heaven." Then the high priest tore his clothes and said, "What further need do we have of witnesses? You have heard the blasphemy! What do you think?" And they all condemned Him to be deserving of death.* (Mark 14:61-64)

This remarkable discovery — for the first time — has provided us with the physical remains of an individual named in the Bible. There is little to see at the site today. The only visible evidence of the tomb is a blue, metal ventilation shaft that pops up into the middle of a children's playground sitting beside a pleasant quiet road in the Peace Garden. However, the ossuary is on display in the Israel Museum in Jerusalem. When we saw it, we realized we were standing in the presence of one of the men responsible for Jesus's death, and this was a moving spiritual experience. The irony of the story wasn't lost on us — two thousand years after the event we can view the ossuary (his remains were reburied on the Mount of Olives) of the man that condemned Christ to death, yet the man he condemned has an empty tomb, and according to the Scriptures, He is alive:

> ... *"Do not be afraid, for I know that you seek Jesus who was crucified. He is not here; for He is risen, as He said. Come, see the place where the Lord lay. And go quickly and tell His disciples that He is risen from the dead, and indeed He is going before you into Galilee; there you will see Him...* (Matthew 28:5-7)

RACHEL

The traditional site of Rachel's tomb is on the northern outskirts of Bethlehem.

So Rachel died and was buried on the way to Ephrath (that is, Bethlehem). And Jacob set a pillar on her grave, which is the pillar of Rachel's grave to this day. (Genesis 35:19-20)

This beautiful little domed structure is frequented by expectant mothers who come to pray. Until the mid-90s the building sat in its own small plot just off the side of the road. Then, after the first Intifada became threatening, a large multi-arched wall was constructed to shield the building from the road, presumably to protect from potential car bombers. However, this traditional location is clearly open to dispute because:

When you [Saul] have departed from me [Samuel] today, you will find two men by Rachel's tomb in the territory of Benjamin at Zelzah; and they will say to you, 'The donkeys which you went to look for have been found. And now your father has ceased caring about the donkeys and is worrying about you…" (1 Samuel 10:2)

This text states explicitly that Rachel's tomb is in the territory of Benjamin, which is located approximately between Jerusalem (Hinnom Valley) and Ramallah. Because of this, some have looked for Rachel's tomb north of Jerusalem. Driving north out of Jerusalem on Route 60, the Patriarchal route, we pass the village of Hizma. About two kilometers beyond there are four huge, rectangular, stone structures, which from ancient times have been referred to as Kubur Bani Isra'il — the Graves of the Children of Israel. Their actual origin and function aren't at all clear. Each structure is about one meter tall, 2–3 meters wide, and up to fifty meters long. Could one of these be the pillar that Jacob set on Rachel's grave?

Our first attempt to find the site was a wild goose chase. Our only guide us was a small black-and-white photograph in a book, which wasn't very descriptive. We drove a few kilometers north from Jerusalem on the main road towards Ramallah. We stopped at a little bakery and showed them the photograph. The two lovely Palestinian women just laughed and laughed. The photograph we were using not only had the structure but included an image of the author. We can only assume that the two women thought we were showing them my photograph — and of course it wasn't me! We went to several more stores, but it was clear that no one knew what we were asking for or recognized the structure in the photograph.

Then finally a glimmer of hope. A little Arab man with a wonderfully wrinkled face was hammering a tin plate on his anvil. He seemed very excited and indicated we should drive the Ramallah bypass road rather than the main road to

Ramallah. We soon came to an Israeli military checkpoint. After producing my identification, I pulled out the photograph, and a soldier, as if it were an everyday request, explained in perfect English exactly where to go and how to get there. It was only three kilometers and we found it easily.

However, this was an extremely busy two-lane road, and there was a guard rail between the road and the large stone structures. I made the mistake of stopping and within seconds seemingly every horn in Israel was blaring at me. I took off in a hurry, drove about another kilometer, turned around, and came back. While the road was much too busy to stop, as I drove past the structures, I noticed a small break in the guard rail. We returned almost to the military checkpoint, turned around once again, and headed back towards the site — this time knowing exactly what to do.

As we approached the opening in the guard rail, I slowed down, indicated, ignored the horns, and made a rather rapid and erratic dive for the opening. Made it! Survived! But I knew I had scratched the underbody of my rental car as I negotiated the steep, but short, ramp from the road. Upon inspection, I had actually pulled the exhaust pipe from the muffler, but thankfully the muffler was still functional (mostly). And somehow, after all of this, we really enjoyed this site.

THE TOMBS OF THE PATRIARCHS AND MATRIARCHS

Casual tourists don't visit Hebron anymore because it is very unsafe. In fact, it has the potential for dangerous violence to erupt at any time. We had lived in Jerusalem for nine months and yet we hadn't been able to arrange a visit to Hebron. With time running short, we decided to ask Pastor Musa, the pastor of the Baptist Church in Ramallah, to take us. His response was quite unequivocal, "No, I haven't been to Hebron in ten years because it is too dangerous."

"But," I replied, "we have to visit Hebron before we leave Israel."

Again he responded, "No, it is too dangerous."

So we started to do what all Middle Easterners are good at — bartering.

"Okay Musa, if you don't take us, we will catch a taxi from Jerusalem and we will go by ourselves."

Again the predictable response, "Absolutely not, this is craziness."

This bartering continued until Musa partially relented and told us that Pastor Naim at Bethlehem Baptist Church owed him a favor. After four aborted attempts, in May 1993 we finally made a journey to Hebron. Alistair's friend, Michael, accompanied us. Both Pastor Musa and Pastor Naim came with us. Pastor Naim tried to persuade Musa that we shouldn't go, and, although he had agreed to take us, he was more than reluctant.

Anyway, he took us, and this way we were with two Arabic-speakers, both Palestinians, and were in a minivan with West Bank license plates. City center Hebron was an incredible cacophony — people, horns, grid-locked streets, shouting, noise — the stereotypical Middle Eastern city. I only wish we could've taken a video or some photos just to capture it, but that wouldn't have been wise. As we traveled through the streets, it was clear that both pastors were uncomfortable; it seems that local Palestinians were shouting abuse at them, probably because Evelyn and Andrea weren't wearing head coverings.

We arrived at the tombs, parked, and just as we were climbing the steps to the Tomb of the Patriarchs we heard bursts of gunfire. Pastor Musa nervously smiled and said, "Jackhammers, just jackhammers." We weren't turning back now, so rather than going back to the minivan we raced into the major synagogue/mosque that houses the tombs. Half an hour later when we emerged, the streets of Hebron were very quiet, shops were closing, and the whole city was under curfew. We had to get out fairly quickly. It was strange to drive through deserted streets that only thirty minutes earlier were chocker blocked. Later, from the evening news, we learned that the Israeli army had shot and killed two wanted Hamas terrorists — about two hundred meters down the street from where we had parked, and where we had driven about five minutes earlier. Some jackhammer! Now we understood the pastors' reluctance to take us to Hebron.

So the field of Ephron which was in Machpelah, which was before Mamre, the field and the cave which was in it, and all the trees that were in the field, which were within all the surrounding borders, were deeded to Abraham as a possession in the presence of the sons of Heth, before all who went in at the gate of his city. And after this, Abraham buried Sarah his wife in the cave of the field of Machpelah, before Mamre (that is, Hebron) in the land of Canaan. So the field and the cave that is in it were deeded to Abraham by the sons of Heth as property for a burial place. (Genesis 23:17-20)

Then Abraham breathed his last and died in a good old age, an old man and full of years, and was gathered to his people. And his sons Isaac and Ishmael buried him in the cave of Machpelah ... (Genesis 25:8-9)

There they buried Abraham and Sarah his wife, there they buried Isaac and Rebekah his wife, and there I [Jacob] buried Leah... And when Jacob had finished commanding his sons, he drew his feet up into the bed and breathed his last, and was gathered to his people. (Genesis 49:31, 33)

ABNER AND ISHBOSHETH

Abner, the leader of Saul's army, came to Hebron to see David and was well received. Later, Abner was killed by Joab. King David wept over Abner and buried him:

> *Now when Abner had returned to Hebron, Joab took him aside in the gate to speak with him privately, and there stabbed him in the stomach, so that he died for the blood of Asahel his brother. ... So they buried Abner in Hebron...* (2 Samuel 3:27, 32)

The tomb of Abner is opposite the entrance to the Cave of Machpelah described above. Abner's tomb is completely uninspiring. You don't enter a complex, but rather peer through a window into a gloomy cave lit by candles. Just around the corner from the tombs, on the main street, is a large, smelly pool. The pool has no flow, so it has stagnant water complete with enormous piles of garbage that have been dumped in and accumulate. It was at this pool in Hebron, known as the Assassin's Pool, that David ordered the execution of the two men who murdered Saul's last son Ishbosheth. David had Ishbosheth's severed head buried in Abner's tomb:

> *So David commanded his young men, and they executed them, cut off their hands and feet, and hanged them by the pool in Hebron. But they took the head of Ishbosheth and buried it in the tomb of Abner in Hebron.* (2 Samuel 4:12)

RUTH AND JESSE

Ruth was a Moabite and an ancestor of the Lord Jesus Christ (Matthew 1:5). Jesse was the grandson of Boaz and Ruth, and the father of King David; the great grandmother of King David was a gentile. The phrase "stem of Jesse" is used for the family of David (Isaiah 11:1), and "root of Jesse" for the Messiah (Isaiah 11:10; Revelation 5:5). Jesse was a man of wealth and position in Bethlehem. The tombs of Ruth and Jesse are located at the top of Tel Rumeida, or Tel Hebron, which is among the most ancient areas of Hebron. We walked up the main street of Hebron, past the Assassin's Pool until we came to an Arab cemetery to our left. We followed a sign to "ancient walls" and climbed up a rough path to an ancient spring called Abraham's Spring. Just above the spring are many remains from ancient Hebron. By now we had at least three million local children following us, all either smiling or looking forlorn, but all with outstretched hands wanting candies or money — and they have this annoying habit of touching cameras and feeling your pockets; we love children, but this is... aagghh!

This is a military zone, with lots of barbed wire, so we had to skirt around the slope of the Tel in a counterclockwise direction until we bumped into a group of about ten Israeli soldiers. The soldiers did two things. First, they pointed us in the direction we should walk, and second, they relieved us of all the children! We passed through a maze of passageways where some Jewish families live in a few trailers, which served an additional purpose of keeping us from lines of sight, and possible sniping, from nearby Arab neighborhoods. We arrived at the tombs only to find an Israeli army outpost on their roof. We were allowed to enter, but there was nothing to see; the tombs are in horrible repair, but at least we got a magnificent view of Hebron and of the Tomb of the Patriarchs.

JONAH

Everyone knows the story of Jonah or some version of it. Jonah was commanded by God to go and preach repentance to the Assyrian city of Nineveh, but he fled in the opposite direction to escape the task. He was trapped by a great storm, and at his own request, he was hurled overboard into the sea, where he was swallowed by a great fish, remaining alive in the belly of the fish for three days. After being vomited by the fish, Jonah finally went to Nineveh to preach to the wicked city. Nineveh is today's Iraqi city of Mosul, in a Kurdish region about 450 kilometers north of Baghdad.

A popular tradition places the tomb of Jonah opposite to Mosul, on one of the large mounds that mark the location of ancient Nineveh. Today the mound is called Nabi Yunus, the mound of the Prophet Jonah. This mound once had an Assyrian Christian church that housed the Tomb of Jonah. The church was destroyed and replaced by a large and magnificent mosque until July 2014, when the mosque was blown up by the Islamic State because "the mosque had become a place for apostasy, not prayer."

A more ancient tradition places the tomb of Jonah in his native village of Gath Hepher, just a few miles north of Nazareth and overlooking the village of Cana of Galilee where Jesus performed his first miracle. As part of our travels, we tried to visit both tombs.

Our visit to Jonah's tomb at Gath Hepher was uneventful because it didn't happen! As usual, we had our rental car with yellow license plates, and we had good maps and knew exactly where we were going. We drove into the little village of Mashhad, biblical Gath Hepher, and straight to the mosque that houses the Tomb of Jonah. Immediately, we had a twofold problem — no parking lot, and lots of children. Simply, we were afraid to leave our car while we visited the tomb.

However, in comparison, our visit to the tomb of Jonah in Nineveh was much more exciting.

It was our third day in Baghdad. On our first day we traveled a round trip of 180 kilometers to Babylon, and on our second day a round trip of 750 kilometers to Ur. So after 930 kilometers in taxis, we questioned whether we wanted to sit for another 850 kilometers to go to Nineveh. But then Davir, one of the clerks at the hotel desk, came up with an idea. Davir was perhaps in his early twenties, spoke very good English, and he'd been responsible for most of our arrangements the previous two days. Davir suggested that we fly to Mosul, ancient Nineveh —and we described that story earlier when we traveled with the prophet Jonah to this region.

When we arrived in Mosul we got a local taxi to take us to the ruins of Nineveh. We had only traveled a few minutes when the taxi stopped in the middle of a busy intersection. Noise, horns, people, and traffic were everywhere. The engine had stalled and the driver was clearly having problems getting it restarted. Then, refreshingly, he simply jumped out of the car, in the middle of all the chaos, and popped the hood — we love the unregulated nature and spontaneity of the Middle East! Whatever he wriggled under the hood didn't work, and we were still stranded. Then he began to weave a piece of wire, which looked like a straightened coat hanger, from the engine compartment through to the accelerator peddle. We were becoming a little less comfortable with this spontaneity. Davir saved the day, and we climbed out of the taxi and jumped into another cab to take us to the taxi rank. We then made our way to the mound called Nabi Yunus, the mound of the Prophet Jonah. An enormous mosque dominates the site, and it is a popular Muslim tradition that Jonah is buried here. We went to the site, but only men were allowed access to the complex, and only Muslim men were permitted inside the mosque which housed the tomb. So we peered in from the outside.

Jonah's tomb stands on one of the southern mounds of ancient Nineveh and has a view looking north over the other ruins that mark the site of this once magnificent city of Nineveh. As we stood there, we tried to recreate a few images in our minds. Jonah preached in its busy streets and markets almost 2,800 years ago. Its mighty walls rose from the east bank of the River Tigris opposite where the modern city of Mosul now stands. Scripture calls it "an exceeding great city." It had 1,500 watchtowers up to sixty meters high. Its kings lived in luxury, it had magnificent palaces, and many of its artifacts are housed in the British Museum in London. But Nineveh was also a cesspool of corruption. The prophet Nahum

(3:1) calls Nineveh "…the bloody city, it is all full of lies an d robbery…" As we looked over the vast area of desolate mounds, we were reminded of the words of the prophet Zephaniah:

And He will stretch out His hand against the north, Destroy Assyria, And make Nineveh a desolation, As dry as the wilderness (Zephaniah 2:13)

And there it was before us and Nineveh was indeed "…a desolation, as dry as the wilderness."

ESTHER AND MORDECAI

The tombs of Esther and Mordecai are located in the city of Hamadan, Iran. Although formerly this was a favored pilgrimage site, today only the occasional Jewish foreigner visits the shrine —and a few tourists. Although the shrine fronts on to a main street, entrance is gained off of a little alleyway. We approached the high metal gate and rang the doorbell. After the third ring of the bell a man looked anxiously through the gate. He quickly let us into the grounds. In broken English and fluent French, he managed to tell us a little about the shrine, its history, and the story of Esther, Mordecai, and Purim. The tombs are ancient, and the current structure was built over the tombs in the thirteenth or fourteenth century AD. There is much discussion about who is actually buried in these tombs, and some scholars argue that Esther is buried in Susa.

The gatekeeper brought us through a small but pleasant garden to the shrine which is protected by a door made of solid granite and weighing four hundred kilograms! He opened it with a large key, and with the enormously heavy door now opened, we had to bend two-fold to get through the low entrance. Inside the door we were immediately inside a small synagogue with white-washed walls adorned with Hebrew writing. Beyond the synagogue were the two sarcophagi, draped in embroidered floral coverings, resting on an elaborately carved ebony pedestal almost two meters tall — the actual tombs are apparently about two meters belowground.

Esther's tomb was draped in yellow and white while Mordecai's was draped in pink. The attendant assured us that the sarcophagi were two and a half thousand years old — I doubt it! We pondered over the significance of the impact these two people had on the history of the Jewish people. This was a beautiful little spot, and we were in no rush to leave. It was easy to tip the gate attendant because we had been warned ahead of time in a Lonely Planet Guide — the gatekeeper didn't want money, rather he wanted a ballpoint pen to add to his collection from around the world. The big metal door clanged shut behind us, and we returned to the modern Iranian street, noisy with mini-vans and motor scooters. Before climbing into our wagon, Evelyn spotted a little store that sold headscarves. We had been in Iran for a week, and she was getting a little tired of the black dress and white headscarf. There wasn't much that could be done about the black dress, but in this little store we managed to get a few more headscarves — in yellow, mauve and blue — and with true Iranian hospitality the lady storekeeper wanted us to have the scarves free of charge "because you are visitors in my country." We paid!

DANIEL

Daniel wrote the book in the Old Testament that bears his name, and he was a prophet during the period of the Captivity of the Jews in Babylon and Persia. According to Shi'ite Muslim tradition, Daniel's tomb is located in today's town of Shush just a few hundred meters west of the entrance to the ancient city of Shushan (earlier chapter); it is conceivably a correct location. We parked on the main street, and as we crossed the street, we slowed to read a slogan written in bold letters on the road. It read "Americans go home," along with a Star of David accompanied by some Arabic script. We smiled to ourselves and proceeded towards the entrance that was blocked by a number of local women in flowing chadors. They smiled, greeted us, and stepped aside to let us in. We entered a courtyard about the size of a basketball court. The yard had a small fountain in the middle and the walls covered with large murals, some depicting scenes from the book of Daniel, and others that were overtly political and rancid anti-American, anti-western, and anti-Israeli propaganda. It was interesting that the murals were all accompanied by English writing, yet in the town itself we couldn't find a soul who spoke a word of English! A rather eye-catching mural depicted a young Muslim woman dressed in her chador accompanied by the words: "A woman modestly dressed is like a pearl in its shell." How woke is that? As usual, there were separate entrances for men and women. The woman's entrance didn't allow cameras but the other side did! The tomb was so highly ornate that it verged on being tacky.

The monument is large, perhaps 2.5 meters tall and four meters long, covered in green and gold tiles, trimmed with wood, and some mirrors and paint, and the whole thing housed in a room in which the walls and ceiling were lined with thousands of tiny mirrors that made the light bounce all over the place in a myriad of interesting patterns. Again we were puzzled at the pilgrims pressing their faces against the tomb, pushing money through the receptive slots, kissing the tiles, and whispering prayers — Daniel was Jewish, he lived one thousand years before the advent of Islam, and he isn't mentioned in the Koran. Why were these Muslims showing such devotion to a Jew? We made our exits from our separate entrances almost simultaneously and bumped into each other because our eyes were adjusting to the intense sunlight. We mused at what we had just seen, walked by the murals with Palestinian fighters wearing keffiyehs, Iranian soldiers, barbed wire, and numerous other images that present a rather biased view of events in the world outside of the Islamic Republic of Iran.

DARIUS, XERXES AND ARTAXERXES

The Old Testament contains many references to the nation of Persia: the kings of Persia (Ezra 9:9), the kings of Media and Persia (Daniel 8:20), the prince of the kingdom of Persia (Daniel 10:13), the powers of Persia and Media (Esther 1:3), and the seven princes of Persia and Media (Esther 1:14). Ezra 6:14 specifically refers to "Cyrus, Darius, and Artaxerxes king of Persia," and it was their tombs we had come to visit. The base for our visit was the city of Shiraz, home of the great poets Sa'adi and Hafez. Shiraz had an elegance beyond any other city we visited (except for the resplendent Esfahan), and it also provided the opportunity to visit the magnificent city of Persepolis which was destroyed by Alexander the Great.

The monumental tombs of Darius I, Xerxes, Artaxerxes I, and Darius II are located at Naqsh-e-Rostam to the west of Persepolis. These are massive, cross-shaped rock tombs, about twenty-five meters high, and impressively carved out and stretched across a limestone cliff high above the ground. The cliff is generously decorated with carvings. The place was alive with local tourists, and it would have been of great interest for us to know how many of these Muslim people were aware that they were visiting the tombs of four biblical kings, and two of them (Darius and Artaxerxes) were specifically very gracious to the Jewish exiles returning to Jerusalem, and the other (Xerxes) along with his Jewish queen and wife, Esther, preserved the Jewish people living in Persia.

DARIUS I

Darius I, also known as Darius the Great, was king of the Persian Empire from 522–486 BC. He made Shushan, or Susa, his new capital and created a code of laws similar to the Code of Hammurabi. He initiated fabulous building projects at Persepolis and at Babylon. In 520 BC Darius assisted the Jews in rebuilding the Temple in Jerusalem.

Then King Darius issued a decree, and a search was made in the archives, where the treasures were stored in Babylon. And at Achmetha, in the palace that is in the province of Media, a scroll was found, and in it a record was written thus: In the first year of King Cyrus, King Cyrus issued a decree concerning the house of God at Jerusalem: "Let the house be rebuilt, ... Also I [King Darius] issue a decree that whoever alters this edict, let a timber be pulled from his house and erected, and let him be hanged on it; and let his house be made a refuse heap because of this. And may the God who causes His name to dwell there destroy any king or people who put their hand to alter it, or to destroy this house of God which is in Jerusalem. I Darius issue a decree; let it be done diligently. (Ezra 6:1-3, 11-12)

Xerxes is the Greek name of Ahasuerus, the king mentioned throughout the Book of Esther. He was the ruler of a vast empire and had great wealth:

Now it came to pass in the days of Ahasuerus (this was the Ahasuerus who reigned over one hundred and twenty-seven provinces, from India to Ethiopia), in those days when King Ahasuerus sat on the throne of his kingdom, which was in Shushan the citadel, that in the third year of his reign he made a feast for all his officials and servants—the powers of Persia and Media, the nobles, and the princes of the provinces being before him—when he showed the riches of his glorious kingdom and the splendor of his excellent majesty for many days, one hundred and eighty days in all. (Esther 1:1-4)

Artaxerxes means "a possessor of an exalted kingdom." Under his rule, Ezra and Nehemiah were authorized to return to Jerusalem to rebuild the temple and the city walls. Early in his reign he halted the rebuilding of Jerusalem, and then changed his mind:

The king sent an answer ... Now give the command to make these men cease, that this city may not be built until the command is given by me. (Ezra 4:17, 21)

So the elders of the Jews built, and they prospered through the prophesying of Haggai the prophet and Zechariah the son of Iddo. And they built and finished it, according to the commandment of the God of Israel, and according to the command of Cyrus, Darius, and Artaxerxes king of Persia. (Ezra 6:14)

Darius II is of minor biblical importance only being referred to once in Nehemiah 12:22.

During the reign of Darius the Persian, a record was also kept of the Levites and priests who had been heads of their fathers' houses in the days of Eliashib, Joiada, Johanan, and Jaddua. (Nehemiah 12:22)

CYRUS

About sixty kilometers north of Naqsh-e-Rostam and 110 kilometers northeast of Shiraz in west-central Iran is the ancient city of Pasargadae. It is here that we went to visit the tomb of Cyrus the Great, the founder of the Persian Empire which he ruled from 559-530 BC. He is best known for his capture of Babylon in 539 BC. Cyrus allowed the Jewish captives to return to their homeland in Jerusalem. The Book of Ezra contains many reports on the progress of the work related to the decree of Cyrus. Cyrus proclaimed the Jewish return from captivity:

> *Now in the first year of Cyrus king of Persia, that the word of the Lord by the mouth of Jeremiah might be fulfilled, the Lord stirred up the spirit of Cyrus king of Persia, so that he made a proclamation throughout all his kingdom, and also put it in writing, saying, Thus says Cyrus king of Persia: All the kingdoms of the earth the Lord God of heaven has given me. And He has commanded me to build Him a house at Jerusalem which is in Judah. Who is among you of all His people? May his God be with him, and let him go up to Jerusalem which is in Judah, and build the house of the Lord God of Israel (He is God), which is in Jerusalem. And whoever is left in any place where he dwells, let the men of his place help him with silver and gold, with goods and livestock, besides the freewill offerings for the house of God which is in Jerusalem. (Ezra 1:1-4)*

Cyrus also issued a decree to rebuild the Temple:

> *Then King Darius issued a decree, and a search was made in the archives, where the treasures were stored in Babylon.2 And at Achmetha, in the palace that is in the province of Media, a scroll was found, and in it a record was written thus: In the first year of King Cyrus, King Cyrus issued a decree concerning the house of God at Jerusalem: "Let the house be rebuilt, the place where they offered sacrifices; and let the foundations of it be firmly laid.., (Ezra 6:1-3)*

Some have questioned whether it is worth the effort to go to Pasargadae. The ruins aren't well preserved, and it is a flat, lonely sort of place. However, the purpose of our visit was to experience the final resting place of Cyrus the Great, and the surroundings didn't matter that much to us. The tomb is the best-preserved structure at Pasargadae and once had an inscription that read, "Oh man, I am Cyrus, the son of Cambyses, who founded the empire of Persia, and was king of Asia." Paul Kriwaczek writes of this tomb:

> … it is worth the journey: an immensely dignified gabled white stone cube, set upon a monumental base, recalling the form of a ziggurat, a Mesopotamian step-temple. The whole ensemble is today some thirty-five feet (ten meters) high. One side is pierced by a doorway, above which there seems once to have been another opening, now filled in. The building stands all alone, isolated in a wide expanse of scrubby plain with only purple thistles as decoration, over which, in this season, the wind whistles across from the khaki-colored

mountain escarpments in the distance, the only features that break the monotonous view.[62]

As we stood before this simple and graceful building, we knew we were standing on the very spot that Alexander the Great stood in the year 330 BC — Alexander had a great admiration for Cyrus. It seemed strange to us that a Persian Empire builder was admired by the Greeks. But then we also recalled that Cyrus was also held in high regard by the Jews and by Almighty God. God had at least two special names that He applied to Cyrus:

Who says of Cyrus, 'He is My shepherd,...' (Isaiah 44:28)

Thus says the Lord to His anointed, To Cyrus, whose right hand I have held... (Isaiah 45:1)

As we stood there we also realized that the mission upon which we embarked almost fourteen years ago was now at an end — this this was the last biblical site that we would visit in our quest to visit most of the sites mentioned in the Holy Scriptures — but we didn't get to Patmos.

MARY, THE MOTHER OF THE LORD JESUS CHRIST

The Gospels provide a clear and vivid image of Mary, but there aren't any other ancient texts that reference her. She was a typical and devout Jewish believer, deeply meditative and with a true heart. From the beginning to the day of Pentecost, she pondered in her heart the meaning of her many puzzling experiences. We are given no indication, scripturally or historically, that Mary was any different from any other Jewish, or Christian woman, other than her unparalleled privilege of being the mother of the Messiah. It wasn't until 1950 that Pope Pius XII declared the dogma of the Assumption of Mary and asserted "that the Virgin Mary, the Immaculate Mother of God, when the course of her life was finished, was taken up, body and soul, into the glory of heaven." The last mention of Mary in the Scriptures is in the upper room in Jerusalem, awaiting the coming of the Holy Spirit (Acts 1:14). We don't know how or when Mary died.

The location of the tomb of the Virgin Mary is disputed. There are claims that Mary died and was buried at Ephesus. This tradition began in 1824 when Catherine Emmerich, a nun, had a vision from God. It was revealed to her that Mary had not died in Jerusalem, but in Ephesus, and that her grave was five hundred meters away from her home a few kilometers from the city.

---

[62] Kriwazek, P. (2002). *In Search of Zarathustra: the first prophet and ideas that changed the world.* Phoenix Publ., London.

However, long tradition has placed the tomb in the Kidron valley adjacent to the Garden of Gethsemane in Jerusalem. The church in the Kidron Valley originated in the fifth century. From this Tomb, according to Catholic and Eastern Orthodox traditions, Mary was taken into heaven. Therefore, she only went through the tomb but didn't stay there. This tomb thus became a shrine commemorating her Assumption into Heaven, and hence the church is called the Church of the Assumption. Also according to the traditions of the Catholic and Eastern Orthodox churches, Mary fell asleep for the last time on Mount Zion and her remains were then transported to the Kidron site for burial. To commemorate this, on Mount Zion stands the Benedictine Basilica of the Dormition (Dormition Abby). The Dormition Abbey is architecturally beautiful and is located just outside the Zion Gate. In the basement of the Abby there is a statue of the sleeping virgin.

From the outside, the Church of the Assumption is dull and foreboding, and inside it's worse. We found this to be the most depressing church throughout the Bible lands. Upon entering the church, you are immediately greeted by a wide set of steps, the entire width of the church, leading down into a dark, underground cave. Our eyes struggled to adjust to the darkness and we coughed as we first encountered the incense smoke rising up the stairs to meet us. Halfway down, the forty-eight steps are two niches on either side, facing each other, and we were told these were the tombs of Mary's parents Anne and Joachim. No one seemed to be interested in these, and we continued to the bottom of the stairs.

An elderly priest stood on the bottom step. He was dressed very simply, and his black gown seemed to be pulled forward over his shoulders by the abundance of heavy chains, crosses and crucifixes he attired. We stood at a distance and watched quietly. The priest appeared absolutely emotionless as an endless string of mostly older women lined up to kiss his outstretched hand. The bottom step leveled out into the floor of a quite large hall which is the church. There was little light except for that filtering through the main door above us. The walls were covered by idols and icons, and from the ceiling hung dozens of chandeliers and incense burners. Everything was black from years of burning incense. Over to the right was a shrine alleged to house the tomb of Mary. The shrine is richly decorated with smoke-covered icons, candlesticks, and lowers. We had to stoop significantly to enter the low door; the inside is quite plain but there is a glassed-off section where pilgrims can reach in to touch the spot believed to be where Mary lay until she was assumed into heaven.

We exited the tomb by a different door and found a distant spot, sat down, and observed. We watched pilgrims for at least half an hour. We were particularly attracted to one young woman who entered the hall. She kissed the priest's hand, stepped down the bottom step, saw the shrine, and immediately dropped to her knees in tears. It took her a full fifteen minutes to cover the ten meters to the shrine alternately crawling, weeping, praying, kneeling, genuflecting, and crossing herself. We admired this special devotion but were a little puzzled by the object of her devotion. Mary was indeed a special young woman, but from Scripture, there is no indication that Mary didn't die just like everyone else — no one deserves worship but God alone and His Son Jesus Christ.

JOHN THE BAPTIST

John was the forerunner of our Lord, and we have but fragmentary accounts of him in the Gospels. He was born six months before Jesus, and Jesus came from Galilee to Jordan to be baptized by John. Perhaps John's most profound words were spoken when he saw Jesus approach:

...Behold! The Lamb of God who takes away the sin of the world! (John 1:29)

His public ministry was brought to a sudden close when he was imprisoned by Herod at the fortress of Machaerus in the lonely hills east of the Dead Sea. Here he was subsequently beheaded in about AD 26).

There seems to be little information, either historical, legend or tradition, about the location of John's tomb. However, a Greek Orthodox Church on Christian Quarter Rd in the Old City of Jerusalem claims to have had the head of John the Baptist. The entrance to the church has a painting of John the Baptist's head above the door. John's head is also supposedly buried in the Omayyad Mosque in the Old City of Damascus. It is a massive and magnificent structure renowned for its multi-colored mosaics of trees and landscapes. In the main sanctuary of the mosque is a structure surrounding what Muslims revere as the place where John's head is buried.

Finding directions around the old city of Jerusalem is not that difficult once a few of the major alleyways have been mastered. The old city of Damascus is a different story. Darb el-Mustaqim in Arabic, Straight Street, is probably so named because it's about the only straight street in an otherwise labyrinthine-twisted jumble of alleys and chaotic markets that constitute the charm of the Old City. The Old City is surrounded by a wall that mostly dates to the thirteenth century. The wall has eight gates, and only the restored Bab Sharqi, meaning East Gate, dates back to Roman times.

Originally we wanted to visit Bab Kisan, which is the traditional site where Paul was lowered over the wall to escape the city. We called a taxi and asked for Bab Kisan. The driver immediately responded with "Bab Sharqi?" "No, no, we want Bab Kisan." No matter how we tried, this driver was going to take us to Bab Sharqi, because this is the most famous of the gates. We finally got through to him that we wanted a different gate and then he proceeded to rattle off the names of all the other gates — except Bab Kisan! On our journey to nowhere, the driver stopped with at least three other taxi drivers before someone knew the name — and it was about a five-minute walk!

Following our visit to Bab Kisan, we ventured into the alleyways of the old city. After getting lost, and asking directions at least six times, we finally arrived at the entrance of the magnificent Omayyad Mosque. We thought that entering the mosque would be easy because Evelyn was modestly dressed in a long skirt down to her ankles; for men, the guards don't seem to mind as long as legs are covered. Even Evelyn's long skirt wasn't adequate, and they provided her with a long, blue shawl, or robe, that reached to the ground. Evelyn pinned the front of it closed but the little guard put a few extra pins in at ground level. So, except for her face, Evelyn was literally covered from the top of her head to the soles of her feet without the faintest whisper of flesh or personal clothing showing. Of course, we can't wear shoes in the mosque so we have to carry them with us — there is a high rate of theft of shoes left in the cubicles at the mosque entrance. This mosque is absolutely stunning, and if there had been nothing else in Damascus, the mosque alone would have been worth the visit — and sitting in a proud place in the center of the cavernous main hall is a structure supposedly housing the head of John the Baptist; you can't actually see anything.

STEPHEN

The only first-hand source of information on the life and death of St. Stephen is the book of Acts. For centuries the location of Stephen's tomb was unknown, but a site was identified in AD 460 just north of the Damascus Gate in Jerusalem, near the place where, according to tradition, Stephen was stoned to death. More recently the Dominican Fathers erected a new church on the foundations of the old church. The church is protected by a high wall, and there is a single, large metal gate. We rang the bell and were invited in, and one of the clerics give us a delightful and extremely informative tour of the basilica[63] and the tomb.

---

[63] A church is any place of worship having a permanent congregation and under the direction of a cleric. A basilica is a church that has been conferred that status by the pope because of some unique or significant characteristic of the church.

PETER AND PAUL

Rome is the eternal city, considered to be the center of Christendom and one of the most beautiful and interesting cities in the world. Not surprisingly, it has numerous basilicas and churches, with over four hundred in the Centro Storico alone. Each of these commemorates someone, something, or some event. Many of them are repositories for some of the world's great artworks, both paintings and sculptures, and many are architectural masterpieces in their own right.

The city is literally packed with frescos, mosaics, and sculptures by many of the great masters — the architectural wonders of Bramante and Bernini, and the works of Michelangelo, Raphael, and many other Renaissance and Baroque artists. Undoubtedly, the jewel in the crown is St. Peter's Basilica which must rank as one of the most spectacular buildings in the world. The interior of the basilica is a showpiece of the great masters, adorned with numerous frescoes, mosaics, sculptures and memorials — and then there is the Sistine Chapel and the Vatican museums. Unfortunately, we see some questionable claims scattered among this architectural and artistic feast, such as fragments of Christ's crib in the magnificent Basilica of Santa Maria Maggiore.

The view of the Roman Catholic Church is that the apostle Peter was executed in Rome and was interred on Vatican Hill. Through the centuries, various structures have been built over the tomb, and today Peter's tomb is argued to be under the High Altar of St Peter's Basilica. A pre-arranged visit to the Vatican Excavations Office, and by appointment only, allowed us to visit the catacombs and excavations on a guided tour. The tour is quite fascinating and ended with us encountering numerous first-century tombs below the high altar in St. Peters, and one tomb, in particular, is believed to be that of Peter.

Historically, this position has been both politically and spiritually important because Catholics teach that the Bishop of Rome, the Pope, holds the keys of the kingdom, passed down from Peter the fisherman who was made chief of the apostles. This is critical in making the argument for the apostolic succession of the bishops of Rome. However, according to Boettner and numerous other scholars "there is in fact no New Testament evidence, nor any historical proof of any kind, that Peter was ever in Rome."[64] It is noteworthy that in Romans 16:21-23 (written AD 56) and in 2 Timothy 4:10-21 (written AD 67) Paul mentions eighteen different co-workers and ministers who were in Rome, and Peter is not named among them, so it is unlikely that Peter ever pastored a church in Rome. It is especially pertinent that Galatians 2:7-8 tells us that Peter was the apostle,

---

[64] Boettner, L. (1989). *Roman Catholicism*. Presbyterian and Reformed Publ. Co.

not to the Romans, but to the Jews — it was Paul who was designated as the apostle to the Gentiles.

Back to our travels. The Basilica of Santa Maria Maggiore is one of Rome's four patriarchal basilicas. We cynically viewed the fragments of the baby Jesus's crib, and then we spotted a priest. We asked him about another basilica, the Basilica di San Giovanni in Laterano. This was the first Christian Basilica constructed in Rome and is one of the most important in the Catholic world. It is the cathedral of Rome, and it is the Pope's official seat as the Bishop of Rome. We told the priest that we would like to visit in order to see the heads of St. Peter and St. Paul. He looked puzzled! So, we pulled out our Lonely Planet travel guide and showed him where it said that the canopy over the papal altar in the basilica contained many relics including the heads of St. Peter and St. Paul. He gave a very interesting response: "Yes, they say. I have also heard that." I think he had as much faith in these relics as we did. But we dutifully found our way to the great basilica and viewed the two heads — we don't know who they belonged to, but we don't believe for a minute that they have anything to do with Peter or Paul.

From the center of Rome, it is only a twenty-minute ride in the underground to the Basilica di San Paolo Fuori-le-Mura which literally means St. Paul's outside of the wall. That basilica is about three kilometers south of the Porta San Paolo (St. Paul's Gate). This is yet another magnificent building, with tremendous artwork, and until the construction of St Peter's Basilica, it was the largest church in the world. Completely encircling the basilica are mosaic portraits of all the Popes from St. Peter to John Paul II; secular historians are of virtually one mind that there is no record of any popes for the first four or five hundred years of church history. The original church di San Paolo Fuori-le-Mura was built in the fourth century by Constantine over the burial place of Paul. Paul is believed to be buried under the main altar and, as we write this, Vatican archaeologists are preparing to announce they have positively identified the tomb of St. Paul the apostle.

JOHN AND LUKE

John and Luke are both buried in the region of the great city of Ephesus. Ephesus was chosen as the site for one of the largest and most complex temples built in ancient times. The Temple of Artemis had a marble sanctuary and a tile-covered wooden roof. The temple's inner space featured a double row of at least 106 columns, each believed to be 12–20 meters high. The foundation was approximately sixty meters by 120 meters. The original temple burned in 356

BC and was rebuilt on the same foundation. Fire devastated the second temple in AD 262, but its foundation, a column, and scanty fragments strewn on the ground are all that remains of one of the Seven Wonders of the Ancient World.

There is also a magnificent Basilica containing a tomb that has been revered since the second century as the tomb of John the Apostle. This is a very early date for such a shrine, reaching back almost into the generations of the successors of the Apostles. The current basilica was built during the sixth century AD by the emperor Justinian and dedicated to John. The plan of the church was cruciform and was covered with six domes supported on columns. Under the central dome was situated the tomb of John.

Off to the side of the upper car park at Ephesus, just opposite the upper entrance, is a foundation and the remains of a circular structure. It is thought to be the foundation of an ancient temple that was later converted into a church. A bull's head carved in the door jamb led people to believe that this was the tomb of Luke (author of the Gospel and Acts of the Apostles) since the bull's head was an ancient symbol for Luke, but it is an identification that is the subject of much conjecture. Somewhere in history, Luke's body was taken to Constantinople (Istanbul) and later moved to the Santa Giustina Church Padua near Venice. However, the body doesn't have a head! There are 'officially' two heads of Luke, one at Prague, which rests in the Cathedral of St. Vitus in Prague Castle, and one in Rome in the Church of St. Peter in the Vatican.

THE LORD JESUS CHRIST

Now in the place where He was crucified there was a garden, and in the garden a new tomb in which no one had yet been laid. (John 19:41)

He is not here, but is risen! Remember how He spoke to you when He was still in Galilee, saying, 'The Son of Man must be delivered into the hands of sinful men, and be crucified, and the third day rise again.' (Luke 24:6-7)

I made my first trip to Israel in 1991 only weeks after the Gulf War. This was in response to an invitation from a colleague at the Ben Gurion University of the Negev, for me to consider spending a sabbatical year in Israel. I spent just a little less than two weeks in the Negev, especially around Sede Boqer, but then my colleague and I spent my last weekend in Jerusalem. But this was no ordinary weekend — this was the Easter weekend. What an incredible time to be in Jerusalem. Friday is the Muslim holy day, and there were thousands of Muslims on the Temple Mount. Friday was also Good Friday, and many of the Christian denominations were remembering Christ's crucifixion with services at the Church of the Holy Sepulchre and parades through the streets and alleys of the Old City. Then on Friday evening, the Jewish people started to gather at the Western Wall for the beginning of the Sabbath. Saturday at the Western Wall was incredible — again, it seems there were thousands of Jews, many of whom were praying, many were going through various rituals, and many were just rejoicing and dancing. And then there was Sunday — resurrection Sunday. We were staying at Christ's Church Hospice just inside the Jaffa Gate, and, among many other things, we planned to visit both of the proposed sites of the Lord's crucifixion, burial, and resurrection — the church of the Holy Sepulchre, and Gordon's Calvary, and the nearby Garden Tomb…

On Good Friday we walked the short distance to the Church of the Holy Sepulchre. This is one of the most important sites in Christendom, and it has inspired both devotion and violence. However, the experience shocked me. I had some romantic idea in my mind of visiting a beautiful church, with beautiful music, and a somber reminder of our Lord's crucifixion. Instead, the church is an ancient jumble of five for six denominations competing for floor space, chapels, and authority. There was no music at all. Instead, there were endless processions of Church dignitaries dressed in all of their colorful regalia, burning countless candles, and pouring seemingly endless smoke from their incense burners. There was so much ritual, so much tradition, so much pushing and shoving, that very little seemed to resemble true worship or reverence. I began to wonder what part Christ played in all of this theater, and even if He was a part of it, even though He was supposed to be the central figure. I will admit that there was a sizeable number of pilgrims who were clearly in a mode of deep devotion. We found a good vantage point and watched this whole event unfold for at least an hour. It was tremendous theater but a method of remembering our Lord to which I was totally unaccustomed. Because the church was busy, we weren't able to visit the sepulcher, but over the next ten years, we would have numerous opportunities to do so.

One such opportunity occurred late one evening when the old city was deserted. In these areas, we developed certain habits. For example, I always carry my wallet and my passport, one in each pocket. To avoid pickpockets, I walk with my hands in my pockets, clutching the wallet and passport. I entered the church, virtually empty, and walked straight to the tomb. I bent over, still with my hands in my pockets, to enter a low door into an outer vestibule. Then I bent over again to enter the actual tomb. An older woman was already in the tomb, dressed totally in black, wearing a black veil, and burning a few prayer candles. As I stood in this confined space, I couldn't help but think of the enormous influence this one man's life had on the history of the world.

As I was contemplating, I realized that the elderly woman was becoming more interested in me than in her candles. I was quite fascinated and intrigued by the number of rituals she performed. She then snapped at me in what sounded like an Eastern European language. In hindsight, I have no idea how I reacted, but I think I simply stood and stared at her and my body language was saying *"what's your problem?"* She then snapped at me again and I realized she was offended by me having my hands in my pockets. I dutifully removed my hands from my pockets, but I guess I had sinned and wasn't about to be forgiven — she snapped again and scolded me for at least thirty seconds. I have no idea what she said, but I realized it was time for me to leave, and thereby committed another crime. I turned, bent down to leave through the low door, and she was at me again — I had turned my back on the tomb. I was now in the outer vestibule, and the woman was coming out from the tomb. However, she did it properly and reversed out, thereby facing the tomb at all times. But as she reversed through the low door, she stood up too quickly and gave her head quite a bang on an overhanging ledge. I knew this was going to be my fault as well, so I hot-tailed it out of there, and I could hear her furiously scolding me across the church as I made a quick exit through the main doors and into the deserted streets of the Old City — with my hands back in my pockets clutching my wallet and passport.

On Good Friday 1993 we had a close scare. Some of Evelyn's family were visiting, and we were in the Old City of Jerusalem near the Church of the Holy Sepulchre. There was a street performance where Christ's journey to the cross was being re-enacted by a group of charismatic Christians. Then, from nowhere, Evelyn's sister felt something whizz past and a young lad standing beside her was hit in the head and started to bleed. He was dragged over to the entrance to a little store where he seemed to collapse to the floor. We don't know what it was and didn't wait to find out. At the very least it was a missile from a catapult, and the lad had quite a head wound. Because of the commotion associated with the performance, most people didn't even realize what had happened. We simply grabbed our group and quickly got out of there.

And now back to that first-weekend visit. Friday had been very disappointing, but Sunday was different. We were up early to go to the Garden Tomb. The service began at 7:00 a.m., but there were few people there. Tourism was low as a result of the Gulf War, which had ended only weeks earlier. We had good seats where we were slightly higher than the speaker and could see both the speaker and the empty tomb very clearly.

The service proceeded through a few songs and prayers and then the sense of the moment hit me. Somehow it finally dawned on me that I was sitting in the Garden (possibly) where Christ rose from the dead on Resurrection Sunday — this was Resurrection Sunday, the tomb was there and Skull Hill (a possible location of Calvary) was only a few meters behind me and over my shoulder. As we sang through the words of the next hymn, I could feel the tears welling up within me and running down my cheeks. And the story became deeper as the preacher spoke and referred to John and Peter running to the tomb. As he spoke, he used his hands and arms to indicate Peter and John coming to the tomb "and John stopped right here," as he pointed to a place outside the door of the tomb, "while Peter just ran right on inside." The stage could not have been clearer, the object lesson could not have been stronger, and the phrase *"He is not here, He is risen"* had the strongest possible impact.

When we returned as a family in 1993, the impact was no less powerful although it was extra meaningful to be there as a family. For the ten months we lived in Jerusalem, on most Sundays we attended morning worship services at the Garden Tomb. For many of those months we were richly blessed by the preaching of Pastor Derek Cook, and also by the singing and the worshipful atmosphere — the backdrop of an empty tomb made the message all that more impacting. It often struck us that there couldn't be a church in the whole world with an 'interior' as nice as this one: often about 25C, under the shade of the trees, yet with sunbeams breaking through, many flowers and shrubs, birds chirping, a few butterflies, quiet, peaceful and serene. This is arguably the tomb belonging to Joseph of Arimathea and the tomb in which Christ was placed and from which He rose from the dead. This is a special place and is a meditative spot in an otherwise noisy and bustling city.

The main attraction in the garden is a tomb that was closed by a rolling stone. Whether this is the actual tomb of Christ, or not, is not important. What matters is that this garden is a tremendously powerful reminder that Christ died, was buried, and was raised again. To be surrounded with this reminder for an entire service, regularly for ten months, was an enormous privilege.

We have visited the Garden frequently and more often than any other biblical site. We have many special memories. On one occasion, a group of about forty black ladies was on a guided tour of the Garden. The guide pointed out a house on the northern wall of the Old City, about one hundred meters distant, and explained that Horatio Spafford once lived there. Spafford wrote the hymn *"When peace like a river"* or more commonly called *"It is well with my soul."* That was a trigger, and the ladies broke into singing the hymn — some of the most heartfelt and joyous singing we've ever heard. The volume almost lifted the roof of the Arab bus station adjacent to the Garden. The third stanza of his hymn beautifully summarizes a core belief of salvation:

> My sin, oh, the bliss of this glorious thought!
> My sin, not in part but the whole
> Is nailed to His cross, and I bear it no more
> Praise the Lord, praise the Lord, o my soul!
>
> It is well (it is well)
> With my soul (with my soul)
> It is well, it is well with my soul

On another occasion, there was a long lineup to the tomb. An independent traveler decided she wasn't going to wait in line but jumped to the front. She peered in through the door, and without going in she turned around and quite astonishingly said, "It's empty." There was a guide present, and she responded, "Of course it's empty; that's our message." Then, as if to check that her eyes weren't deceiving her, the lady peered into the tomb a second time, and again, "It's empty," and as she walked away she muttered, "It's a fake." The poor lady was probably perplexed as to why everyone else was smiling, and she obviously didn't know the story! Until recently there was a door on the tomb[65], and on the door a sign which read "He is not here, He is risen." That's the core message of Scripture and the message a confused and messed up world needs.

> ...Christ died for our sins according to the Scriptures, and that He was buried, and that He rose again the third day according to the Scriptures, (1 Corinthians 15:3-4)

Yes, the tomb is empty!

---

[65] To facilitate the movement of the increasing number of visitors, this door was removed in 2018 and is currently in storage.

XII.
JERUSALEM

The city of Jerusalem is central to much of the biblical narrative. Jerusalem is given many names in Scripture, such as Salem (Genesis 14:18), Jebus (Joshua 18:28; Judges 19:10; 1 Chronicles 11:4), Ariel (Isaiah 29:1, 2, 7), the City of David (1 Chronicles 11:7) and Zion (1 Kings 8:1). The actual "name" Jerusalem is first used in Joshua 10:1:

> Now it came to pass when Adoni-Zedek king of Jerusalem heard how Joshua had taken Ai and had utterly destroyed it... (Joshua 10:1)

This is the Holy City (Isaiah 52:1), the city of the great King (Matthew 5:35), the city of truth (Zechariah 8:3). Every corner and every alley of the Old City, and of the region directly to the south of the Old City (the Ophel and the City of David), seems to have some historical significance, much of it biblical. Jerusalem is mentioned over 770 times in the Bible,[66] and The City of David is used forty-four times in the Old Testament. Jerusalem was the capital of the ancient, southern kingdom of Judah. The original City of David was on the spur of land immediately to the south of the Temple Mount. It was first built on the hills bordered by two converging valleys, the Valley of Hinnom (Gehenna) to the west and south, and the Kidron Valley to the east. The Kidron Valley separates the Old City from the Mount of Olives. Today's Old City is about one-kilometer square. The wall averages twelve meters high and has eight gates: seven open and one closed.

There are many wonderful Scripture verses referring to the city:

> This is Jerusalem; I have set her in the midst of the nations and the countries all around her. (Ezekiel 5:5)

> ...Jerusalem, the city which the Lord had chosen out of all the tribes of Israel, to put his name there... (2 Chronicles 12:13)

> ... the Lord had said, "In Jerusalem shall My name be forever." (2 Chronicles 33:4)

> Beautiful in elevation, The joy of the whole earth, Is Mount Zion on the sides of the north, The city of the great King. (Psalm 48:2)

---

[66] It is intriguing that Jerusalem is also so central to Islam, yet Jerusalem is not mentioned in the Koran.

…Jerusalem shall be called the City of Truth, The Mountain of the Lord of hosts, The Holy Mountain. (Zechariah 8:3)

It shall be in that day that I [the Lord] will seek to destroy all the nations that come against Jerusalem. (Zechariah 12:9)

The people shall dwell in it; And no longer shall there be utter destruction, But Jerusalem shall be safely inhabited. (Zechariah 14:11)

…O Jerusalem, the holy city!… (Isaiah 52:1)

…Jerusalem, the holy city… (Nehemiah 11;1)

…the city of the great King. (Matthew 5:35)

The first mention of the city is in Genesis 14:18 where we are introduced to Melchizedek, the King of (Jeru) Salem. This was the city that David conquered, where Araunah had his threshing floor, where David and some of the other kings of Judah are buried, where it was attacked and destroyed by Nebuchadnezzar, and where our Savior was tried, crucified, arose from the dead, and ascended to Heaven. Jerusalem is an intriguing city, full of contrasts and contradictions. The contrasts are largely due to the fact that the world's three great monotheistic religions — Judaism, Christianity, and Islam — all claim Jerusalem as a special holy city. The contradictions often come from competing groups of Christians — mostly Roman Catholic, Greek and Russian Orthodox, and Armenian — but we will visit these in a subsequent chapter.

We are immediately faced with two problems as we describe our travels in this city. First, we have already written about our visits to many sites in the city in other parts of this book. Secondly, many of the biblical sites are on the main tourist itinerary, so we experienced few difficulties, dangers, or adventures in finding them. So in this chapter, we will briefly pick our way through our memories of the city, and we won't dwell on every biblical site, but rather on those not described elsewhere.

WESTERN WALL TUNNELS

One of the first things we did upon our arrival in Jerusalem in 1992 was to take a guided walking tour of "underground Jerusalem." The tour was led by an energetic tour guide called "David." Trying to absorb all the information that David supplied was like drinking from a fire hose, and listening to his piercing high-pitched voice was akin to a fingernail on a blackboard. David brought us to see various Herodian, Roman, Byzantine, and Crusader structures, mostly walls and pavements, under the current Old City. The most exciting part of this tour was a visit to excavations of the Western Wall, a retaining wall that supported Herod's temple platform.

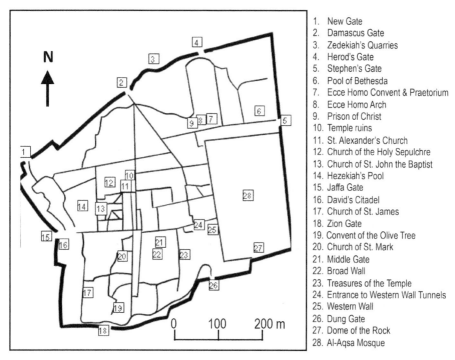

1. New Gate
2. Damascus Gate
3. Zedekiah's Quarries
4. Herod's Gate
5. Stephen's Gate
6. Pool of Bethesda
7. Ecce Homo Convent & Praetorium
8. Ecce Homo Arch
9. Prison of Christ
10. Temple ruins
11. St. Alexander's Church
12. Church of the Holy Sepulchre
13. Church of St. John the Baptist
14. Hezekiah's Pool
15. Jaffa Gate
16. David's Citadel
17. Church of St. James
18. Zion Gate
19. Convent of the Olive Tree
20. Church of St. Mark
21. Middle Gate
22. Broad Wall
23. Treasures of the Temple
24. Entrance to Western Wall Tunnels
25. Western Wall
26. Dung Gate
27. Dome of the Rock
28. Al-Aqsa Mosque

Major biblical locations in the Old City of Jerusalem.

We walked almost three hundred meters along the base of the Western Wall to the Antonio Fortress.[67] This walk is as much as thirty meters below today's city and is completely below the Muslim quarter. We were able to touch the humongous monoliths — the biggest building stones known in Israel, and some of the largest in the world — one is twelve meters long, up to 4.5 meters wide, three meters high, and almost four hundred metric tons. This stone and a few other massive stones are part of the second course of stones in the Western Wall.

The stone used for the temple building projects by King Solomon and by King Herod the Great was taken from an underground quarry just a short distance to the north, one hundred meters east of the Damascus Gate. It seems to be nearly always closed with piles of rubbish accumulating around the metal gate guarding the entrance. However, we were finally able to enter in late 1993, and it is a massive cavernous hole extending under the Muslim Quarter almost

---

[67] In the mid-1990s the tunnel was extended and provided an exit on to the Via Dolorosa in the Muslim quarter of the Old City.

as far as the Temple Mount. Sadly, some graffiti artists had been there before us.

And the temple, when it was being built, was built with stone finished at the quarry, so that no hammer or chisel or any iron tool was heard in the temple while it was being built. (1 Kings 6:7)

Things changed a lot over the intervening years so that during the Festival of Lights in 2018, deep inside the quarry we listened to a performance on a grand piano with lighting provided by hundreds of candles.

WESTERN WALL

Shortly thereafter we went to visit the Western Wall and plaza. The first time I set my eyes on the Western Wall I had goosebumps. In just a few seconds, all that I'd read and heard about this structure, and its centrality to the Jewish people, went whizzing through my mind, and I was overcome. The plaza below the wall is divided into two unequal parts, the larger one for men, and the smaller one for women. The area is under the auspices of the rabbis, and is more or less considered a synagogue, so modesty is required, including head coverings for men. Being new, we didn't know the rules and didn't know if we, as non-Jews, were allowed to enter this sacred precinct.

We stood and watched for a long time as both men and women entered their respective areas. We became quite absorbed watching the rituals — the people bobbing rhythmically as they prayed, many were singing, others paraded what looked like Torah Scrolls in beautifully ornate cases, many kissed the wall, and soldiers prayed against the wall with M-16s slung over their shoulder. We wanted to enter the precinct and experience all of this close-up, but were we allowed to? Everyone in there had a head covering, everyone seemed to be Jewish, and yet there were no signs of prohibition. A few men approached the entry to the precinct without head coverings, and they were able to borrow a small disposable cardboard head covering (called a kippah, or in Yiddish a yarmulke). We were fascinated by the diversity of kippahs (strictly, the plural of kippah is kippot). It wasn't unusual to see knitted images of Homer Simpson and Donald Duck.

We finally decided to "try it." Alistair and I confidently walked towards the entry, looked the attendant in the eye, smiled and nodded, placed a cardboard kippah on our heads, and kept moving. Within less than two minutes, a jolly green giant of a man approached us. He was well over six feet tall, quite rotund, and a rather imposing figure. He was dressed in black from head to toe, wore a large hat, and supported a huge beard and tassels. "Are you Jewish?" he asked. I was deeply embarrassed because I thought we were to be ejected "No," I replied, "we are not Jewish." Then he turned his question into a statement and said, "You are Jewish?" "No," I replied, "we are not Jewish." Then he smiled, tapped himself on the nose (while looking at mine; I have a big nose), and said, "Yes, you are Jewish. Welcome," and he smiled and walked off. So it was fine to be here after all. Subsequently, we discovered that everyone is welcome and can wander in and out.

Off to one side of the men's precinct is an archway called Wilson's Arch named after Charles Wilson, a nineteenth-century British explorer, who discovered it in 1864. The arch was one of many great arches that supported Bridge Street, a private road built by King Herod, which led from his palace to the top of the Temple Mount. Some of the original arch stones from the time of Herod can be seen from inside the arch. Alistair and I went through the arch and immediately saw numerous orthodox Jews praying, reading, and many had just fallen asleep. It is definitely a quieter, more contemplative place than outside, but it smelled like an overly ripe locker room. In subsequent visits, we walked all through this place clicking cameras and taking videos, and nobody cared a hoot. This was a particularly exciting place to be during the major festivals at Passover and Succoth. However, the swaying and bobbing of the devout reveal the powerful attraction this place has on the minds and hearts of the Jewish people.

The Western Wall is not, as many assume, a wall from the ancient Jewish temple. Rather, it is a retaining wall. King Herod the Great rebuilt the Second Temple on the exact site of its predecessor and expanded the sacred enclosure by constructing a massive rectangular retaining wall on the slopes of the hill known as Mount Moriah. He filled the inside with thousands of tons of rubble and created the huge sixteen-hectare plaza still known today as the Temple Mount. This is especially significant to the Jewish people because they don't have their temple, but the western wall is the closest spot to where they can approach the location of their ancient temple without adventuring onto the Temple Mount, an area now under Muslim control. But, being non-Jewish, we aren't barred from visiting the Temple Mount.

TEMPLE MOUNT
Until the mid-1990s, the Temple Mount was a wonderful place to visit. This is the place where Abraham was going to sacrifice his son Isaac. This was the site of Araunah's threshing floor, and of Solomon's, Zerubbabel's, and Herod's temples. This place was destroyed by Nebuchadnezzar's armies in 586 BC, and six hundred years later Jesus Christ overturned the tables of the money changers

Then He said, "Take now your son, your only son Isaac, whom you love, and go to the land of Moriah, and offer him there as a burnt offering on one of the mountains of which I shall tell you." (Genesis 22:2)

Now it came to pass in the Ninth year of his reign, in the tenth month, on the tenth day of the month, that Nebuchadnezzar king of Babylon and all his army came against Jerusalem and encamped against it; and they built a siege wall against it all around. (2 Kings 25:1)

Then Jesus went into the temple of God and drove out all those who bought and sold in the temple, and overturned the tables of the money changers and the seats of those who sold doves. (Matthew 21:12)

The Romans finally reduced it to scorched ruins in AD 70. Today, it is occupied by what some ultra-orthodox Jews refer to as a geopolitical reality — i.e. by Muslims and their imposing, beautiful, golden-domed ornamental shrine known as the Dome of the Rock. King Hussein of Jordan paid for a new gold covering for the dome in 1992. We were amused that the job was being done by Mivan construction from Northern Ireland. Mivan had two large cranes on site — an orange one, and a green one. I wonder how many of the locals recognized the raw sense of Irish humor.[68]

The Mount was also a special place to visit because of some scholarly activities attempting to precisely locate the original site of the Holy of Holies[69] and the temple. There are a number of competing hypotheses, but two seem to carry the most support. One proposes that the Holy of Holies was located precisely over the "foundation stone," which is in the middle of the Dome of the Rock. The other proposes that the temple was on the large plaza to the north of the current Dome of the Rock and that the Holy of Holies may have been centered on a small structure which today looks like a large-domed wishing well known as the Dome of the Spirits or the Dome of the Tablets. In the absence of indisputable evidence, devout Jews will not approach the area for fear of desecrating the inviolable temple precincts. But it is a fascinating exercise to go to the Mount with both hypotheses in hand, or in head, and walk around like Sherlock Holmes looking for clues, testing the evidence posited by the respective proponents.

---

[68] We were both born in Northern Ireland and grew up there until we were married. The colors orange and green are perceived to be the colors of Protestant Unionists and Catholic Nationalists respectively.

[69] This was the most inner sanctum of the Jewish temple. It contained the Ark, the mercy seat, the cherubim, and the Shekinah glory, and only the High Priest could enter the Holy of Holies, and only on one day each year — on Yom Kippur, the Day of Atonement.

BROAD WALL

We will now stroll up into the Jewish Quarter of the Old City and visit two amazing archaeological sites — the Broad Wall and the Middle gate. Neither is very impressive in appearance, but historically and archaeologically these are remarkable.

During the War of Independence, in 1948, Jordanian legions acted irresponsibly and despicably and systematically set out to eradicate any vestige of Judaism from the Old City.[70] In the process, they demolished homes and synagogues but provided an unprecedented opportunity for archaeologists to excavate in otherwise inaccessible places. In the early 1970s, archaeologists unearthed part of the city wall from the period of King Hezekiah.

And he strengthened himself, built up all the wall that was broken, raised it up to the towers, and built another wall outside;... (2 Chronicles 32:5)

The city's population had increased, and when the Assyrian army approached, the king decided to fortify the city and wall in the newly built areas. The wall is about seven meters wide and still stands up to three meters tall.

MIDDLE GATE

Only minutes away are the remains of a First Temple period tower or gate eight meters high, almost twelve meters long, and three meters wide. This structure bears silent witness to the destruction wrought by the Babylonian army, and this may be the "Middle Gate" through which King Nebuchadnezzar entered Jerusalem.

Then all the princes of the king of Babylon came in and sat in the Middle Gate... (Jeremiah 39:3)

Some arrowheads were found near the tower, and these testify to the battle that took place here in 586 BC.

THE TEMPLE INSTITUTE

Just around the corner from these two sites is a small, rather inauspicious-looking museum/tourist center called The Temple Institute. Here, a group of Jewish artisans are zealously preparing all of the vessels and instruments required for a new Jewish temple that they believe will be built on the Temple Mount — when that geopolitical reality is removed! They have painstakingly followed all

---

[70] At the conclusion of the War in January 1949, Jordan occupied east Jerusalem, including the Old City, and Judea, and Samaria (the West Bank).

the detailed instructions from the Bible, the Torah, and from tradition, making all sorts of implements of gold, silver, bronze, and copper. They make it very clear that these aren't show-pieces or replicas — these are the real thing, awaiting a temple to put them in — we saw the High Priest's robe,[71] the High priest's twenty-four-carat gold crown, silver trumpets, menorah, various chalices, and implements for preparing the sacrifices and for preparing the priests, e.g. the bronze laver. We don't get terribly excited about many museums, but this one is fascinating.

Since 1992, this museum has moved across the street, was renovated, expanded, and then moved again to the current location about fifty meters to the south. In our opinion, while these upgrades were necessary, the place has lost much of its original charm. At the time of our first visit, a rabbi simply gave an oral presentation describing each article one by one as he lifted them out of a display cabinet. There were about ten visitors in a small room, and it was informal, cozy, and relaxed. At the end of the presentation, various visitors chatted to the rabbi and asked more questions. Meanwhile, Alistair, who was fourteen years old, reached into the cabinet and held the High Priest's crown. Today, the whole place is thoroughly modernized with video presentations and gift stores, and it has totally lost that personal, informal touch — but still fascinating.

ANCIENT RUINS

We now leave the Jewish Quarter and walk for five minutes through the Arab souk, past stores crammed with spices and other consumables, butchers selling animal heads and entrails, craftsmen of every type working with leather, wool, copper, and other metals, and the ever-persistent hawkers selling souvenirs. The smells are at once both aromatic and obnoxious; the noise and bustle are very Middle Eastern. Soon we arrive at a little bakery called Zalatimo's Sweets[72] located on the Via Dolorosa where the stairs to the ninth Station of the Cross leave from Suq Khan ez-Zeit St. Thousands of pilgrims and other tourists pass this spot every day, but only locals go in. We went in, but not to buy sweets; we had other motives. We purchased and enjoyed a piece of baklava, and while paying, we asked the store owner if he would allow us to visit his storeroom. He was a little puzzled at first, but he had enough English to understand what we wanted, and he escorted us in. After removing a few crates of empty Coca-Cola bottles and other stuff, we were able to view a few scant ruins of ancient

---

[71] The High Priest's robe is made of Irish linen because Ireland is the only place in the world that produces flax of sufficient quality.
[72] Now under new ownership and no longer a bakery.

structures that once stood here. There are some remains from the ancient Temple of Venus which occupied the site before the Church of Holy Sepulchre was built, about AD 336. There are also a few remnants from the original Church of the Holy Sepulchre. We replaced the Coke bottles, said a big thank you, gave him a tip, and walked around the corner to another neglected site that is passed by thousands of pilgrims.

CHURCH OF ALEXANDER NEVSKY

This Russian Orthodox Church[73] is located about sixty meters east of the Church of the Holy Sepulchre. After a couple of rings on the doorbell and a period of very persistent knocking, the door was opened, and we were invited in by a delightful young nun. Inside are some of the best-preserved ruins in Jerusalem. There is an arch from the time of Hadrian, and this was possibly a major entry to the city in Roman times. There is also a fairly sizable chunk of the wall from King Herod's time along with some Roman columns, and part of the entrance to the original Church of the Holy Sepulchre. But the highlight of this place is a slit-like hole in the wall adjacent to the gate at Hadrian's arch. The hole is about half a meter long and perhaps half as wide. This, the nun explained, is an eye of the needle referred to by Jesus:

And again I say to you, it is easier for a camel to go through the eye of a needle than for a rich man to enter the kingdom of God." (Matthew 19:24)

Scholars disagree on the meaning of Christ's statement, some arguing that Christ meant exactly as He said — the eye of a literal needle. Others argue that this structure beside the gate was typical. A shepherd returning to the city late at night, after the city gates were closed, could squeeze his sheep, and himself through the hole, but never a camel. Either way, it's a wonderful object lesson. This visit to St. Alexander's came with a price. The nun, although delightful, insisted on showing us around the chapel. Oh, my! We can visit most churches, temples, shrines, mosques, and synagogues in less than two minutes flat. Most of them are uniformly scripted to a religious pattern and get tedious after the third or fourth one. Nevertheless, so as not to offend the enthusiastic young lady we endured a one-hour description of every nut and bolt in every icon and idol. This was one time where I almost fell asleep while still standing.

---

[73] Through the late 1990s this church looked to be permanently closed and no amount of ringing or knocking got a response. Then in about 2010 it reopened as a bona fide tourist attraction which sadly most tour groups walk past in their rush to other places.

JERUSALEM ARCHAEOLOGICAL PARK

The Jerusalem Archaeological Park, the Ophel, is situated along the southern wall of the Temple Mount. Topographically, ancient Jerusalem had three components: the hill of the City of David, the Ophel ridge, and the Temple Mount — the Ophel connects the City of David with the Temple Mount. For purely historical purposes, the Ophel is well worth a visit. It provides an opportunity to see the remains of shops, markets, homes, ritual baths, and streets from ancient Jerusalem. It also allows you to experience a feel for the enormity of some of the stones used in the construction of the retaining wall of the temple. The great stones near the southwestern corner aren't held together with mortar, and their sheer weight gives the structure its stability. We were dwarfed as we stood at the base of the wall and looked up, and yet the original wall may have been one-third higher than it is today. To the left of the corner are the pavement of a main street and commercial area from Roman times. As dramatic evidence of the Roman destruction of AD 70, on the street is a pile of building stones from the top of the original wall that have been left lying where they were found. Among the pile is a replica of a stone engraved with the words "Place of the Trumpeting" (the original is in the Israeli Museum, Jerusalem). High above us at the top of the wall is where a priest stood to blow the trumpet to begin and end the Sabbath.

> *For days will come upon you when your enemies will build an embankment around you, surround you and close you in on every side, and level you, and your children within you, to the ground; and they will not leave in you one stone upon another, because you did not know the time of your visitation.* (Luke 19:43-44)

We then walked about one hundred meters along the base of the southern wall to a wide staircase, much of it original. This once brought hordes of pilgrims through the gates and up onto the Temple Mount. Although the gates are now built up, and there are no longer hordes of pilgrims, this didn't stop our imaginations from running wild as we stood and watched and listened to that imaginary group of people singing the Psalms of Ascent (Ps 120-134) as they went to the temple to worship.

CITY OF DAVID

It is only a short walk across the road to the City of David, which to us is the undiscovered[74] gem of the Bible lands. King David captured the Jebusite city of Jebus and it became the City of David. The phrase 'The City of David' is used

---

[74] The area is now fully developed into one of Jerusalem's paramount tourist attractions.

forty-four times in the Old Testament and overlooks the Kidron valley to the east. Parts of the original Jebusite wall and of David's additions are visible. Most tour buses park right here; however, until about 2005, most pilgrims headed off in the opposite direction to see the Western Wall. So close, and yet they miss this gem called the City of David. We will now visit Warren's shaft, Gihon Spring, Hezekiah's tunnel, and the Pool of Siloam.

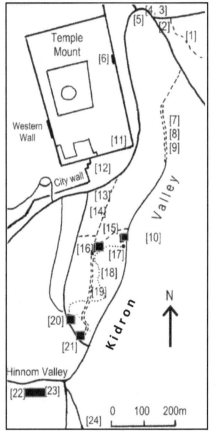

1. Church of Mary Magdalene
2. Garden of Gethsemane
3. Grotto of Gethsemane
4. Church of the Assumption
5. Church of St. Stephen
6. Beautiful Gate, Golden or Eastern Gate
7. Absalom's Pillar & Cave of Jehoshaphat
8. Bnei Hezir Tomb
9. Zechariah's Monument
10. Shebna's Tomb
11. Pinnacle of the Temple
12. Ophel Archaeological Park
13. Jeremiah's Cisterns
14. City of David Excavations
15. Jebusite Wall
16. Warren's Shaft
17. Gihon Spring
18. Hezekiah's Tunnel
19. Tombs of the Kings of Judah?
20. Pool of Siloam
21. The King's Garden
22. Akeldama
23. Tomb of Annas of the High Priest
24. En Rogel

Major biblical locations in the Kidron Valley, Jerusalem.

WARREN'S SHAFT

The first thing we visited was a sloping stone "stepped structure," which probably supported a palace or fortification on the crest of the ridge, possibly the palace of King David. Just a few minutes later we came to Warren's shaft. Charles Warren was a British army engineer who discovered a sloping access tunnel that burrowed under the city wall to a point twelve meters above the Gihon Spring. A narrow, vertical shaft dropped from this point down into the spring. Until the late 1990s, it was thought this was the way that water was hauled up into the city in ancient times, and perhaps this was the actual biblical water shaft through which David's warriors penetrated the city, ca. 1000 BC.

Now David said on that day, "Whoever climbs up by way of the water shaft and Defeats the Jebusites (the lame and the blind, who are hated by David's soul), he shall be chief and captain." Therefore they say, "The blind and the lame shall not come into the house." (2 Samuel 5:8)

Now David said, "Whoever attacks the Jebusites first shall be chief and captain." And Joab the son of Zeruiah went up first, and became chief. (1 Chronicles 11:6)

Recent archaeological finds around the Gihon Spring at the bottom of the hill have cast serious doubt on this interpretation. The biblical story of David's commander, Joab, entering the city remains intact — but he didn't climb up this shaft.

KIDRON VALLEY, GIHON SPRING, AND HEZEKIAH'S TUNNEL
We continue along this access tunnel and then down a long set of steps past enormous stone structures to the Gihon spring below, located in the Kidron valley. Depending upon the political climate, this can be an anxious and nervous place to be.

Also he removed Maachah his grandmother from being queen mother, because she had made an obscene image of Asherah. And Asa cut down her obscene image and burned it by the Brook Kidron. (1 Kings 15:13)

And the king commanded Hilkiah the high priest, the priests of the second order, and the doorkeepers, to bring out of the temple of the Lord all the articles that were made for Baal, for Asherah, and for all the host of heaven; and he burned them outside Jerusalem in the fields of Kidron, and carried their ashes to Bethel... The altars that were on the roof, the upper chamber of Ahaz, which the kings of Judah had made, and the altars which Manasseh had made in the two courts of the house of the Lord, the king broke down and pulverized there, and threw their dust into the Brook Kidron. (2 Kings 23:4, 12)

Solomon was anointed king of Israel at the Gihon Spring.

The king also said to them, "Take with you the servants of your lord, and have Solomon my son ride on my own mule, and take him down to Gihon. There let Zadok the priest and Nathan the prophet anoint him king over Israel; and blow the horn, and say, 'Long live King Solomon!'...So Zadok the priest, Nathan the

prophet, Benaiah the son of Jehoiada, the Cherethites, and the Pelethites went down and had Solomon ride on King David's mule, and took him to Gihon...So Zadok the priest and Nathan the prophet have anointed him king at Gihon;...
(1 Kings 1:33-34, 38, 45)

The spring is a gusher and releases its waters into what is known as Hezekiah's tunnel. In the 1990s the only access to the tunnel was to enter via the spring from the Kidron Valley. The first time we walked the tunnel we were accompanied by an official guide who chased some annoying, pestering children away. A few years later, we had stones thrown at us while we were entering. And we did actually go into the spring; in fact, up to the knees at first and later right up to our waists. From here it was a 533-meter walk along the rather sinuous Hezekiah's tunnel to the Pool of Siloam. The tunnel was built in 701 BC in anticipation of a siege by King Sennacherib of Assyria.

Now the rest of the acts of Hezekiah—all his might, and how he made a pool and a tunnel and brought water into the city—are they not written in the book of the chronicles of the kings of Judah? (2 Kings 20:20)

The tunnel drops only thirty-five centimeters (some sources cite anything up to 2.1 meters; <½% grade) over its length. It averages 1.75 meters high, about seventy-five centimeters wide, and flows from the Gihon Spring to the Pool of Siloam. It takes approximately forty-five minutes to wade waist-deep through the length of the tunnel.

We have waded through the tunnel on numerous occasions but the first time was the most exciting. We had a good flashlight, clothes, and footwear that we didn't mind getting wet, and we did it on a hot day so that we could drip-dry at the Pool of Siloam! This is not a place for claustrophobics. Even though it is an easy walk, and there is no chance of getting lost, it is nevertheless totally enclosed, cramped, dark, wet, and a long way to the other end. Today it is very different. In the 1990s one almost had to have permission from young Arab lads to take you to the tunnel or even lead us through it. Now it is all part of the City of David site and tourists go through the tunnel by the busload, and water levels rarely are more than mid-calf.

When those who first cut the tunnel had finished their task they described the completion of their work. The inscription was originally on the wall of the tunnel near the Pool of Siloam and is now in the Istanbul Archaeological Museum. This was an inscription we really wanted to see. But there was a problem; the gallery housing the artifact in Istanbul had been closed to the public for about three years because of insufficient funds to adequately curate the collection.[75] In early 2000 we were living in Antalya in southwestern Turkey, and we were offered an opportunity to get to the museum in Istanbul. A few days later we jumped in a bus for the twelve-hour journey to Istanbul. When we arrived at the museum it was like a mystery novel as the security guard brought us past "no entry" signs, opened huge doors, switched off various security alarms, unlocked doors, and finally took us into a gallery that was quite dusty. It had obviously been closed for some time. And what a collection. Not only was there the Siloam Inscription, we also saw the Gezer calendar and the Soreg Inscription. We had our own private viewing, and it was exciting for us to see these pieces which are so old and have such an important bearing on biblical history.

POOL OF SILOAM

Okay, back to wading through the tunnel. Although we thoroughly enjoyed the journey through the tunnel, it's a relief to reach the far end at the Pool of Siloam. It takes a few minutes for the eyes to adjust from the blackness of the tunnel to the bright summer Israeli sun: even so, the hot sun brought rapid drying to our dripping clothes. The Pool of Siloam[76] has been badly neglected and is a bit of a cesspool with garbage, a couple of old chairs, and bicycle frames. Never again can we keep a straight face and sing the hymn *"By cool Siloam's shady rill, how fair the lilies grow…"* Evidently, the author, Reginald Heber, didn't visit the pool, although his words may have been accurate in 1811 when he penned the words.

> *Shallun the son of Col-Hozeh, leader of the district of Mizpah, repaired the Fountain Gate; he built it, covered it, hung its doors with its bolts and bars, and repaired the wall of the Pool of Shelah by the King's Garden…* (Nehemiah 3:15)

> *He answered and said, "A Man called Jesus made clay and anointed my eyes and said to me, 'Go to the pool of Siloam and wash.' So I went and washed, and I received sight."* (John 9:11)

---

[75] There were three artifacts in this gallery that we wished to see. First, the Siloam Inscription, a 2,700 year-old Hebrew inscription describing the meeting of two crews of hewers who had begun digging from opposite ends of the tunnel.. Second, there was the Temple or Soreg Inscription which is a two thousand year-old stone tablet from the temple in Jerusalem warning non-Jews that they would be killed if they entered the sacred precinct of the temple. A low wall, the Soreg, surrounded the inner sacred precinct of the temple and defined the area beyond which only Jews could go. The third piece was the Gezer Calendar (from Gezer which is between Jerusalem and Tel Aviv) is a small, stone tablet inscribed with the oldest (three-thousand year-old) extant piece of Hebrew writing. Ironically, all three pieces were right beside each other in the same gallery in the Istanbul Archaeological Museum.

[76] In 2005 archaeologists identified what is probably the real Pool of Siloam at the time of Christ about fifty meters south of the one that tourists have been visiting for years, i.e. the wrong one. The seventy-meter-long pool was uncovered when workmen were digging an irrigation trench.

And we have another indelible memory of the pool. I wanted to get a photograph of the exit from the tunnel with the pool in the foreground. To get the proper angle I decided to step into the pool, and immediately sank to my shins in mud. I was totally stuck and Evelyn and some friendly neighbor had to drag me out with the mud desperately trying to hold on to me.

On one occasion as we left the pool we met a young Jewish lad who was alone, dressed completely in black, with kippah and peyos.[77] This might not seem unusual in Jerusalem, but this was the Arab village of Silwan. This is a Palestinian hotbed, and at times it is not even safe for tourists and visitors, never mind a conspicuous Jewish lad on his own. We felt prompted to keep an eye on him as he walked towards the Old City, a walk of perhaps ten minutes up a steep road. In a short distance, a fork in the road leads off to the left and more or less runs parallel to our road, and both eventually arrive near the Dung Gate. The young man turned left, but we weren't going there. As we walked on our two parallel roads, we could see Arab youths taunting him and throwing stones.

We were in a dilemma. We had our two children with us, aged twelve and fourteen years, and we couldn't put them at risk, yet this Jewish lad was clearly in danger. We hurried up the hill and went to a spot where we knew the young lad would arrive. He approached us, looked quite scared, and just gazed through us. We asked, "Are you okay?" No response. We asked again but he just kept walking, and to our utter shock he turned to walk back down the road that we had just come up. We knew that there are always police and army inside the Dung Gate near the entrance to the Western Wall Plaza. We raced through the gate, spotted a few soldiers, and before we had more than two sentences out we heard: "What, he's gone down towards Silwan?" and they were into their jeep and off like a whirlwind. We hung around for a few minutes but didn't "see" the end of the story.

EN ROGEL

From the Pool of Siloam, we proceeded farther down the Kidron Valley in search of En Rogel. This is a thirty-eight-meter-deep well in the Kidron Valley near the junction of Hinnom Valley where Jonathan and Ahimaaz stayed and where Adonijah sacrificed sheep:

---

[77] The Torah says, "*You shall not round off the peyos of your head*" (Leviticus 19:27). The word peyos refers to sideburns i.e. the hair in front of the ears that extends to underneath the cheekbone which is level with the nose.

Now Jonathan and Ahimaaz stayed at En Rogel, for they dared not be seen coming into the city;... Then the woman took and spread a covering over the well's mouth, and spread ground grain on it; and the thing was not known. (2 Samuel 17:17, 19)

And Adonijah sacrificed sheep and oxen and fattened cattle by the stone of Zoheleth, which is by En Rogel; he also invited all his brothers, the king's sons, and all the men of Judah, the king's servants. (1 Kings 1:9)

Now given that this well is thirty-eight meters deep and that there are very few sources of water in Jerusalem, this should be easy to find. No way. We had a reasonable idea of the general location. We arrived and entered a very tiny mosque but no one had any idea what we were talking about, and even the Arabic name, Bir-Ayyub, didn't help. We asked a number of people, but no one knew the location. Then we went to the door of a humble home that had a small garden. Three women emerged, and they indicated that they knew the well. We accompanied them, along with an aged gentleman, for about fifteen minutes farther down the Kidron, and sure enough, we arrived at the site of a former well. This one was filled in, and it wasn't the one we were looking for. At this stage, we gave up, and it was only three years later that we decided to try once again. We found it almost instantly, and it was in the little garden where we met the three women three years earlier — literally five meters away and just around the corner of the house. And this little garden was on the other side of a wall from the tiny mosque! What's up with these people?

HINNOM VALLEY — HELL

The En Rogel well is at the junction of the Kidron and Hinnom Valleys, and it is the Hinnom we wanted to visit next. It was probably September 1992, and we'd arrived in Jerusalem only recently. We rented a car to drive down the Valley of Hinnom. From the abbreviated name we get the Hebrew ge'hinnom, and the Greek 'gehenna' which is consistently translated in the New Testament as "hell." We entered from the upper west end of the valley and slowly drove down towards the Kidron valley. As we drove down the valley, we couldn't help recalling that this was the valley where child sacrifices occurred. We will let the Scriptures tell the story:

And he defiled Topheth, which is in the Valley of the Son of Hinnom, that no man might make his son or his daughter pass through the fire to Molech. (2 Kings 23:10)

Ahaz was twenty years old when he became king,.... He burned incense in the Valley of the Son of Hinnom, and burned his children in the fire, according to the abominations of the nations whom the Lord had cast out before the children of Israel. (2 Chronicles 28:1, 3)

Also he caused his sons to pass through the fire in the Valley of the Son of Hinnom;... (2 Chronicles 33:6)

And they have built the high places of Tophet, which is in the Valley of the Son of Hinnom, to burn their sons and their daughters in the fire, ... (Jeremiah 7:31)

And that is more-or-less our Jerusalem. For us, Jerusalem is one of the most wonderful cities in the world — history, geography, archaeology, rioting, religion, politics, culture, museums, McDonald's — it has everything — and before McDonald's, there was a McDavid's!

XIII.
THE LIFE OF JESUS CHRIST

DETOUR THIRTEEN:
WHAT IS THE BIBLE ALL ABOUT?

If you were to be asked, "What is the New Testament about?" you might respond that the Gospels are four different versions of the life of Christ and the remaining books focus on early missionaries spreading the gospel. But what about the Old Testament? What is that about? It would be difficult for most people to encapsulate that into one simple sentence. Most Christians are unaware of how central Jesus is in the mind of God. They know that Christ came to be our Savior and that He died on the cross to forgive us our sins. But for many Christians, it stops there, and they are now waiting for some time in the future when they die and can go to heaven to be with the Lord for eternity. That's the basic understanding many Christians have of the Christian life. But let's look at what Jesus Christ had to say:

You search the Scriptures, for in them you think you have eternal life; and these are they which testify of Me. But you are not willing to come to Me that you may have life. (John 5:39-40)

Jesus was speaking to the Pharisees who were familiar with the Old Testament Scriptures, and he told them that even though they had studied the Scriptures, they missed the whole point, because they didn't recognize that those Scriptures were talking about Him. Jesus says: "For if you believed Moses, you would believe Me; for he wrote of Me" (John 5:46).

Christ came more than one thousand years after Moses, but Jesus says that Moses wrote of Him. Moses wrote Genesis, Exodus, Leviticus, Numbers and Deuteronomy. So, according to Jesus, they're about Him. A story in Luke is one of our favorite passages. Jesus had risen from the dead, and He appeared alongside two disciples on the road to Emmaus, but they didn't recognize Him. After some conversation, Jesus interrupted and said to them:

Then He said to them, "O foolish ones, and slow of heart to believe in all that the prophets have spoken! Ought not the Christ to have suffered these things and to enter into His glory?" And beginning at Moses and all the Prophets, He expounded to them in all the Scriptures the things concerning Himself. (Luke 24:25-27)

Then Jesus continued:

Then He said to them, "These are the words which I spoke to you while I was still with you, that all things must be fulfilled which were written in the Law of Moses and the Prophets and the Psalms concerning Me." And He opened their understanding, that they might comprehend the Scriptures. (Luke 24:44-45)

So, even the Psalms and the Prophets are about Christ! The plain and obvious central teaching of the bible is:

For I delivered to you first of all that which I also received: that Christ died for our sins according to the Scriptures, and that He was buried, and that He rose again the third day according to the Scriptures, (1 Corinthians 15:3-4)

The key to understanding the Bible is to see Jesus Christ on nearly every page.

––––––––––––––––

JESUS'S EARLY YEARS

These chapters on Jesus will be the most difficult parts to write. The majority of Old Testament sites are in Iran, Iraq, Syria, Lebanon, and in Judea and Samaria (the West Bank), and most of these had a certain amount of exploration, adventure, and even danger. In contrast, the life and ministry of our Lord mostly centered on Galilee and Jerusalem, and these are two of the safest parts of Israel outside of the Negev desert. Although there wasn't the same sense of adventure, there was definitely an overpowering sense of being on a journey, of being on an exciting pilgrimage, and this also raised the adrenaline levels — at many sites, our emotions ran high as we slowed down to contemplate and to meditate on the events that occurred.

As with our visit to Jerusalem, we will treat the life of Christ as a journey. But this tour is fraught with problems. The major Christian denominations, such as Greek Orthodox and Roman Catholic, have different sites for the location of many New Testament events. Consequently, there are two Shepherd's Fields, two rooms for the Last Supper, two houses for Caiaphas the High priest, two locations for Christ's crucifixion, two burial locations, two places of Ascension, two locations for the martyrdom of Stephen, and two places for the burial of Mary the mother of Jesus. There are two chapels at Capernaum, and in their zeal to own locations, there are two chapels at Cana of Galilee, and both of them are in the wrong location!

Much of the confusion has arisen because in AD 325 the Jerusalem patriarch, Bishop Macarius, urged Constantine's[78] mother Helena to take responsibility for the Holy Land's neglected Christian sites. A year later, Helena and the Bishop toured the Holy Land together and identified many Christian sites including the cave in Nazareth where Mary was told that she would give birth to Jesus, the cave in Bethlehem where Jesus was born, the field where the shepherds saw the star, the room where Jesus turned water into wine at Cana, the stump of the tree that provided the wood for Jesus's cross, the Via Dolorosa,[79] etc.

There can be no doubt that some of the sites that Helena identified were already well known and some of them were marked by pagan temples. In AD 135 Emperor Hadrian, in his attempt to wipe out Christianity and to eradicate the holy sites, tore down Christian shrines and replaced them with pagan temples, which, ironically, marked their locations for future generations. Nevertheless, some of Helena's identifications have to be treated with caution because she had no credentials as a historian or archaeologist. This, unfortunately, confuses and serves to blemish the greatest story ever told. Quite frankly, the exact locations don't matter — the events that happened are what matter, and they concern issues of eternal significance.

The Christmas story begins in Nazareth, a small Jewish village that Mary and Joseph set off from to Bethlehem. Today, Nazareth is a busy Israeli-Arab city with seventy thousand Arab Christians and Muslims. Our tour begins at the Basilica of the Annunciation which marks the location where the angel Gabriel appeared to a young woman called Mary:

> *Now in the sixth month the angel Gabriel was sent by God to a city of Galilee named Nazareth, to a virgin betrothed to a man whose name was Joseph, of the house of David. The virgin's name was Mary. And having come in, the angel said to her, "Rejoice, highly favored one, the Lord is with you; blessed are you among women!" But when she saw him, she was troubled at his saying, and considered what manner of greeting this was. Then the angel said to her, "Do not be afraid, Mary, for you have found favor with God. And behold, you will conceive in your womb and bring forth a Son, and shall call His name JESUS. He will be great, and will be called the Son of the Highest; and the Lord God will give Him the throne of His father David. And He will reign over the house of Jacob forever, and of His kingdom there will be no end." (Luke 1:26-33)*

---

[78] The Roman Emperor Constantine legalized Christianity in the Roman Empire in 313 AD.

[79] The Via Dolorosa, or the Way of Suffering, retraces Christ's alleged route to Calvary. Helena identified the precise spots along the route where certain events took place, and these became accepted by Christian tradition. But she not only identified where the known events took place, she also introduced some new events, thereby creating some of the fourteen Stations of the Cross.

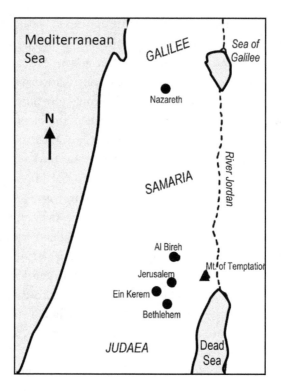

Major locations associated with the early life and ministry of Jesus Christ.

The modern basilica was built in 1969. It is an enormous, cold concrete monolith that looks much more like a lighthouse than a church, and it dominates the city. The church has two levels. The lower level contains the grotto, which, according to tradition, was the home of Mary and the Site of the Annunciation. If you are looking for a solitary moment to contemplate the visitation, good luck! Busloads of tourists jam the small shrine, jostling for a good photograph. Cameras click, flash, and whirr, and pilgrims rush on only to be replaced by another busload. The upper level of the church has an enormous 170-foot high cupola through which natural light flows to illuminate the entire interior, which is adorned throughout by mosaics and works of art contributed from around the world.

Our story now takes us on a journey with Mary to visit her cousin Elizabeth in the village of Ein Kerem. Tradition identifies this village as the birthplace of John the Baptist. Scripture is vague on the birthplace of John other than to say:

Now Mary arose in those days and went into the hill country with haste, to a city of Judah, (Luke 1:39)

Some commentators read "City of Juttah" rather than "City of Judah" in which case, John may have been born in today's city of Yatta about eight kilometers south of Hebron. Nevertheless, there are two churches in Ein Kerem. The Church of the Visitation is built over the home of John the Baptist's parents, Zechariah and Elizabeth. The church sits high on the hillside with a wonderful view of the valley and the surrounding wooded hills. This is probably one of the most beautiful churches in Israel. This is where Mary, pregnant with Jesus, went to visit her cousin Elizabeth. The Scriptures tell us that:

> Now Mary... entered the house of Zacharias and greeted Elizabeth. And it happened, when Elizabeth heard the greeting of Mary, that the babe leaped in her womb; and Elizabeth was filled with the Holy Spirit. (Luke 1:39-41)

Mary then proceeds to proclaim what we now call the Magnificat:

> And Mary said:
> "My soul magnifies the Lord,
> And my spirit has rejoiced in God my Savior.
> For He has regarded the lowly state of His maidservant;
> For behold, henceforth all generations will call me blessed.
> For He who is mighty has done great things for me,
> And holy is His name.
> And His mercy is on those who fear Him
> From generation to generation.
> He has shown strength with His arm;
> He has scattered the proud in the imagination of their hearts.
> He has put down the mighty from their thrones,
> And exalted the lowly.
> He has filled the hungry with good things,
> And the rich He has sent away empty.
> He has helped His servant Israel,
> In remembrance of His mercy,
> As He spoke to our fathers,
> To Abraham and to his seed forever." (Luke 1:46-55)

One wall of the church courtyard is covered with ceramic tiles quoting the Magnificat in more than forty languages.

Just a short distance away is the Church of John the Baptist, and here's a fine example of where "holy sites" become embarrassing. Again, this is a fairly nice little church, but as we enter a fairly conspicuous sign informs us that the village of Ein Kerem isn't specifically mentioned in the New Testament and that it's not clear where John was born. Nevertheless, we are directed to a grotto where John the Baptist is said to have been born, and a large silver star marks the spot!

Now Elizabeth's full time came for her to be delivered, and she brought forth a son. (Luke 1:57)

It is fitting that Bethlehem is only a short distance from Ein Kerem. Bethlehem is the City of David, and the city where Samuel called David to be king of Israel. Our first visit to Bethlehem was memorable. We jumped onboard a sherut, a shared taxi, from Jerusalem and asked to be dropped off at Rachel's tomb on the northern outskirts of Bethlehem. We visited Rachel's tomb, then walked along the main road into town popping into several souvenir stores en route. After exploring a rather vibrant Manger Square, we visited the Church of the Nativity. Our first visit to the church was memorable because we had the whole church to ourselves, except for the brightly clothed priests scurrying back and forth.

There is evidence of a cave in Bethlehem being venerated as Christ's birthplace since around AD 160, and in AD 326, Constantine commissioned a church to be built over the cave. Portions of the beautifully ornate floor mosaic survive from that period. Constantine's church was destroyed by Justinian in AD 530, who built the much larger church that remains today. We enter the huge church through the very small rectangular Door of Humility. This low door forces all who enter to bend over as an act of humility. However, the door has little to do with humility and more to do with practicality. It was created in Ottoman times to prevent horses, camels, and carts from being driven into the church.

This is an interesting church, but it stands scarred by age and conflict. It has some ornate mosaics, gilded chandeliers, lamps, and artwork, although centuries of burning candles and incense are taking their toll making the general unpleasantness of the place a little overpowering. The focal point of this church is the Grotto of the Nativity, a small cave beneath the church altar. It is entered by a flight of steps and this cave has been honored as the site of Christ's birth since at least the second century. A silver star in the marble floor marks the spot where Christ is believed to have been born.

Now after Jesus was born in Bethlehem of Judea in the days of Herod the king, behold, wise men from the East came to Jerusalem, saying, "Where is He who has been born King of the Jews? For we have seen His star in the East and have come to worship Him." (Matthew 2:1-2)

In the Grotto, as in other parts of the church, the various denominations continue to fight over turf. The crypt has fifteen lanterns: six for Greek Orthodox, five for Armenian Orthodox and four for Roman Catholics. Steps away from the birthplace shrine is the Chapel of the Manger, owned by the Roman Catholics.

It struck us, perhaps incorrectly, that the Catholics were saying: "You (Greek Orthodox and Armenian) may have the spot where Christ was born, but we have the manger."

Subsequent visits to the church weren't as peaceful, and frequently there were lengthy lines to enter the grotto. Now imagine the scene: hundreds of people have spent perhaps thousands of dollars to be here, and for most, this will be a once in a lifetime visit. The lineup is long and moves slowly. It is hot and stuffy, with incense and smoke choking off the few remaining atoms of oxygen still floating around. You slowly move step by step down the stairs and finally, the grotto is in sight. Just at that moment, two things occur. Other visitors decide to avoid the lineup by going against the one-way system that is in place, and your tour guide is coercing everyone to hurry along because he wants to herd you to your waiting bus to take you to some tacky souvenir shop. Tour guides and priests out-compete each other for volume in shouting, and this all generates a lot of unchristian behavior.

For us, we usually had time, and on more than one occasion we simply stood back and watched the unholy show happen — on top of what many consider to be the holiest spot on earth. This was both very funny yet sad at the same time. We just waited for the time when a priest would swing his censor and take out a visitor, or even another priest! We didn't witness it but it has happened — just go to YouTube and search "Bethlehem fight: Priests brawl."

Adjacent to these main chapels is the Roman Catholic chapel which is open, bright, simple with fine architecture, and a much more inviting environment. From this chapel, stairs lead down to the residence of the scholar Jerome who was commissioned in AD 382 to translate the Bible into Latin from the original Hebrew and Greek. This translation became known as the Vulgate and was widely adopted and remained the standard version of the Bible in the Western world for more than a thousand years.

Then on Christmas Eve 1992 we went by bus to Bethlehem to attend a carol service in the Church. It was a privilege to visit Bethlehem at Christmas, but the city was deserted. The residents were under strict curfew, and there were more soldiers and police than visitors. However, with such tight security, it was probably the safest spot in the Middle East. The carol singing was wonderful, but the 'preacher' was dreadful, and the only redeeming feature about the sermonette was that it only lasted ten minutes.

Then, on Christmas morning we went to Christ Church Cathedral just inside Jaffa Gate in the Old City. This was a worshipful service, the preaching was good, and the singing was wonderful with many of the old favorite carols accompanied by a trumpet and by a fellow who walked all over the piano keyboard. From Christ Church, we went directly to the Mount of Olives for Christmas dinner.

Because of the total lack of Christmas Spirit in Israel, we felt that Christmas dinner in our apartment might be a little lifeless. Grandma and Grandpa Turkington were visiting, so we decided to book Christmas dinner in a hotel. None of the major hotels provide Christmas dinner because the Jewish rabbis will withdraw the hotel's kashrut (kosher) certificate. Without this certificate, a hotel would suffer financially — observant Jewish people couldn't eat there. But, we found three good places that did provide Christmas dinner: the YMCA (Christian), the American Colony Hotel (Palestinian), and the Intercontinental (known as the seven arches) on the top of the Mount of Olives.

The Intercontinental doesn't worry about losing their certificate because they never had one. This hotel was built when the Mount of Olives was occupied by Jordan before the1967 war. The main driveway to the hotel runs through a part of the large Jewish cemetery on the Mount of Olives. When the Israelis captured the Mount of Olives in 1967 they did a mammoth job of removing bones etc. from under the driveway and relocating them — but this sacrilege made the hotel ineligible to hold a kashrut certificate. Ironically, all of this history allowed us to have Christmas dinner in the most beautiful setting imaginable — on the Mount of Olives with an incredible vista over the Old City of Jerusalem. And the actual seven-course meal was the best. Even now, almost thirty years later, we don't recall ever having a finer meal than that in the 7-arches. As expected, Christmas was very different that year. Perhaps it wasn't all we had hoped for, but it is one we will never forget.

To the east of Bethlehem lies the village of Beit Sahour, where we find the Shepherds' Field. This is identified as the place where the Angel of the Lord visited the shepherds and informed them of Jesus's birth:

> Now there were in the same country shepherds living out in the fields, keeping watch over their flock by night. And behold, an angel of the Lord stood before them, and the glory of the Lord shone around them, and they were greatly afraid. Then the angel said to them, "Do not be afraid, for behold, I bring you good tidings of great joy which will be to all people. For there is born to you this day in the city of David a Savior, who is Christ the Lord. (Luke 2:8-11)

The Roman Catholics and the Greek Orthodox each have their own Shepherds' Field. The Roman Catholic chapel is designed to resemble the shepherds' tent, and there are a few sizeable caves nearby. The Greek Orthodox site has a fifth-century church built over a cave. The Orthodox site is adjacent to the traditional field where Ruth and Boaz romanced. Both sites sit amid olive trees and are appealing. The interiors of both churches have, as expected, paintings depicting various aspects of the birth of Jesus. The majority of tourists visit the Catholic site, so if you want peace and quiet, the Orthodox site is a nice alternative – if it's open.

Jesus grew up and spent His boyhood in Nazareth, and at the age of twelve was presented at the temple in Jerusalem:

> *Now when the days of her purification according to the law of Moses were completed, they brought Him to Jerusalem to present Him to the Lord.* (Luke 2:22)

On the journey home from Jerusalem Scripture records:

> *When they had finished the days, as they returned, the Boy Jesus lingered behind in Jerusalem. And Joseph and His mother did not know it; but supposing Him to have been in the company, they went a day's journey, and sought Him among their relatives and acquaintances. So when they did not find Him, they returned to Jerusalem, seeking Him.* (Luke 2:43-45)

We have no idea where they were when Mary and Joseph realized Jesus was missing, but one tradition identifies the location as Al Bireh: a southern suburb of Ramallah and lying in the shadow of the fairly large mound of Mizpah, where Samuel gathered all of Israel together and where Saul was chosen as Israel's first king (1 Samuel 10:21-24). We have often mused with the possible question — did Mary and Joseph point out the sites of the great Old Testament stories to Jesus as they walked between Jerusalem and Nazareth?

Our story shifts back to Nazareth and Jesus's boyhood. Earlier we visited the Church of the Annunciation. Every Christian tour group visits this church in the belief that this is where the angel Gabriel announced to Mary that she would bear a child who would be Israel's Messiah. However, less than one hundred meters from the entrance to the church is the Sisters of Nazareth Convent.

In the bowels of the earth below the convent is a tomb with one of the most magnificent rolling stones in all of Israel. Beside the tomb are the remains of a building dating to the first century AD, which appears to be a typical family home of its time and place. All of this is found beneath the remains of the 5th–6th century AD Byzantine church. Ken Dark, a professor of archaeology and history at England's Reading University, believes that a strong case can be made for this house being the boyhood home of Jesus Christ. Visualize this — a convent constructed over the ruins of a Byzantine church which in turn is built over a first-century house. Important?

In 2017 Evelyn and I had heard about this tomb in the Sisters of Nazareth Convent. We were in the area and decided to pay a visit. We rang the bell a few times then a small gate opened and we entered. We went to reception and asked the nun if it were possible to see the Rolling Stone tomb. She was reluctant because the only nun who spoke good English wouldn't be available for thirty minutes. However, the nun arrived and led us down a little narrow staircase deep beneath the convent. We made two or three stops, and in her limited broken English she tried to explain what we were viewing. Little of what she told us made much sense because she was evidently talking about a church and a house while we were looking for a Rolling Stone tomb. We finally reached the tomb, and it lived up to its reputation — beautiful.

Our tour being over, the nun escorted us back upstairs and out into the bright glaring Nazareth sun. She kindly provided us each with a glass of cold water. When we left the convent we began to read the brochure that the nun had given us when we were leaving. When we started to read about a church and a home we were puzzled. When we read about the possible claim of this being Jesus's boyhood home we were skeptical. But then we came across the reports by Professor Dark and our skepticism rapidly faded; this could be a valid identification.

JESUS'S PRE-MINISTRY YEARS

The next part of the story jumps about eighteen years in Christ's life to where he is baptized in the River Jordan by John the Baptist and begins His public ministry:

> *Then Jesus came from Galilee to John at the Jordan to be baptized by him. And John tried to prevent Him, saying, "I need to be baptized by You, and are You coming to me?" But Jesus answered and said to him, "Permit it to be so now, for thus it is fitting for us to fulfill all righteousness." Then he allowed Him. When He had been baptized, Jesus came up immediately from the water; and behold, the heavens were opened to Him, and He saw the Spirit of God descending like a dove and alighting upon Him. And suddenly a voice came from heaven, saying, "This is My beloved Son, in whom I am well pleased." (Matthew 3:13-17)*

This is one site where the evidence is quite strong and points to a specific location.[80] The unfortunate tensions between Jordan and Israel made this a difficult site to visit because it means crossing the River Jordan, into the country

---

[80] The Scriptures relate various events that took place in, or near, this section of the River Jordan. It was near here that Joshua led the Children of Israel across the Jordan and into the Promised Land. Elijah, and later Elisha, divided the waters of the Jordan, Elijah was taken up to heaven in a chariot of fire, and Elisha made an ax head float.

of Jordan. In 1992 this option wasn't available because Jordan and Israel were still officially at war, and it was virtually impossible to cross over to Jordan. The only option was to view the site from the Israeli side. On the third Thursday of October every year, the Roman Catholic Church had an arrangement with the Israeli military to allow a pilgrimage to the baptismal site of Jesus Christ. A wood worker in the Christian Quarter of the Old City had tickets.

The baptismal site is on the river Jordan about five kilometers east of Jericho, on the Israel-Jordan border. Militarily this is a sensitive zone. It was quite amusing traveling from Jerusalem to Jericho, and back, in a bus full of nuns, monks, and Jesuit priests! Quite frankly, we don't think we have ever been among a group of people where the air was so blue with profanity. There were only a few tourists among the group. There were five buses from Jerusalem, and we joined about fifteen more buses in Jericho. We then moved together in a convoy with a military escort to the River Jordan. Who knows how many barbed wire fences we traveled through in this heavily protected zone?

About a kilometer from the river, the buses parked, and we walked to the river. Despite all the fuss, it was still beautiful to see this site: tranquil, slow-flowing, and one of the nicer parts of the Jordan River. I'm sure Jesus was aware of what lay ahead for His baptismal site — barbed wire fences galore, sentry posts, fox holes, land mine warnings, and a blown-up bridge (this used to be a road link between Israel and Jordan).

It was seventeen years before we were able to visit the baptismal site on the Jordanian side, more likely to be correct than the Israeli claim. How bewildering to walk down to the banks of the River Jordan and look across the river to the Israeli side —a distance of perhaps five meters! A quick jump and a few strokes and one could cross the border in either direction. Not likely; there are lots of armed soldiers on both sides to ensure no one tries such a stunt.

Immediately after His baptism, the Scriptures tell us that Jesus was led into the Judean wilderness where He fasted for forty days and was tempted by the devil:

Then Jesus, being filled with the Holy Spirit, returned from the Jordan and was led by the Spirit into the wilderness, being tempted for forty days by the devil.... (Luke 4:1-2)

Two of these temptations were at physical locations — the Pinnacle of the Temple in Jerusalem, and the high mountain, but first we will visit the Judean wilderness.

Perhaps as many as 70% of biblical narratives include wilderness or desert and a visit to the Bible lands is not complete without a visit to the Judean wilderness. This is the region where David hid from King Saul, and it is also the setting for the parable of the Good Samaritan.

The wilderness lies south of Jerusalem and west of the Dead Sea. It is arid with some springs, can be very cold with some rain in the winter, and is blisteringly hot in summer. In mid-March 1993 we took an organized day trip into the Judean wilderness. We went in a 'desert safari truck' with a high clearance, and we jaunted throughout various parts of the Judean hills: desolate apart from scattered Bedouin encampments and the odd, lone shepherd. In this vast emptiness, it was easy to envisage our Lord, fasting and praying, and being tempted to turn stones into bread. It was winter, and the open-sided vehicle allowed the biting wind to chill us to our cores. Nevertheless, this was an extraordinary experience of the Bible lands.

Our ultimate destination was the hill of Azazel or 'Scapegoat Mountain," which was the location of the scapegoat ceremony during Old Testament times. Each year on Yom Kippur the scapegoat had all the sins of Israel placed on it. Jewish tradition teaches that the goat was brought to this location, had its feet tied, and was thrown from the top of the mountain as a sacrifice, and thereby covered the sins of the people. Actually, Azazel isn't a mountain but rather the top of a steep cliff. From the top of Azazel, looking backward to the west, there is a wonderful panorama of the central spine of mountains that runs through Israel, with both Jerusalem and Bethlehem very clear, and Hebron a hazy distant view.

The Bible continues to tell us that Jesus was taken to the pinnacle of the temple in Jerusalem:

> *Then he brought Him to Jerusalem, set Him on the pinnacle of the temple, and said to Him, "If You are the Son of God, throw Yourself down from here..."* (Luke 4:9)

This is generally regarded as the top of the southeastern corner of the wall of the Temple Mount from which there was a forty-five meter drop to the Kidron Valley below. Many times we have walked along the road that skirts the eastern wall of the Temple Mount, and invariably when we got to the southeast corner we would lean back, bend our necks to an excruciating angle, and look up — it's a long way up.

Jesus was then taken to a high mountain, the Mount of Temptation that sits as a backdrop to the city of Jericho.

> *Then the devil, taking Him up on a high mountain, showed Him all the kingdoms of the world in a moment of time. And the devil said to Him, "All this authority I will give You, and their glory; for this has been delivered to me, and I give it to whomever I wish. Therefore, if You will worship before me, all will be Yours."* (Luke 4:5-7)

About halfway up the slope of the mountain is a cryptically colored Greek Orthodox monastery, an incredible structure hanging off the edge of the cliff. Between the fourth and the seventh centuries, the place was inhabited by hermits who lived on the side of the hill in caves, which they turned into cells, chapels, storage rooms, and water reservoirs. Some of these caves can be seen in the monastery. Only a few monks now inhabit this large monastery, and if you visit on a day with few visitors you can be treated to a personal tour. In the monastery is a stone on which, according to tradition, Jesus sat during his temptation.

The summit of the mount is reached by a footpath that passes through the monastery. The monk almost seemed reluctant to unlock the door, but soon we were on our way climbing steeply for about thirty minutes to the summit. There are some ruins of an old monastery at the summit along with what remains of an aborted attempt to build a church. The view from this prominent mountain includes Jericho Valley, the Dead Sea, and the mountains of Moab — it's breathtaking. But the experience also brings to reality the statement in Scripture:

> ... on a high mountain, showed Him all the kingdoms of the world in a moment of time. (Luke 4:5)

JESUS'S MINISTRY

In 1965, George Stevens directed the Hollywood blockbuster film *"The Greatest Story Ever Told."* Without argument, the birth, life, death, and resurrection of Jesus Christ has had a greater impact on human history than any other story, event, or person. More blood and ink have been spilled over Jesus than any other human being that ever walked this planet. The life of Christ can be viewed like a sandwich, with the major part of the Gospel narratives focussing on His ministry, sandwiched between two infinitely important bookmarks: His birth; and His death, resurrection, and ascension. In the next few pages, we'll focus on the sites associated with Christ's ministry. Our journey does not always follow a chronological sequence, yet we'll mostly describe things in an geographical order.

Jesus performed His first miracle at Cana of Galilee where He turned water into wine:

> On the third day there was a wedding in Cana of Galilee, and the mother of Jesus was there. Now both Jesus and His disciples were invited to the wedding. And when they ran out of wine, the mother of Jesus said to Him, "They have no wine."... Now there were set there six waterpots of stone, according to the manner of purification of the Jews, containing twenty or thirty gallons apiece. Jesus said to them, "Fill the waterpots with water." And they filled them up to the brim. And He said to them, "Draw some out now, and take it to the master of the feast."

And they took it. When the master of the feast had tasted the water that was made wine... (John 2:1-3, 6-9)

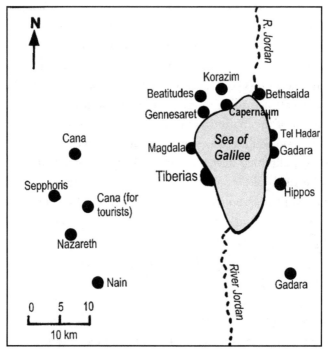

Major locations in Galilee associated with the ministry of Jesus Christ.

Today's village of Kefr Kenna is northeast of Nazareth. Because of Kefr Kenna's convenient location on the main road from Nazareth to the Sea of Galilee, it is a scheduled visit for virtually every Christian tourist group. Two wedding churches sit almost opposite each other across a laneway. The Greek Orthodox Church, which is seldom open, and a Roman Catholic Church. There is a third church commemorating that Nathaniel was from Cana (John 21:2). On our first visit to the Roman Catholic wedding church, we were fortunate enough to receive an amusingly offensive tour by one of the priests. He showed us the "actual jars used by Jesus to turn the water into wine." Now give me a break! This was doubly amusing because this is probably an erroneous identification of Cana and the "real" Cana of Galilee is probably about five kilometers farther to the northwest.

To access the real location required a lot of effort. We drove to the Arab village of Kafr Manda. This is where paved roads end, and we then bumped and bounced our way along a rough farm track for almost an hour. We really should have parked in Kafr Manda and walked because we only traveled about five kilometers. The thought of parking and walking entered our minds many times as we scraped the car's underbelly — but then, we possibly risk returning to a car stripped of wheels and other necessary components, or perhaps no car at all!

When we arrived within about three hundred meters of the site we spotted a Bedouin encampment right on the spot where we wanted to visit. As far as we know, there are no ruins today, just a small rounded hill, with Bedouin tents, marking the original site. We decided that to view the site from three hundred meters was sufficient. In hindsight, this was a mistake. We should have trekked into the Bedouin encampment and savored the moment because the Bedouin are typically a welcoming people. An hour later we had retraced our tracks and arrived at the great antiquity site of Sepphoris, the traditional home of Joachim and Anne, Mary's parents, and the birthplace of the Virgin Mary. And from the theater at Sepphoris, we could see Cana and its Bedouin tents straight north across the valley below us.

Our journey now takes us to Mount Tabor, the traditional site of the Transfiguration of Christ. Tabor is a five-hundred meter steep-sided mountain rising from the Plain of Jezreel. Evelyn was driving, and we could see Mount Tabor in the distance. According to our map, there was a single road encircling the mountain near its base, and on the northern edge a road branched off towards the summit. The short, ten-minute drive to the summit was nightmarish and negotiated seventeen hairpin bends. The road is slightly more than a single lane, but it's not double lanes. We met numerous stretched Mercedes barreling down at such excessive speeds we thought the devil was chasing them. Evelyn learned very quickly that Mercs were much bigger than our little Fiat Uno, and although priority should always go to uphill traffic, the rules didn't apply on this road. After pulling off to the side of the road at least fourteen million times and praying that we would always meet speeding Mercedes on a straight stretch of road, rather than on a bend, we finally reached the summit.

The view is spectacular and it seemed as though we could see forever, which is probably a good thing because the priest refused us entry to the church because we were wearing unholy short pants. To the west, Nazareth is perched delicately on the top of the hill, and we could clearly see the traditional cliff where the natives of Nazareth tried to kill Jesus. There are questions about the authenticity of this location being the place of transfiguration. It might be, but we think it is more likely that Christ was transfigured on Mount Hermon in northeastern Israel. Matthew and Mark both record that it was a high mountain — at 2,750 meters Mount Hermon is a high mountain, whereas Mount Tabor is only five hundred meters high. The proximity of Mount Hermon to Caesarea Philippi, today's Banias, also argues in its favor. It was at Caesarea Philippi that Peter made his great confession, and said of Jesus those immortal words:

> ... *"You are the Christ, the Son of the living God."* (Matthew 16:16)

... and the next chapter begins with:

> *Now after six days Jesus took Peter, James, and John his brother, led them up on a high mountain by themselves;* (Matthew 17:1)

Mount Hermon is in the extreme north of Israel and is 2, 750 meters high. We visited Mount Hermon in springtime and the question was how would we ever get to the summit because with ski season over lifts wouldn't be operating. On our way to the mountain, we detoured to the friendly Druze village of Majdal Shams. We had gone there to deliver a letter for a friend in Canada. The envelope was simply labeled "persons name, Majdal Shams." What were the chances of finding a specific person with only a village name as an address? We entered the village and stopped in the main street. We stopped a random individual and showed him the envelope. "Oh that's my bother Amin!" We were convinced this was one of these Arab responses based on the fact that everyone is their brother, including cousins, second cousins and close friends.

As it turned out, this was his real brother, he took us to his home, and we were invited in for a light meal and were treated like royalty. Samir's brother Amin was a maintenance worker on the ski lifts on Mount Hermon. We drove to the ski area, found Amin, who turned on the ski lift at no cost, and ferried us up to almost the highest point in Israel. The Syrian Hermon rises another eight hundred meters but is in a strict military area. It was beautiful, with scattered pockets of snow remaining from the winter, and we are compelled to believe that this is where Christ was transfigured:

> *Now after six days Jesus took Peter, James, and John his brother, led them up on a high mountain by themselves; and He was transfigured before them. His face shone like the sun, and His clothes became as white as the light. And behold, Moses and Elijah appeared to them, talking with Him.* (Matthew 17:1-3)

At the southern base of Mount Hermon is the site of Caesarea Philippi located at Banias Springs. The springs are quite beautiful and are one of three major sources of the River Jordan. This location witnessed one of the most pivotal dialogs recorded between Christ and His disciples:

> *When Jesus came into the region of Caesarea Philippi, He asked His disciples, saying, "Who do men say that I, the Son of Man, am?" So they said, "Some say*

John the Baptist, some Elijah, and others Jeremiah or one of the prophets." He said to them, "But who do you say that I am?" Simon Peter answered and said, "You are the Christ, the Son of the living God." (Matthew 16:13-16)

DETOUR FOURTEEN:
THE THREE SOURCES OF THE RIVER JORDAN

The River Jordan has three major sources, the Hasbani River which arises in Lebanon, the Banias spring at the base of Mount Hermon, and the Dan springs bubbling to the surface in the Dan Nature Reserve. The Dan and Banias sources are easy and beautiful to visit but the Hasbani is more difficult. Through a quirk of history the main street of the village of Ghajar in northern Israel forms the border between Israel, to the left, and Lebanon, to the right. But even before we entered the village, we had to pass through an Israeli road check. The soldier on duty spoke good English, had time to chat, and explained to us how it came to be that this village was half in Israel and half in Lebanon. We were thoroughly searched, had our identity checked, and had to go through passport control even though we weren't leaving Israel. He took our passports and explained that he would hold on to them until we returned. He also told us that under no circumstances were we to turn right from the main street (that would be going into Lebanon) but could only turn left and remain in Israel. The Hasbani can be seen from a parking lot at the far end of the village. In a more recent visit in 2018, we were stopped at the checkpoint and were told, very politely but firmly, that there was no chance of getting into Ghajar.

The name Banias is a corruption of Paneas, a sacred place to the god Pan. At the site one can still see many reminders of pagan worship with numerous idol niches carved into the rock face. The most obvious feature is the large opening to a cave called "The Grotto of the God Pan." This was a place of animal sacrifices from the third century BC until about the fifth century AD. Various stories are rumored about this cave and one is that this cave was called "The Gates of Hell" and that when Christ was speaking to His disciples he was using this cave both as an object lesson and as a backdrop.

> *And I also say to you that you are Peter, and on this rock I will build My church, and the gates of Hades shall not prevail against it.* (Matthew 16:18)

One can easily imagine Christ standing at the springs speaking to His disciples and explaining to them that He would build His church on the foundation that He (Christ) is the Son of the Living God. And as he speaks he waves His arm in a large arc pointing at all the pagan idolatry and says that even the gates of Hell and idolatry can't prevent it from happening.

During His ministry, the Gospels record three people that Christ raised from the dead —Jairus's daughter (Luke 8:40-56), the widow's son (Luke 7:11-44), and Lazarus (John 11:1-32). The story of the widow's son occurred in the village of Nain which lies on the northern slopes of Mount Moreh, just off the main road from Afula to the Sea of Galilee.

> *Now it happened, the day after, that He went into a city called Nain; and many of His disciples went with Him, and a large crowd. And when He came near the gate of the city, behold, a dead man was being carried out, the only son of his mother; and she was a widow. And a large crowd from the city was with her. When the Lord saw her, He had compassion on her and said to her, "Do not weep." Then He came and touched the open coffin, and those who carried him stood still. And He said, "Young man, I say to you, arise." So he who was dead sat up and began to speak. And He presented him to his mother.* (Luke 7:11-15)

We visited this quaint little village specifically to visit a commemorative church. We quickly found the church, after almost being bulldozed off the road by an enthusiastic truck driver. The church was locked, but the Muslim family beside the church had the key. The lad unlocked the door and showed us in. We found it in disuse with no altar, no pews, and not even a mat: empty except for a beautiful painting. Hanging above the door this work of art depicted the story of Christ restoring life to the widow's son. The Muslim family no longer keeps the keys, and that responsibility now lies with the priest at the church on the summit of Mount Tabor.

We now return to Nazareth to what locals refer to as the Mount of Precipice. There is a car park near the summit, and the viewpoint offers unparalleled views of Tabor, Endor, Nain, Shunem, and Armageddon. Jesus spent his boyhood years in Nazareth before beginning his ministry. After moving to Capernaum, Jesus returned to teach in the synagogue of Nazareth on two occasions but was rejected both times. On one occasion the townspeople were so outraged that they tried to throw him off a cliff.

> *So He came to Nazareth, where He had been brought up. And as His custom was, He went into the synagogue on the Sabbath day, and stood up to read... Then He closed the book, and gave it back to the attendant and sat down... So all those in the synagogue, when they heard these things, were filled with wrath, and rose up and thrust Him out*

of the city; and they led Him to the brow of the hill on which their city was built, that they might throw Him down over the cliff. (Luke 4:16, 20, 28-29)

This is the traditional location of this attempt on Christ's life. We don't know if this is the real location, but it seems reasonable, and it provides a clear visual of this event in the Lord's life.

Many of the events in Christ's ministry happened in unspecified locations around, or on the Sea of Galilee. The Sea of Galilee is fed by the Jordan River, it is twenty kilometers long, eleven kilometers wide, and forty-five meters at its deepest point. A one-day tour around the Sea of Galilee offers the traveler access to many of the sites visited by Jesus during His ministry years. The first site we visit is the Mount of the Beatitudes, a site that has undergone much upgrading and renovation over the years. This is the site where Christ taught the Sermon on the Mount recorded in Matthew chapters 5-7. Among some of the more famous and well-loved passages are:

Matthew 5:1-12	The beatitudes
Matthew 5:3-11	"Blessed are the poor in spirit .."
Matthew 5:13-16	"You are the salt .. the light .."
Matthew 6:5-15	Jesus taught about prayer
Matthew 6:9-13	"Our Father in heaven .."
Matthew 6:19-23	"Lay up for yourselves treasure in heaven"
Matthew 6:24	"No man can serve two masters .."
Matthew 6:33	"But seek ye first the kingdom of God .."
Matthew 7:7-12	Ask, seek, and knock
Matthew 7:13-14	Narrow and wide gates
Matthew 7:24-27	The wise and foolish builders

This is a beautiful church in a serene setting, overlooking the Sea of Galilee, and ruined only by a stream of noisy tourists. The octagonal church sits in a small garden that seems to have something in flower all year round. The nuns on site do a reasonable job controlling the noise levels inside the church. Periodically, visiting tour groups break into song as they praise and worship God *a cappella* using the words of some of the old favorite hymns. On numerous occasions, we had lunch in a large natural theater behind the church with uninterrupted views of the Sea of Galilee. We had been told on a previous visit that this theater was the likely site of Christ's sermon. A speaker using a moderate voice, standing fifty meters downslope, can be heard over a large area. Sadly, and we aren't sure why this happened, on our last visit the theater had been planted to bananas.

Below the Beatitudes church on the shores of the Sea, is the Church of the Multiplication of the Loaves and Fishes.

> *After these things Jesus went over the Sea of Galilee, which is the Sea of Tiberias. ... And Jesus went up on the mountain, and there He sat with His disciples... Then Jesus lifted up His eyes, and seeing a great multitude coming toward Him, He said to Philip, "Where shall we buy bread, that these may eat?"... Andrew, Simon Peter's brother, said to Him, "There is a lad here who has five barley loaves and two small fish, but what are they among so many?" Then Jesus said, "Make the people sit down." Now there was much grass in the place. So the men sat down, in number about five thousand. And Jesus took the loaves, and when He had given thanks He distributed them to the disciples, and the disciples to those sitting down; and likewise of the fish, as much as they wanted.* (John 6:1, 3, 5, 8-11)

The Arabic name for this area is Tabgha, meaning seven springs from the earlier Greek Heptapegon. Fishermen have frequented this area for thousands of years. As we entered the parking lot, two violinists greeted us with soothing music. There was also a magnificent, deep red bougainvillea, always blooming whenever we visited. This is another beautiful church that has not succumbed to the gaudy and gloomy atmosphere of the larger churches.

We entered through a cool courtyard with a small pool that provided welcome cooling from the intense heat. Most of the floor was composed of a fractured Byzantine mosaic, highlighted with an intricate basket of loaves and two fish. However, it is not clear why the Byzantine pilgrims chose this location to commemorate this miracle because the Gospels place the miracle near Bethsaida (Luke 9:10-17).

Tabgha is also the traditional location for the calling of the disciples. It is believed that Jesus walked along the shore and called out to Simon Peter and Andrew who were casting their nets into the lake. Jesus then saw two other brothers, James and John, who were mending their nets, and Jesus called them to follow him.

As we returned to our car, we noticed a suspicious-looking character hovering around and then moving off as we approached. We saw him again at our car as we returned from the Church of the Primacy of Peter.[81]

---

[81] This church commemorates an event that took place after Christ's resurrection and we will visit it at that time.

We continued along the northern shore of the Galilee to Capernaum where Jesus made his home during the years of his ministry:

And leaving Nazareth, He came and dwelt in Capernaum, which is by the sea, in the regions of Zebulun and Naphtali, (Matthew 4:13)

Matthew the tax collector and Peter's mother-in-law lived here in Capernaum, which was one of three cities cursed by Jesus for lack of faith. It was also in Capernaum that the centurion's son was healed, the paralyzed man was let down through the roof, and Peter's mother-in-law was cured:

Then He began to rebuke the cities in which most of His mighty works had been done, because they did not repent: "Woe to you, Chorazin! Woe to you, Bethsaida! For if the mighty works which were done in you had been done in Tyre and Sidon, they would have repented long ago in sackcloth and ashes. (Matthew 11:20-21)

Now when Jesus had entered Capernaum, a centurion came to Him, pleading with Him, saying, "Lord, my servant is lying at home paralyzed, dreadfully tormented."... Then Jesus said to the centurion, "Go your way; and as you have believed, so let it be done for you." And his servant was healed that same hour. (Matthew 8:5-6, 13)

Then behold, men brought on a bed a man who was paralyzed, whom they sought to bring in and lay before Him. And when they could not find how they might bring him in, because of the crowd, they went up on the housetop and let him down with his bed through the tiling into the midst before Jesus... Immediately he rose up before them, took up what he had been lying on, and departed to his own house, glorifying God. (Luke 5:18-19, 25)

Now when Jesus had come into Peter's house, He saw his wife's mother lying sick with a fever. So He touched her hand, and the fever left her... (Matthew 8:14-15)

Capernaum has some wonderful remains, chief of which is the large synagogue. The dating is debated, but it is clearly later than the first century, and it sits on top of an earlier synagogue from the time of Jesus. It was in this synagogue that Jesus preached His sermon on the bread of life (John 6:35-59).

Another great attraction is the remains of a residence that stood out from the others. This house was the object of early Christian attention with second-century graffiti. Pilgrims referred to this as the house of the apostle Peter. We are skeptical about many unsubstantiated claims, but this one actually has compelling evidence. If so, this might be the actual home where Christ and Peter lived, where Peter's mother-in-law was healed, and where the paralytic was lowered through the roof. The best place to view the remains of this house is from inside the Franciscan church built on supporting legs right over the top of the house. A large glass panel allows pilgrims to look down on top of the house.

One of the more unusual contrasts at Capernaum is the two modern churches representing the two denominations that oversee the site. The Franciscan church looks like a spaceship, and has to be the most our-of-context architectural feature in all of the Bible lands. The Greek Church has very few visitors and is tiny in comparison. It is an elegantly simple, white church with red domes sitting picturesquely in an orchard on the edge of the water.

We left Capernaum, only to see our friend hovering around our car again! However, we knew he couldn't follow us anymore because it's a long walk to Bethsaida, another of the cities that Jesus cursed, and we would be driving.

When we first traveled in this area we couldn't find Bethsaida even though today it's a well-visited pilgrimage destination. This was the hometown of Philip, Andrew, and Peter. It was here that Jesus healed a blind man, and he also cursed the city:

> Then He came to Bethsaida; and they brought a blind man to Him, and begged Him to touch him... Then He put His hands on his eyes again and made him look up. And he was restored and saw everyone clearly. (Mark 8:22, 25)

We continued west hugging the shores of the Galilee, and then the road swung north and we crossed the Jordan River. We made it across on a rumble bridge constructed of nothing more than a series of tightly fitting planks that banged, bounced and rumbled as we drove over. We continued for about another kilometer across the edge of a fertile plain on the northeastern shore of the lake, and it was probably in this area that the feeding of the five thousand took place. We swung left up to the Jordan park and recreational area.

Our maps indicated that Bethsaida was in here somewhere, but all we had was a very grainy photograph of a bolder-strewn slope. It was getting late in the afternoon, so the gateman didn't charge us an admission fee. I showed him the photograph and explained what I was looking for. Even though he spoke relatively good English, I didn't get a glimmer of hope. We proceeded, and after seeking help from at least a dozen people, we decided to give up. And then, as we were driving towards the exit I spotted the bolder-strewn hillside on my photograph; it was identical. How did no one know about this, especially the gatekeeper? I got out of the car to photograph the hillside, and I climbed almost to the top of the slope for a better angle. It was then I noticed a broken fence, with a broken gate, with a rough hand-painted sign saying "Bethsaida excavation; no entry."

Having seared my exploration conscience to the point of no redemption, I threw my leg over the fence and walked to the ruins. The place was a mess with the piles of archaeological debris making it look like it had been bombed.

But ten years later, on a return trip, this was a well established tourist site along with signposts and information boards. There is still debate on the correct identification of this site as Bethsaida, but let's believe it for now. The most impressive remains are the Iron Age gate and two large Hellenistic houses: homes of a fisherman and a winemaker. Most significantly, a small section of a Roman street has been uncovered. If this is Bethsaida, then Jesus walked right along this street — awesome!

We often took great pleasure in finding sites that most would never visit. Such is the case with Tel Hadar, a small excavation on the eastern shore of the Galilee about two kilometers north of Kursi, also on the grounds of the Dugit Beach and Resort holiday park. Excavations at the site indicate that this was a major Geshurite stronghold and perhaps the one to which Absalom fled after murdering Amnon (2 Samuel 13:37-39). Of more immediate interest, this is the traditional site of the feeding of the four thousand:

Jesus said to them, "How many loaves do you have?" And they said, "seven, and a few little fish." So He commanded the multitude to sit down on the ground. And He took the seven loaves and the fish and gave thanks, broke them and gave them to His disciples; and the disciples gave to the multitude. So they all ate and were filled, and they took up seven large baskets full of the fragments that were left. Now those who ate were four thousand men, besides women and children. (Matthew 15:34-38)

When we first visited this site in 1993 it was barely noticeable just after the entrance to the park. It was unkempt, badly overgrown, and previous excavators seemed to have walked off and left debris behind them. But there, at the edge of the road, partially hidden by unclipped bushes, was a large boulder inscribed "Tel Hadar, feeding of four thousand with bread and fish." Our daughter Andrea jumped onto the rock and said, "Dad, take my photo." And a little way behind that was another block of inscribed basalt — hewn with a basket with seven loaves, another basket with a few fish, seven baskets full of bread, and a reference to Matthew 15:29. Sadly, on two subsequent return visits, we couldn't even locate the ruins, so the site went off of our radar until Fergus and I returned in 2018.

By this time, the Luna Gal Water Park was closed and abandoned, but the adjacent Dugit Beach and Resort appeared to be open. We drove to the entry kiosk, but there wasn't any way the two admissions/security women were going to lift the barrier. We tried to explain that we didn't want access to the beach or the resort but simply to drive one hundred meters into the park. We were looking for two rocks with scriptural inscriptions, and we showed them the photographs taken many years earlier. It seems the photographs made them think we were crooks because there were definitely no rocks or archaeological ruins one hundred meters up the driveway.

After much discussion, we parked the car off the side of the road and were permitted walking access. I knew we were in approximately the correct location, but I couldn't see either of the large inscribed boulders or any of the previous scant ruins. However, my bones told me that this was the correct place but badly overgrown. Fergus took a little convincing, but we ventured into the shoulder-high vegetation, pushed and shoved our way through it realizing that we were slowly going uphill possibly to the excavation. After about fifteen minutes clambering, we had covered about fifty meters and there in front of us was the identical photograph of ruins I had taken more than twenty-five years earlier. Definitely the correct site —but where were the inscribed boulders?

By this time I had dropped my camera three times and lost my lens cap. And then we spotted "some vague shape" behind high vegetation about twenty meters distant. We clambered over a few walls and through some thick vegetation to emerge at a beautiful new monument showing the story of the loaves and fishes. We don't know when this monument was made or when it was placed here, but it looked very recent even though overgrown. We excitedly took photographs and then went back to the original location of the two, large, inscribed boulders —they were not to be seen, and we don't know where they've been taken. We retraced our one hundred meter walk to the kiosk and showed the two ladies the photographs we had just taken. "No way. There is no way that monument is in this park." We offered to take them back and show them but to no effect. There was no monument, and they knew because they worked here! C'est la vie.

Two kilometers south is the rather interesting site at Kursi. Located at the base of a beautiful valley coming down from the Golan Heights, and looking out over the Galilee, this is the setting of a favorite story from my childhood. The site is enhanced by the presence of the remains of a beautiful Byzantine church from the fourth or fifth century with a baptistery, archways, pillars, and an exquisite mosaic floor.

> When He had come to the other side, to the country of the Gergesenes, there met Him two demon-possessed men, coming out of the tombs, exceedingly fierce, so that no one could pass that way. And suddenly they cried out, saying, "What have we to do with You, Jesus, You Son of God? Have You come here to torment us before the time?" Now a good way off from them there was a herd of many swine feeding. So the demons begged Him, saying, "If You cast us out, permit us to go away into the herd of swine." And He said to them, "Go." So when they had come out, they went

into the herd of swine. And suddenly the whole herd of swine ran violently down the steep place into the sea, and perished in the water. (Matthew 8:28-32)

Just a few kilometers south of Kursi is Tel Sussita which was one of the cities of the Decapolis. The Greeks called it Hippos meaning 'a horse,' and Jews called it Sussita, Aramaic for 'mare.' Hippos is not specifically mentioned as a biblical site, but it was probably visited by Jesus during His ministry in Galilee. I can't get anyone to agree with me on this, but it makes more sense to me that Hippos was the city set on a hill in Matthew 5:14 rather than the traditional identification with Safed.

You are the light of the world. A city that is set on a hill cannot be hidden. (Matthew 5:14)

When Jesus said that a city set on a hill cannot be hidden, He was delivering the Sermon on the Mount. If the traditional location of the sermon is correct, there is no way Christ could have seen the city of Safed. In contrast, Hippos would have been clearly visible in the distance.

The ruins of Hippos are high on the hill above Kibbutz En Gev, and there is a clear, steep zig-zagging path up the hill. The task was to find the beginning of this path which we estimated to be about eight hundred meters away and probably at the back of an orange grove. There was a well-used farm track through the grove and we drove this, winding our way around the trees, deliberately ignoring the bewildered look from the farmworkers. We passed from an orange grove into a banana plantation, more bewildered looks, and then finally came to an absolute dead-end against a rusty fence and impassable pile of overgrown debris —and still couldn't find the path. We retraced our tracks, waving and smiling sheepishly to the workers.

Then, to our delight, we found a road just south of En Gev climbing up towards Hippos! This road was in a fairly bad state and restricted to farm vehicles. Having determined that our rental car was, in fact, a tractor, we drove almost to the top of the hill. We parked and walked a three-hundred-meter trail to the summit. There was little to see except for a few newer buildings, probably Turkish, and there was an active dig in progress. Walking westwards, we came to a location with nine pillars all lying flat on the ground, but parallel, testimony to some large earthquake that rattled this region. From this vantage point, we also had a magnificent view of Kibbutz En Gev, the Sea of Galilee, and the site of the Sermon on the Mount!

Part of Christ's ministry took him to Tyre and Sidon, both of which are in Lebanon. In 1992 Israel was officially at war with all of its neighbors except

Egypt. Although Tyre was only about thirty kilometers north of the Israeli border it was impossible to get to without doing a circuitous journey from Israel to Egypt, through Jordan and Syria into Lebanon.

We made the journey to Tyre and Sidon on a separate trip when we were visiting Syria. We took a taxi from Damascus, Syria, to the remarkable site at Baalbek. Baalbek is Lebanon's greatest Roman treasure and can be counted among the wonders of the ancient world. Today, you can see the remains of some of the largest and noble Roman temples ever built, and they are also among the best preserved.

I wish there was some way that I could capture in words our journey from Baalbek to Beirut by microbus. The eighty-five-kilometer journey took two hours, and I'm still not sure how we survived. The driver was crazy; no, he was insane. The entire journey was single-lane highways, horns, tailgating, and even passing vehicles on the wrong side — along very rough shoulders. We well remember catching up on a funeral procession of about five or six cars. It took a while but with weaving and swerving, we finally passed all the cars. At that moment, one of our passengers indicated he wanted out of our bus. A sudden screech to a halt, doors opened, the funeral procession passed, and our passenger exited the bus. The doors closed and then we had another ten minutes swerving and weaving until we passed the funeral procession ... and then you guessed, another passenger wanted out. This happened four times. We spent half of the journey passing this funeral procession.

However, the real excitement was reserved for the last twenty minutes into Beirut. The road passed over a mountain ridge and then dropped precipitously for about twenty minutes to the coast at Beirut. The road winds and twists, and for most of the journey the swerves and weaves of the driver matched the winds and twists on the road — although on a few occasions they were perilously close to being out of sync. But we made it; definitely another situation where the Lord protected us.

And we did all this just to visit Tyre and Sidon, Zarephath, and Byblos. Tyre and Sidon were an easy day trip from Beirut by taxi. Nothing remains of ancient Sidon although there is a rather interesting Crusader castle and adjacent market area. Tyre was the principal seaport of the Phoenician coast and is about forty kilometers south of Sidon. There are three major archaeological parks at Tyre, only two of which are open to the public. Tyre was strange in that there is a lot to see and yet nothing memorable aside from one great arch. However, we are reminded that it is precious to walk in Christ's footsteps.

Then Jesus went out from there and departed to the region of Tyre and Sidon. And behold, a woman of Canaan came from that region and cried out to Him, saying, "Have mercy on me, O Lord, Son of David! My daughter is severely demon-possessed."... Then Jesus answered and said to her, "O woman, great is your faith! Let it be to you as you desire." And her daughter was healed from that very hour. (Matthew 15:21-22, 28)

The vast majority of Christ's ministry occurred either in Jerusalem or in Galilee. Even so, a famous event was His encounter with the woman at the well near the village of Sychar, which is today's Askar, an eastern suburb of Nablus. Nablus is the site of biblical Shechem. The well where Jesus spoke with the woman is on the plot of land referred to in Genesis 33:

Then Jacob came safely to the city of Shechem, which is in the land of Canaan, when he came from Padan Aram; and he pitched his tent before the city. And he bought the parcel of land, where he had pitched his tent, from the children of Hamor, Shechem's father, for one hundred pieces of money. (Genesis 33:18-19)

The thirty-five meter deep well sits at the base of Mount Gerizim, about three hundred meters from the ruins of ancient Shechem. When we first visited in 1993, it was located inside an unfinished Orthodox church. There was nothing particularly memorable about the trip other than the rather grumpy priest who would not allow us to photograph the well but did sell us a postcard. Two years later we returned amid a lot of trouble in Nablus, and we weren't sure about traveling in the West Bank in a rental car with the tell-tale yellow plates. However, at that time a number of sites were under the control of the Palestinian Authority (PA) so we decided to press ahead and use the PA checkpoints as our litmus test on the safety of our travels. We reasoned that the last thing the Palestinians wanted was the publicity of harmed or injured tourists, so if the situation was unsafe, they would stop us.

We were stopped a few times and after brief and friendly encounters we were waved through and arrived at the church. This time we decided to try and chat up the priest. We chatted for about ten minutes, but again no photographs were allowed. When we thought he wasn't looking, we tried to sneak a photograph, but he caught us, chased us out, and closed the doors. We didn't even have time to purchase another postcard —oh, well; forgive the pun!

A few years later we were back yet again, and this time there was a film crew at the well. We watched retake after retake as the presenter[82] wandered over to the

---

[82] The presenter was David Hulme and as best we can tell this was part of the quite unremarkable movie called "*The Quest for the Real Jesus*." If so, then the shoot taken at Jacob's Well didn't make the final cut.

well, picked up a cup of water, had a sip, and then told the story of Jesus and the Samaritan woman. Surely this time we could take a photograph — no!

After an interlude of almost twenty years we returned again, and to our surprise an enormous, striking new church had been built over the site. The landscaping and gardens were beautiful and the interior spared no expense. And yes, we had a drink of water and this priest did allow a photograph — for a donation. We took a few photographs and although the priest was agitated by our meager $10 USD donation, we placed it in the offering box, smiled, and departed.

The story involves more than Jesus and the woman, and also involves the disciples going to buy bread in the village of Sychar. The best place to "see" the entire story is from the top of Mount Gerizim which offers an awesome view. From the summit, you can see Mount Ebal, the city of Nablus, the ruins of biblical Shechem, Jacob's well, the tomb of Joseph, and the village of Sychar. It's easy to imagine the whole story unfold of Jesus and the woman at the well:

> So He came to a city of Samaria which is called Sychar, near the plot of ground that Jacob gave to his son Joseph. Now Jacob's well was there. Jesus therefore, being wearied from His journey, sat thus by the well. It was about the sixth hour. A woman of Samaria came to draw water. Jesus said to her, "Give Me a drink." For His disciples had gone away into the city to buy food. (John 4:5-7)

And when the woman said to Jesus, "Our fathers worshipped on this mountain" (John 4:20), you can easily envisage the two of them turning around as the woman pointed at the mount; the well is at the base of Mount Gerizim.

Jesus had probably less trouble on his journey to Jerusalem than we had. In a story we will describe later, Evelyn had her handbag stolen. Thankfully, we didn't lose our travel documents, and the police made it clear that since we were living in Israel we should keep our passport and other important documents in a safe place, preferably at home. Within a few days, we were on our way from Jericho up to Jerusalem when we were stopped at an army road check. We got one almighty bollocking for not having our passports and were told in no uncertain terms that we should never leave home without them!

On another occasion, we were traveling the same road in a rental car. There was quite a line of traffic being held back by a slow-moving Arab truck loaded with produce. As we approached the Good Samaritan's Inn,[83] the four cars in front of us all had the same idea. They all pulled out, accelerated, and passed the tuck. Unfortunately for all of us, although there was quite a length of clear road,

---

[83] Identifying this building as the site of Christ's parable is highly speculative.

there was a solid white line, the police were watching, and they signaled us to pull onto the hard shoulder. One by one the police argued quite loudly and forcibly with each of the four drivers in front of us. All of the exchanges were in Hebrew so we could only spectate in ignorance. Each driver was given a ticket and then the police turned to us.

He was only a half-sentence in to his barrage when I handed him my British Columbia driver's license and my passport. Meanwhile, Alistair and Andrea had their noses pressed against the car window wondering if daddy was going to jail. I played total ignorance. When he asked in Hebrew "Do you speak Hebrew?" I put on my best puzzled face and indicated with hands, arms, and facial expression that I had no idea what he was asking. He had no English; I had no Hebrew. With a lot of pointing and other gestures we were able to explain, I think, that we were visitors at the Hebrew University in Jerusalem and were living in Jerusalem for one year. He seemed totally exasperated, which is exactly what I wanted. At that, he took my driver's license, pressed it into my hand, said in slow deliberate English, "Have a good day," and walked off! We escaped once again!

Jesus taught the Lord's Prayer while delivering the Sermon on the Mount (Matthew 6), and also again as part of the Olivet Discourse, on the Mount of Olives, in Matthew chapters 25 and 26. The traditional site of Christ's teaching is a grotto in a Carmelite convent called the Church of Pater Noster (Our Father), or the grotto of the teaching. Of note is the real attraction here: there are beautifully colored ceramic plaques adorning the cloister walls, with the Lord's Prayer written in over one hundred different languages (Luke 11:2-4).

On one occasion, we decided to visit the Church of Pater Noster by car rather than walking or by taxi. We knew this was risky because at that time rental car insurance didn't cover cars in Arab east Jerusalem or the West Bank, and the Mount of Olives is in both. We were nervous as we drove around looking for a 'safe' parking site. Then we spotted two large tour buses parked outside the Chapel of the Ascension, and we were able to tuck our car in behind them, more or less out of sight. Pater Noster was only a few minutes downhill, and we reasoned that we could be there and back for a quick visit before the eighty or so tourists returned to their buses. When we returned, the buses were gone and our rental car was attended by four or five Israeli soldiers. We really shouldn't have parked there, and we shouldn't have had an Israeli rental car on the Mount of Olives. So, after a mild but stern reprimand, we were on our way.

Perhaps one of the best-known stories from Christ's ministry is the healing of the paralytic man at the Pool of Bethesda.

Now there is in Jerusalem by the Sheep Gate a pool, which is called in Hebrew, Bethesda, having five porches... Now a certain man was there who had an infirmity thirty-eight years. When Jesus saw him lying there, and knew that he already had been in that condition a long time, He said to him, "Do you want to be made well?" The sick man answered Him, "Sir, I have no man to put me into the pool when the water is stirred up; but while I am coming, another steps down before me." Jesus said to him, "Rise, take up your bed and walk." And immediately the man was made well, took up his bed, and walked. (John 5:2, 5-9)

This pool is inside the grounds of the Crusader Church of St. Anne in the Muslim section of the Old City of Jerusalem just inside the Lion gate. As we left the raucous cobbled streets and relentless vendors, we transitioned abruptly into a beautiful flower garden with flowering trees and shrubs, accompanied by the singing of birds and tourists in the church. The interior of the church is austere and unadorned, but it has exquisite capitals on pillars supporting the arches. The extraordinarily reverberant acoustics surpass any sound stage, and it was a favorite pastime to sit in the church while groups toured through; depending on the numbers, most groups had an opportunity to sing two or three pieces. The Pool of Bethesda is beside the church. The imposing remains of a pool with two baths and five porches confirm the story told in the Gospel according to John.

Now there is in Jerusalem by the Sheep Gate a pool, which is called in Hebrew, Bethesda, having five porches. (John 5:2)

JESUS'S FINAL DAYS

These were probably the most pivotal five days in all of recorded human history. The journey begins in Bethany followed by what is popularly called the Triumphal Entry of Jesus into Jerusalem. For many, the journey ends at Calvary. In reality, this is only the beginning! We will retrace the footsteps of Christ in these last days on the earth, then after His resurrection, we will follow Him to Galilee, and His ascension from the Mount of Olives.

Ancient Bethany is the present-day Arab village of el-Azariyeh, located three kilometers east of Jerusalem. We hadn't been in Jerusalem very long when we decided to visit Bethany. Surprisingly, anyone we told about our plans either advised us not to go or gave us a detailed lecture about the potential dangers of going into the West Bank, especially populated areas, or parts of east Jerusalem. Being the Jewish Sabbath there were no buses, so we took a taxi to the Damascus Gate and then an Arab taxi to the village of Bethany, just over the top of the Mount of Olives and into strong Palestinian territory. The driver delivered us right to the door of the church commemorating the site.

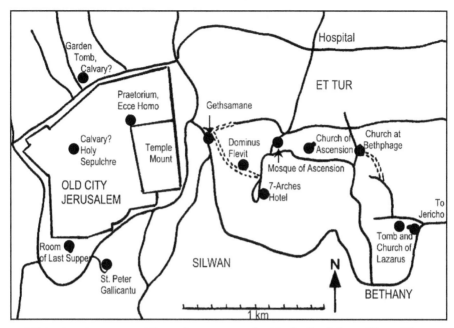

Major locations around Jerusalem associated with the final days of Jesus Christ.

Jesus's first recorded event at Bethany was the raising of Lazarus from the dead. The tomb that visitors are shown is a very interesting little spot descending twenty-four steep steps beneath a Muslim mosque. Entry to this tomb is not for the overweight, the tall, or the inflexible. After descending the flight of steps, it takes a fairly agile body to crouch and wiggle into the small cave.

> *Now a certain man was sick, Lazarus of Bethany, the town of Mary and her sister Martha... Therefore the sisters sent to Him, saying, "Lord, behold, he whom You love is sick."...Now Martha said to Jesus, "Lord, if You had been here, my brother would not have died... Then, when Mary came where Jesus was, and saw Him, she fell down at His feet, saying to Him, "Lord, if You had been here, my brother would not have died."...Then Jesus, again groaning in Himself, came to the tomb. It was a cave, and a stone lay against it. Jesus said, "Take away the stone."...Martha, the sister of him who was dead, said to Him, "Lord, by this time there is a stench, for he has been dead four days." Then they took away the stone from the place where the dead man was lying... He cried with a loud voice, "Lazarus, come forth!" And he who had died came out bound hand and foot with graveclothes, and his face was wrapped with a cloth. Jesus said to them, "Loose him, and let him go." (selected verses from John 11:1-44)*

A few meters downhill from the tomb is a Franciscan church built over the traditional site of the home of Mary, Martha, and Lazarus, and according to tradition, this is where Mary anointed Jesus.

And when Jesus was in Bethany at the house of Simon the leper, a woman came to Him having an alabaster flask of very costly fragrant oil, and she poured it on His head as He sat at the table... For in pouring this fragrant oil on My body, she did it for My burial. Assuredly, I say to you, wherever this gospel is preached in the whole world, what this woman has done will also be told as a memorial to her." (Matthew 26:6-7, 12-13)

After visiting the church, we walked up the eastern side of the Mount of Olives, up a steep road. The road then became a rough track,[84] and we walked along between two high walls for about one kilometer until we emerged at the Church at Bethphage. It was here that Jesus mounted the colt that would take Him on His triumphal entry,[85] on Palm Sunday, to Jerusalem.

Now when they drew near Jerusalem, and came to Bethphage, at the Mount of Olives, then Jesus sent two disciples, saying to them, "Go into the village opposite you, and immediately you will find a donkey tied, and a colt with her. Loose them and bring them to Me. And if anyone says anything to you, you shall say, 'The Lord has need of them,' and immediately he will send them." (Matthew 21:1-3)

It was along this route that Scripture records:

Then the multitudes who went before and those who followed cried out, saying: "Hosanna to the Son of David! 'Blessed is He who comes in the name of the Lord! 'Hosanna in the highest!" (Matthew 21:9)

Despite perhaps ten attempts between 1992 and 2000, we never found the Church at Bethphage open. We didn't return to the church until 2018 when it was renovated, and it was surprisingly open. It's a lovely little church,[86] but, as so often happens, it goes overboard and has on display "the stone that Jesus stood on to climb on to the foal." From the front of the church, we kept walking, continuing uphill until we reached the main road at the top of the Mount of Olives. From here, we followed Christ's route and descended the western slope of the Mount of Olives to the beautiful little Church of Dominus Flevit.

---

[84] In the early 2000s the Israeli security barrier was constructed and transected the Mt. of Olives at this point. Here, the wall is almost ten meters high and separates Bethany and Bethphage. Today it is not possible to walk from Bethany to Bethphage.

[85] Many commentators believe that Daniel 9:24-27 allows us to predict the exact day of Christ's triumphal entry into Jerusalem. Daniel cpt. 9 predicts that it will be 173,880 days (seventy biblical weeks; 490 years) after *"the going forth of the commandment to restore and to build Jerusalem.* The only decree in Scripture to rebuild the city is in Nehemiah 1:1-4, 2:1-8, and Nehemiah states explicitly that the decree was given *"in the month Nisan, in the twentieth year of Artaxerxes the king."* In our calendar this was March 14, 445 BC. If we now move forward 173,880 days, then Jesus rode into Jerusalem on April 6, 32 AD. Others have proposed March 30, 33 AD.

[86] In the garden behind the church is an ancient tomb with a rolling stone.

The name Dominus Flevit literally translated means "The Lord wept," and the name of the church is taken from the Gospel account of Christ weeping before a city unaware of its fate:

Now as He drew near, He saw the city and wept over it, saying, "If you had known, even you, especially in this your day, the things that make for your peace! But now they are hidden from your eyes. For days will come upon you when your enemies will build an embankment around you, surround you and close you in on every side, and level you, and your children within you, to the ground; and they will not leave in you one stone upon another, because you did not know the time of your visitation." (Luke 19:41-44)

This small chapel has a beautiful garden growing seasonal flowers, and there's often a marvelous display of red geraniums — the priest has his own brown pet hen that follows him around. The interior of the church has a simple elegance, and the window over the altar offers an incomparable panorama of Jerusalem — a photograph through a black metal trellis that adorns many books, calendars, postcards, and screen savers.

During this week Jesus moved around the area teaching and condemning the Pharisees and Sadducees. He returned to Bethany at least once. We will fast forward towards the end of the week when Jesus and his disciples celebrated the Passover Seder that would become known as "the Last Supper" in the so-called Upper Room.

Tradition has enshrined a fourteenth-century second-story room, beside the Dormition Abbey just outside the Zion Gate, as the location of the upper room. This building has been traditionally accepted as being on the original location of the home of Mary, the mother of John Mark, and may also have been the headquarters of the early church. Because of Jewish devotion for the Tomb of King David,[87] which is believed to be located beneath the Upper Room, the whole area has been transformed into various Yeshivas (Schools of the Torah). In the same place, seven weeks later, the Holy Spirit appeared to Mary and the Apostles at Pentecost.

When the Day of Pentecost had fully come, they were all with one accord in one place. And suddenly there came a sound from heaven, as of a rushing mighty wind, and it filled the whole house where they were sitting. Then there appeared to them divided tongues, as of fire, and one sat upon each of them. And they were all filled with the Holy Spirit and began to speak with other tongues, as the Spirit gave them utterance. (Acts 2:1-4)

---

[87] The traditional burial place of King David is immediately downstairs from the Room of the Last Supper. However, there are questions because David was *'buried in the City of David'* (1 Kings 2:10).

The Upper Room is a large hall, with the ceiling supported by three pillars that divide the room into three naves. On one visit we came across a group of tourists who were singing "God be with you till we meet again." It was beautifully harmonious and reverberated throughout the old building, and this clearly wasn't an average tour group. The significance of the events surrounding the Last Supper mustn't be lost. It was here that Christ inaugurated what would become one of the major sacraments of the Christian church, variously known as the Eucharist, Communion, or the Lord's Table. But it was also during this meal that Jesus predicted that Judas would betray Him, an event that would happen just a few hours later in the Garden of Gethsemane.

The Garden (John 18:1 calls it an olive grove) of Gethsemane is at the bottom of the Mount of Olives, across the Kidron Valley and opposite the Temple Mount. Gethsemane holds an important place in the Gospel story because Jesus went there after the Passover Seder with His disciples, on the night of his arrest.

It is a small garden and has numerous, twisted and gnarled olive trees that are hundreds of years old. Some of the faithful believe that these may be the same olive trees that witnessed Jesus's last night before his arrest, but this is highly dubious. However, a three-year study was conducted by the Italian National Research Council along with some Italian universities.[88] Three of the eight olive trees were examined and results indicate the trees are around nine hundred years old dating back to the mid-twelfth century, although it is thought that the roots may be even older. Carbon dating indicated that the three samples came from the years 1092, 1166, and 1198. The remaining five trees couldn't be analyzed. DNA analysis showed that the three trees had an identical genotype, indicating they likely originated from a common 'parent' tree. This suggests that the trees were originally branch cuttings taken from a larger tree, possibly in an attempt to sustain their lineage. In the garden is the Church of All Nations built over a large rock where tradition says Christ prayed in anguish:

> *Then Jesus came with them to a place called Gethsemane, and said to the disciples, "Sit here while I go and pray over there." And He took with Him Peter and the two sons of Zebedee, and He began to be sorrowful and deeply distressed. Then He said to them, "My soul is exceedingly sorrowful, even to death. Stay here and watch with Me." He went a little farther and fell on His face, and prayed, saying, "O My Father, if it is possible, let this cup pass from Me; nevertheless, not as I will, but as You will." (Matthew 26:36-39)*

---

[88] Petruccelli, R. et al. (2014). Observation of eight ancient olive trees (*Olea europaea* L.) growing in the Garden of Gethsemane. *Genetics.* (337: 5), 311-317.

Bernabei, M. 2015. The age of the olive trees in the Garden of Gethsemane. *Journal of Archaeological Science.* (53), 43-48.

And immediately adjacent is the Grotto of Gethsemane, the site of Christ's betrayal and arrest. Regardless of how often one visits, you can do little else but stand in awe and wonder.

And while He was still speaking, behold, Judas, one of the twelve, with a great multitude with swords and clubs, came from the chief priests and elders of the people. Now His betrayer had given them a sign, saying, "Whomever I kiss, He is the one; seize Him." Immediately he went up to Jesus and said, "Greetings, Rabbi!" and kissed Him. (Matthew 26:47-49)

On one occasion we had just left the garden, it was hot, and we bumped into three young Arab lads who were probably about ten years old. They were pushing a rickety old cart and selling soft drinks and other snacks. We recognized them because we had bought soft drinks from them about three months earlier. To our surprise, one of them said: "Ah, our English friends." I smiled and put my right hand on the young man's shoulder and said, using typical Arab parlance, "My friend, we are from Northern Ireland. We are Irish. You never want to call an Irish man English." It was as much as we could do to keep a straight face because many of our best friends are English. I continued, "You calling me English is the same as me calling you an Israeli." "Ah, no, no, no!" he said. "I'm sorry. We love the Irish, but we hate the English. We don't like the English because they gave our land to Israel. But when we see them we say 'welcome' and try to sell them soft drinks. But we hate the English!" After settling this little misunderstanding, we bought some soft drinks, chatted for a few moments, and then walked off to the Kidron Valley knowing that the next time the young lads would meet someone from England they would say "We hate the Irish, but we love the English!"

Immediately behind the Garden of Gethsemane is the Church of Mary Magdalene, and it is recognizable by its onion-shaped golden domes. This church has very restricted opening hours, but one day we managed to get in. It doesn't have a particularly nice interior, but it sits in beautiful grounds. It is a Russian Orthodox Church that has a coffin on display, that of, "Alice, Princess Andrew of Greece, Princess of Battenburg," the mother of Prince Philip the Duke of Edinburgh. However, also on the property are about five, ancient, rock-cut steps that originally led to the top of the Mount of Olives, and these may have been the route taken by the priests for the sacrifice of the red heifer (Numbers 19:1-22).

After Jesus's arrest, His disciples deserted Him and He was taken before Caiaphas the High priest. To get to the house of Caiaphas, the angry mob would have taken Christ down the Kidron Valley, past Absalom's monument, the cave of Jehoshaphat, Zechariah's Monument, the Bnei Hezir tomb, the Gihon Spring, and the Pool of Siloam, before climbing the steps up the slope of Mount Zion. The section of steps that we see today may well be the same Roman steps, called the Scala Sancta (sacred steps), where Christ would have been taken after His arrest. These steps lead directly to the Church of St. Peter at Gallicantu.[89] This is also the traditional site of the home of Caiaphas the high priest, where Christ was put on trial, and where Peter denied the Lord.[90]

> And Peter remembered the word of Jesus who had said to him, "Before the rooster crows, you will deny Me three times." So he went out and wept bitterly. (Matthew 26:75)

It is probable that the house of the high priest Caiaphas once stood on this site, even though archaeological support for this is sparse. However, excavations have revealed the remains of an ancient Byzantine basilica below the current church. Down in the bowels of the church is a prison and possibly where Christ would have been held. More ominously, beside the prison is an area where prisoners would have been scourged and mistreated. It was always noticeable to us that amid all the hustle and bustle of the streets and tourist sites of Jerusalem, it was always silent in the scourging chambers as the harsh reality of Jesus's treatment became more tangible to those who chose to visit.

> And those who had laid hold of Jesus led Him away to Caiaphas the high priest, where the scribes and the elders were assembled. But Peter followed Him at a distance to the high priest's courtyard. And he went in and sat with the servants to see the end. Now the chief priests, the elders, and all the council sought false testimony against Jesus to put Him to death, but found none. Even though many false witnesses came forward, they found none. But at last two false witnesses came forward and said, "This fellow said, 'I am able to destroy the temple of God and to build it in three days.'" And the high priest arose and said to Him, "Do You answer nothing? What is it these men testify against You?" But Jesus kept silent. And the high priest answered and said to Him, "I put You under oath by the living God: Tell us if You are the Christ, the Son of God!" Jesus said to him, "It is as you said. Nevertheless, I say to you, hereafter you will see the Son of Man sitting at the right hand of the Power, and coming on the clouds of heaven." Then the high priest tore his clothes, saying, "He has spoken blasphemy! What further need do we have of witnesses? Look, now you have heard His blasphemy! What do you think?" They answered and said, "He is deserving of death." Then they spat in His face and beat Him; and others struck Him with the palms of their hands, (Matthew 26:57-67)

---

[89] The literal meaning is 'the cock crowed' and the curious name of the church recalls the fact that the cock crowed after Peter had denied the Lord three times.

[90] Oskar Schindler is buried in the graveyard directly over the wall to the west of this church, and the final scenes from the movie "Schindler's List" were taken in this graveyard.

But there is an amazing twist to this story. In the late 1980s or early 1990s, the ossuary of "Joseph, son of Caiaphas" was discovered in a tomb at the Peace Forest at the Sherover Promenade near East Talpiot in southern Jerusalem. Inside were the bones of six people, including those of a sixty-year-old man, most likely Caiaphas. The ossuary is on display at the Israel Museum, Jerusalem.

December 30th, 1992 was a memorable day. The weather had turned nice, and we decided to take Grandma and Grandpa Turkington to various sites on Mount Zion including the Church of St. Peter at Gallicantu. After leaving the church, I stopped to change a film in my parents' camera. Meanwhile, Evelyn and my parents walked a farther fifty meters to the top of the hill and sat down on a low wall.

Two young Arabs came along and lifted Evelyn's handbag along with the camera bag, which had my video camera, passports, videotapes taken during the previous four months, film, etc. The two lads took off running. These guys were so slick that Evelyn and my parents initially weren't even aware of what had happened. Meanwhile, fifty meters downhill I didn't know that this had happened, and I saw these fellows running towards me. Initially, I assumed that they were a couple of tourists running to catch their bus. Then something caught my eye (it was quite likely the two images of maple leaves on a bag one of the fellows was carrying). An inner voice told me that these fellows had my video camera bag.

Even now, many years later, I can still relive the speed at which thoughts went flying through my mind. Is this my bag — or not? I didn't think, I simply reacted. I reached out and grabbed the bag from the fellow as he ran past. I can still see this all transpire in slow motion, and yet it all happened so fast. And the conclusion — yes this was indeed my camera bag.

A group of soldiers arrived about two minutes later. Then the police came and drove us back to the Jaffa Gate police station for a statement. Evelyn lost her handbag, but it only had about $20 USD in it. I've often wondered what went through the minds of those two fellows. No doubt they were proudly running off with a video camera and handbag which they had just stolen from some vulnerable dumb tourists, only to be ripped off by another dumb tourist! I've also often wondered what I might have said to those fellows if it wasn't my camera bag.

As we retrace Christ's final days, it seems that the sites become progressively more meaningful as we approach Calvary. Our next site was especially moving. The Praetorium was assumed to be in the Antonio Fortress which was the residence of the Roman procurators. The proposed site today is in the Ecce Homo

Convent of the Sisters of Zion at the beginning of the Via Dolorosa. However, most scholars argue that either this site is not old enough or it's in the wrong location. This was also known as the Lithostratos or Stone Pavement (Gabbatha in Aramaic; John 19:13), and this was the site of Jesus's civil trial before Pontius Pilate.

> *Then the soldiers of the governor took Jesus into the Praetorium and gathered the whole garrison around Him. And they stripped Him and put a scarlet robe on Him. When they had twisted a crown of thorns, they put it on His head, and a reed in His right hand. And they bowed the knee before Him and mocked Him, saying, "Hail, King of the Jews!" Then they spat on Him, and took the reed and struck Him on the head. And when they had mocked Him, they took the robe off Him, put His own clothes on Him, and led Him away to be crucified.* (Matthew 27:27-31)

This site was always high on our agenda when we had visitors. We visited so often that the nun at the admissions desk began to wave us through without charge. On one occasion, we were there at the same time as a tour group from Pittsburgh and they sang two verses of *"On a hill far away, stood an old rugged cross"* accompanied by a female vocalist with the most beautiful voice. In such a highly emotional atmosphere we were moved to tears as we reflected on the events that happened here — regardless if it's in the proper location.

Within this same convent complex is a chapel containing part of an old archway called the Ecce Homo Arch, and the arch continues outside and stretches over the Via Dolorosa. *Ecce Home* is Latin for 'Behold the Man,' and this is the traditional site where Pilate tried to wash his hands of the whole affair with Jesus:

> *Pilate then went out again, and said to them, "Behold, I am bringing Him out to you, that you may know that I find no fault in Him." Then Jesus came out, wearing the crown of thorns and the purple robe. And Pilate said to them, "Behold the Man!"* (John 19:4-5)

Christ was then led to Calvary.[91] The traditional route that Christ took on His journey to Calvary is called the Via Dolorosa or the way of suffering. It winds through the Muslim and Christian Quarters of the Old City ending at the fourteenth Station of the Cross inside of the Church of the Holy Sepulchre.

> *Then Pilate said to them, "Why, what evil has He done?" But they cried out all the more, "Crucify Him!" So Pilate, wanting to gratify the crowd, released Barabbas*

---

[91] It is interesting that Calvary is so central to the gospel message, yet the name appears only once in the KJV and NKJV, and not at all in the NIV, ESV or NASB. "And when they had come to the place called Calvary, there they crucified Him, and the criminals, one on the right hand and the other on the left" (Luke 23:33, NKJV).

to them; and he delivered Jesus, after he had scourged Him, to be crucified. (Mark 15:14-15)

There are serious questions about the legitimacy of this route and whether most of the route that is followed existed two thousand years ago. Notably, this route and its streets are not marked on the sixth-century Madeba map. Unfortunately, this extremely important event has become marred and to a certain extent over-shadowed by traditions that have been superimposed on it. The route marks at least three places where Jesus fell and where Veronica wiped Jesus's face.

We realize the whole event is only a re-enactment and meant to be a poignant object lesson for the devout, but why not restrict the event to what we know? On Friday afternoons the Franciscans lead a procession winding through the streets that witnessed Christ's suffering. We had to do this at least once. This in itself was an eye-opener. The priests that led it that day had done it so many times that it had become a mere routine, another thing on the "to do" list for Friday. They raced along the Via Dolorosa explaining the events at the various stations, praying, and they did it all so fast that we were out of breath trying to keep up.

The final five Stations of the Cross are inside the Church of the Holy Sepulchre. On our first family visit to the Church of the Holy Sepulchre we were thoroughly bewildered; finding our way around was a truly frustrating experience. We leafed anxiously through our Lonely Planet guidebook trying to locate Calvary on a tiny map of the church. And where was Christ's Tomb?

The Church of the Holy Sepulchre is a curious conglomeration of altars, chapels, and architectural styles that could confuse anyone. Periodically throughout the day, colorful religious processions take place. These, along with hundreds of visitors who are constantly wandering in and out of the church, create an atmosphere of religious fervor, noise, and confusion that is all exacerbated by the building's dark and gloomy interior.

On the day before the Orthodox Easter, Orthodox Christians celebrate a festival of Holy Fire. As we entered the church, a priest was standing by the Anointing Stone with a large ring on one finger of an extended hand. Dozens of people, mostly elderly women, were lined up to kiss the ring. We didn't find out the meaning or reason for this activity, but the priest's totally indifferent attitude wasn't very encouraging. A short time thereafter we met a parade of priests coming through the church led by the Greek Orthodox Patriarch. We watched in astonishment as some priests pushed people, sometimes aggressively, to one side to make way for the parade. The mostly elderly ladies seemed to apologize for obstructing the parade route.

Then, they made a mistake! A priest grabbed Evelyn with an intent to brush her to one side: "Get your hands off me," Evelyn spoke loudly and firmly. I almost felt sorry for the priest because he was evidently shocked and perhaps even offended that a lady had challenged his behavior. And yes, the priests do get into brawls; just search YouTube for "Christian monks brawl at holy site."

In spite of all the confusion, activity, and gloom, this is the most visited church in the country. Much of the Christian world believes this church to be built over the site of Calvary and Christ's tomb, hence the name Holy Sepulchre.

And when they had come to a place called Golgotha, that is to say, Place of a Skull, they gave Him sour wine mingled with gall to drink. But when He had tasted it, He would not drink. Then they crucified Him, and divided His garments, casting lots, that it might be fulfilled which was spoken by the prophet: "They divided My garments among them, And for My clothing they cast lots." Sitting down, they kept watch over Him there. And they put up over His head the accusation written against Him: THIS IS JESUS THE KING OF THE JEWS. (Matthew 27:33-37)

Now from the sixth hour until the Ninth hour there was darkness over all the land. And about the Ninth hour Jesus cried out with a loud voice, saying, "Eli, Eli, lama sabachthani?" that is, "My God, My God, why have You forsaken Me?" Some of those who stood there, when they heard that, said, "This Man is calling for Elijah!" Immediately one of them ran and took a sponge, filled it with sour wine and put it on a reed, and offered it to Him to drink. The rest said, "Let Him alone; let us see if Elijah will come to save Him." And Jesus cried out again with a loud voice, and yielded up His spirit. (Matthew 27:45-50)

Now when evening had come, there came a rich man from Arimathea, named Joseph, who himself had also become a disciple of Jesus. This man went to Pilate and asked for the body of Jesus. Then Pilate commanded the body to be given to him. When Joseph had taken the body, he wrapped it in a clean linen cloth, and laid it in his new tomb which he had hewn out of the rock; and he rolled a large stone against the door of the tomb, and departed. (Matthew 27:57-60)

Now after the Sabbath, as the first day of the week began to dawn, Mary Magdalene and the other Mary came to see the tomb. And behold, there was a great earthquake; for an angel of the Lord descended from heaven, and came and rolled back the stone from the door, and sat on it. His countenance was like lightning, and his clothing as white as snow. And the guards shook for fear of him, and became like dead men. But the angel answered and said to the women, "Do not be afraid, for I know that you seek Jesus who was crucified. He is not here; for He is risen, as He said. Come, see the place where the Lord lay. And go quickly and tell His disciples that He is risen from the dead, and indeed He is going before you into Galilee; there you will see Him. Behold, I have told you." (Matthew 28:1-7)

The place called Calvary and the nearby tomb were lost to Christians a century after Christ's Crucifixion. In AD 135 the Roman emperor Hadrian destroyed Jerusalem, rebuilt the city as Aelia Capitolina, and covered the sacred sites with idolatrous shrines. It is said that when Constantine's mother, Queen Helena, came to Jerusalem in AD 326, she razed the pagan shrines and in the process discovered Calvary and the Holy Sepulchre beneath Hadrian's idolatrous temples. In addition, she found the three crosses on which Christ and the two thieves were crucified, the crown of thorns, the nails used for pinning Jesus to the cross, and the inscription above Jesus's head. She then began construction of a much larger building that encompassed the Holy Sepulchre, Calvary, and the cave in which she discovered the crosses.

Little remains of the original basilica which has been repeatedly ravaged by fires and wars. Over the centuries, various denominations contended and struggled for the privilege of praying next to the holy sites. During periods of restoration, each denomination altered the interior according to its own particular styles while at the same time grabbing as much property as possible. The church today is divided among the Roman Catholics, Greek Orthodox, and Armenians, but the Copts, Syrian Jacobites, and Ethiopians can hold religious ceremonies at specified hours.

The Armenian chapel is dedicated to Helena, and it is constructed over the cave where Helena is said to have found the artifacts. Today, the cave is a chapel with the rather unimaginative title of the Chapel of the Invention of the Cross. The keys to the church are in the hands of a Palestinian Muslim family who open the doors each morning at 7:00 a.m. and close at 8:00 p.m. This ceremony is performed in the presence of a Greek Orthodox, Armenian, and Roman Catholic priest.

Many protestant denominations and evangelicals prefer to visit another location proposed as the site of Christ's entombment and resurrection. This is called the Garden Tomb (check out their website), near a place often called Gordon's Calvary, after Charles Gordon, a British general who endorsed the location in 1883. Gordon was convinced that Skull Hill was the site of crucifixion, but he wasn't the first to claim this, and he had virtually nothing to do with the promotion of the Garden Tomb.

This tomb is situated outside the walls of the Old City of Jerusalem, to the north of the Damascus Gate. There is some circumstantial evidence corroborating this location, but no hard, archaeological evidence. Regardless, this is a special, quiet, and contemplative spot in the middle of a noisy and busy Jerusalem, and the contrast with the Church of the Holy Sepulchre could not be greater. It is a beautifully tended garden with flowers, shrubs, olive trees, seating areas, an olive press, and the centerpiece is a tomb which was closed by a rolling stone. Until late 2018, the tomb had a door,[92] and on the door a sign which read, "He is not here, He is risen."

> *Now in the place where he was crucified there was a garden; and in the garden a new sepulcher, where was never man yet laid.* (John 19:41)

If that were the end of the story, then Jesus would be reduced to a man with a mission on the wrong planet. But Jesus's burial wasn't the end, and His resurrection was supported by more than five hundred eyewitnesses:

> *and declared to be the Son of God with power according to the Spirit of holiness, by the resurrection from the dead.* (Romans 1:4)

> *For I delivered to you first of all that which I also received: that Christ died for our sins according to the Scriptures, and that He was buried, and that He rose again the third day according to the Scriptures, and that He was seen by Cephas, then by the twelve. After that He was seen by over five hundred brethren at once, of whom the greater part remain to the present, but some have fallen asleep. After that He was seen by James, then by all the apostles. 8 Then last of all He was seen by me also, as by one born out of due time. For I am the least of the apostles, who am not worthy to be called an apostle, because I persecuted the church of God.* (1 Corinthians 15:3-9)

DETOUR FIFTEEN:
JESUS SAID TO NICODEMUS "YOU MUST BE BORN AGAIN.'"
(JOHN 3:7)

"Do not marvel that I said to you, 'You must be born again'" (John 3:7). At its core, the gospel is simple. It is the good news that Christ died for the sin of mankind, and to all who believe that this is true, He gives eternal life in Heaven. But the gospel is also deep, extremely deep, and innumerable books have been written on the subject. Here, we will provide three different gospel presentations.

---

[92] The door was removed and placed in storage to facilitate the movement of the increasing number of visitors to the Garden and the Tomb.

1. THE GOSPEL IN ONE MINUTE

The following was transcribed from a television panel discussion, and is available on-line:

John Ankerburg: Dr. Kennedy, with a minute left, for people that again are listening, the gospel is always good news. When you start to grasp it, it really grabs your soul. And the fact is in this one minute that we've got left, for the person that's listening and saying. Hey, don't leave me hanging now, how do I get into this relationship with Jesus? Tell me more.

James Kennedy: Delighted to do it! The great joy of my life! God is Holy and we are sinful—that's the problem. If that were all there were to the problem—God would solve it very simply—He would send us all to Hell! But God is also loving, infinitely so, and because he loved us, He sent His own Son into the world. And He imputed, or laid upon Jesus Christ all of our guilt and sin. And then, something which astounded me when I first learned it, as a Father, God poured out all of His wrath for sin, upon His own Son. And Jesus Christ in body and soul suffered infinitely in our behalf and paid for the penalty for our sins. As I have told many, the problem for you is simple—your sins are going to be punished by God. The question is, are they going to be punished on you, in Hell forever, or on Jesus Christ on the Cross? If you would prefer the latter—you need to abandon all trust in yourself, repent of your sins, and receive Him into your heart as Savior and Lord, trusting in His atoning death and perfect life as your only hope of salvation. And His promise is, "He that trusts in Me, already has everlasting life." [93]

2. THE GOSPEL IN THREE MINUTES

Dr. Donald Grey Barnhouse said that "The highway to the cross is firmly established in Genesis 4.[94] Here the first lamb is seen. One lamb for one man."

Here the first lamb is seen. One lamb for one man.

Then she bore again, this time his brother Abel. Now Abel was a keeper of sheep, but Cain was a tiller of the ground. And in the process of time it came to pass that Cain brought an offering of the fruit of the ground to the Lord. Abel also brought of the firstborn of his flock and of their fat. And the Lord respected Abel and his offering, but He did not respect Cain and his offering. And Cain was very angry, and his countenance fell. (Genesis 4:2-5)

---

[93] Dr. Kennedy, J., Dr. MacArthur, J., Dr. Sproul, R. C., and Ankerberg, J. *Irreconcilable Differences: Catholics, Evangelicals, and the New Quest for Unity.* Roundtable discussion, Ft. Lauderdale, Florida, 1995. Accessed 22 February 2021 from https://www.biblebb.com/files/ECTDOC.HTM

[94] Donald Barnhouse, *Genesis, a Devotional Exposition* (Zondervan Publishing Company, January 1, 1970).

Later, at the Passover, there was one lamb for one household.

Then Moses called for all the elders of Israel and said to them, "Pick out and take lambs for yourselves according to your families, and kill the Passover lamb. And you shall take a bunch of hyssop, dip it in the blood that is in the basin, and strike the lintel and the two doorposts with the blood that is in the basin. And none of you shall go out of the door of his house until morning. For the Lord will pass through to strike the Egyptians; and when He sees the blood on the lintel and on the two doorposts, the Lord will pass over the door and not allow the destroyer to come into your houses to strike you. And you shall observe this thing as an ordinance for you and your sons forever. It will come to pass when you come to the land which the Lord will give you, just as He promised, that you shall keep this service. And it shall be, when your children say to you, 'What do you mean by this service?' that you shall say, 'It is the Passover sacrifice of the Lord, who passed over the houses of the children of Israel in Egypt when He struck the Egyptians and delivered our households.'" So the people bowed their heads and worshiped. (Exodus 12:21-27)

And he shall take from the congregation of the children of Israel two kids of the goats as a sin offering, and one ram as a burnt offering. Aaron shall offer the bull as a sin offering, which is for himself, and make atonement for himself and for his house. He shall take the two goats and present them before the Lord at the door of the tabernacle of meeting. (Leviticus 16:5-7)

Then on the Day of Atonement, there was one sacrifice for the nation.

Then he [Aaron] shall kill the goat of the sin offering, which is for the people, bring its blood inside the veil, do with that blood as he did with the blood of the bull, and sprinkle it on the mercy seat and before the mercy seat. (Leviticus 16:15)

Finally, it is Christ, the lamb of God who takes away the sin of the whole world.

The next day John saw Jesus coming toward him, and said, "Behold! The Lamb of God who takes away the sin of the world!" (John 1:29)

3. THE GOSPEL IN FIVE MINUTES

God is absolutely and perfectly holy,[95] all of us are sinful,[96] and that is a problem. Because God is holy, He cannot commit or approve of evil,[97] and our sin repels us from Him. But God is also loving, and infinitely so, and that attribute of God draws us to him. So God's holiness repels us from Him and

---

[95] ..."Holy, holy, holy is the Lord of hosts; The whole earth is full of His glory!" (Isaiah 6:3)

[96] "for all have sinned and fall short of the glory of God" (Romans 3:23).

[97] "… God cannot be tempted by evil, nor does He Himself tempt anyone" (James 1:13).

His love draws us to Him. The problem is that a holy God demands that all sin must be punished.[98]

The wrath of a holy God can't be appeased by good works that we do,[99] and His wrath could only be satisfied by a perfect sacrifice without spot or blemish, and the only acceptable sacrifice was His own Son, Jesus Christ, who came into the world as a mediator between God and mankind.[100] Christ was sacrificed by crucifixion on a Roman cross, and by this act God imputed or laid upon Jesus Christ all of our guilt and sin. God poured out all of His wrath for sin upon His own Son.

And Jesus Christ suffered infinitely in body and soul on our behalf, paying the penalty for our sins. But that is not all. God not only placed all my sin on Jesus, but in a great exchange, God clothed me in Christ's righteousness. My sin in exchange for His righteousness![101] So when a holy God now looks at me, I'm still a sinner deserving of punishment — but now covered by the righteousness of Jesus – God does not see my sin, but rather He sees Jesus's righteousness. The problem of a sinner in the eyes of a holy God has been solved.

The question is, do you believe this? Do you believe that Christ died for your sin, was buried, and rose from the dead on the third day? Will you repent and believe in Jesus Christ as your Lord and Savior? Romans 10:9 says, "that if you confess with your mouth the Lord Jesus and believe in your heart that God has raised Him from the dead, you will be saved." Confessing Jesus as Lord means humbly submitting to His authority,[102] abandoning all trust in yourself, repenting of your sins, and receiving Him into your life as both Savior and Lord, trusting in His death and resurrection as your only hope of

---

[98] "For the wages of sin is death, but the gift of God is eternal life in Christ Jesus our Lord" (Romans 6:23).

[99] "But we are all like an unclean thing, And all our righteousnesses are like filthy rags;" (Isaiah 64:6). For by grace you have been saved through faith, and that not of yourselves; it is the gift of God, not of works, lest anyone should boast. (Ephesians 2:8-9)
not by works of righteousness which we have done, but according to His mercy He saved us, through the washing of regeneration and renewing of the Holy Spirit, whom He poured out on us abundantly through Jesus Christ our Savior, that having been justified by His grace we should become heirs according to the hope of eternal life. (Titus 3:5-7)

[100] "For there is one God and one Mediator between God and men, the Man Christ Jesus" (1 Timothy 2:5).

[101] "For He made Him who knew no sin to be sin for us, that we might become the righteousness of God in Him" (2 Corinthians 5:21).

[102] "that at the name of Jesus every knee should bow, of those in heaven, and of those on earth, and of those under the earth, and that every tongue should confess that Jesus Christ is Lord, to the glory of God the Father" (Philippians 2:10-11).

salvation. Moreover, our failure to obey God places us in danger of eternal punishment.[103]

On the day that Jesus rose from the dead the Scriptures tell us that he met two disciples on the road to Emmaus.

> *Now behold, two of them were traveling that same day to a village called Emmaus, which was seven miles from Jerusalem. And they talked together of all these things which had happened. So it was, while they conversed and reasoned, that Jesus Himself drew near and went with them. But their eyes were restrained, so that they did not know Him. And He said to them, "What kind of conversation is this that you have with one another as you walk and are sad?" Then the one whose name was Cleopas answered and said to Him, "Are You the only stranger in Jerusalem, and have You not known the things which happened there in these days?" And He said to them, "What things?" So they said to Him, "The things concerning Jesus of Nazareth, who was a Prophet mighty in deed and word before God and all the people, and how the chief priests and our rulers delivered Him to be condemned to death, and crucified Him. But we were hoping that it was He who was going to redeem Israel. Indeed, besides all this, today is the third day since these things happened. Yes, and certain women of our company, who arrived at the tomb early, astonished us. When they did not find His body, they came saying that they had also seen a vision of angels who said He was alive. And certain of those who were with us went to the tomb and found it just as the women had said; but Him they did not see."* (Luke 24:13-24)

They were dismayed and discouraged because they thought that the one who was going to deliver them, had been killed by the Romans. Jesus didn't tell them who He was, and they evidently didn't recognize Him, but He went on to explain to them from their Old Testament Scriptures that their Redeemer would be crucified. It goes on to say:

> *… "O foolish ones, and slow of heart to believe in all that the prophets have spoken! Ought not the Christ to have suffered these things and to enter into His glory?" And beginning at Moses and all the Prophets, He expounded to them in all the Scriptures the things concerning Himself.* (Luke 24:25-27)

Scripture does not tell us what Christ told them, but that is a conversation I would love to have heard!

So where is Emmaus? According to Scripture Emmaus is about eleven kilometers from Jerusalem (Luke 24:13), or perhaps it is twenty-eight kilometers

---

[103] "These shall be punished with everlasting destruction from the presence of the Lord and from the glory of His power" (2 Thessalonians 1:9).

(160 stadia in the *Codex Sinaiticus)*. This disparity in distance has caused fairly predictable confusion. Four modern towns have been proposed as being Emmaus: today's villages of Amwas, Abu Gosh, El-Qubeibeh, and Motza.

Firstly, today's village of Amwas, at the Latrun interchange, is about twenty-three kilometers from Jerusalem on the main highway to Tel Aviv. There was an Emmaus here in Roman times, and a village of Imwas until 1967. This site lay almost abandoned until about 2015 at which time the site was brought up to tourist standards, including quite extensive excavation and a small museum.

Second, the Crusader Church in Abu Gosh is about ten kilometers west of Jerusalem just off the main highway to Tel Aviv. This is one of the best-preserved Crusader churches in the country and is set in beautiful gardens. Inside the church steep steps go down to a spring and well. Tradition teaches us that it was here that Christ had a meal with the two disciples.

The third option is in the village of El-Qubeibeh, beyond the Prophet Samuel's tomb, at Ramah about eleven kilometers from Jerusalem. This was probably one of the more dangerous sites we visited. We had an Israeli rental car and we drove to the village, and we were naive enough to stop in the village to ask for directions to the church. It was only a few hundred meters down the road, and we arrived at a huge, black, heavy iron gate — closed. We rang the bell, a janitor appeared, and I have never seen a man run so fast. In seconds, the gate was opened, we were inside, and the gate was rapidly slammed tightly shut behind us. "How did you get here?" was his only concern. He was flabbergasted that we had stopped in the village and asked for directions. He explained that El-Qubeibeh is a dangerous Palestinian village and what sort of a place we were in — we didn't know! Tourists aren't brought here because safety can't be guaranteed. We then met the priest who was equally aghast and was more concerned about how we would get back out. He showed us some remains which he claimed to be of the house of Cleopas, one of the two men who walked along with Jesus (Luke 24:18).

Fourth, results from excavations in the early 2000s lead some scholars to favor Colonia near the modern village of Motza. Excavations confirm that the first-century Jewish village was called Emmaus.

We aren't told much about Christ after His resurrection and before His ascension but we are told that He went to Galilee and there he performed yet another miracle:

> *And He said to them, "Cast the net on the right side of the boat, and you will find some." So they cast, and now they were not able to draw it in because of the multitude of fish.* (John 21:6)

The site of this miracle is marked by a little church, sitting in beautiful grounds, with the waters from the Sea of Galilee lapping at the front door. It would remain like this until a series of dry years caused water levels of the Sea of Galilee to drop and the 'lapping waters' moved about seventy-five meters from the church. The church is called the Primacy of Peter because of the dialog that occurred there between Christ and Peter:

So when they had eaten breakfast, Jesus said to Simon Peter, "Simon, son of Jonah, do you love Me more than these?"

He said to Him, "Yes, Lord; You know that I love You."

He said to him, "Feed My lambs."

He said to him again a second time, "Simon, son of Jonah, do you love Me?"

He said to Him, "Yes, Lord; You know that I love You."

He said to him, "Tend My sheep." He said to him the third time, "Simon, son of Jonah, do you love Me?" Peter was grieved because He said to him the third time, "Do you love Me?"

And he said to Him, "Lord, You know all things; You know that I love You."

Jesus said to him, "Feed My sheep. Most assuredly, I say to you, when you were younger, you girded yourself and walked where you wished; but when you are old, you will stretch out your hands, and another will gird you and carry you where you do not wish." This He spoke, signifying by what death he would glorify God. And when He had spoken this, He said to him, "Follow Me." (John 21:15-19)

We only got into "trouble" here twice: once our daughter Andrea was refused admission because she was wearing shorts, and once I was reprimanded for climbing a fence to take a photograph — a small price for seeing this lovely site.

The last events of Christ's earthly sojourn are recorded in the book of Acts:

Now when He had spoken these things, while they watched, He was taken up, and a cloud received Him out of their sight. (Acts 1:9)

Two different churches commemorate this event. Most tourists are taken to the Chapel of the Ascension near the top of the Mount of Olives. On a rock inside the chapel, we were shown a footprint which Jesus is supposed to have left as he ascended to Heaven. This is highly unlikely because Scripture tells us that Jesus ascended to heaven from Bethany (Luke 24:50), so this is someone else's footprint, if it is a footprint at all!

About one hundred meters away is the Russian Orthodox Church of the Ascension. In the multitude of times we visited the Mount of Olives, we only found the gate to this church opened once. I was alone, and I desperately wanted to see inside the gardens and the church. People would arrive at the gate, ring a bell, a small door would open, and then they were ushered inside.

I waited until I saw two vulnerable, older women. I walked along beside them and just pretended I was with them. The women rang the bell, the door was opened, they waved a piece of paper, and they were in. I followed right on their heels and when the attendant opened his mouth to say something, I confidently said, "I'm with them," and kept walking.

And what a surprise awaited. Hidden away behind shops and homes on the Mount of Olives is one of the most beautiful gardens in Jerusalem. There was a ceremony happening, so I viewed the interior of the church from the entrance.

But let's not forget the profound significance of this site, wherever it is. Not only did Jesus leave the earth from here, but He will also return to this same spot — He is coming again:

And while they looked steadfastly toward heaven as He went up, behold, two men stood by them in white apparel, who also said, "Men of Galilee, why do you stand gazing up into heaven? This same Jesus, who was taken up from you into heaven, will so come in like manner as you saw Him go into heaven." (Acts 1:10-11)

XIV.
PAUL'S MISSIONARY JOURNEYS

The apostle Paul, born as Saul, was the earliest and most influential messenger of Christ's teaching. Paul was born in Tarsus in southeastern Turkey. He was a competent pupil, surpassing many of his fellow students in his enthusiasm and zeal for the Jewish law (2 Corinthians 11:22-28). This zeal was demonstrated as he assaulted the fledgling church of Jerusalem. The church was a threat to all that Paul cherished, and this demanded that the followers of Jesus be eliminated.

Stephen was one of the most outspoken leaders of the young church, and he became its first martyr. The book of Acts records how Paul publicly associated himself with Stephen's executioners and then embarked on a campaign to suppress the church.

> *Then they cried out with a loud voice, stopped their ears, and ran at him with one accord; and they cast him out of the city and stoned him. And the witnesses laid down their clothes at the feet of a young man named Saul. And they stoned Stephen as he was calling on God and saying, "Lord Jesus, receive my spirit." Then he knelt down and cried out with a loud voice, "Lord, do not charge them with this sin." And when he had said this, he fell asleep.* (Acts 7:57-60)

The most accepted location for Stephen's martyrdom is at, or close to, Skull Hill. This is beside today's Arab bus station in Jerusalem, adjacent to the Garden Tomb. This was a traditional place of execution in Roman times and is close to Damascus gate, previously called St. Stephen's Gate. Immediately north of the Garden Tomb is the Basilica of St. Etienne (St. Stephen) and Ecole Biblique et Archaeologique Francaise under the direction of the French Dominican Fathers. The compound is behind a high wall and you can only get in if someone opens the security door on Nablus Rd. or attend Sunday services. A friendly priest showed us around parts of the compound, including the tomb of Stephen inside a rather lovely little basilica. The first church on this site was built in the fifth century to house relics of Stephen. It was also built here, as the priest told us, to memorialise the site of Stephen's martyrdom, which was identified by the Empress Eudocia in the fifth century AD.

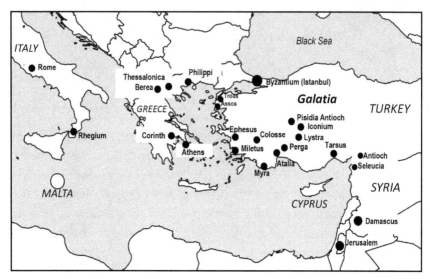

Major cities visited by the apostle Paul on his missionary journeys.

At the height of Paul's assault on the Jerusalem church, he was confronted on the road to Damascus by the risen Lord Jesus, and in an instant his life was changed — he became the leading defender of the cause which he had tried to destroy. After one aborted attempt, we made two journeys to Damascus. The aborted attempt was in 1993 when, long with our children, we went from Israel to Egypt and, by playing a little passport-shuffle, we entered Jordan, which was still officially at war Israel. While in Jordan we applied for visas for Syria. It only took two days to process our request, but when we received our visas we developed cold feet — what would happen to us and the children if we were caught in Syria with Israeli stamps in our passports?

The first visit was in 1996. Jordan and Israel had now signed a peace deal, so getting to Amman from Jerusalem was relatively easy. And from Amman, by playing passport shuffle, Evelyn and I made a day trip to Damascus. We were nervous about an overnight stay just in case someone found the Israeli stamps in our British passports.

The second visit was easy, and in 2001 we flew straight into Damascus from Amsterdam and were legally in Syria. The details of all of these attempts to enter Syria are described in earlier chapters.

Acts 9:3 and 22:6 tell us that Paul's conversion happened "near Damascus," and unfortunately that is all we are told. Consequently, various sties have been proposed. One traditional site is near Bab Sharqi, a gate into the Old City of Damascus. Here there is a rather magnificent edifice marked as the memorial of

St. Paul. The church is a memorial, and the traditional site of Saul's conversion is in a grotto in a garden behind the church. Someone must have gone through a lot of bother and expense to identify this site, to build this church, to construct the grotto, and to maintain this whole complex. But forgive us for asking a simple question: if Paul was converted on the road to Damascus from Jerusalem, how did Paul come to be at the eastern end of the city while the road from Jerusalem approaches from the southwest! Not only was Paul approaching Damascus, he was also already through it and leaving the other side. There seems little likelihood this can be the site.

> *As he journeyed he came near Damascus, and suddenly a light shone around him from heaven. Then he fell to the ground, and heard a voice saying to him, "Saul, Saul, why are you persecuting Me?" And he said, "Who are You, Lord?" Then the Lord said, "I am Jesus, whom you are persecuting. It is hard for you to kick against the goads." So he, trembling and astonished, said, "Lord, what do You want me to do?" Then the Lord said to him, "Arise and go into the city, and you will be told what you must do."* (Acts 9:3-6)

Some scholars favor a site near the village of Atrouz, about fifteen kilometers southwest of Damascus on the road to Quneitra, which not coincidentally also happens to be the road from Jerusalem. Since Crusader times, the village has been regarded as the traditional site of the conversion of Saul of Tarsus.

Finding this site wasn't easy. All we had as a reference was a black-and-white photograph of a small rotunda church with a cross. The hotel staff knew what we wanted but couldn't offer any indication where the church was. We went to the little chapel that marks the location of the home of Ananias and spoke to the lady that ran the gift shop as well as the resident priest, and they couldn't help us. Actually, we are convinced that the priest knew exactly what we wanted, but he had a keener interest to send us to the wrong location that we described above.

Out of desperation, we walked along Straight St., out through Bab Touma, and stopped a taxi. We showed him the photo, he nodded more-or-less knowingly, and beckoned us into his cab. Rather naively we hopped in, and he sped off spending more time looking at the photograph than he was looking at the road. We emerged from Damascus into the countryside, and I had the sense we were heading in the correct general direction. After about ten kilometers of driving around secondary roads our driver pulled up to a home. They chatted in Arabic, looked at the photograph, arms waved and fingers pointed, and after a few minutes we were on our way again.

We rounded a corner, and there in front of us in the open fields was the small rotunda church marking the traditional site of Saul's conversion. The gate was locked, but, not to be deterred, our driver jumped the wall and gave us a leg up-and-over as well. The church was locked, so our driver went to a house on site and began banging the door. Sure enough, a custodian appeared, and we were ushered into the beautiful little church. This is quite a special site because, firstly, it commemorates one of the most momentous events of the early Christian church. Second, the site isn't covered by a huge, ugly building. Third, the site is in the countryside and hasn't been encroached by urban spread.

As a result of Saul's encounter with Christ on the Damascus road, he was temporarily blinded. He was led into Damascus, and the biblical narrative introduces us to Ananias, Straight St., and the House of Judah.

> *Now there was a certain disciple at Damascus named Ananias; and to him the Lord said in a vision, "Ananias." And he said, "Here I am, Lord." So the Lord said to him, "Arise and go to the street called Straight, and inquire at the house of Judas for one called Saul of Tarsus, for behold, he is praying."* (Acts 9:10-11)

The traditional House of Ananias is easy to find and is frequented by tourists. It's a quaint little chapel belowground that has been the site of church gatherings from the third century. There is no admission fee, but there is a donation box. There are perhaps five rows of small pews, and the chapel holds about 20–30 people at a squeeze. There was no one else there, and the priest came to chat to us. He was from Chicago,[104] had plenty of time to sit and chat, and he was a jolly out-going chap until we told him that our son was a graduate of the Moody Bible Institute in Chicago. Then he had to go! He didn't go far because he was watching the donation box! We scrambled around in our pockets to find as much change as possible that would be worth as little as possible but would make a lot of noise in the box. We donated, then moved swiftly to Straight St. before the priest could find out that we had left him less than ten cents.

Straight Street is probably so named because it is the only straight street in an otherwise labyrinthine-like twisted jumble of alleys and markets that make up the Old City of Damascus. The street starts at Bab Sharqi and runs for over one kilometer through the Christian quarter, passing a Roman Arch, and eventually becoming Madhat Pasha Souq (market). A local tradition indicates that the House of Judas was located in the area of this souq. The site today is a gate into a caravanserai, and inside the gate is a small mosque.

---

[104] This priest is not to be confused with another priest at the Greek Orthodox monastery of St. Onuphrius in the Hinnom Valley, Jerusalem, who was also from Chicago and who also broke off conversation when he heard that our son was a graduate of Moody Bible Institute.

The narrative continues to record that Paul immediately began to preach and to proclaim Jesus as the Son of God. After a lot of confrontation there was a plot to kill Paul:

> *But their plot became known to Saul. And they watched the gates day and night, to kill him. Then the disciples took him by night and let him down through the wall in a large basket.* (Acts 9:24-25)

The account of Paul being lowered over the city wall is commemorated by St. Paul's chapel, which is built into one of the city gates, Bab Kisan. This should have been easy, but taxi driver after taxi driver wanted to take us to Bab Sharqi and to Bab Touma. None of them seemed to know Bab Kisan. After seeing the city walls of Damascus from every possible angle and perspective, and having driven past our destination at least twice in our quest, we finally were delivered to Bab Kisan. Finally there, we found an austere and elegantly simple chapel with wall motifs depicting the story. About one hundred meters east along the city wall there is a beautiful example of a home built into the city wall, perhaps just like the one Paul was lowered from.

DETOUR SIXTEEN:
WHERE IS QUNEITRA AND HOW DO WE GET THERE?

Quneitra was a war-ravaged city in the UN buffer zone between Israel and Syria on the Golan Heights. By visiting a government office in Damascus, we could get a pass to visit the city. What a mess; everything was in ruins: a church, a hospital, many homes, and the main street — but this is the price of war.

Unfortunately, Syria uses this as anti-Israeli propaganda, but there were two problems. Firs, most tourists are simply not interested in seeing the place, and it would never become a destination of the regular tour bus routes. Second, the Syrians had deliberately, and not too skilfully, exaggerated the devastation. For example, if this was how the Israelis left it, and if children were bombed in their desks at school, and patients were bombed in their hospital beds, as we were told, then why were there no desks or beds sticking out from the rubble? Hmmm? Why was the roof and exterior walls of one end of the hospital intact but the interior walls demolished? Hmmm? And where did the 1.5 meter deep pile of rubble in some of the buildings come from? The walls and roof were damaged, but intact. Was the rubble actually shipped in? Hmmm?

———————

Before we continue Paul's journey and leave Damascus, there are a few other places to visit. In a wonderful Old Testament story, a Syrian general named Naaman had leprosy, and the prophet Elisha told him to bathe in the River Jordan. Scripture indicates that he was angry and said:

> *Are not the Abanah and the Pharpar, the rivers of Damascus, better than all the waters of Israel? Could I not wash in them and be clean?* ... (2 Kings 5:12)

Presumably, the rivers of Damascus were more impressive then than they are today. The River Abanah currently flows alongside the northern wall of the old city and is a rather filthy spectacle. I would almost rather die of leprosy than bathe in that cesspool, which has become a garbage dump for many local residents. While I was positioning myself to take a photograph, a local was passing by and he stopped to ask: "Why are you taking a photograph of that?" Why indeed?

Back to Damascus. In the Old City of Damascus is the Omayyad mosque. This was built in the eighth century AD and is the oldest stone mosque in the world. It is a massive and magnificent structure renowned for its multi-colored mosaics of trees and landscapes. It replaced an earlier cathedral church of St. John and is possibly built on the site of the temple of Rimmon (2 Kings 5:18). In the main sanctuary of the mosque is a structure surrounding what Muslims revere as the tomb of John the Baptist. Although it isn't visible, we are told that John's head is buried here. Visitors are free to enter this mosque but only after being appropriately attired.

Appropriate attire for men is quite relaxed and flexible, but for women, it's defined by the officious little men at the entrance. Evelyn was handed a full-length black dress and a handful of safety pins. When she was covered, the dress-custodian did an inspection and pinned the neckline a little tighter, and just in case the bottom of the dress might blow and expose a square centimeter of sinful female ankle, he pinned the dress a little tighter at the bottom as well. C'est la vie!

We rented a car in Damascus and spent a week visiting various sites in Syria. Driving in Damascus was insane. So much so that we requested the car rental agent to drive us to the edge of the city before we took over the wheel. After we left Damascus, the driving was quite normal, and major roads were in good condition. While searching for sites, Evelyn does the driving and I do the map reading.

In Syria, although women are permitted to drive, very few do so. Consequently, we got a vast number of stares when we passed other vehicles, especially when we passed them "on the inside" — Syrians have an irritating habit of driving quite slowly in the fast lane.

Most sites were fairly well marked with bilingual signs, but the Syrians have the annoying habit of pasting political posters on road signs! The highlights of this trip were our visits to the great antiquity sites of Ebla, Ugarit, Carchemish, and Palmyra. There was also a lot of adventure searching for the more insignificant Bible sites of Helbon (Ezekiel 27:18), Arvad (Ezekiel 27:8,11), Arpad (2 Kings 18:34), Pethor (hometown of Balaam, Numbers 22:5), Gozan (Isaiah 37:12), and the River Habor (1 Chronicles 5:26). But we can't leave Syria without a visit to Hamath and Tadmor.

Hamath is today's city of Homs. In the eleventh century BC, the city became the capital of the Syro-Hittite principality. Today it is best known for its giant water wheels, called norias, that lift water out of the Orontes River and move it into aqueducts to supply water to local agriculture. It was here that the Princes of Judah were executed:

> So Nebuzaradan, captain of the guard, took these and brought them to the king of Babylon at Riblah. Then the king of Babylon struck them and put them to death at Riblah in the land of Hamath. Thus Judah was carried away captive from its own land. (2 Kings 25:20-21)

We reached Homs on the fourth day of our car rental. We were planning to drive to Homs, have lunch, and then drive across the desert to the amazing ruins at Palmyra, biblical Tadmor. I had been driving about fifty kilometers from Homs when I began to feel that there was something wrong with the steering in our rental car. It felt as though the car just wanted to go in its own direction and that the wheels weren't always connected to the steering. We slowed our pace and parked upon arrival in Homs. It didn't take long to see that something was wrong because the two front wheels were pointing in different directions. We went immediately to a tourist information office, and the staff were very efficient at getting a mechanic to come to our aid. We followed him in our wonky car across the city to his garage, and three hours later we were on our way to Palmyra. I'm not a mechanic, but something had snapped, and the steering wheel was only directing one of the front wheels, while the other wheel just turned in whatever direction momentum pushed it.

It was an uneventful drive across the desert to Palmyra, and we arrived just in time to see the most magnificent sunset. Solomon built the city at the northeastern boundary of his empire on an oasis in the heart of the Syrian Desert, astride the main east-west trade route which ran from Mesopotamia to Canaan.

And Solomon went to Hamath Zobah and seized it. He also built Tadmor in the wilderness, and all the storage cities which he built in Hamath. (2 Chronicles 8:4)

The city was also situated on the main north-south trade route. Because of its strategic location, Tadmor became an important commercial center and military station. The Greeks and Romans renamed the city Palmyra. Tadmor is one of the most impressive and magnificent archaeological sites in the Middle East. It is often described as the bride of the desert, and there are remains of temples, a triumphal arch, theater, baths, Straight Street, and cemeteries. Sadly, in 2015, ISIS terrorists destroyed many tombs, statues and other ancient artifacts at this magnificent site.

That's enough of a detour, now it's time to return to Paul. After Damascus, Paul began to carry out his commission to preach and spread the gospel of Jesus Christ. He probably spent about ten years in and around Tarsus, actively evangelizing Gentiles, and also a short time in Jerusalem. Few details of those years have been preserved. At the end of that time, Paul went to Antioch, and this was followed by what is popularly known as his three missionary journeys. These took place primarily in what we today call Turkey and Greece. In a narrative such as we are telling here, it isn't possible to follow this route precisely without considerable duplication of material; instead, we will visit the sites going in an approximately east to west direction, with a few deviations when warranted.

For most of these locations there was little sense of adventure because many of them are signposted and marked, and our drive to these sites were uneventful. Our first stop is Antioch, which is today's city of Antakya in southern Turkey, about fifty-five kilometers north of the Syrian border. In the northeastern part of the city is Senpiyer Killsesi, or the Church of St. Peter. This one definitely fits the small and ugly category. The church is located in a cave, and both the site and the cave held little beauty or visual appeal.

Tradition says that this cave was owned by Luke, the author of Luke and Acts, a resident of Antioch, who donated the cave to the growing church. This church has been dubbed "The World's First Cathedral," and early church history is closely connected with Antioch. Believers in Jesus were first called Christians in Antioch. Paul began his three missionary journeys here, and his first and second journeys ended here.

And when he [Barnabas] had found him [Saul], he brought him to Antioch. So it was that for a whole year they assembled with the church and taught a great many people. And the disciples were first called Christians in Antioch. (Acts 11:26)

It was exciting to visit Antioch. Even so, one scene left an indelibly sad impression upon us. As we exited the church, we walked over the paved courtyard, and after tripping on a number of paving stones we came to a viewpoint over today's city where we counted the minarets and domes of twenty-eight mosques. What went wrong? This was one of the cradles of Christendom — today the fire has gone out and Islam dominates the nation of Turkey. We address the question of "What happened, what went wrong?" in the final chapter.

After leaving the church at Antioch, we drove about thirty kilometers to the port city of Seleucia (although "city" might be a grandiose term for this run-down dilapidated little fishing town). The last six kilometers to the town were horrible. The road was unpaved and pot-holed, and it became exhausting to simultaneously avoid potholes and maniac drivers coming in the opposite direction.

As it often happened, the only information we had was a photograph, and this time we were looking for a long, fairly high wall, sitting in the middle of a field! Amazingly, this wall is what remains of the old harbor from which Paul and Barnabas probably began their first missionary journey. We arrived at the port and had the usual rummage around to get a feel for the place. Frankly, we didn't care much for either the feel or smell. We showed the photograph to a number of locals, including a few policemen and a hotel manager, but none of them seemed to recognize it. This was disappointing because we really wanted to see this harbor wall, and yet we had no other clues to help us find the site.

We jumped into the car and started driving, and then, no more than 200–300 meters away was our photograph. It was exact and unmistakable — how couldn't those locals have recognized it? They pass it every day! The wall was about thirty meters off the side of the road, and we pulled in and just contemplated. A farmer was plowing his land in front of the wall. We couldn't help but think: "Does that farmer know that he is plowing on the site of an ancient port? Does he know that Paul and Barnabas sailed from his field? Has he ever heard of Paul and Barnabas? Did he know anything of the significance of his village and the nearby Antioch?"

> *Now in the church that was at Antioch there were certain prophets and teachers: … the Holy Spirit said, "Now separate to Me Barnabas and Saul for the work to which I have called them." … So, being sent out by the Holy Spirit, they went down to Seleucia, and from there they sailed to Cyprus.* (Acts 13:1-2, 4)

Our next destination is Tarsus, the hometown of the apostle Paul. Tarsus is also the city where Mark Anthony met Cleopatra. There are a number of interesting sites at Tarsus including an ancient road, dated 300 BC; it was excavated in the mid-1990s while digging the foundations for a parking lot in the city center. About 150 meters to the northeast is St. Paul's well. Although its connection to Paul isn't clear, there are some rather dubious claims that it was in Paul's home.

But Paul said, "I am a Jew from Tarsus, in Cilicia, a citizen of no mean city; and I implore you, permit me to speak to the people." (Acts 21:39)

In September 1999 we took a few days to go traveling in south-central Turkey. En route, we took a few detours off the main routes, and we were rewarded. Think about the most miserably poor place you have ever visited. Now double that image, and some of these places were probably worse than that. One particular place looked like a Hollywood movie set based in medieval England, but it was real. It is in this area that we find Iconium, Lystra, Derbe, and Antioch of Pisidia.

Iconium is today's Turkish city of Konya, and there aren't any ruins from ancient times. Iconium is another example of what we described for Antioch. The city has innumerable large, often impressive mosques, but there is only one Christian church in the city-center region, the Church of St. Paul. All other Christian activities are banned. What went wrong? Paul preached and was persecuted in this city. He even had to flee the city, but he had an impact:

Now it happened in Iconium that they went together to the synagogue of the Jews, and so spoke that a great multitude both of the Jews and of the Greeks believed. (Acts 14:1)

Lystra is about thirty kilometers south-southwest of Iconium and is an easy drive. The unexcavated mound of Lystra is non-descript, and we climbed up and over it for twenty minutes, and drove around it a few times, but it is non-descript. The cattle and horses nearby were much more attractive and interesting than the featureless mound! Yet, two thousand years ago this was the site of some great biblical narratives, and it was the hometown of Timothy:

And in Lystra a certain man without strength in his feet was sitting, a cripple from his mother's womb, who had never walked. This man heard Paul speaking. Paul, observing him intently and seeing that he had faith to be healed, said with a loud voice, "Stand up straight on your feet!" And he leaped and walked. (Acts 14:8-10)

Then Jews from Antioch and Iconium came there [to Lystra]; and having persuaded the multitudes, they stoned Paul and dragged him out of the city, supposing him to be dead. (Acts 14:19)

And when they had preached the gospel to that city and made many disciples, they returned to Lystra, Iconium, and Antioch, strengthening the souls of the disciples, exhorting them to continue in the faith, and saying, "We must through many tribulations enter the kingdom of God." So when they had appointed elders in every church, and prayed with fasting, they commended them to the Lord in whom they had believed. (Acts 14:21-23)

Derbe stumped us, it really did. We left Karaman driving east on the main road to Niğde. After about twelve kilometers, we spotted a signpost to Derbe. We were able to find today's village of Derbe, we think, but couldn't find any hint of the ancient mound — and apparently there is one. We were shown a mound that was about eight hundred meters away across roughly plowed fields, but we had no way of getting there. It's a real handicap to travel in these countries and not have the native tongue to communicate. Handwaving, sign language, and pointing can go a long way, but it's not always sufficient. It was at Derbe that Timothy joined Paul and Silas on their missionary journey:

> Then he came to Derbe and Lystra. And behold, a certain disciple was there, named Timothy, the son of a certain Jewish woman who believed, but his father was Greek. (Acts 16:1)

Antioch of Pisidia is a different story from those of Iconium, Lystra, and Derbe. In Antioch there are some impressive ruins at the northern edge of today's town of Yalvac. However, getting to Yalvac wasn't easy, and it took us over an hour to drive the winding, twisting, mountainous road to get there. On entering Yalvac, the site of Antioch of Pisidia is clearly marked with those lovely yellow signs.

> But when they [Paul and Barnabas] departed from Perga, they came to Antioch in Pisidia, and went into the synagogue on the Sabbath day and sat down. (Acts 13:14)

Getting to Antioch in Pisidia was slow, but leaving it was a racetrack. It was approaching dusk as we left, and we wanted to reach Iconium that evening. This particular road was relatively good, with the odd surprise, but with Evelyn at the wheel, anything is possible. Two hours later, and almost 160 kilometers, we were in Iconium. Evelyn's knuckles were white on the steering wheel, and mine were just white! Andrea slept through it all.

We continued westward and slightly south to the twin cities of Perga and Attalia. Attalia is today's resort city of Antalya. We lived there for eight months from July 1999, and we will have lots to share in a few moments.

Perga was the capital city of Pamphylia and is only twenty kilometers northeast of Antalya. Perga was on Paul's first missionary journey, and Paul and Barnabas preached here, but Perga is best known as the place where John Mark deserted Paul:

> Now when Paul and his party set sail from Paphos, they came to Perga in Pamphylia; and John, departing from them, returned to Jerusalem. (Acts 13:13)

When Paul began his first missionary journey, one of the first places he visited in about AD 46 was Perga; it's possible that he preached his first sermon here. Perga became an important city, and to understand its importance it is necessary to visit its remains. For us, Perga is one of Turkey's best-kept secrets, and one of Turkey's most under-appreciated sites. It is a sprawling site containing a number noteworthy things: a stadium for twelve thousand people, the remains of the first church built in Perga, an agora surrounded by Corinthian columns, a basilica, and a Roman Bath. The main street is lined with columns, many of which have beautifully carved inscriptions.

The star attraction is the ruins of the ancient theater which had a capacity of twelve thousand people. Unfortunately, for safety reasons, it was closed on both occasions we visited. Not to be deterred, we were able to scramble up a steep slope to get to the back of the theater. Here we found a small opening we could slip through to get into the theater. The stage has absolutely magnificent marble relieves depicting the life of Dionysus. However, on both occasions, we only had a short time to absorb the scene before being evicted. Paul was mistreated in many cities, but there is no record of him being kicked out of Perga.

Moving on from Perga is Attalia. It is only mentioned once in Scripture:

Now when they had preached the word in Perga, they went down to Attalia. From there they sailed to Antioch, where they had been commended to the grace of God for the work which they had completed. (Acts 14:25-26)

Antalya is a beautiful resort city. It servers conveniently as a center for short trips to other sites, such as Aspendos, Side, Perga, Myra, Patara, and others. The city has a Roman harbor from which Paul probably sailed to Antioch. And notably, Antalya has a small but wonderful museum featuring many artifacts from Perga, which displays a few jaw fragments of St. Nicholas — Santa Claus is dead? For us, our most memorable times in Antalya were Christmas and New Year.

Christmas in Turkey was very different and very quiet; in a 99% Muslim country, this was a regular work day. While none of the hotels provided a Christmas dinner on Christmas Day, most of them did so on Christmas Eve. On Christmas Eve, we had a delightful meal at The Falez, a quite elegant five-star hotel overlooking the Mediterranean. After dinner we jumped into a taxi and went to the St. Paul's Center for the Christmas Eve Carol service.

This was a very special occasion. The pastor gave a wonderfully encouraging message, and at about five minutes before midnight we all lit candles and paraded single file down to a beautiful little garden attached to the church. It was cool, but not cold, and all forty of us stood around and sang old, favorite Christmas carols for about half an hour — a beautiful and meaningful time of worship. On Christmas morning there were just the three of us: Evelyn, our daughter Andrea, and me. Evelyn made a nice breakfast, we opened our gifts, and went downtown. It was very pleasant out, probably about 17-18C, so we decided to go out on a boat trip for about two hours along the coast to a fairly impressive waterfall. We returned to the harbor and then went to Burger King for dinner on Christmas Day; I suppose it could have been worse, we could have gone to McDonald's.

A few days later was the end of the second millennium and then it was New Year's Day 2000. Evelyn, Andrea, and I arranged to go to a beautiful little restaurant/hotel in the Old City called Alp Pasha. In its former days, this was a summer home of the Sultans, and some of today's hotel rooms were the former rooms of the Sultan's harem. The hotel was built around an elegant little courtyard with a small, central swimming pool.

We arrived at about 8:00 p.m., and I was silently wondering how we were going to put in four hours until midnight. However, that didn't turn out to be a problem. The waiters were all a little on the crazy side and obviously having an enjoyable time. This was a buffet dinner, and for one of the few times in recent years, we probably got our money's worth. The buffet provided a wonderful diversity of foods including a dessert buffet. Of course, throughout the evening, artists came around the tables singing and playing instruments. At the stroke of midnight, we all sang something, a number of fireworks were shot off to the heavens, the restaurant manager was pushed, fully-clothed into the pool, and we had a very civilized, enjoyable, and quite unique entry to the year 2000.

Continuing south and west along the rather tortuous, although scenic coast, we soon came to Myra and then a little farther on to Patara. The site of Myra, with its elegant Roman theater and rock tombs, is on the outskirts of the town of Demre. Near the town center of Demre is the Church of St. Nicholas. St. Nicholas was born in Patara and became the bishop of this area; he is remembered in history as Santa Claus. Paul was on his way to Rome when his ship docked in Myra.

And when we had sailed over the sea which is off Cilicia and Pamphylia, we came to Myra, a city of Lycia. There the centurion found an Alexandrian ship sailing to Italy, and he put us on board. (Acts 27:5-6)

The ruins at Patara aren't very impressive but the beach is!

Now it came to pass, that when we had departed from them and set sail, running a straight course we came to Cos, the following day to Rhodes, and from there to Patara. (Acts 21:1)

As we traveled farther along the coast, we headed northwards and arrived at Miletus. The city of Miletus was originally situated on the coast, but because of the siltation, the site is now about ten kilometers inland. Aside from the rather magnificent Roman Theater, Miletus has little to offer the visitor. A reconstructed gate from Miletus is on display in the Pergamon Museum in Berlin. This gate dates from AD 120 and is 16.78 meters tall. It's one of the most famous examples of Roman façade architecture in existence.

... The next day we came to Miletus. For Paul had decided to sail past Ephesus, so that he would not have to spend time in Asia; for he was hurrying to be at Jerusalem, if possible, on the Day of Pentecost. (Acts 20:15-16)

From here it is a seventy-five-kilometer drive north to Ephesus. The ruins at Ephesus are among some of the best anywhere, especially the colonnaded street, the enormous theater, and the Celcus library. Ephesus, along with six other places — Smyrna, Pergamum, Thyatira, Sardis, Philadelphia, and Laodicea — are collectively known as the Seven Churches of the Revelation. We will describe our visits to the seven churches in the next chapter. As we left Ephesus and continued north along the Aegean coast, we passed through Smyrna, today's Izmir; and Pergamum, today's Bergama, before arriving at Assos. Paul arrived at Assos on foot from Troas, which is a healthy sixty kilometers.

Then we went ahead to the ship and sailed to Assos, there intending to take Paul on board; for so he had given orders, intending himself to go on foot. And when he met us at Assos, we took him on board ... (Acts 20:13-14)

Assos is today's village of Behramkale. It is a lovely place, facing the Gulf of Edremit and looking offshore to the Greek Island of Lesbos. The village has two sections. The upper village is built on a steep slope, and a driver requires nerves of steel to negotiate some of the steep sharp corners. Here you can find the reasonably good remains of a Temple of Athena built in the sixth century BC.

We visited in January when it was biting cold, and we led the on-site tour guide around the entire site in less than three minutes; I'm sure it's the fastest tour he has ever taken. Just below the acropolis is a block-paved road. Following this for two kilometers leads you past the massive city walls, a basilica, and a theater, to the lower village and the ancient harbor. We stayed overnight in a beautiful little guest house overlooking the modern harbor. The place was memorable because we had a real, open fire in our bedroom, with an endless supply of small logs. Fire marshals in North America would have had a fit, but to us it was cozy and gorgeous, especially as we heard the wind and driving rain beating against our windows.

As we drove towards Troas we entered a more pastoral region. The ruins are singularly unimpressive and scattered on both sides of the road amid trees and fields. Nevertheless, it was a fairly nice day, cool but sunny, and we took the opportunity to explore. Most of the ruins are of more recent origin but that didn't prevent us from imaging Paul's long sermon:

...Paul, ready to depart the next day, spoke to them and continued his message until midnight... And in a window sat a certain young man named Eutychus, who was sinking into a deep sleep. He was overcome by sleep; and as Paul continued speaking, he fell down from the third story and was taken up dead. But Paul went down, fell on him, and embracing him said, "Do not trouble yourselves, for his life is in him." (Acts 20:7, 9-10)

It was also here at Troas that another pivotal event occurred in the early Christian church. Paul had a vision, and the gospel was brought to Europe.

And a vision appeared to Paul in the night. A man of Macedonia stood and pleaded with him, saying, "Come over to Macedonia and help us."... Therefore, sailing from Troas, we ran a straight course to Samothrace, and the next day came to Neapolis, (Acts 16:9, 11)

The ruins of Troas are sixteen kilometers southwest of the ruins of ancient Troy, famous for the legendary Trojan horse. The remains of the city were lost for centuries and were eventually uncovered by a German archaeologist, Heinrich Schliemann, who used Homer's Iliad to locate the site. The ruins include a temple, a theater, and many foundations. The most notable feature of the site today is the totally inappropriate and ugly life-size reconstruction of the wooden Trojan horse. Oh, it really is ugly. This region has witnessed two important battles in history. Not only was there the war of Troy, immortalized in Homer's Illiad, but this was also the area of the Gallipoli campaign in 1915 during World War I.

Paul went from Troas to Macedonia, present-day Greece, and so introduced the gospel to Europe. We will now go to Greece and begin our tour of New Testament sites with a visit to Athens. Our task was to get from Antalya to Athens on a tight budget, and it turned out to be more difficult than anticipated.

We began with a six-hour overnight bus journey from Antalya to Izmir. Due to a lot of language and communication problems, we were put on the wrong bus to the port town of Cesme about thirty-five minutes west of Izmir. We arrived in Cesme early enough to buy breakfast and board the 10:00 a.m. ferry for the one-hour trip across to the Greek Island of Chios. Once on Chios, we discovered that the ships sailing the next leg of our journey, ten hours across the Aegean Sea to Athens, were fully booked for two days, except for a deluxe first-class suite that we couldn't afford. Flights were infrequent, and there was nothing for two days. When we worked out the finances, although it was too expensive, our cheapest option was to take the first-class suite. Luckily, when we returned to the travel agent, there was one suite left — we took it!

It was now just after midday, and the ship didn't depart for ten hours. What can anyone do in a nowhere town on a nowhere island for ten hours? We visited a number of restaurants, walked up and down the main street many times, counted dogs, counted scooters, went to a park, slept on a bench, counted more dogs, went to a supermarket, and counted more dogs! Eventually, the enormous ferry came into the harbor which is right alongside the main street of town. Although we paid too much, it was a wonderful suite, and we had a good night's sleep before arriving in Athens early the next morning.

Athens is one of those cities with a rich, deep history, but after visiting the Acropolis and a few other nearby sites, Athens runs out of appeal. Athens is named after the goddess Athena, and it developed around the 185-meter-high Acropolis. In AD 49 Paul disputed daily in the Agora. Of biblical interest, Athens has the Areopagus, otherwise known as Mars' Hill, the Agora, and the Church of the Holy Apostles built to commemorate Paul's teaching.

> Now while Paul waited for them at Athens, his spirit was provoked within him when he saw that the city was given over to idols. Therefore he reasoned in the synagogue with the Jews and with the Gentile worshipers, and in the marketplace daily with those who happened to be there... And they took him and brought him to the Areopagus, saying, "May we know what this new doctrine is of which you speak?... Then Paul stood in the midst of the Areopagus and said, "Men of Athens, I perceive that in all things you are very religious; (Acts 17:16-17, 19, 22)

Although I'm not a preacher, it was a moment of fantasy to stand on Mars' Hill and imagine Paul preaching to the people of Athens.

It's a short drive from Athens to Corinth, with a short stop to view the remarkable Corinth canal. It was the Roman Emperor Nero who first attempted to cut a canal through the Isthmus, but the project was abandoned. There were other attempts, but it wasn't until 1893 that it was completed by a Greek company. The Canal is 6,343 meters long, twenty-five meters wide, and has a maximum height (depth) of sixty-three meters — impressive.

Modern Corinth, rebuilt northeast of the ancient site, is little more than a dreary little town. Corinth is located on the Isthmus of Corinth between the Ionian Sea and the Aegean Sea on a narrow strip of land connecting the Peloponnesus peninsula of southern Greece with central Greece. The massive and fortified Acrocorinth can be seen towering to the south of the ruins. Corinth was one of the most important trade cities in ancient Greece. It is estimated that the city had a population of approximately 500,000 people at the time of Paul's arrival. Paul wrote at least two letters to the church of Corinth, both dealing with divisions in the church and with immorality. Among the archaeological finds at Corinth is the bema, or judgment platform, a marble podium from which Roman officials addressed the people. It is likely that this is where Paul was brought before Gallio and acquitted:

> When Gallio was proconsul of Achaia, the Jews with one accord rose up against Paul and brought him to the judgment seat, saying, "This fellow persuades men to worship God contrary to the law." (Acts 18:12-13)

In addition, the pavement below the bema seat is probably the site where the Greeks beat Sosthenes:

> Then all the Greeks took Sosthenes, the ruler of the synagogue, and beat him before the judgment seat... (Acts 18:17)

Along the southern side of the agora is a large stoa filled with shops, probably where Paul told the Corinthians they could buy meat with a clear conscience. At the eastern end of the agora and south of the stoa are two basilicas used as law courts, and this may have been where the Corinthian Christians went to court against their brethren (1 Corinthians 6:1-11).

From Corinth, we literally drove as fast as we could, directly north to the region of Macedonia. In biblical times this was a region north of Greece, then Achaia. Today it is the northeastern region of Greece, centered on Thessalonica. Cities of Macedonia that are mentioned in the New Testament consist of Thessalonica, Berea, Apollonia, Amphipolis, Neapolis, and Philippi. Its capital was Thessalonica where the governor resided.

When we arrived in Thessalonica we ran into a few problems. Our travel bible is a collection of Lonely Planet guidebooks, and we rely on them extensively for accommodation and restaurants. The first order of business is always to find somewhere to sleep. Unfortunately, the first recommended hotel had been burned to the ground, the second had been demolished, the third was closed for renovation,[105] and, finally, the fourth was able to give us a room. Finding

---

[105] These were not problems with the Lonely Planet guidebook because travelers all understand that most guidebooks are, at best, one year out of date when they are first published.

somewhere to eat was even more problematic because most places seemed to close early, so we ended up eating in a cheap hamburger-salad joint.

The next morning it took us all of thirty minutes to see the few, scant remains of ancient Thessalonica, right in the city center, where major excavations were taking place. Unfortunately, the dig was behind some hoarding and barricades, and we could only see from a viewpoint on the main street. It is an amazing juxtaposition to see modern stores and boutiques overlooking two-thousand-year-old ruins. It was here that the house of Jason was attacked followed by a near-riot in the city:

> *But the Jews who were not persuaded, becoming envious, took some of the evil men from the marketplace, and gathering a mob, set all the city in an uproar and attacked the house of Jason, and sought to bring them out to the people. But when they did not find them, they dragged Jason and some brethren to the rulers of the city, crying out, "These who have turned the world upside down have come here too."* (Acts 17:5-6)

Scripture records that Paul and Silas were brought before the 'Politarchs,' which is translated in Acts as 'city officials' (NIV) or 'rulers of the city' (NKJV). Critics of the Scriptures argued that the title 'Politarchs' (Acts 17:6, 8) was a biblical error because there wasn't any known title of this name. However, a Greek inscription from a Roman gateway in Thessalonica dating from the time of the apostles is on display at the British Museum — it is called the *Politarch Inscription.* The inscription lists the civic officials of the city in the second century AD and includes six Politarchs (Rulers of the Citizens), the Tamias (Treasurer) of the city, and the Gymnasiarch (Director of Higher Education). Another blow to biblical minimalists.

Biblical Berea is modern Veria, seventy-five kilometers west of Thessalonica. Between the two cities, we had the opportunity to visit Pella, the birthplace of Alexander the Great, and one of the most important archaeological sites of Greece. Unfortunately, with rental car time pressures, we didn't have time for a detailed visit before racing on to Berea.

Remnants of the ancient Roman Egnatian Way have been preserved along Mitropoleos Street. At the beginning of the 1900s the city had seventy-two Byzantine and post-Byzantine churches; today there are forty-eight, hence Veria is sometimes called "Little Jerusalem." Near Plateia Raktivan is "St. Paul's Altar" where it is believed that Paul delivered many of his daily sermons to the Bereans.

> *Then the brethren immediately sent Paul and Silas away by night to Berea. When they arrived, they went into the synagogue of the Jews. These were more fair-minded than*

those in Thessalonica, in that they received the word with all readiness, and searched the Scriptures daily to find out whether these things were so. (Acts 17:10-11)

Our journey that day had every expectation of being exciting. We drove due east, most of the time following the route of the ancient Roman Egnatian Way, for about 150 kilometers, traveling from Thessalonica through Amphipolis, Apollonia, and Neapolis to Philippi. The only reminder of Apollonia today is a signboard as you pass the village at one hundred kilometers per hour. There were only a few ancient ruins at Amphipolis; however, since our visit, the remains of four early basilicas have been discovered, so Amphipolis must have been a notable religious center.

Amphipolis was one of the most important cities of Macedonia in antiquity. The Egnatian Way, a major Roman roadway, ran through the city. On the outskirts of the town is the "Lion of Amphipolis," a large 2–3 meter tall stone lion sitting on top of a 2–3 meter high pedestal. This has been dated from the fourth century BC, so there is little doubt that Paul stopped to have a look as he walked by. Its purpose isn't clear although popular ideas are that it was a funerary monument or a monument erected to commemorate some military victory.

We then raced on to visit Philippi but before doing so we stopped at a high viewpoint that provided a panoramic view over Kavala, biblical Neapolis, and the port city of Philippi, which is about fifteen kilometers inland. Although we were in a hurry, we took time to contemplate that this was the landing port in Europe for visitors from the Orient and the beginning of the great Egnatian Way which went to Rome. Paul came through here in AD 49 on his way to Philippi in response to the vision he had while at Troas.

Therefore, sailing from Troas, we ran a straight course to Samothrace, and the next day came to Neapolis, (Acts 16:11)

Leaving Kavala he traveled north to Philippi. Excavations have revealed ruins of Roman baths, a colonnaded street, basilicas, temples, a Roman forum, a fourth-century theater, remnants of several Christian churches, and an acropolis. It was at Philippi that Paul had his first European convert, Lydia. About 1.5 kilometers west of the ruins, on the Krenides River, is a small chapel and baptismal site, to commemorate the traditional location where Lydia was converted and baptized.

Now a certain woman named Lydia heard us. She was a seller of purple from the city of Thyatira, who worshiped God. The Lord opened her heart to heed the things spoken by Paul. (Acts 16:14)

Our most cherished remembrance of Philippi was that archaeologists had uncovered parts of a Roman building that may have been a prison; it is rather cautiously referred to as "the prison of Paul." This is one of the best-known stories in Scripture related to the apostle Paul, so we will provide the whole story:

> Then the multitude rose up together against them; and the magistrates tore off their clothes and commanded them to be beaten with rods. And when they had laid many stripes on them, they threw them into prison, commanding the jailer to keep them securely. Having received such a charge, he put them into the inner prison and fastened their feet in the stocks. But at midnight Paul and Silas were praying and singing hymns to God, and the prisoners were listening to them. Suddenly there was a great earthquake, so that the foundations of the prison were shaken; and immediately all the doors were opened and everyone's chains were loosed. And the keeper of the prison, awaking from sleep and seeing the prison doors open, supposing the prisoners had fled, drew his sword and was about to kill himself. But Paul called with a loud voice, saying, "Do yourself no harm, for we are all here." Then he called for a light, ran in, and fell down trembling before Paul and Silas. (Acts 16:22-29)

And then we read the most important question for all humanity, followed by its only answer:

> And he brought them out and said, "Sirs, what must I do to be saved?" So they said, "Believe on the Lord Jesus Christ, and you will be saved, you and your household." (Acts 16:30-31)

We will now briefly move our geography back to Jerusalem. Paul had been attacked by a mob in the area of the Temple. He was rescued by a detachment of Roman soldiers and kept in custody at the Roman governor's headquarters in Caesarea for the next two years. Here he exercised his privilege as a Roman citizen and appealed to Caesar to have his case transferred to the emperor's tribunal in Rome. And so, Paul set out for Rome in the fall of AD 59. Paul's journey took him to Malta, then to Syracuse on the island of Sicily. Then, after a brief stop at Rhegium on the Italian mainland, Paul sailed up the western coast of Italy and finally landed at Puteoli, which today (now Pozzuoli) is a southwestern suburb of Naples. We will pick up the story from there.

In 2003 we were attending a conference of the International Association of Vegetation Science in Naples. We arrived a few days early to do some traveling. We rented a car and went to the summit of Mount Vesuvius, the remarkable ruins at Pompeii, and then to Pozzuoli. There are two harbors at Pozzuoli, but we couldn't determine if either of these was the ancient harbor where Paul landed. Puteoli was famous for its Roman baths, portions of which remain today, across the road from the harbor.

From there we circled round and reached Rhegium. And after one day the south wind blew; and the next day we came to Puteoli, where we found brethren, and were invited to stay with them seven days. And so we went toward Rome. (Acts 28:13-14)

The last few words of those verses say "…so we went toward Rome," and they would have done so along The Appian Way or Via Appia. This road, constructed in 312 BC, is one of the most famous roads built by the ancient Romans. The road ran south from Rome to Terracina and later was extended to modern Brindisi; it was more than 560 kilometers long. From Rome to Terracina the road is nearly straight, and the forty-kilometer stretch from just south of Cisterna, almost to Terracina, is without a bend and almost continuously lined with pine trees. Many parts of the road have been renovated and are still in use. Today, the Appian Way has kilometer markers and not the expected Roman-mile markers! Scripture records that Believers from Rome came out to meet Paul at Appii Forum and at Three Taverns, neither of which have been satisfactorily identified.

And from there, when the brethren heard about us, they came to meet us as far as Appii Forum and three Inns. When Paul saw them, he thanked God and took courage. (Acts 28:15)

The exact location of Appii Forum is unclear. It has been described at locations ranging from fifty-three kilometers to seventy-seven kilometers south of Rome. The best guesses are at a memorial church at Triponti at kilometer sixty-six, or at Foro Appio at kilometer seventy-one. The location of Three Inns is even more elusive, but for us, it was sufficient to simply drive along this tree-lined road and to try and capture the spirit and atmosphere surrounding Paul and his friends as they traveled this road almost two thousand years ago.

Paul finally arrived in Rome. He had planned to visit Rome at least twice, but he ultimately ended up in Rome as a prisoner and was martyred.

When these things were accomplished, Paul purposed in the Spirit, when he had passed through Macedonia and Achaia, to go to Jerusalem, saying, "After I have been there, I must also see Rome." (Acts 19:21)

Now when we came to Rome, the centurion delivered the prisoners to the captain of the guard; but Paul was permitted to dwell by himself with the soldier who guarded him. (Acts 28:16)

From Rome, Paul wrote letters to the Ephesians, Colossians, 2 Timothy, Philemon, and probably Philippians. Under Nero, the city of Rome was burned and Christians were persecuted. In the second century, Ignatius of Antioch and Justin Martyr were martyred here along with many other prominent Christians.

Rome is probably one of the most beautiful cities we have visited. There is an enormous number of Christian churches scattered throughout the city, each commemorating someone, something, or some event — many of them rather dubious — and few are of direct scriptural relevance. Those of direct significance are St. Peter's Basilica and St. Paul's Outside the Walls.

St. Peter's Basilica is the largest and most imposing church in the Christian world. The interior of the church is a showpiece of the great masters — it is adorned with numerous frescoes, mosaics, sculptures, and memorials. There isn't any positive documentary evidence that Peter was ever in Rome; however, tradition claims that the high altar of the basilica is centered over the tomb of Peter. The guided tour of the tomb, related Roman ruins, and the catacombs under St. Peter's was fascinating. And while the climb to the top of Michelangelo's dome was tough, it offered a stunning view of the city of Rome. Many sites in Rome were awe-inspiring such as the Vatican Museums, the Sistine Chapel, and many of the churches, particularly the Basilica di San Paola Fuori-le-Mura (Paul outside the wall) which is believed to contain Paul's tomb and the site of his martyrdom. After four days we were literally churched-out, and when our resistance would weaken we would visit yet another church and find it to be as incredible as most of the previous ones we had visited.

And of course, when in Rome, one has to visit the catacombs and the Colosseum. Although neither of these are direct biblical sites, each has a strong connection to the history of the early Christians in Rome. The catacombs are kilometers of tunnels carved out of the soft rock and were the meeting and burial places of early Christian in Rome from the first to the fifth centuries.

Again, the Colosseum isn't a biblical site, but many Christians were martyred here. The massive amphitheater seated over fifty-thousand spectators who watched bloody gladiatorial contests and other blood sports. Interestingly, only a short five-minute walk from the Colosseum is the triumphal Arch of Titus, built in honor of Titus's victories against Jewish rebels in Jerusalem in AD 70. On a relief inside the arch, the spoils of Jerusalem are displayed, and these include an image of a menorah — this is one of the earliest known depictions of a menorah. Some scholars believe that proceeds from the sale of the spoils of Jerusalem may have been used to fund the building of the Colosseum.

And while we visited all of the things that people visit in Rome, we had two extra-special "insights." We sat for two hours in the Basilica of San Giovanni in

Laterano witnessing the ordination of about half-a-dozen priests, and we decided it would be interesting to have an audience with the pope. An audience with the pope is not like it sounds. Typically, you would think of an audience as being one or a few people meeting, but at this event, there must have been up to ten thousand people in the audience in St. Peter's Square. In addition, you must have tickets. How would Canadian Protestants acquire tickets to have an audience with the Pope?

Tickets were available, free of charge, two days in advance. So, Evelyn and I pranced off to St. Peter's Square and joined the long lineup that was rapidly growing. After about ten minutes, we noticed that most people were clutching sheets of paper that looked suspiciously like a letter. We ventured to inquire of those just ahead of us in line, and they told us that these were letters from their local priest confirming that they were Roman Catholic and in good standing in the church. Oh, my!

We devised a plan. Evelyn held our place in the lineup and I walked about sixty meters to the head of the line. The ticket booth wouldn't open for another ten minutes, but I explained to the attendant that we had no letter. He ushered me through the turnstile and pointed me in the direction of two Swiss Guards standing at ease in a beautiful, arched doorway. I approached them and explained our problem. The only words from the guard were: "How many people?" and within a few minutes I was back with two tickets just before the booth opened. So there is at least one advantage to being a Protestant in Rome!

Two days later we arrived early to get a ringside seat to watch Pope John II glide past in his popemobile. We had a good view and then we sat through a ninety-minute "audience" with the Pope. It was all very interesting, especially when one of the Swiss Guards fainted in the hot Roman sun.

The book of Acts comes to an abrupt end much like an unfinished story, and what happened to Paul in Rome is left unclear. He seemed to be free to proclaim the gospel but under some form of loose house arrest:

> *Then Paul dwelt two whole years in his own rented house, and received all who came to him, preaching the kingdom of God and teaching the things which concern the Lord Jesus Christ with all confidence, no one forbidding him.* (Acts 28:30-31)

We aren't told if this semi-captivity ended in his execution or his release. The general assumption is that he was executed, but there is also a school of thought that he was released for two or three years (AD 60-61), during which time he probably wrote the books of 1 Timothy and Titus. The book of 2 Timothy clearly states that Paul is (back) in prison:

For I am already being poured out as a drink offering, and the time of my departure [death] is at hand. (2 Timothy 4:6)

If Paul was released, he was rearrested about AD 67 and eventually executed by Nero in Rome. Paul is most likely buried in the Basilica di San Paolo Fuori-le-Mura which literally means St. Paul's outside of the wall. This was the largest church in the world until the construction of St Peter's Basilica, and it is a resplendent building with tremendous artwork. In his final epistle, Paul left his legacy to Timothy when he wrote:

I have fought the good fight, I have finished the race, I have kept the faith. (2 Timothy 4:7)

However, Paul's final victory lap is captured by:

We are confident, yes, well pleased rather to be absent from the body and to be present with the Lord. (2 Corinthians 5:8)

XV.
THE SEVEN CHURCHES OF REVELATION

In Revelation chapters 2 and 3, the Apostle John was inspired by the Holy Spirit to give us the Revelation of Jesus Christ. This God-breathed writing begins with letters to the seven churches in Asia Minor (in what is now western Turkey), addressing their strengths and weaknesses. From a simple reading of these chapters, it is clear that Jesus is the author of these letters.

By AD 96, only a few decades after their establishment, the churches were already getting into trouble. We toured twice to visit the sites of these seven churches. Today, Ephesus and Pergamon[106] are archaeological wonders, but the remaining sites are singularly uninspiring.[107] Actually, Laodicea is such a mess that, in a perverse way, it is quite enjoyable just to muddle through the ruins. Having said that, there have been extensive archaeological excavations and renovations since our last visit. In addition, traveling the roads between the cities offered little by way of excitement, mystery, adventure, or intrigue, so we have few stories that parallel our travels in Israel and other parts of the Middle East.

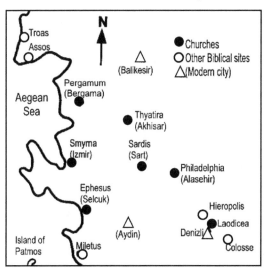

Location of the Seven Churches named in chapters 2 and 3 of the book of Revelation.

---

[106] Pergamon or Pergamum, also referred to by its modern Greek form Pergamos.

[107] It is an eye-opener to meet tourists that are very disappointed because not a small number believe they are going to visit the actual churches!

However, to the Christian believer, a visit to these sites is spiritually uplifting, and there are many insightful lessons to be learned from the letters to these churches. The most impressive ruins are at Ephesus, so we will begin our tour there and drive in a circular, clockwise direction, ending with Laodicea, following the same order as they appear in the Bible.

EPHESUS

During Roman times Ephesus was a city of trade, and the Agora was the largest market in the east. Ephesus was an extremely wealthy city, and the theater seated 25,000 people. But at the time of Paul, Ephesus was immoral because of all its wealth from trade and from the worshipping of Artemis. Paul's preaching was powerful. And because so many people turned to the Lord, sales of silver statues of Artemis decreased. The silversmiths were becoming bankrupt and could no longer trade, so they staged a riot against Paul as described in Acts 19.

The church at Ephesus was The Loveless Church. In the letter to this church, Jesus told the Believers that he was aware of all that they had been through and that times weren't easy for them. He also commended them for hating the teachings of the Nicolaitans.

> *and you have persevered and have patience, and have labored for My name's sake and have not become weary.* (Revelation 2:3)

Yet despite their faithfulness, there was a criticism:

> *...you have left your first love.* (Revelation 2:4)

About three kilometers to the east of the ruins of Ephesus lies the city of Selcuk, and most travelers and tourists find accommodation in Selcuk. Selcuk has almost one hundred small pensions that compete vigorously for business. On both occasions, we stayed at the immensely popular (with good reason) Homeros Pension. This pension had lots of character and characters. The food is great, and the rooftop terrace provides a great vantage point for beautiful sunsets and a view of the site of the ancient Temple of Artemis. We had arrived, were settled in our room, and went up to the rooftop terrace to await the evening meal. Our hosts appeared with a complimentary glass of wine — but we don't drink alcohol! It would have been offensive to have refused the wine and so we cautiously lifted our glasses from the tray. We had assumed that our hosts would soon go off downstairs, but they stayed and chatted to us. Meanwhile, we were standing holding these drinks and our hosts were watching us. When they finally left we fed a potted ornamental cedar tree with a little extra juice it wasn't accustomed to, and then we enjoyed a most spectacular sunset in the western sky.

SMYRNA

When Polycarp became the Bishop of Smyrna, the city's population was close to 100,000 people. The modern city of Izmir is built on the ancient site, so little excavation is possible. John informs the Christians that Jesus is familiar with both the suffering and poverty of their community. The church at Smyrna was the Rich Little Poor Church. In the letter to this church Jesus said of them:

I know your works, tribulation, and poverty (but you are rich… (Revelation 2:9)

To be faithful to what they believed, the believers at Smyrna had to stand against emperor worship. For many of them, this meant the loss of their trade and inheritances and caused many of them to become poor. Under Nero, many of them were martyred; however, they were spiritually rich despite their material poverty. Their most celebrated martyr was Polycarp who was a disciple of John. When interrogators tried to force him to denounce his faith he said: "Eighty and six years have I served Him, and He has done me no wrong. How can I blaspheme my King and my Savior?"[108]

Ancient Smyrna is today's city of Izmir about one hour north of Ephesus. Izmir is the second-largest city in Turkey, and trying to get around can be utter confusion. If you don't have a good map, then don't even think of going into Izmir; even with a map, you'll probably get lost because there are no obvious street names or direction signs. It is difficult getting used to traffic circles (roundabouts) that have eight sets of traffic lights! At some intersections, there are lights as each major road joins the circle, and then another set of lights on the circle where each road enters. It's an amazingly unworkable system and invariably leads to clogged traffic. It's rather strange on occasions to see traffic in almost every direction at a standstill, nothing moving, yet horns blasting loudly because everyone wants to get somewhere, but the lights are red, and if you happen to have a green light you probably can't move anyway!

On our first visit to Izmir, we made a fortuitous mistake. We had misread our maps and had already missed two exits into downtown Izmir. Then unexpectedly, we saw a signpost to "Tepekule (Smyrna)" to the right. We were excited as we actually saw the name Smyrna even though it was in parentheses on a signpost.

---

[108] Polycarp's Martyrdom (ca. 69–ca. 155). *The Martyrdom of Polycarp*. Translated by J.B. Lightfoot. Abridged and modernized by Stephen Tompkins. Edited and prepared for the web by Dan Graves. https://christianhistoryinstitute.org/study/module/polycarp (accessed July 21, 2021).

We followed the sign, but alas, this was the last sign we ever saw to Smyrna. We ended up in the suburb of Bayrakli. We drove around this neighborhood for close to an hour. The streets were narrow, twisting around as this neighborhood hugged the contours of a large hill. We asked directions repeatedly, we were sent this way and that, we ended up in many dead-end streets, and on more than one occasion found ourselves driving the wrong way along one-way streets.

Finally, we got the response we needed from a middle-aged man waiting for his taxi. "Ah, I know where that is," he said. While he was speaking to us, his taxi arrived, he jumped in and told us to follow him. We did. Turkish drivers are fast, dangerous, and reckless, and taxi drivers are probably twice as bad. We blindly belted after this taxi driver, making some questionable maneuvers, and ended up in downtown Izmir at the Hilton Tower Hotel. This kind gentleman was correct, but he was also incorrect. From the Hilton Hotel, it is an easy walk to the church of Polycarp and to the ancient Agora. However, while we wanted to visit these sites, and did, we also wanted to visit the few traces of the original acropolis of Smyrna which were now about half an hour away. And yes, we found our way back to Tepekule and Bayrakli and visited the ruins which were about two hundred meters from where we started to follow the taxi.

On our second visit to Izmir, we had better maps, but again we became confused while trying to leave the city. We spotted a police officer, so I quickly stopped the car, applied the parking brake, jumped out, and asked the officer for directions. While we were chatting, I ignored the clanging bells that indicated an approaching train. Meanwhile, Evelyn was frantically trying to get my attention as the barrier was slowly coming down on the roof of our car — I had parked under the barrier!

PERGAMON

Another hour north of Izmir takes us to today's city of Bergama, situated below the ancient site of Pergamon that sits high atop an adjacent hill. Unlike Ephesus and Smyrna, Pergamon was a center of politics, and the people of Pergamon had to be faithful to the emperor and imperial Rome. It was a city where idolatry was at its climax, with temples or altars to at least six Greek gods including Zeus, Dionysus, Demeter, and Athena. According to Greek mythology, Zeus was the father and greatest of all gods, the ruler of the heavens, thunder and lightning, and he was born in Pergamon.

The great altar to Zeus stood on the Acropolis. The altar was erected about AD 190, was thirty-six meters wide, thirty-four meters long, and had twenty-one steps up to the place of sacrifice. In the late 1800s, the altar was excavated, and today it's on display at the Pergamon Museum in Berlin. Some scholars believe that when John refers to Satan's throne (Revelation 2:13) he had this great altar in mind. Others argue it is called Satan's throne because this was the birthplace of Zeus who is considered the father of all Greek gods.

The church at Pergamon was the Compromising Church. In the letter to this church Jesus commends the believers because:

> *...you hold fast to My name...* (Revelation 2:13)

Christ knew their situation, and he knew what they had been through; some of them had even been martyred. Yet, Christ holds them to account and says:

> *...you have there those who hold the doctrine of Balaam ...and the Nicolaitans...* (Revelation 2:14-15)

It seems that in the midst of all the pressures of this city, some Believers faltered in their faith. They followed the teachings of Balaam and Nicolas, and ultimately compromised with the world. Balaam was the Old Testament prophet who caused Israel to turn against God (Numbers 22:5ff).

THYATIRA

This is today's city of Akhisar, situated between Pergamon and Sardis. Thyatira was materially the most insignificant of the seven cities. It wasn't a city of politics or culture, rather it was a city of industry. The city was known for the popularity of its pagan trade unions, and the church here must have felt their strong pressure.

In the letter to this church, Jesus commends the Believers because:

> *...as for your works, the last are more than the first.* (Revelation 2:19)

However, the church at Thyatira was the Corrupt Church. They were reprimanded for allowing a false teacher into their midst:

> *...you allow that woman Jezebel, who calls herself a prophetess, to teach and seduce My servants to commit sexual immorality..."* (Revelation 2:20)

It is not clear whether this false prophetess was actually called Jezebel or was given this name to tie her to the Old Testament character of the same name. Jezebel was the wife of King Ahab and had angered God by worshipping false gods, killing God's prophets, and indulging in immorality.

SARDIS

The ruins of Sardis are scattered widely along a valley, and those that are worth seeing are at the city of Sart. The church at Sardis was alive but dead. At Sardis, believers had become lazy in their faith. They became lost in the luxuries of the world because there was so much wealth, and they considered themselves self-sufficient.

The church at Sardis was the Dead Church. In the letter to this church Jesus said that there were only a few worthy:

> *you have a few names…and they shall walk with me in white, for they are worthy.*
> (Revelation 3:4)

Historians tell us that this was a wealthy area and, with so much wealth, believers became absorbed in the luxuries of the world. Subsequently, they became lazy in their faith. Sadly, they are described as:

> *…you have a name that you are alive, but you are dead.* (Revelation 3:1)

The church had all the trappings and had all the proper outward signs. In today's vernacular, it probably had a large roadside signboard, plans, programs, church bulletins, all sorts of activities, and perhaps a large platform party. But despite all the outward signs of life, Jesus pronounced the church of Sardis to be dead.

PHILADELPHIA

Philadelphia is today's city of Alasehir, one hundred kilometers northwest of one of Turkey's premier vacation resorts, Pamukkale. Philadelphia was a small city, the people were mainly in agriculture, and grapes were the most important produce of the region.

The church at Philadelphia was the Faithful Church, and just like the church at Smyrna, the church at Philadelphia was a persecuted church. When Polycarp was being martyred in Smyrna, many believers in Philadelphia were also being martyred. The church at Philadelphia was commended, and had no reprimands:

> *… for you have a little strength, have kept My word, and have not denied My name.*
> (Revelation 3:8)

That Jesus Christ found nothing to condemn in the Philadelphia church must have been a great encouragement to them.

LAODICEA

Laodicea is sixteen kilometers from Colossae and eleven kilometers from Hierapolis. It was situated on the most important trade and military route from Ephesus on the Aegean coast to the interior of Anatolia and on to Syria. It had an ample water supply from nearby rivers, which was a major source of the region's agricultural wealth. The Christians of Laodicea are accused of being "lukewarm." Laodicea received hot water piped from nearby Hierapolis (today, Pamukkale) and cold water from Colossae, but by the time the water reached Laodicea, especially in the hot summer, it was lukewarm.

The church at Laodicea was the Lukewarm Church. Kim[109] says:

> ...in the church in Laodicea there were no weak people, false apostles or Nicolaitans like there were in the church in Ephesus. They didn't have the pressure of those who claim to be Jews like the church in Smyrna had. Also they didn't have people who disobeyed and ate of the sacrifices offered to idols listening to Balaam and Jezebel's teachings as the church in Pergamos and Thyatira had, nor did they have liars like the church in Philadelphia had. It had been criticized by Jesus Christ for being a church that lived and yet was dead, just like the church of Sardis. This church was neither hot nor cold, it was lukewarm.

Laodicea was a rich city, and bankers, traders, and many rich people gathered there. Because of its wealth, like Sardis, the people of Laodicea thought they needed nothing. Indeed, John recorded them self-declaring: "I am rich, have become wealthy, and have need of nothing" (Revelation 3:17). Jesus told them bluntly:

> ...*you are lukewarm, and neither cold nor hot...you are wretched, miserable, poor, blind, and naked.* (Revelation 3:16- 17)

This was the church that had it all, yet it had nothing. In its own eyes, it was rich, but they didn't understand what God wanted from them, and God declared that they were wretched, pitiful, poor, and blind. What a horrible indictment. This was a church that was purely going through the motions, and it is doubtful if they had any true believers among their ranks.

The ruins of ancient Laodicea are on the outskirts of modern Denizli and should have been easy to find. However, we missed a turn and ending up at Colossae instead. Colossae formed a triangle with two other New Testament cities, Hierapolis and Laodicea. After a brief visit to the featureless mound of Colossae, we retraced our route to Denizli, and then saw the direction sign

---

[109] Kim, J. (1999). *Seven Churches in Asia Minor* (2nd ed.). Okhap publishing Co., Korea.

to Laodicea. From here, it was just a short drive to the edge of the sparse and sprawling site. There was a rough track onto the site, so we decided to park and walk.

This was a mistake. It was hot, we walked for perhaps twenty minutes, and we couldn't see any sign of anything with the exception of one or two small, ruined buildings. We met a shepherd who spoke as much English as we spoke Turkish — none! But we didn't need a spoken language, all we needed were photographs. The old man's eyes lit up, and he beckoned us to follow him. Within a few minutes, we were standing on top of a large theater. A few minutes after that, we were at a small theater, and then he pointed us in the direction of the gymnasium, stadium, odeon, and part of a main street, which we found quite quickly.

All of these ruins are exactly that — ruins. This isn't a tourist site, and there isn't an entrance fee or information kiosk. And perhaps it's this unspoiled mess that made Laodicea one of our favorite sites. It's interesting that part of the ruins is an ancient aqueduct that carried water from the nearby Pamukkale. Pamukkale is one of Turkey's premier tourist resorts with hot springs and baths. It was from this region that hot water was brought to Laodicea, and it was "lukewarm" by the time it arrived here. On seeing these pipes, we couldn't help but stand and think about the words that the Lord Jesus Christ wrote to the church at Laodicea and the lessons that we can learn from it today.

EPILOGUE

Our story shouldn't end with the failures of the church at Laodicea — although we should make note of this as a picture of what happens to those who believe they can go to heaven on their own merits.

Our focus should be on the great hope that we have. The future hope of heaven is based on the fact of a crucified, dead, buried, and risen Lord Jesus who left behind an empty tomb in Jerusalem some two thousand years ago. Our belief in those events, and the eyewitness accounts surrounding them, provide our hope for the present, the future, and for eternity.

This book was designed to introduce you, our readers, to many of the major stories of the Bible beginning with Abraham in Ur and ending with John's letters to the Seven Churches in Revelation. In writing this book, it was never our intention to provide a detailed archaeology or history but, with our limited capacities, to have you share in the exhilaration and excitement we experienced as we saw the Bible come to life.

Some readers will have traveled with us by reading most of the text while others will have cherry-picked their way through. Either way, we trust that you will have been persuaded that the Bible is not a dry, theological text composed of a jumble of disconnected and sometimes unreliable stories. Instead, it reliably conveys a singular message set in the contexts of geography, history, and prophecy.

We've traveled together over wide geography, from Iran and Iraq in the east, through Egypt, Jordan, Israel and Syria, to Turkey, Greece, and Italy in the west. We've had a glimpse into history from ancient Ur, about four thousand years ago, to the more recent journeys of Paul about two thousand years ago. We've have had a few snapshots of prophetical events and episodes — but much of prophecy is yet to come.

The singular message throughout the Bible is the scarlet thread of redemption — God's plan of redemption, fulfilled by the life, death, and resurrection of its central figure, the Lord Jesus Christ, and the promise of His return and eternity. When history, geography, or archaeology comes to life it stirs our mental emotions — but when theology and Scripture come to life, it stirs our heart and soul. We trust that for many of you, our readers, your heart and soul have been stirred and refreshed, and that in some small way we have helped you see Jesus and the Scriptures with a fresh, newly stirred heart.

ABOUT THE AUTHORS

Roy and Evelyn Turkington were born in Northern Ireland and lived there until they were married. Roy has a degree in Biological and Environmental Studies from the New University of Ulster and completed his doctorate at the University College of North Wales. He was a Professor of Botany (specialty in Plant Ecology) at the University of British Columbia, Vancouver, from 1977–2015 and is now Professor Emeritus. From 1990–2004 he made many research-related trips to the Negev desert. Evelyn was a Registered Nurse with specialized training in midwifery (Scotland) and operating room technique (Bristol, England). They immigrated to Canada in 1976. Roy and Evelyn have been married forty-six years, have two children, Alistair and Andrea, and seven grandchildren. They were involved in the AWANA ministry for about thirty years as leaders, commanders, conference speakers, camp team leaders, and Canadian board members. Since retirement, their ministry shifted its focus to Christian volunteer opportunities in Jerusalem. They have led a number of Christian tours to Israel. They have traveled widely in about eighty-five to ninety countries, including Iran, Iraq, and North Korea, and they have lived for one year each in Wales, Israel, Turkey, China, and Argentina. From 1992–93, their family lived in Jerusalem, which was the unintentional springboard for the travels described in this book.

INDEX

C

D

U

V

W

X

Y

Z

CPSIA information can be obtained
at www.ICGtesting.com
Printed in the USA
LVHW081136140622
721237LV00016B/682